The Roots of Modern Japan

The Roots of Modern Japan

Jean-Pierre Lehmann

St. Martin's Press   New York

ISBN 0-312-69310-9

Library of Congress Cataloging in Publication Data

Lehmann, Jean-Pierre, 1945-
  The roots of modern Japan.

  Bibliography: p.
  1. Japan—History—Tokugawa period, 1600-
1868. 2. Japan—History—Meiji period, 1868-
1912. I. Title.
DS871.L43   1982   952′.025   82-743
ISBN 0-312-69310-9   AACR2

For Françoise

Contents

vii

Preface

As Western-style capitalism faces its worst crisis since the Great Depression and Eastern European-style socialism appears manifestly bankrupt, Japan seems to offer a dynamic alternative to a post-industrial society. Not only has Japan in the last twenty-five years or more, with the brief exception of the year 1974, been able to sustain an enviable degree of economic growth, but certainly in the last decade or so she has also proved a paragon of social stability and national cohesion.

Arising out of the seemingly incurable cancer which is affecting most, if not all, Western societies on the one hand and Japan's comparative success on the other, there has occurred, not surprisingly, a certain curiosity and indeed admiration in the West towards Japan. To the historian there is an element here of *déjà-vu*. As Europe in the eighteenth century faced severe political, economic, social and moral crises, there developed a tendency among some of the *philosophes* to portray China and more specifically certain elements of her political philosophy as a viable model for European societies to emulate. In the meantime, as is well known, Europeans managed to do rather well, conquering a good deal of the world, while any talk of emulating foreign societies would have appeared ridiculous at a time when, on the contrary, authors ranging from Marx to Macaulay and others preached that the only road to salvation for non-European societies was to undergo a thorough process of occidentalisation. The Western sense of self-confidence has, for obvious reasons, waned. Now, in the 1980s, some two centuries after the Chinese mirage, it is Japan which has become the focus of attention. Reflecting at least one of the differences in the later eighteenth and later twentieth centuries, however, on this occasion it is not philosophers seeking a political solution to European problems, but their modern counterparts, namely the gurus of business studies, seeking to unravel with a view to transplanting the secrets behind Japan's commercial and industrial success.

The objectives of this book are somewhat different. It is above all an historical study. While the first two chapters seek to develop and illuminate some of the more significant patterns in Japanese history and principally in terms of the formation and nature of the Japanese nation, the subsequent chapters address themselves to the causes and consequences of Japan's transformation to modernity. The late sixteenth and early seventeenth centuries, when Japan first came into contact with the West, correspond to a period of conception. The two centuries and more of isolation which followed in the course of the Edo era are a period of incubation, but in a manner in which the incubatory process should be perceived not as stagnant, but dynamic. In other words, the foundations for transformation to modernity were being laid and certain characteristics which were to mark the more advanced society that Japan became in the second half of the nineteenth and early twentieth centuries were in the process of formation. This last period is that of full-scale modernisation, illustrated by the rate of economic growth, the process of industrialisation, the development of political and administrative modes of organisation and behaviour in response to the challenge of modernity, Japan's absorption into the international economy and diplomatic relations, and the intellectual and social ferment which these forces give rise to. In assessing the particular Japanese historical development, efforts have been directed towards distinguishing between those elements which may be deemed peculiar, or unique, to Japan and those which can be more readily understood in a universal or comparative context. Similarly, the process of modernisation should be perceived as arising out of a combination of external stimuli and internal responses. The term occidentalisation or westernisation appears inappropriate as it implies a comprehensive and linear process. Rather, external forces and internal reactions provided Japan with a dynamic and dialectical process of more or less constant change. Another major theme has been to seek to contest the perception of Japanese history in terms of a dichotomy between tradition and modernity. Japan's history in this respect is no different from that of other nations: it is an evolutionary, occasionally revolutionary, process, where different forces mesh together; these can, often do, give rise to contradictions, but that is something different from seeking to establish contrasting and conflicting forces between that which is allegedly traditional and that which is supposedly modern. In other words, something 'traditional' can, under certain circumstances, be very 'modern'.

The scope of the book is extensive. The objective was to try to cover a broad canvas with a view to presenting as full a picture as possible. The economic, political, social, intellectual and moral dimensions of Japanese society are generally given equal distribution throughout. A major aim here was to seek at least to avoid falling into the pitfall of either economic determinism or cultural determinism. A major theme in this book is to underline the extent to which culture and economy have exerted reciprocal influences but without giving overall a greater predominance to one or the other.

While Japan's success may be worthy of admiration in the 1980s, concern has been expressed here to show to what extent the actual process of modernisation, the laying of roots, was brutal. To that end, the angle has been double in that history is perceived both from above and from below. There were some remarkable entrepreneurs in Japanese history – indeed without them the country would never have successfully industrialised – but this should not be allowed to mask the realities so far as the workers were concerned. Japanese society, at least until recently, was highly exploitative especially in regard to poor peasants, to the minority *eta* people, to women in general and to most members of the industrial labour force. Among other things, a proper appreciation of these facts should prevent people from speaking of contemporary Japan's highly harmonious industrial relations and social stability as being embedded in Japanese culture and traditions.

Japanese history, like that of all nations, can only perhaps be written in terms of exploitation and conflict. This should not, it should be stressed, imply that history as it is studied in this book is presented from a Marxist optic. It is rather an admittedly subjective impression, but arising from what are objective facts, that history is no more than the evolving reflection of human nature. Exploitation and conflict, as they are portrayed here, exist not only in terms of managers and workers, landlords and tenants, men and women, Japanese society in general and the *eta* people, but also exploitation and conflict between nations. While the Japanese in the course of modernisation may have justifiably felt aggrieved that they were or risked being exploited by the predatory Western imperialist nations, this did not prevent the Japanese themselves from exploiting others, namely the Chinese and Koreans to begin with, later most of the societies of South-east Asia.

A degree of exploitation persists in Japanese society to this day, although it is admittedly minimal when compared to most other countries, at least for the time being. The fairly high degree of social cohesion and egalitarianism which exist in Japan today, however, are needless to say born from the experience of the past, and in this case total defeat in 1945 ultimately proved an extremely salutary lesson. Even then, however, as the history of post-war Japan would show, success has been achieved not because of the absence of conflict, but rather the extent to which compromises were made in the face of conflict, compromises which arose out of necessity. While Japan and the Western powers are unlikely to be at war with one another in the foreseeable future, a sense of conflict nonetheless remains. The cultural chasm between Japan and the West is still substantial.

The conflict arises partly out of ignorance. No historian can delude himself that his voice is likely to be heard – and indeed it may not necessarily be a voice worth hearing. Nevertheless the aim in writing this book was partly as a means and in the hope of achieving a greater diffusion of knowledge and understanding about the evolution of the modern Japanese nation. Japanese readers may object that the history of their nation is written here from a biased Western perspective. They may also object that certain elements, perhaps especially the *eta* problem, which are rather black spots in the Japanese record, are given disproportionate importance. The bias of one's culture in studying that of another is inevitable, though the degree of the bias may vary; thus the same problem faces the Japanese historian in writing about another culture but surely this should not prevent him from so doing. Given the cultural chasm which does exist, however, it may be in fact more beneficial for the sake of a reasonably wide Western audience, that is, not the small circle of Japanological specialists, to have a Western interpreter. Other tendencies in this book may not simply reflect the angle of perception of a Westerner but that of a Westerner writing in the early 1980s. Questions ranging from the status and role of the female in society, of minority groups, of industrial relations are ones which are posed pretty much throughout the world. Many social and economic problems are of a universal character, though the solutions to these vary between cultures. Hence it was felt that the approach to Japanese history should consist of a fairly universal perspective even if the detailed assessment provides a more peculiarly indigenous colour.

In summary, therefore, the purpose in writing this book was to present a solid historical framework for modern Japan. It will be clear that certain features of this process have been retained. The first chapter, for example, sets out the extent to which Japan developed a highly cohesive and homogeneous society. Geographic, linguistic and ethnic factors of unity were reinforced by historical experiences, whether the extended period of isolation during the Edo era or the sense of national vulnerability and identity which occurred as the country was opened and faced the challenge of the militarily and economically far superior Western powers. In subsequent chapters it is stressed how all of these forces combined to witness the development in Japan, as in no other country, of a strong and sustained nationalistic policy. While Japanese policies and attitudes in the contemporary age could not be described as being overtly nationalistic, the sense of national cohesion accompanied by that of exclusivism remain strong: out of a population today of close to 116 million, just about three-quarters of a million are foreigners and more than 90 per cent of these are Koreans. Japan remains open to numerous foreign influences – in dress, food, art, and so on – and therefore in that sense it is a highly international country, while on the other it is still very much of a closed society – witness, for example, Japanese policies in regard to the 'boat people' arriving on their shores. Another strong pattern of continuity is the prestige and power accorded to the bureaucracy: Japan in the 1980s can still be described as a highly bureaucratic society. The influential role of the bureaucracy throughout the Edo era and during the transformation to modernity and the initiatives it took in laying the infrastructure for economic development can account for, among other things, the close relationship which persists between government and business. The all-powerful MITI (Ministry of International Trade and Industry) is a post-war creation, but the aura that surrounds it and the power that it wields can be traced back for centuries.

Japan possesses a truly unique history; it is long and it is rich. It goes without saying that this powerful historical tradition has deeply influenced the character of contemporary society and will no doubt continue determining the nature of the future. At the same time, however, that which is perhaps most remarkable about Japanese history – and also unique – is the degree to which on important occasions and in the course of major turning points the past has been discarded in favour of entirely new directions. Although obviously this is a matter open to debate and in any case impossible to prove, one could nevertheless seek to argue that no society, all the while maintaining a certain respect for a traditional order, has altered so profoundly as has Japan over the last two centuries or more. As is suggested in Chapter 5, the Meiji Restoration was in its consequences far more revolutionary than the events following 1789 in France or those following 1917 in Russia. The remarkable propensity for adaptability in the face of new circumstances has been both a feature and a great strength of Japanese society. The institutional innovativeness of Japan is perhaps the key factor lying behind her present success. The sources of innovativeness invariably include a combination of borrowings from abroad with certain indigenous traits. The current and much vaunted system of industrial relations in Japan is perhaps the best and most dynamic example of this process. The weaknesses in the West today are in a large measure due to excessive europocentricism and an inability to break the chains of the past, hence a preoccupation, possibly an obsession, with fighting yesterday's battles. If there is anything at all that should be learned from Japan it is this: the study of external models and a certain institutional and social radicalism can bring a great deal of vitality to society.

Acknowledgements

During the fifteen years that I have been studying modern Japanese society I have received a great deal of help from many different sources. To Professor and Mrs Richard Storry I shall always remain exceedingly grateful for the strong friendship and support they have given me over the years. The assistance and generous hospitality that my family and I have received from Professor Ikeda Kiyoshi and Mrs Ikeda have been invaluable.

In 1974 and again in 1977 I was attached to the Faculty of Law of Tohoku University, Sendai; the hospitality and help that I received on both occasions were nothing short of overwhelming. In 1974 I was fortunate in being the recipient of a Japan Foundation Fellowship. In 1977 I received a grant from the Japan Foundation Endowment Committee and also from the University of Stirling.

Over this last decade I have been certainly stimulated and indeed enriched by the students it has been my good fortune to teach at Stirling University. I am sure that they would all agree that the one who deserves special mention is Mrs Madge Niven, who came to university late in life and whose enthusiasm was not only infectious but rejuvenating.

The Librarian, Mr Gordon Peacock, and his staff at the University of Stirling Library have not only been of great assistance, but deserve to be applauded for their efforts on my behalf and for their tolerance. I also wish to record my thanks to my colleagues in the History Department and especially to Dr Robin Law, Dr John McCracken and Dr Neil Tranter.

That excellent organisation, The British Association for Japanese Studies, has provided an ideal forum for the development of Japanese studies and I have certainly gained a great deal from its annual conferences.

The individuals to whom, for one reason or another, I owe a particular debt are many. I did not want to allow the opportunity to pass to express my gratitude especially to Mr Hagihara Nobutoshi, Professor Maruyama Masao, Professor Oka Yoshitake, Professor Tsuzuki Chushichi, Professor Takeda Kiyoko, Professor Itoh Koichi, Professor Matsuzawa Hiroaki, Mr Yokoyama Toshio, Professor Harafuji Hiroshi, Professor Higuchi Yoichi, Professor

xvii

Okano Yukihide, Professor Mochitsuki Reijiro, Mr Ezoe Takayoshi, Professor Yasui Tatsuya, Mr Ichiro Hotani, Professor Ian Nish, Professor Robert Ballon, Dr Louis Allen, Dr Carmen Blacker, Professor Ben-Ami Shillony, Dr Theodore Zeldin, Miss Betty Neech, Mr Jean-Marc Pottiez, Professor Johannes Hirschmeier, Professor Ronald Dore, Mr and Mrs Eugène Demont. My parents have also been a constant source of encouragement.

The revision of the manuscript was carried out in Fontainebleau, France, where I have been Visiting Professor at the Euro-Asia Centre, INSEAD (European Institute of Business Administration). This has been a highly enjoyable and stimulating experience for which I wish to express my thanks to the Director of the Centre, Professor Henri-Claude de Bettignies, and his staff.

So far as the production of this book is concerned, there is no way that I can adequately express my great debt and very sincere thanks to Miss Wong Chiu-Yin of the Macmillan Press who has been not only an excellent editor but also and especially a superlative friend.

I should like to thank Miss Wilma Hunter for her help in typing the manuscript.

Above all I wish to express my deep gratitude to Françoise, Alexandra, Fabrice and Mahaut: a most supportive quartet.

NOTE

Japanese personal names are given, as is the custom in Japan, with the family name first.

Macrons, the sign which when placed above a vowel in a Japanese word indicates that it is long, have not been used in the text; they are, however, used in the Glossary of Japanese terms.

Full publishing details of works cited in the text will be found in the Bibliographical Note.

PART 1

THE HISTORICAL SETTING

1 Formation of the Japanese Nation

THE NATURE OF NATIONHOOD

In the modern era major transformations of an economic and political nature have largely taken place within the confines of what is termed the nation-state. Visions of a new order transcending national barriers ultimately proved to be chimeric. Pan-Islam, Pan-Asianism, Pan-Africanism were dreams, hardly realities. The internationalism of Trotsky was abandoned in favour of the nationalism of Stalin. Nationalism has been one of the major historical forces in the course of the nineteenth and twentieth centuries. The 'ism', however, can only be derived from a reasonably widespread acceptance on the part of the inhabitants of any given territory of what constitutes the nation: are there a sufficient number of ingredients, and are they sufficiently strong, to make the people believe that they are bound together in solidarity, that together they constitute a national identity, and that the symbol of that identity is worthy of their allegiance? For nationalism to exist, there must be a nation; for the nation to exist, the population must acquire a national consciousness.

It is not the intention here to suggest that the emergence of a national consciousness predetermines economic development; it should perhaps be more clearly seen as a dialectical process. Yet even so far as economic development is concerned, the importance of national consciousness cannot be over-stressed. If a government seeks to impose national unity over an area, while the inhabitants refuse to recognise that any such unity exists, then revolt is bound to occur. A government which is constantly harassed by regional or sectarian or ethnic revolts will find that a considerable amount of its energy and its treasury will be drained in order to 'solve' these problems. The chances, therefore, of passing successful legislation for economic, social, political and military policies are limited.

In the pages that follow we will seek to establish how the conditions for establishing a Japanese nation – and hence the development of a viable and credible ideology of nationalism – were particularly propitious, in fact almost unparalleled. In the course of the late nineteenth century, at a time when

3

highly emotional debates raged throughout most of the globe on the subject of what constituted a nation, Ernest Renan (1823–92) suggested the following composition (*Qu'est-ce qu'une nation?*, Paris, 1882): *'Avoir des gloires communes dans le passé, une volonté commune dans le présent; avoir fait des grandes choses ensemble, vouloir en faire encore'* 'To share common glories in the past, a common will in the present; to have accomplished great things together, and desire to accomplish more'. By the end of the nineteenth century, the Japanese could quite convincingly claim the applicability of this formula to their own achievements and aspirations. In the course of the nineteenth century, Japan was the only non-Western nation to have successfully industrialised, but she was also the only non-Western nation to have elaborated a popularly respected and upheld ideology of nationalism. For the nationalist leaders of other non-Western societies, Renan's dictum remained a dream to be fulfilled, not a reality to be beheld.

What are the criteria for the establishment of this sense of a common national identity and solidarity? Albert Hourani (*Arabic Thought in the Liberal Age*, 1962) suggests a distinction between three types of nationalism: (1) that which is religious, namely based on a common faith; (2) that which is territorial, a sense of community and love for a defined piece of land, (3) that which is linguistic, in the manner advocated by the Syrian writer Sati àl-Husri who argued that all Arabs were of the same nation on the grounds that they all spoke the same language. To these three one might add a fourth criterion, namely the ethnic, in the sense of the unifying concept of a common race.

Modern nationalism, born in Europe, spread out in all directions until eventually it covered the entire globe. There are today approximately 150 'nations'. How many of these, however, are not plagued by internal divisions of varying degrees of severity? In many states it is clear that the centrifugal forces resisting the centripetal nature of the 'nation' fall under one or more of Hourani's three categories, along with the additional ethnic dimension. The nation in this context may be no more than an arbitrary creation and devoid of a national consciousness. This phenomenon is no doubt most visible in sub-Saharan Africa where the process of decolonisation brought about new 'nations', incorporating different ethnic, tribal or linguistic groups, whose only *raison d'être* was as a result of boundaries delineated at the Conference of Berlin or some other imperial settlement.

An important element in the creation of a national consciousness can be found in what may be described as mythology. The myth may, for example, play an important role in masking certain uncomfortable elements of reality. The fact that an Algerian would find it impossible to converse with a Syrian did not prevent àl-Husri from insisting that they should be brothers in the same nation since they both speak Arabic. More significant, however, is the projection of the myth on to the past. The development of modern nationalist ideologies have, to greater or lesser extents, depended on the romanticisation of alleged golden ages of the past. Yet at the same time this may involve a danger which will threaten the very fabric upon which it is intended to weave the national identity. The erudition of Ram Mohan Roy (1772–1833) helped bring about the Hindu Renaissance; yet when the Hindu standard was grasped by the demagogic nationalist Balgangadhar Tilak (1856–1920), and others of comparable persuasion, ultimately the result came in sectarian killings, leading to the partition of 1947, and a hostility between Hindu and Muslim which continues to plague the Indian 'nation' to this day. In appealing to the national heritage, the outcome in many cases can be more divisive than cohesive. Most of the countries of Latin America, for example, are divided by gulfs separating the Indians from the *mestizos* from the whites. In his murals the Mexican painter Diego Rivera (1886–1957) glorified the Aztec past and depicted the horrors of the *conquista*; the potential here, however, was clearly divisive, as his compatriot and fellow painter José Orozco (1883–1949) pointed out, in that Indian would be turned against Spaniard at a time when they should all be seeking to establish their Mexican identity in order to create a viable Mexican nation.

In the latter half of the nineteenth century the questions relating to the nation and nationalism were perhaps most pertinent in the various areas under the suzerainty or protection of the Ottoman Empire. The question of the Balkans, partly arising out of the declaration of the principle of self-determination by Woodrow Wilson (1856–1924), occupied a good deal of the time of those negotiating the post 1914–18 war settlement. The religious, territorial, linguistic and ethnic divisions constituted a maze of labyrinthine proportions. It is, however, with the problems posed by Arab nationalism that the development of Japanese nationalism might be most fruitfully compared.

It was noted earlier how Sati àl-Husri sought to combine all Arabs into one nation on the basis of their alleged linguistic uniformity. More common among many Arab nationalists was to seek religion as the unifying bond: all Muslims are brothers in Islam. Yet, although the general area of North Africa and the Middle East may have had a preponderance of Muslims, there were also significant minorities, both in terms of influence and numbers, such as the Jews, the Maronites, the Druzes, the Orthodox, the Copts, and so on. As in the case of India, therefore, a religious-based nationalism risked unleashing strongly divisive forces – to wit the fate of Lebanon today. Leaving that particular problem aside, however, it was also the case that in attempting to define the concept of the nation and its territorial boundaries Arab nationalists were the inheritors of two conflicting traditions. The *umma* was perceived as embracing all the world of Islam and therefore universal in scope. The *watan*, on the other hand, was more particularistic; in the words of Albert Hourani (*op. cit.*), '[it] has the same meaning as '*asabiyya* in the doctrine of Ibn Khaldun – the sense of solidarity which binds together those who live in the same community and is the basis of social strength'. An emphasis on the universality and unifying force of the *umma* leads to the doctrine of Pan-Islam, while an emphasis on the group solidarity as evinced in the '*asabiyya* (or *watan*) finds expression in Egyptian, or Syrian, or Iraqi, etc. nationalism. The conflict and the confusion between the two persisted throughout the nineteenth and twentieth centuries. The degree of nationalist intensity and determination among the Arabs was no less acute than among the Japanese. The problem for the Arabs, however, was in great part a difficulty in agreeing wherein lay the nation: was it the universal *umma* or a series of particular *watan?*

It is possible to project these terms on to Japan as a means of understanding the evolutionary process of the formation of the nation and the national consciousness. The process will be looked at more closely in subsequent chapters. For the time being one can posit the following. In the pre-modern period the territory of Japan (the *umma*) was divided into some 300 semi-autonomous fiefs (the *watan*) where the strength of feeling of '*asabiyya* varied considerably in degree from one to the other – it was, for example, particularly strong in the southern fief of Satsuma. In the case of Japan, however, the particularistic *watan* (the fiefs) blended fairly rapidly into the more universal *umma* (the whole country), so that the two, *umma* and *watan*, became indistinguishable: the feeling of '*asabiyya* (the sense of community from which strength is derived) of the Japanese extended, in due course, to the whole of Japan. This phenomenon must not be brusquely disposed of simply because today it has become such a glaring reality. It is true that Japan has retained practically no residue of local particularism, as is the case in even the much older nations of Europe. It would not be correct, however, to assume that this transference of fief solidarity to national identity was achieved without a struggle nor that the latter was necessarily a foregone conclusion: indeed, a good deal of the political history of Japan in the decade preceding the revolution of 1868, and the three or four which followed it, can be written in terms of rivalries between the sons of the various fiefs.

The victory, so to speak, of the centripetal over the centrifugal forces in such a short time and in such a categorical manner is one of the more important features of the 1868 revolution. As a preliminary understanding, however, it is useful to apply to Japan the various criteria for the development of nationalism referred to earlier: the religious, the territorial, the linguistic and the ethnic. It will be seen how all combined to allow Japanese nationalism to develop untrammelled by barriers which have beset, in one way or another, most other societies attempting to form themselves into nations.

Territory

The Japanese territory is clearly defined, even if it has slightly expanded or contracted over time. Essentially the Japanese nation comprised the three islands of Kyushu, Shikoku and Honshu. In the latter part of the nineteenth century a programme of colonisation was carried out in the northern island of Hokkaido; although the Russians may have occasionally cast an expansionist glance in that direction in the past, Hokkaido nonetheless indisputably became recognised as part of Japan. To the majority of the Japanese these four islands are effectively what is meant and included in the nation of Japan. Both to the north and the south there are areas of some ambiguity.

To the north-west of Hokkaido lies the elongated island of Sakhalin, while to the north-east are the Kuril islands, stretching all the way up to Kamchatka. Sakhalin was visited by both Russian and Japanese navigators from the seventeenth century onwards. In the modern era sovereignty over Sakhalin has alternated between the Japanese and the Russians, while at times they divided it into half. At the end of the Second World War there were somewhere in the region of 400,000 Japanese living in Sakhalin, the great majority of whom were repatriated to Japan, and the island is now, along with the Kurils, a separate *oblast* of the USSR with Yuzhno-Sakhalinsk as its capital. The Japanese do not dispute Russia's jurisdiction over Sakhalin. The question of the Kurils is different. Here again, possession has alternated between Japan and the USSR; at the Yalta Conference the Russians were ceded the Kurils at the same time as their jurisdiction over the whole of Sakhalin was recognised. Today, however, the Japanese claim the two islands in greatest proximity to Japan, Kunashiri and Etorofu (Kunashir and Iturup as they are known in the USSR) and this is a matter of dispute between Japan and the Soviet Union; it is unlikely, however, to lead to war between the two countries. The ordinary Japanese will not think of Etorofu and Kunashiri in terms comparable to, say, the way the ordinary Frenchman felt about Alsace-Lorraine in the period 1871–1918. The Soviet presence on these islands is strategically uncomfortable, economically unfortunate (fishing) and psychologically upsetting. In the consciousness of the Japanese, however, these islands are not an integral part of the Japanese nation.

The same comment might be made of another chain of islands which extends for approximately 400 miles from southern Japan to the northern tip of Formosa, collectively known as the Ryukyu islands, the largest of which is Okinawa. Originally the Ryukyus formed an independent kingdom. By the fourteenth century Chinese supremacy was established; but in keeping with Chinese custom the king of Naha (capital of Okinawa) retained a degree of sovereignty as long as he paid tribute to the Chinese emperor. The Ryukyus served as a meeting place and trade entrepôt between China and Japan and by the fifteenth century the Shimazu realm (Satsuma) of Southern Kyushu had already established a special relationship with the islands. In 1609 the Satsuma fief actually conquered the Ryukyus, annexed the northern islands of the chain, and made the king at Naha a vassal of the *daimyo* (feudal lord) of Satsuma; a strange situation developed whereby the king of Naha paid tribute both to Peking and to Kagoshima (capital of Satsuma). After the revolution of 1868 the king was brought to Tokyo and in 1879 the Ryukyu islands were administratively metamorphosed into the Okinawa prefecture. The Chinese put up only token resistance and so both *de facto* and *de jure* the Ryukyus became administratively a part of Japan. This does not mean, however, that the Ryukyus figure in the Japanese perception of what constitutes their nation. In April 1945 two Allied offensives converged on the island of Okinawa which capitulated in June. It is true that 85 per cent of the defenders died in battle and it is also true that the fall of Okinawa was instrumental in the resignation of the Cabinet of General Koiso Kuniaki (1880–1950). At the same time, however, the government could still claim that the sacred soil of Japan had not been trampled upon by an enemy foot. The Ryukyus lie on the periphery of the true Japanese nation.

So far as the four main islands are concerned, however, the territory of the Japanese nation is both clearly defined within the Japanese consciousness and internationally recognised. The advantages of this situation cannot be over-emphasised. Territorial wars have plagued many of the nations of the world; Japan has been immune from these. This clear recognition of what constitutes the national territory has also been a major factor in developing a concept and ideology of territorial nationalism. Nor, and this is a very important point, are there rival nationalisms claiming attachment to any piece of territory. Japanese territorial nationalism is also singularly reinforced by linguistic, religious and ethnic considerations.

Language
Sati àl-Husri's definition of the most important unifying precept of a nation, a common language, admirably fits the Japanese case. It is true that a fisherman from Tohoku (north-east Japan) would have had difficulty conversing with a farmer from the southern part of Kyushu; there were regional dialects, but no significant linguistic barriers. In this respect again Japan stands out in stark contrast to many of the countries of the world. In fact one can go further than this. Not only do the Japanese have a single unifying language, spoken by no other nation, but it is a very difficult language for a foreigner to master. Francis-Xavier (1506–52), the Basque Jesuit missionary, described the Japanese language as an invention of the devil in order to impede the progress of Christian proselytism. The Japanese language, therefore, is not only a

unifying factor, but also a defence mechanism. Hence linguistic nationalism could also be a potent force.

Religion
The religious factor in Japan is a somewhat complicated one. At the risk of some oversimplification, one can say that it consists of an amalgam of the purely indigenous Shinto along with the importation from outside of Buddhism and Confucianism – the latter two, however, in spite of being originally extraneous have, over the centuries, taken on a marked indigenous hue. Leaving aside matters of metaphysics, as far as national consciousness is concerned the following points can be made. The Shinto religion is inextricably associated with both the territory and people of Japan. Just as the Japanese language is spoken in no other nation, similarly Shinto is practised only in Japan; it is not an evangelising religion. (The only exception here was the establishment of Shinto shrines in Taiwan, Korea and Manchuria in the pre-Second World War years as part of the programme of the 'japanisation' of these colonised people.) Japan was perceived both in esoteric literature and in popular mythology as the 'land of the gods' (*shinkoku*). The initial xenophobic resistance to the Western incursion of the mid-nineteenth century – *joi*, or the movement to 'expel the barbarians' – had a certain millenarian coloration to it.

Having said that, it is also the case that although religion, mainly in the form of Shinto, may have contributed to a sense of national consciousness, religious nationalism as such, in a manner akin to Christian or Islamic societies, is not a characteristic feature of Japan in the modern era. As noted above, the Japanese embraced both Shinto and Buddhism – Confucianism is more of a moral philosophy than a religion. On the whole the two religions have co-existed quite harmoniously and in fact have exerted reciprocal influences over each other. Although one or the other may have experienced periods of ascendancy, the Japanese people are not divided between Shintoists and Buddhists in the sense that, say, the Indians are between Muslims and Hindus and the Northern Irish between Catholics and Protestants. Religious fervour, though discernible in a few sects, is not a marked feature of Japanese history, philosophy or society, nor is there a tradition of religious exclusivism. There have been conflicts in Japanese history in which monks and temples were involved; it would not be accurate, however, to describe these as religious wars, since the fighting was primarily concerned with the temples' temporal powers, not their spiritual beliefs.

Japan, in contrast to so many societies, has been spared the problem of significant religious minorities and the violent confrontations that these seem invariably to invite or provoke. While religion in Japan, therefore, has not been a determining influence on the development or coloration of Japanese nationalism, it has been a contributory factor, even if only passively, to modernisation. Thus, Japan's progress was not to be significantly impeded by strong reactionary religious groups – such as the *ulema* in parts of the Islamic world, for example the *mollahs* in Iran today, or, for that matter, the Roman Catholic Church in Europe and Latin America – nor by deeply held popular religious shibboleths. This is not to say that the process of modernisation was enthusiastically embarked upon by one and all, far from it, but that the forces of opposition did not enjoy the degree of religious sanction which they had in other societies.

Race

There is no such thing as the Japanese race, in the sense of a distinct racial species. The Japanese, however, have perceived themselves as a distinct racial group and this perception has played an important function in the development of Japanese national cohesiveness and nationalism. This unifying concept of a common race is further underlined by the absence of significant ethnic minorities, something which in so many other societies has acted as a disruptive force. There are groups which are discriminated against: the aboriginal inhabitants of Japan – the descendants of whom, the Ainu, are contained exclusively in the northern island of Hokkaido; Koreans living in Japan; and an indigenous outcaste group known as the *eta*, whose origins and role will be discussed in a later chapter. Without in any way wishing to minimise the plight of these people, nevertheless from an historical perspective the point is that they were not of a sufficient magnitude to threaten the viability of the nation.

In the age of nationalism the Japanese arrived on the scene singularly well equipped. The potential for creating a unified nation was certainly there. Ultimately the strongest manifestation of Japanese nationalism is the territorial, though it is buttressed by the linguistic and racial. What this means in real terms is that the instinctive reaction is to defend the territory and to preserve Japanese sovereignty over it. Cultural considerations, though by no means totally insignificant, are nevertheless of secondary importance. Religion in Japan may not have been a strong force for nationalism, nor, however, was it a significant impediment to change. It is the combination of these factors which set out Japan's uniqueness.

PATTERNS OF HISTORICAL DEVELOPMENT

When one considers a number of features of Japan's historical development from earliest times, the emergence and the nature of the nineteenth- and twentieth-century nation-state become more understandable. Some of the more prominent characteristics, or patterns, of Japanese history will be studied in the following pages with a view to shedding light on the background of Japan as she entered the modern era.

Japan and the Outside World

The first point to highlight is that in the course of recorded history Japan had never been the victim of successful military invasion until the late summer of 1945. There are a number of reasons for this, obviously, though at this stage it might be useful to interject a little geography. It was fashionable in the late nineteenth and early twentieth centuries to refer to Japan as the 'Britain of the East', partly on the grounds that she was an island off the mainland of Asia, as the British isles lie off the mainland of Europe. Among (many) other things, however, it needs to be pointed out that the distance between Pusan at the southern tip of Korea and Kita-kyushu, the two points of closest proximity between Japan and the continent, is seven times the distance from Dover to Calais, and the seas are much rougher – one does not swim across the Tsushima Straits. The Japanese islands themselves do not offer hospitable terrain to the would-be invader, with more than three-quarters of the land-mass being mountainous. Invasion along conventional lines is a daunting proposition – which is one of the alleged reasons for the dropping of the atom bomb on Hiroshima, though why Nagasaki two days later remains rather a mystery.

Japan is far more of an island fortress than Britain ever was. This is not to say that an invasion of Japan was never attempted. The most celebrated abortive invasion in the chronicles of Japanese history is that of the great Kublai Khan (1214–94) at the end of the thirteenth century. As is well known, the Khan's great armada was defeated more by the elements – in the shape of a great typhoon – than by the valour or military skills of the Japanese defenders. As is equally well known, the Japanese dubbed the salvational wind *shinpu*, otherwise pronounced as *kamikaze*, meaning 'the wind of the gods', the spirits of which they unsuccessfully tried to resurrect in 1944.

Japan, with the exception of the brief interval of the years 1945–52, has never been governed by a foreign power. This, in the nineteenth century, was something of which the Japanese were powerfully aware and a situation they intended to maintain. Consider the pattern of foreign invasions, from Roman times to the 1968 Soviet invasion of Czechoslovakia, which have been a marked feature of the history of every European nation. Japan also stands in stark contrast to other regions of Asia. At the time of the British invasion of India most of the country was ruled by the foreign Mughal (Persian) dynasty; China from 1644 to 1912 was under the reign of the foreign Ch'ing (Manchurian) dynasty, while most of the Middle East and south-eastern

Europe were under the suzerainty of the Sublime Porte, namely the Turkish Ottoman Empire. Thus, for example, Chinese nationalism in its embryonic form as witnessed in, say, the Taiping revolution (1851–64), was anti-Manchu, rather than anti-Western; it was believed that with the removal of the foreign dynasty, China as a nation would emerge strong and powerful. The Japanese had no foreign over-lords to dispose of prior to facing the West.

   As a concomitant of this historical phenomenon, one can argue, though with a number of reservations, that there is also in Japan a political and psychological tradition of isolationism. A few of the qualifications to this statement will be looked at shortly, while others will be elaborated at greater length in the following chapter. The point here is that if the Japanese were not invaded, nor did they often try to invade, the abortive conquest of Korea and Ming China by Toyotomi Hideyoshi (1536–98) being more of an aberration of pre-nineteenth-century Japanese history than a pattern. Also if one considers the frequent marriages between members of diverse European monarchical families in order to cement alliances or gain territory, no such phenomenon has occurred in Japan. Europeans, of course, tend here to be the exception rather than the rule. For example, the Manchu rulers of the Chi'ing dynasty were not only forbidden to marry Chinese women, but they were even proscribed from having intercourse with them; a taboo broken by the lecherous Emperor Hsien Feng in 1852 when he indulged himself with Chinese maidens, collectively known as the Four Springs – Peony Spring, Cherry-apple Spring, Apricot Spring and Hangchow Spring – a sacrilege perceived by some as the source of the decline and ultimate eclipse of the dynasty six decades later.

   If political and military isolationism is a feature of pre-nineteenth-century Japanese history, this hardly applies to intellectual currents, in fact quite the reverse. When placing Japan in the pantheon of the 'great' cultures of the world, namely with Egypt, Greece, Rome, India, China, down to more modern times with France, Germany, Britain, Russia and so on, there is one characteristic which they all share and which in Japan is conspicuous by its absence. Japan has never, in all her history, produced a towering religious or philosophical figure of universal repute and influence. Not only is there no Japanese equivalent to Confucius, Christ, Buddha, Muhammad, there is also no Japanese equivalent to Rousseau, Adam Smith, Marx, Nietzsche, nor even to Lenin or Mao. In historical terms, Japan has tended to be a beneficiary, rather than a benefactor, of the great intellectual currents of the world. This is not to say that Japan has been devoid of original thinkers, but rather that generally speaking originality has been more involved in adaptation and innovation than in invention.

   Japan, as the historian Richard Storry (*A History of Modern Japan*, 1978) has pointed out, though not subjected to military invasions, has experienced a series of cultural invasions. The most fundamental consists of the Japanese absorption of Chinese culture in the period roughly corresponding to the seventh to the ninth centuries AD. Throughout the ensuing centuries Japan continued to absorb, though with very varying degrees of intensity, cultural imports from the outside world, predominantly China and Korea, to some extent from the Iberians and the Dutch in the sixteenth and eighteenth centuries and, of course, from the major Western powers in the latter part of the nineteenth. All these cultural importations were subsequently assimilated into the indigenous environment – or 'japanised' in the jargon of the profession – with the result that occasionally the resulting product bore only the vaguest resemblance to the source from whence it came.

The Imperial Institution

While scanning the Japanese landscape and attempting to place it in the perspective of an international horizon, there remains one wholly indigenous, unique and historically significant institution which demands attention. That is the Japanese imperial institution. The first thing that marks it off as quite exceptional is that it is the longest-surviving monarchical dynasty. Even if one is sceptical about the claims that the first occupant of the imperial throne, Jinmu, ascended to it on 11 February 660 BC and settles for the more plausible second or third centuries of the present era, the unique distinction of longevity remains valid. That in itself is a consideration of utmost importance in an understanding of the emergence of the modern Japanese nation-state, but there is far more to it than that.

The Japanese 'Emperor' or 'Empress' (in the sense of reigning monarch, not in the sense of consort to the Emperor) were referred to by the Japanese in the course of history with a variety of euphemisms. They might be called *Gosho*, the name of the palace they lived in in Kyoto and which could be translated as 'hallowed place'; *Mikado*, 'sacred gate' leading to the palace; *Dairi*, the part of the palace where the Emperor resided; *Tenshi*, 'child of heaven', etc. In the modern era, however, the current appellation has been *Tenno*, not an entirely satisfactory translation of which might be 'lord of heaven'. In this book we shall use the term tenno (without italicising it) for two reasons. The more practical is that this will obviate the necessity of having to refer to the 'Japanese' emperor when wishing to distinguish him from, say, Napoleon (I or III) of France, Franz-Josef of Austria–Hungary, Theodoros II of Ethiopia or, for that matter, from Bokassa I of the Central African Empire. The second reason is that 'emperor' is not really a proper translation of tenno in that it does not in any way convey the numerous connotations derived from the use of the term nor the aura with which it is enshrouded. In Japanese the term tenno is exclusively reserved for their monarch, other emperors being called *kotei*. We refer (or referred) to the Sultan of the Ottoman Empire, the Kaiser of Germany, the Czar of all the Russias, the Shah of Iran, and so forth, so that even from the point of view of consistency it would seem that it is more appropriate to use the term tenno rather than emperor.

Article II of Chapter I of the 1889 Constitution of Japan declared a salic law. The present operative Constitution, of 1947, is mute on the matter of female monarchs, but it is unlikely, at least in the foreseeable future, that a woman will be invested with the imperial regalia. In the past, however, there have been ten female occupants of the throne; although eight of these were concentrated in the seventh and eighth centuries, there have been two in more modern times – Meishŏ (1623–96) and Go-Sakuramachi (1740–1813). Neither of the two, however, was married nor did they bear children. For the purposes of modern history it is correct to visualise the tenno as a fundamentally male, indeed phallocratic, institution to a degree paralleled perhaps only by the papacy in Rome. Indeed just as the Pope is presented as the 'father' of all Catholics, so is the tenno presented as the 'father' of all Japanese.

In the opening paragraph of this section we referred to the tenno institution as 'wholly indigenous'. Strictly speaking this is not entirely correct, although in the course of history, and certainly in modern times, it has been perceived by the Japanese as such. In early Japanese history there were rivalry and warfare between various families or clans (*uji*) in the course of which one was emerging *primus inter pares*. It was at the time that this family was consolidating its power that the first and most fundamental cultural invasion took place. Japanese scholars went to visit China and they were as awed by the cultural splendour of the T'ang dynasty (618–907) as more than a millennium later they were to be overwhelmed by the material power of the West. From the point of view of the tenno institution the timing is of considerable significance.

The first T'ang monarch, Li Yuan (reigned 618–26), came to power after the short-lived Sui dynasty (589–618) and after an extensive period of civil disorder and warfare had plagued China. The T'ang dynasty set about on a vigorous programme of national reorganisation and regeneration with many of the institutions which it established, especially the crucial civil service examination system, *mutatis mutandis*, surviving until the beginning of the twentieth century. Not only were China's cultural attributes splendid, including the Buddhist religion recently imported from India, but it was equally clear that her political system, and the ideology upon which it rested, could serve as a viable model for Japan.

Traditionally, both the Chinese and Japanese monarchs were supposed to act as intermediaries between the world of mortals below and the heavens above. Their ministrations would include praying for rain at times of drought, for victory at times of war, and so on. Thus, as has often been pointed out, but still requires stressing, both in China and Japan there was an absence of an independent authoritative ecclesiastical institution, as was the case, for example, in the Christian or Islamic world. The Chinese or Japanese monarchs were supposed to be both pope and sovereign, both caliph and sultan. According to Japanese mythology, Jinmu-tenno was descended from the sun-goddess Amaterasu and from the male deity Izanagi and the female deity Izanami who between them created the land of Japan. Thus all descendants of the imperial line are ultimately born from the deity at the apex of the Shinto pantheon. Chinese influence in the evolution of the Japanese imperial institution should be seen chiefly in two respects: first, in the way secular authority was bestowed on the tenno; secondly, albeit perhaps more indirectly, in the methods with which the secular and spiritual legitimacy of the tenno were proclaimed.

For the first 432,000 years of China's history the reign was established by a succession of twenty-four celestial monarchs, the first dozen of whom concerned themselves mainly with the affairs of heaven, while the second dozen set about putting in order earthly matters. The first recognised Chinese ruler as such, however, was Huang Ti, who is to the Chinese what Jinmu-tenno is to the Japanese. In early recorded history, however, Chinese rulers ascribed to themselves the humbler equivalent of 'king', rather than 'emperor'. Prince Shih founded the Ch'in dynasty (221–207 BC), which brought about the unification of China, involving the standardisation of the script, weights and measures, and included the beginning of the erection of the famed Great Wall. It was also Shih, however, who proclaimed himself Shih Huang Ti (translated as Emperor) and thereby invested a divine status to his rule and one which, in theory, remained with the occupant of the imperial throne until 1912. It should be emphasised here that the power of the Chinese 'Emperor' was always perceived as both spiritual and temporal; the Chinese monarch both reigned and ruled.

The situation in Japan was somewhat different. By the time of the Chinese cultural invasion it would appear that the position of the tenno had developed for some time and in such a fashion that his sacerdotal role was clearly of much greater significance than his administrative one. In fact, it was held that the tenno should be above these vulgar mundane matters; he was, therefore, little more than a kind of chief priest. It is here that the Chinese influence came to bear. During the height of Chinese influence, roughly mid-seventh to early ninth centuries, two things happened.

The first is that it is precisely during this period that the person of the tenno enjoyed the greatest temporal power, or at least so far as recorded history is concerned. This point is important to bear in mind. As will be seen, from the late twelfth century to 1867 temporal power was in the hands of succeeding dynasties of *shogun* (military commanders – hereafter not italicised), who actually ruled, while the emperor reigned. During these centuries, however, there were a number of movements favouring 'restoration', by that meaning the act of 'restoring' both spiritual *and* temporal power to the person of the tenno. The perception was that the legitimate right to rule of the tenno had been usurped by the shogun and that this was a highly unsatisfactory situation. This perception, it should be clear, bore only scant resemblance to reality; but then a sense of reality is not necessarily an important vehicle of history.

The second thing, however, and intimately connected with the first, is that it is during this same period that the legitimacy of the tenno was traced and put into writing. This is of course a universal phenomenon. When the upstart parvenu Francesco Sforza (1401–66) established himself as Duke of Milan he had the court historians compile a twelve-volume chronicle of his family history. The tenno of this period could claim far more legitimate and longer lineage than the Sforza, but this was simply by oral tradition and the evolution of native custom. Thus, among other things, this is an age of codification. The court had two family histories compiled: the *Kojiki* (Record of Old Things) and the *Nihon-shoki* (Chronicle of Japan), both completed in the early eighth century. There is a substantial difference between the two works, the former being more of a literary exercise, while the latter is more a history. Both, however, reflect the spirit of the age; both related the age of the gods down to the origins of the tenno and his descendants.

In these records, as in the codes which were promulgated in the first year of the eighth century, both the secular and sacerdotal power of the tenno were not only asserted, but held to be indivisible. This was the concept known as *saisei-itchi,* which might be translated as 'the unity of rights and administration'. The *Taiho Ritsu* (Penal Code) and *Taiho Ryo* (Civil Code) of 701, based on their equivalent Chinese models, went into considerable detail in defining administrative offices and laws, but both equally emphasised that ultimate responsibility and all power resided in the person of the tenno. In this way, to borrow New Testament phraseology, in the tenno God and Caesar were made one.

If there are significant similarities between the Chinese and Japanese imperial institutions, there are also crucial differences and it is as important to understand the latter as it is the former.

In order to do this, however, it is important to say a few words about Confucianism. An exercise of this kind inevitably involves generalisation, even the risk of caricature; it must, nonetheless, be attempted. If the three pillars upholding Western civilisation can, to a certain degree, be distinguished from one another – Judaeo-Christian religion, Greek philosophy and Roman law – Confucianism combines the three elements. Although there are other schools and influences within the East Asian civilisation, Confucianism is the most dominant. Confucius (K'ung Fu-Tzu, 551–479 BC) lived in a period of great political and military anarchy. He shares with Jesus, Muhammad and Shakyamuni (the Buddha) the quality of never having written anything himself, but to have had his message recorded by his disciples; these writings came in the form of what are called *The Analects.* The message of Confucius was subsequently revised and considerably regenerated by Mencius (Meng-tzu, 371–289? BC). That loose body of doctrines referred to as Confucianism has, needless to say, considerably evolved over the ages and, as in the case of all religions and philosophies, various aspects of its creed may have meant different things to different people at different times. Also, as suggested above, Confucianism is universal in its concern: it seeks to dictate political organisation as well as social organisation, including, for example, the proper relationship between husband and wife.

Confucius deplored the anarchy which surrounded him and his efforts were chiefly directed at restoring *harmony* to society. The term harmony has been italicised here for, in terms of Western understanding of the East Asian civilisation, it is perhaps one of the most crucial concepts to have uppermost in one's mind. What this means, among other things, is that in the Confucianist perspective conflict cannot be constructive; conflict exists when society is not at peace with itself, when harmony has ceased to prevail, and therefore all efforts should be directed at restoring social harmony. Perhaps the cardinal injunction for the maintenance of harmony is 'Know thy place'. Thus the ideal Confucianist society is a highly vertical one and, indeed, founded on what are called the Five Basic Relationships. Of the five – ruler and subject, father and son, husband and wife, elder brother and younger brother, and friends – only the fifth relationship is conceived of on equal terms; the other four were absolute relations of superior to inferior. It should be clear, therefore, that Confucianism is the very antithesis of egalitarianism – and the status of woman is definitely relegated to a very lowly position.

Confucianism, especially in the works of Mencius, sees man as fundamentally good – and it is here that one can see the attraction that Confucianism had for Rousseau. Man should be guided by principles of *virtue*, rather than by laws – a position vigorously denounced by the chief contending philosophy in China generally placed under the title of Legalism. Again we have italicised the word virtue, for, along with harmony, it is another key concept in the Confucianist philosophy. The five chief virtues were those of benevolence, righteousness, reverence, wisdom and sincerity. It was incumbent on all men to practise the virtues, but it was primarily the responsibility of those who enjoyed the position of superiority in any given relationship.

If there occurred calamities – from earthquakes or famines to civil wars or political anarchy – this was due to either of two causes; society was not properly following the rules of harmony or the rulers were not practising virtue. And it is here that one comes to a most fundamental position and one where the Chinese and Japanese paths completely diverge. In the Chinese interpretation, if it is social elements which are behaving in an unruly fashion and thus responsible for the calamities afflicting society, then they must be suppressed forthwith. If, on the other hand, it would appear to be the case that it is the ruler who is responsible, then that is an altogether different matter. And it is here also perhaps that the divine status of the Chinese sovereign is somewhat reduced when compared to his Japanese colleague. The Chinese sovereign is the agent of heaven and he reigns and rules according to the mandate of heaven. So long as he practises virtue he retains the mandate. Once he ceases being virtuous, however, then he loses the mandate and it becomes incumbent upon the people, in order to carry out heaven's will, to change the mandate of heaven. When the dynasty has changed, the founder of the new dynasty is the possessor of a new mandate, which he and his descendants shall continue to enjoy so long as they practise virtue.

It is on the importance attached to the concept of heredity that the Japanese and Chinese traditions differ almost totally. This is not to say that the Chinese attached no importance to heredity, but as seen in the case of the mandate of heaven outlined above, it is clear that it was not the sole, nor even necessarily the prime, source of legitimacy. Two quick examples can be presented to clarify further the contrast – though it should be made abundantly clear that here we are speaking of theory, not necessarily always of reality. The first is that of primogeniture. The Chinese have generally not practised primogeniture, while in Japan it has tended to be the norm – in economic terms this was to have clear implications in regard to capital accumulation. Secondly, one feature of the Chinese system which was conspicuously absent in Japan (until after the revolution of 1868) was that of the civil service examination. Confucius and his disciples, along lines parallel to the Platonic ideal, believed that power should be combined with wisdom and that the latter was not necessarily the monopoly of any specific layer of society. As was seen earlier, it was during the T'ang dynasty that recruitment to the civil service by competitive examination was institutionalised and that this survived until its abolition in 1905. In theory the humblest peasant could aspire to the highest administrative office as long as he was able to prove his superior wisdom by passing the examinations. In Japan the important element in determining the bearer of a particular civil or military office was heredity and not merit. It should again be emphasised that one is here talking about the theory, not necessarily the reality – and, as will be seen, one of the more powerful causes of the revolution of 1868 was the conflict between the two principles of merit and heredity which emerged in the century or so which preceded the revolution.

For the tenno, therefore, the source of legitimacy was above all hereditary. A change of dynasty was unthinkable since this would obviously sever the link with Jinmu-tenno. The tenno had one chief consort, but numerous other concubines, thus improving the possibility of producing numerous imperial offspring. The successor to the throne need not be the child of the chief consort – in fact the present crown prince will be the first of the modern tenno to be the son of his 'official' mother. Of course it could – and did – happen that the reigning tenno might be sterile or impotent or die in infancy. In this case the successor was adopted from within the imperial family. The question of who should inherit the throne did occasionally lead to war. Adoption, in order to perpetuate the family name, was (and is) a widespread phenomenon in Japan; the paternal–filial relationship need not be a blood one. In society at large an adoption could be secured from people other than relatives – though, as in the Edo period (1603–1867), the choice was theoretically circumscribed by social rank; in the case of the tenno, however, adoption must be from among members of his family.

In the course of history the imperial institution experienced numerous vicissitudes and indeed at times languished not only in obscurity but even in poverty. Its fundamental nature, however – its link with the gods and its principle of heredity – were never challenged. It was a remarkable institution and, from the historical perspective of creating a viable modern nation-state, it played a fundamental role.

Power in Japanese History
It is difficult (and generally always has been) to define the locus of power in Japan. For, among other things, there is generally a considerable disparity between form and substance. If one takes the example of the contemporary Japanese family, by relying exclusively on appearance it would seem clear that not only is the husband the boss, but a tyrannical one to boot. Here, however, one is presented with one of the starkest contrasts between form and substance, in that the chief female of the houschold – today generally the wife, but in the past more commonly the mother of the husband – rules with an iron hand, while the husband is flattered with courtesies in regard to his (impotent) reign. The pattern can be situated in practically any institution. The presumed head of a family, corporation, university is generally little more

than a figurehead. In this context one should introduce one of the operative terms of Japanese historical study, namely *gekokujo*; this literally translates as 'the victory of the lower over the higher¹, more figuratively as the rule of the higher by the lower.

This term has been used with particular effect by Maruyama Masao (*Thought and Behaviour in Modern Japanese Politics*, 1963) in analysing the convulsions of the 1930s. There were, during this decade, a number of young officer movements whose avowed aim was to change the direction and nature of government. The phenomenon of the military putsch is (unfortunately) fairly universal. What sets the Japanese case, certainly of the 1930s, apart is that the young officers did not presume to take over control themselves; it was generally expected that once the coup was successful some figurehead, for example, a general believed to be sympathetic to the 'cause', would assume power. Megalomania is somewhat different in Japan to what it is in most other places.

A possible correlative of the *gekokujo* phenomenon is that, generally speaking, Japanese history has not been marked by great charismatic political leaders. In the course of the seismic transformations of the mid-nineteenth century, no single figure can be said to have dominated the arena. In the convulsions of the 1930s and early 1940s, there was no Japanese counterpart to Hitler, Mussolini or Franco. Japanese leaders do not tend to be white-plumed knights in the forefront of battles, but generally furtive figures in the background. There are exceptions, perhaps most notably that triumvirate of the late sixteenth/early seventeenth centuries, Oda Nobunaga (1534–82), Toyotomi Hideyoshi (1536–98) and Tokugawa Ieyasu (1542–1616). In the Japanese consciousness, however, and indeed as would appear to be the case in the nation's chronicles, great heroes are more associated with failure than with victory – the theme of Ivan Morris's *the Nobility of Failure* (1975). Perhaps the two most popular heroes of Japanese history are Minamoto Yoshitsune (1159–89) and Saigo Takamori (1827–77). Both, however, failed in their mission, both suffered untimely deaths, the first by order of his brother (Yoritomo, 1147–99), the second at the hands of his kinsmen.

As to the 'man at the helm' in most periods of Japanese history he is hardly visible. Or rather there will be a person visibly at the helm, except when a decision regarding which direction to take is needed, and then he will be conveyed to the privacy of the cabin below. This pattern, though not applicable to the first two of the triumvirate mentioned above, was observed by the third. The battle of Sekigahara (1600) is generally regarded as the occasion on which the period of civil war was definitely brought to an end. Three years later the victor, Tokugawa Ieyasu, secured from the tenno Go-Yozei (1571–1617) the appointment of shogun and thus the Tokugawa dynasty was established. Within two years, however, Ieyasu abdicated in favour of his son Hidetada (1579–1632); the latter, in turn, abdicated nine years before his death and was replaced as shogun by his son Iemitsu (1603–51), who is one of the very few to have actually preserved the throne until his death.

This pattern of abdication stretches far back into Japanese history and has continued to exist until comparatively recently. The practice of the reigning tenno abdicating in favour of his successor became well established during the Nara period (709–84) and was prevalent during most of the Heian period (794–1185) and indeed was institutionalised as the *insei* (cloister government) by the tenno Shirakawa, who lived from 1053 to 1129, but reigned only from 1072 to 1086, leaving as his successor to the throne a seven-year-old boy. In more modern times one can cite the example of the Meiji *genro* (elder statesmen, though meant more in terms of prestige than actual age) who, having set the ship of state on an even keel, retired to the background and placed their protégés at the helm. The most recent case perhaps is that of Yoshida Shigeru (1878–1967), the prime minister and main political figure of the immediate post-war era, who resigned office in 1954 and spent his (many) remaining years at the seaside resort of Oiso.

While we did say that megalomania takes a different form in Japan, we did not say it does not exist. Ostensibly the retired sovereigns, shoguns, *genro* or prime ministers left the hurly-burly of the affairs of state in order to give themselves up to meditation, the arts, learning, or simply to enjoy more fully the company of their concubines. The reality, however, was generally of a different order. In alleged retirement, power nevertheless continued to be exercised with as much effect as, if not more than, when in office. Why did this system develop? The answer is difficult and in any case varies according to the times, places and circumstances. In fact in the cases of all the tenno who had never actually exercised any power, that is, the vast majority, it was generally a result of ennui and impatience at having constantly to perform the sacred rituals; abdication in their case did literally mean greater freedom to enjoy the arts or whatever aspects of court entertainment most took their fancy. In other cases it might be as a means of ensuring the succession.

What has been written here may appear to contradict the phenomenon of *gekokujo* raised earlier on. One might try to explain it in the following manner. When the 'boss' and his entourage effectively exercise power, then the phenomenon of *gekokujo* is in abeyance or indeed in extinction. When this is no longer the case, then the forces of *gekokujo* go into operation. In the course of the Edo period (1603–1867), for example, in the early decades the shoguns, retired or otherwise, effectively exercised power. In the latter half, however, real power was increasingly devolved further and further down the scales of the feudal hierarchy. The revolution of 1868 is to a very great extent an assertion of *gekokujo*. It might be objected that this is a universal phenomenon; that surely Robespierre, Danton, Marat & Co. were exercising a gallic version of *gekokujo*. We have seen earlier on, however, how the universal phenomenon of the military putsch had its peculiar variant in Japan in the 1930s. It is not a question that revolt and subsequent transference of power are unique to Japan, but that the manner in which they have occurred is remarkable and that this is turn has had important ramifications in the course of Japanese history and especially in the revolution of 1868.

In introducing this subject it might be appropriate to say just a few words about the traditional system of periodisation in Japan. Earlier, we had occasion to mention the Nara period, the Heian period and the Edo period. Generally periods are named either after the place in which the government is alleged to be located or after the family who are, in form if not necessarily always in substance, in control. Three caveats must be entered. This periodisation is obviously not descriptive of social or economic conditions; for these purposes Japanese historians are more likely, in say the modern or pre-modern era, to distinguish between feudal, early modern, modern and contemporary as a means of illustrating the socio-economic conditions rather than the political. Secondly, two periods may be at least partly coincidental. Thus the Heian period is generally reckoned to have been in existence from 794 to 1185; Heian-kyo (the modern city of Kyoto) was the new capital designed for the tenno and his court in imitation of the capital of T'ang China, Ch'ang An. The tenno and his court in fact remained in residence there until in 1868 they moved eastwards to Tokyo (the former city of Edo). The reason why the Heian period ends in 1185, however, is that in theory secular power was transferred to the new institution of the shogunate which established its capital in Kamakura, thus inaugurating the Kamakura era which lasted from 1185 to 1333. In fact, however, the tenno had long ceased exercising secular power and this was firmly in the hands of a family, the Fujiwara, who had assumed and inaugurated the office of *kanpaku* (chief councillor); thus the period 858–1160 is sometimes referred to as the Fujiwara period, but also as the Heian period in that this power continued to be exercised from Heian-kyo (Kyoto). Name and place therefore can both be used, thus the same period can be called the Edo era (after the place) or the Tokugawa era (after the name of the dynasty).

The third caveat is that Japan was not a unified state during most of the periods in question. In the so-called feudal period, which in strictly political terms extended from 1185 to 1869 (the year the *daimyo*, feudal lords – hereafter not italicised – 'returned' their domains to the tenno), Japan was parcelled into numerous fiefs. The degree of autonomy of the fiefs varied considerably throughout these centuries of political feudalism; fief autonomy was particularly strong in the course of most of the Ashikaga or Muromachi era (1338–1573) – Ashikaga being the name of the shogunal dynasty, Muromachi the district in Kyoto where they built their castle – while it was correspondingly weak throughout most of the Edo era. Finally, it should be made clear that even here dates are arbitrary and correspond generally to the final acquiescence (or submission) to what had become an overpowering reality. This reality was determined by strategic and economic factors, not political fiat. In real terms the beginning of 'feudalism' can be said to have predated 1185 by more than two centuries, while its erosion was well under way before 1869.

It was shown earlier in this chapter how succession to the tenno's throne was retained in the same family for, in the words of the 1889 Constitution, 'ages eternal'. At the same time it was pointed out how the tenno's actual temporal rule was in existence for only a very limited time. Power in Japanese history has generally been devolved from the alleged ruler to some other office. This pattern of devolution has taken many guises which in its modern context will be scrutinised to some degree. Here, however, we will limit our consideration to only two offices, the first very briefly, the second in somewhat greater detail. The first office is that of *sessho* or *kanpaku*; the two are in strict theory separate offices, the first being somewhat akin to the term 'regent', the second to 'chief councillor'; for our purposes, however, they can be treated together. One should note here again the extreme importance of heredity attached to these offices as already indicated in the case of the tenno's legitimacy. There has been only one imperial dynasty, while the dynasties of *kanpaku-sessho* have varied and altogether there have been three shogunal dynasties. The *sessho* (regent) was an office which had been held by members of the imperial family; in 858, however, it was assumed by the noble Fujiwara Yoshifusa (804–72). The office of *kanpaku* was inaugurated by Fujiwara Mototsune (836–91). From the ninth to the middle of the nineteenth century both offices could be held only by descendants of the Fujiwara family, indeed generally reserved to only five descending families (referred to as the *go-sekke*). The office of shogun was inaugurated in 1192 by Minamoto Yoritomo. All succeeding shogunal dynasties were related to the Minamoto family. Oda Nobunaga became neither *kanpaku* nor shogun as he was not a descendant of either of these families. Hideyoshi was really the son of his own works and nothing more. He did, however, assume the office of *kanpaku*; indeed he was generally referred to in Japanese history as *taiko-sama*, *taiko* being the term applied to a retired *kanpaku* (*sama* is a title of respect), Hideyoshi having retired in order to secure the succession for his son. Hideyoshi, however, claimed to be descended from the Fujiwara, a claim which was clearly fraudulent, but here perhaps was an instance of *force majeure* and the tenno Ogimachi (1517–93) assented to recognise the fabricated genealogy without which the title of *kanpaku* could not have been legitimately bestowed. Ieyasu's claims to Minamoto descent were equally implausible, nevertheless the fiction had to be accepted. Once again one must distinguish between form and substance.

The time when the Taiho codes were promulgated, known as the era of the *ritsu-ryo* society, as we have seen, corresponded to the height of Chinese influence when both temporal and spiritual power were firmly in the hands of the tenno and his court. The secular authority gradually came to be challenged, especially by the Fujiwara family. A very important precedent was set by the Fujiwara and followed by Japan's political leaders for the ensuing centuries. The Fujiwara did not seek to usurp the imperial throne, they simply established a new institution, the *kanpaku*, and monopolised control over another, the *sessho*. The all-important principle of heredity was not only preserved, but indeed expanded since heredity became the sole basis of legitimacy for the *kanpaku-sessho* offices as well. The Fujiwara did not have to fight the tenno, but in order to cement closer relations with the throne the Fujiwara resorted to placing their women either as chief consorts to the tenno or somewhere reasonably high in the imperial harem. The Fujiwara, therefore, might well have made their own the famous dictum of the Habsburg Emperor Maximilian I (1459–1519): *Belli gerant alii, tu felix Austria nube* ('Let others make war, you, fortunate Austria, marry'). And indeed in this respect the Fujiwara were eminently successful in that almost three-quarters of the reigning tenno from the eighth century to the present were the offspring of Fujiwara women.

The power of the tenno declined and until 1868, with a few small exceptions, temporal power resided elsewhere both in fact and in theory. The prestige of the imperial family and of the tenno in particular continued to be great throughout the ages and of course the fiction was maintained, with varying degrees of zeal, that the power exercised by the alternative ruler was invested in him by the tenno. Thus the shogunal dynasties also frequently contrived to establish close relations with the imperial family through marriage or concubinage. The position, however, can be roughly stated in the following terms. The more firmly established the shogunal dynasty and their power, the less they bothered about securing the investiture or indeed access to the imperial bedchamber. When shogunal fortunes declined, however, the imperial prestige ascended. One of the dying gasps of the Tokugawa regime was to try to secure a firmer and more legitimate foundation to their rule by marrying the penultimate shogun Iemochi (1846–66) to Kazu, the young sister of the tenno Komei (1831–66).

The highly individual political arrangement of Japan in comparison with most other societies was that of the dual structure and reciprocal relations of the shogunal and imperial institutions. In European terms, had Oliver Cromwell, instead of ordering Charles I's decapitation, confined him to the regal palace with nothing but ceremonial duties to perform, or Napoleon I recalled Louis XVIII from Hartwell and installed him with impotent pomp in Versailles, then Oliver and Napoleon would have been respectively shoguns of England and France. In terms of modern history what this meant was that the Japanese had something which (say) the Chinese lacked: a residual alternative source of political legitimacy. The century of Chinese history from the mid-nineteenth to the mid-twentieth can largely be written in terms of a search for an alternative and acceptable source of political legitimacy. The Japanese had no such problem and partly as a result of this their revolution was able to take place far more quickly and far more smoothly than the Chinese.

The Institution of Shogun

What were the origins of this shogunate and how did it develop? In order to answer this question one must turn to changing patterns of land tenure and to internal warfare. In the *ritsu-ryo* period the land and the people belonged to the tenno. The area under imperial control extended from the southern island of Kyushu to just north of the Kanto plain. The northern part of the island of Honshu was still inhabited by the aboriginal natives of the Japanese islands; the conquest of Japan by what we today call the Japanese began in the south and over the centuries extended northwards. Thus fighting with the natives was still taking place during the Heian period.

It is important at this point to explain the distinction between the *kuge* and the *buke*. The *kuge* literally means public families, but might be more precisely defined as civilian nobility. The *buke* are military families. The *bu* can mean military, martial, or arms. Thus from *bu* we have *bushi*, a warrior; *bushido*, the way of the warrior or the code of knightly chivalry; *budo*, the martial arts, namely such sports as *judo*, *kendo*, and so on. An alternative word for *bushi*, warrior, is *samurai*, etymologically derived from the verb 'to serve', or 'wait upon'. The Japanese warrior (and henceforth we shall alternatively use either bushi or samurai and no longer italicise them), therefore, is perceived as both a man of arms and a retainer. The history of the latter part of the Heian period can be seen in terms of the *buke* challenging the power of the *kuge*. They were successful and from the twelfth to the mid-nineteenth centuries power was almost exclusively in the hands of the *buke*, though the *kuge* occasionally sought to reassert themselves. Power and prestige, however, do not necessarily always go hand in hand. The Heian period had witnessed a very rich and flourishing culture and the inhabitants of Heian-kyo were looked upon with awe as paragons of civilisation and sophistication. In modern British terms one might say they were beheld in a fashion comparable to the aura which the Oxbridge don enjoys when seen from the perspective of a provincial university lecturer. Likewise, the bushi were held to be rustic, ill-mannered ignorami, which by and large of course they were. Although life in Kyoto had become very decadent and tended to remain so, and although in the course of time at least some of the bushi lost their rustic manners and acquired great learning, the prestige of the *kuge* remained unaffected. From the late Heian period onwards the leading *buke*, from the shoguns downwards, sought marriage or concubinage arrangements with the *kuge*. Of the fifteen Tokugawa shoguns, one third chose as their chief consorts *kuge* girls, while just under half were married to imperial princesses; and this, with the exception noted earlier of the hapless Iemochi, was at a time when Kyoto was perhaps at its most impotent.

Returning to the latter part of the Heian period, what was happening was the following. While the *kuge* and the imperial court were luxuriously engaged in frivolity and sensuality of all kinds, the *buke* were having to fight hard campaigns. In return for their services they were given estates or else they simply appropriated them. These private estates, *shoen*, enabled the proprietor to collect taxes and in due course to raise troops. The proprietor might in turn grant parts of his estate to the more powerful leaders of his army. This is what in Japanese is called *onkyu*, meaning the granting of fiefs to vassals as a reward for military services. Thus one can see here the transition which is gradually taking place. From a position where in theory all the land and all the people belonged to the tenno, the land is in fact being parcelled out by the *buke* who in turn are also establishing their own vassalage. The fiction was retained that land and people belonged to the tenno, but in reality this was so only very indirectly. The concept of 'restoration' here must be seen, therefore, not only as 'restoring' temporal power to the tenno, but also 'restoring' to him both the land and the people.

The late Heian period witnessed the ascendancy of the military–landlord families, *buke*, over the tenno and the *kuge*. This also meant that Japanese society was bound to become overwhelmingly patriarchal. If the *kuge* were still respected for their (alleged) intellectual superiority, the question of moral values was altogether different. The moral code of conduct to which all sections of society should aspire was that of the *bushido*. *Bushido* was derived from the nature of a martial society and from the social ideology of Confucianism to which we referred earlier in this chapter. The woman's position was one of total subservience to her male lord, according to the well-known Japanese adage that in childhood she belongs to her father, in marriage to her husband and in widowhood to her son. Also, as invariably happens in misogynic martial societies, where the physical and moral attributes of manliness are so much admired, there was a tendency for male homosexuality to proliferate – that is of a Spartan, rather than Athenian variety – thus further undermining the position of women. That paragon of samurai virtues, Saigo Takamori, was a notorious sodomite. We shall have more to say about the situation of women in the following chapters. But for the time being, one might simply note in passing that although a number of women occupied the imperial throne, no woman ever became shogun.

All aspects of society, therefore, were changing even though Heian-kyo continued to enjoy a residual charm and prestige which endured throughout the subsequent ages. Nevertheless, the late Heian period definitely marked the end of an era. As the *buke* were consolidating their proprietorship over land and vassals, they were also, as is the case with warriors, fighting not only against the aborigines but also among themselves. In simple terms one can say that the Minamoto family emerged as the most powerful of the *buke*. Once this position was asserted *vis-à-vis* the *buke*, it only remained for it to be legalised by the tenno. Minamoto Yoritomo had established his headquarters in Kamakura on the east coast of Japan at a considerable distance from Kyoto. Minamoto Yoritomo was granted in 1192 the title of *sei-i-tai-shogun* by the Emperor Go-Toba (1180–1239) and thus officially began the institution of the shogunate.

The term *sei-i-tai-shogun* literally means 'commander-in-chief in charge of the suppression of barbarians'. The nomenclature and the post date back to the Nara period. The barbarians in this instance were the Ebisu, the aboriginal inhabitants of Japan, the shogun being entrusted with their suppression so that the Japanese could occupy more territory. The title, however, remained the same long after the barbarians had either been suppressed, driven to the northern island of Ezo (now called Hokkaido), or assimilated through miscegenation. There was an interval of some centuries between the ending of one barbarian threat and the appearance of another. As coincidence would have it, Europeans were also referred to as barbarians. This too was derived from China; the Chinese distinguished between the barbarians from the north, such as the Mongol and Manchu nomadic tribes and against whom they were (supposed to be) protected by their Great Wall, and the barbarians from the south, namely Europeans. Europeans were 'southern-barbarians' in the sense that they reached China from South-East Asia and to the southern port of Canton. In the mid-nineteenth century, therefore, the chief administrative officer of Japan was still the possessor of the title *sei-i-tai-shogun*; when Perry and others came knocking at the Japanese door, it was strongly felt in certain quarters that the *sei-i-tai-shogun* should live up to his responsibilities and go about suppressing these barbarian intruders.

Although the title of shogun predated the establishment of the Kamakura

government by four centuries or more, the crucial point to note here is that
hitherto this had been a temporary *ad hoc* arrangement. With Yoritomo,
however, it was recognised as a permanent and hereditary office, hence one
has here the foundation of the first of the shogunal dynasties. The government
of the shogun was called the *bakufu*, 'tent government', since earlier shogun in
the course of their campaigns had no fixed residence but administered from
their camps. The term (hereafter not italicised) survived even after the
shogun's headquarters were installed in a well-fortified castle on a fixed site.

The shogun was the *primus inter pares* of the *buke*, though in the course of the
bakufu's seven-century existence the extent of his power varied considerably.
Temporal power devolved away from the imperial institution in Kyoto. The
shogun exercised jurisdiction and the right to collect taxes only over that area
which his family controlled, namely his domain. Japan, therefore, was
parcelled up into a series of fiefs. The doctrines purporting to prove the secular
power of the tenno were quietly put to one side. As opposed to universal bonds
of loyalty between the tenno and his subjects, namely the people of Japan,
there developed particularistic ties between each lord and his retainers. One
sees this phenomenon illustrated in a number of practices of the feudal ages.
The case of *junshi*, self-immolation, is indicative of a number of characteristics
of these centuries. The term originates from antiquity when it was the practice
to have slaves buried with some great figure when he died in order that they
might minister to him in his travels in the world beyond. In the feudal era it
took a slightly different form, though the term was retained. When a shogun
died it might be considered incumbent among some of the feudal lords more
closely associated with him to commit *seppuku* – the more refined term for
hara-kiri, disembowelment – in order to keep the dead shogun company.
Similarly, when a great feudal lord died, it would be the privilege of his more
important retainers to follow suit. *Junshi*, as practised in the feudal era, also
underlines what was said earlier about the declining status of women.
Although it was the custom that widows should not remarry, they were
nonetheless not considered worthy of accompanying their deceased husbands
(as in the case of suttee in India); *junshi*, like so many other facets of Japanese
society, became an exclusively male preserve.

2 The *Ancien Régime*

THE EMERGENCE OF FEUDALISM

Japanese history in the centuries predating the emergence of the modern era –
the second half of the nineteenth century – can largely be written in terms of
opposing centrifugal and centripetal forces. The *ritsu-ryo* system, referred to in
the preceding chapter, had witnessed a high degree of political,
administrative, military and economic centralisation. In the latter half of the
Heian period, however, strong centrifugal forces asserted themselves with
both political and military power, along with a degree of economic autonomy,
devolving away from the centre, that is, the imperial court of Kyoto. In this
process of transition and especially in the course of the twelfth century a series
of wars – for example, the Hogen (1156) and Heiji (1159–60) insurrections –
broke out, further eroding imperial power; indeed the most significant result
was the transfer of administrative power from the court nobles to the military
chiefs. In this manner was feudalism brought about in Japan. The imperial
court was gradually stripped of land and people. Under the feudal system, the
lord exercised exclusive rights of tenure and taxation over the areas under his
jurisdiction and his retainers owed allegiance to him, not to the tenno. In the
evolution of Japanese feudalism, increasing stress was placed on the lord–
vassal relationship; that which arose as the result of a military arrangement
would, especially during the Edo period, receive ideological sanctification.

As the locus of power evolved away from the imperial court, paramountcy
in military and administrative affairs was hotly contested between rival
families and factions. In the years leading to the establishment of the
Kamakura bakufu, the main rivalry was that between the Taira and
Minamoto families; the outcome was the Genpei wars, lasting from 1180 to
1185, culminating in the largest naval conflict hitherto witnessed in the Far
East – the battle of Dan-no-ura in 1185 in which the Taira were completely
routed. Thus was order restored with the setting up of the Kamakura bakufu
which enjoyed a degree of central power, the legitimacy of which arose from
its investiture by the tenno in the new and completely innovative shogunal
dynasty of the Minamoto. The establishment of the Minamoto set a pattern in
Japanese history which might be described in the following manner: the
establishment of the Minamoto shogunal dynasty in 1185, of the Ashikaga

dynasty in 1338 and of the Tokugawa dynasty in 1603 can be seen as efforts to contain the over-extension of the feudal centrifugal forces and restore, with varying degrees of authority and success, a modicum of central administration.

Great military confrontations produce great military heroes, who, in turn, provide inspiration for epic tales, narrated, sung and acted for posterity. The most famous of these legends in Japan was the *Heike Monogatari* (written in the early thirteenth century), a work dramatically relating the rise and fall of the house of Taira. In terms of its impact it is perhaps comparable to the French medieval *chansons de geste*, for example the *Chanson de Roland* (which in fact was composed at roughly the same time as the *Heike Monogatari*). Thus one needs to emphasise here that the earlier great epic, the *Genji Monogatari*, written by a woman, Murasaki Shikibu, in the early eleventh century, was exclusively concerned with the affairs of the civil Heian court; while the *Heike Monogatari*, exclusively concerned with matters of warfare and individual bravado on the battlefield (as opposed to the bedchamber), emphatically announces the coming of a new age. The emergence of the bushi as the ruling élite of Japan was reflected not only in a new literary genre, but also in the birth and development of religious sects more attuned to martial values: *Zen-shu* (the Zen Sect of Buddhism) was introduced in Japan from China during the Kamakura period, while in the thirteenth century, Nichiren (1222–82) preached a more indigenous but militant gospel. The age of the bushi had begun and was faithfully illustrated in all spheres of Japanese cultural activities.

The Kamakura settlement, however, did not eliminate real or potential tensions within Japanese society; conflict continued between rival *buke* and indeed between *buke* and *kuge*, the latter not easily satisfied with being relegated to impotent, albeit prestigious, political oblivion. The intricate details of Japanese political history in the three centuries following the establishment of the Kamakura bakufu need not detain us here. Suffice it to note the following points and trends. Shortly after the death of Yoritomo, the founder of the dynasty, political power devolved to yet another military family, the Hojo. The latter did not seek to supplant the Minamoto dynasty, but simply created a new office, that of *shikken*, namely regent to the shogun. A pattern often repeated in the course of Japan's political history and serving as illustration of the *gekokujo* phenomenon, described in the preceding chapter, established itself whereby an impotent tenno theoretically reigned in Kyoto, while an equally impotent shogun theoretically ruled in Kamakura, whereas in fact administration was, for a while at least, firmly in the hands of a completely different family and office: the Hojo. The complacency, power and prestige of the Hojo were significantly undermined by the two Mongol invasions of 1274 and 1281. Although these proved abortive, the threat from the outside and the ruling family's apparent inability to cope effectively provided more than ample ground for revolt. The Kamakura bakufu and the Hojo regency were overthrown simultaneously in 1333.

In a brief, albeit significant, interval tenno and *kuge* power reasserted themselves. The years 1333–6 are known as the Kenmu Restoration, during which the tenno Go-Daigo (1288–1339) sought to re-establish central administrative control in Kyoto. This imperial interlude was short-lived; it provided both fodder and a model, however, for subsequent restorationist thinkers and movements. The immediate result was the near total eclipse of the imperial household and *kuge* until they were rehabilitated in the latter part of the sixteenth and early part of the seventeenth centuries. This decline of Kyoto reached its nadir in the course of the Onin civil wars.

The causes of the latter need not concern us here; the consequences, however, were of great significance as far as our understanding of the prelude of Japan's modern era is concerned. Although the period following the attempted Mongol invasions witnessed almost ceaseless warfare, these were not as extensive and devastating as the civil war which followed the Onin war of 1467–77. On the one hand, during the Onin war central government, theoretically under the sovereignty of the Ashikaga shogun, ceased to exist for all intents and purposes. On the other hand, the manor system (*shoen*), which had emerged in the course of the later Heian period and was the major feature of feudalism under the Kamakura bakufu, collapsed. What this meant was that the *shoen*, hitherto to be counted in the thousands, were being absorbed into vaster but numerically far inferior territorial fiefs under the jurisdiction of great military landlords. Thus came about the period of a century of civil warfare, referred to as the *sengoku* era (the period of the country at war with itself).

Local warlords (the daimyo) became completely independent and fought each other for the aggrandisement and consolidation of their fiefs, with the ultimate aim of imposing their will on the whole of the nation. The latter endeavour, however, could not be achieved by any single daimyo alone; hence came into operation on a grand scale the converse of warfare, namely the creation of alliances. Reduced from the thousands to a few hundred, the daimyo coalesced round a much smaller number of the most prominent families. These in turn exercised power, directly or indirectly, over extensive provincial areas: the Shimazu consolidated their position in the southern part of Kyushu, the Date on the eastern part of northern Honshu, and so forth. The political map of Japan was not only changing, it was being simplified. On the other hand, the social picture was also rapidly evolving. This era of incessant warfare allowed a high degree of social mobility from the lower bushi estate to positions of high military rank and even the rise of commoners –

Toyotomi Hideyoshi was of peasant stock. With the demands created by warfare ample opportunity was provided for the enrichment and gain in influence of artisans and merchants; the latter also benefited considerably from the vast extension of foreign trade (to be seen below). Thus, among other things, the *sengoku* period witnessed urbanisation. The opportunities for rapid social promotion and the chaotic instability of the country acted as powerful inducements to self-seeking opportunism involving frequent cases of treachery; in return for a promise of a higher rank, a vassal would betray (or indeed kill) his lord for the sake of another. The feudal ideal of the lord–vassal relationship was completely submerged in an anarchic sea of rising individualism. This occurred at all levels of society; indeed, Hideyoshi achieved power by violating Oda Nobunaga's will, while Tokugawa Ieyasu, Hideyoshi's erstwhile closest and most faithful vassal, betrayed his oath and ultimately had Hideyoshi's appointed heir, Hideyori, assassinated. Finally, in this general chaos, it should be noted that opportunities were even presented to women to play influential roles in political intrigue; indeed the *sengoku* era is not without its heroines, as well as its heroes. The state of complete disorder must be emphasised, for only when this is appreciated is it possible to understand the political, social, economic, ideological and moral rigidity which the founders of the new Tokugawa dynasty sought to impose. Peace and unification were eventually achieved. Before examining the consequences of the latter, however, another important facet of the *sengoku* era needs to be examined: the arrival of Westerners and with them the introduction of firearms, ·Christianity and the extension of Japan's maritime and foreign trade.

EXPANSION IN EUROPE

Before proceeding with Japanese affairs, however, it may be worthwhile to pause briefly in order to consider, in lightning fashion, developments in Europe. The Renaissance led to the Reformation which in turn produced the Counter-Reformation. The Roman Church, after suffering considerable setbacks, re-emerged with strong militant and mercantile determination. Most illustrative of this new mood was the founding of the Society of Jesus (the Jesuits) by the Basque Ignatius of Loyola (1491–1556) in 1540. The ambitions of Christian expansionism were to be significantly aided by other developments, notably in the sciences of navigation, cartography, geography and so on. Needless to say these were not always perfect. In late October 1492, Christopher Columbus (1451–1506) set foot on an island and solemnly declared it must be Japan – in fact, it was the island which came to be called Cuba. Nevertheless, while the *Santa Maria*, the *Pinta* and the *Niña*, irrespective of their captain's intentions, were heading West, Vasco da Gama (1469–

1524), Fernand Magellan (*c.* 1480–1521) and others set their sails in an easterly direction.

The age of explorers rapidly metamorphosed into the age of conquerors. Similarly, new economic demands arose. The luxuries of the past – spices, tea, sugar, silks, etc. – were becoming the necessities of the day. The spirit of mercantilism required to be nourished by the acquisition of gold – symbolised in the passionate quest for *el dorado*. In the course of time, and as a result of military and conjugal campaigns, the European nation-states came into being, led by monarchs, such as Francis I (1494–1547), Philip II (1527–98) and Elizabeth I (1533–1603), whose ambitions were matched by their ability.

All these factors combined in enabling these new powers to dispense with hitherto indispensable Levantine and Italian traders. Thus were the great European seaborne empires born. Initially quasi-monopolised by the Spaniards and the Portuguese – who, in spite of Lusitanian reluctance, were united under a single crown from 1580 to 1640 – the defeat of the Spanish Armada and the death of Philip II finally broke the bonds and unleashed the full fury of the Dutch, the English and eventually the French to expand round the world.

For our purposes we can ignore developments in the New World and concentrate our attention briefly on what happened in the East. The Portuguese, after having established themselves in such outposts as Goa on the Malabar Coast (1510), moved to more eastern horizons and decided to settle permanently in Macao (1557). Spain in 1564 sent the *conquistador* Miguel Lopez de Legazpi to subdue and colonise a group of islands in the East which collectively came to be known as the Philippines (after Philip II). Rapidly following in their train came the Dutch who established themselves in Batavia (Djakarta today), while the English contented themselves temporarily with a few outposts on the Coromandel coast, eventually to be joined there by the French. The process which the Japanese subsequently labelled as the eastern advance of Western power (*seiryoku-tozen*) was under way. By no means, however, should Japan be seen as nothing but a passive onlooker to these developments. In fact, in the same period of European history which has been described here, events in Japan also seemed to be propelling her to become a great seaborne empire.

THE IBERIAN INTERLUDE AND IMPACT

Earlier in this chapter it was stated that Japanese history could be written largely in terms of contending centrifugal and centripetal forces. The most acute and lengthy period of breakdown of central or quasi-central power occurred in the century which followed the Onin wars. As the second half of the fifteenth century set in, the Ashikaga shogunate of the Muromachi bakufu

was in a parlous state; the shogun Yoshimasa (1434–90) behaved in a manner
not unremarkable among sovereigns presiding over chaos – he enjoyed
himself. When he died a power-struggle over the succession broke out. This
marks the beginning of the *sengoku jidai*. It was a period of total anarchy:
contending daimyo strove to gain supremacy as their samurai armies fought
battles all over the country. Armed bandits roamed the countryside, causing
havoc to the agricultural economy, as they tore into villages, pillaging,
burning, raping.

   In this period of political and military anarchy, however, there were also a
number of important social ramifications. The first, as noted earlier, was that
a significant degree of social mobility did occur. Secondly, there was a good
deal of trade, which allowed merchants to acquire wealth; and indeed, in a
manner comparable to medieval Europe, there emerged a number of
autonomous commercial towns, notably those of Sakai, Yamaguchi and
Osaka. There was also another interesting development. As will be indicated
shortly, this period also witnessed the introduction of firearms. Indispensable
as a raw material for the warfare being waged was leather. Traditionally, the
only group in Japan who worked with leather, and the same who slaughtered
animals, were the *eta*. The origins of the *eta*, who are in fact completely
indigenous to the Japanese population, are obscure; suffice it to say here that
they were a despised outcast group and, in spite of a number of legal changes,
remain so to this day. Given the nature of their work, however, not
surprisingly their popularity was considerable during the *sengoku jidai*, as a
result of which the feudal war-lords sought to attract *eta* to their domains.
Hitherto mainly localised in the Kansai region, the effect of the demand for
their services was to scatter them throughout most of the country.

   The political settlement which brought the *sengoku jidai* to an end will be
looked at later in this chapter. In terms of the 'roots of modern Japan',
however, one of the most influential factors was the establishment of the policy
of *sakoku* (closed country, namely isolationism) which lasted from 1639 to
1854. This isolationism came as a complete reversal to an expansionism which
Japan had been experiencing for some time, the extent and effects of which
were remarkable. The background of the policy of isolation, therefore,
requires consideration.

   The traditional order of foreign relations in East Asia was centred on
China. In the preceding chapter a few words were said in regard to the
internal social arrangement which comes under the general label of
Confucianism. The basic principles of the internal order were applied to
external relations – in theory, if not always in practice, this system remained
operative until the latter part of the nineteenth century, its executors being
initially the Western powers, but ultimately imperial Japan. Thus, as in the

realm of social affairs, the world from a traditional Chinese optic was perceived in hierarchical fashion. China was the middle kingdom, the *huang-ti* (emperor) was the Son of Heaven, the supreme ruler; all surrounding territories were tributary states of China, whose monarchs were vassals of the *huang-ti*, who paid him tribute of both a ceremonial and material nature. Among other things, the *huang-ti* could be called upon to arbitrate between the disputes of tributary monarchs whose claims for legitimacy rested on the power that was invested in them by the *huang-ti*. Japan, as has already been pointed out, owed a very significant cultural debt to China and there can be little doubt that China's overall superiority in terms of civilisation was recognised by Japan at least until the latter half of the nineteenth century. Strictly speaking, however, Japan had remained outside the Chinese tributary orbit; this may be accounted for partly by reasons of geography – had the Mongol invasions proved successful the nature of the relationship would presumably have changed – but also for indigenous institutional reasons, namely that Japan had her own emperor, the tenno, whose legitimacy was derived from his divine ancestors, and who himself had the power to invest others to rule, whether *kanpaku* or shogun. Nevertheless, there are instances in which the *huang-ti* saw fit to exercise his imperial power over the Japanese, as in, for example, the case of the Ming emperor Chu Ti (1360–1424) conferring upon the third Ashikaga shogun Yoshimitsu (1358–1408) the title of King of Japan in 1404.

The honour thus granted to Yoshimitsu, which in fact he had not requested and indeed did not welcome, was not, however, without reason. In the course of the middle of the fourteenth century onwards, piracy became a lucrative business in which a good number of lords and their retainers from the western coast of Japan engaged. These pirates – referred to as the *wako*, the 'wa' being the Chinese character for *Yamato*, the ancient appellation of Japan – plundered the coasts of China and Korea and indeed extended their activities throughout most of South-East Asia. They obtained goods such as silks, porcelains, iron, and precious metals and other luxury goods – the Muromachi era was a highly colourful one, the ruling élite of which were much addicted to luxury goods and luxurious living. In the Philippines, for example, one of the most prized treasures were ancient Chinese ceramic wares which could be found buried in old graves, as these were much appreciated by the participants of the tea ceremony (*cha-no-yu*); the tea ceremony, though probably originating some time in the early thirteenth century, was initially a mainly religious exercise, closely identified with the Zen Buddhist sect. Under the Ashikaga shogunate, however, it became an exercise in aesthetics, not, as is the case today, of simplicity, but on the contrary of opulent luxury.

Both China and Korea sent missions to Japan to ask that these piratical plunderings be brought to an end. Yoshimitsu proved reasonably successful in this endeavour, hence the token of gratitude he received from China. In connection with the *wako* of the mid-fourteenth century there is one interesting tangent. Japanese plunder in Korea caused havoc to the already disintegrating Koryo dynasty (935–1392). A Korean general, by the name of Yi Sŏng-gye, had risen to some prominence partly because of the success he had achieved in repelling the Japanese pirates; in 1392 Yi Sŏng-gye had the last Koryo king deposed, usurped the throne and thus founded the Yi dynasty in Korea, which was to last for over five centuries but was ultimately, in 1910, brought to an end when the Japanese annexed Korea and turned her into a colony.

Piracy, temporarily suppressed, resurfaced as the Ashikaga shogunate weakened and lost effective control. By the early sixteenth century it had resumed on such a scale that China suspended official relations with Japan and severed them completely in 1557. Two points, however, should be noted. The first is that from the mid-fourteenth century Japan became an expansionist commercial nation and Japanese colonies were established throughout most of East Asia, notably in Korea, Formosa, Luzon – which a band of Japanese pirates tried to conquer in 1540, but failed – Annam, Siam – where Japanese mercenaries became the King's palace guard – Borneo, Sumatra. Even after *sakoku*, these colonies remained, though dwindling in number, ultimately to be absorbed into the local populations for lack of new Japanese blood being exported. The second point is that Japanese expansionism, then, had origins comparable to those of Elizabethan England, the exploits of the *wako* being somewhat reminiscent of those of, for example, Sir Francis Drake (*c.* 1543–96).

It was in the course of the early/mid sixteenth century that one of the more convulsive events in Japanese history was to occur, namely the arrival of the Portuguese. The impact, both direct and indirect, on the course of Japanese history was substantial. The story itself is a reasonably familiar one and only a very brief summary will be given here. It is important, however, to assess, albeit quickly, some of the major areas in which the Portuguese presence mostly made itself felt and thereby influenced developments within Japan – warfare, medicine and the sciences in general, trade and navigation, religion and politics, and ultimately *sakoku*.

In 1542 the first Europeans to touch Japanese soil landed on the small island of Tanegashima off the southern coast of Kyushu; their arrival, however, was not predetermined, but the result of an accident, their ship having been diverted from their route to Macao by strong winds. A papal Bull of 1502 gave Portugal the exclusive right of proselytisation in the Far East; the propagation of Christianity by the two Iberian kingdoms was seen as an important element in their mercantile and political expansionism, thus missionaries operated under what was known as the *Padroado Real* (Royal Patronage) for Portugal and *Patronato Real* in Spanish. In 1564, as noted earlier, Spain undertook the conquest of the Philippines and thus sent her own missionaries eastwards. Generally speaking the Jesuit order (Society of Jesus) operated under the patronage of the Portuguese monarchy, while such mendicant orders as the Franciscans were under the patronage of the Spanish monarchy. The recipient of this patronage was not necessarily a native of the country from which he received it, though he would probably be the subject of the monarch. Thus Christopher Columbus, a Genoese Jew by origin, nevertheless placed himself under the patronage of Queen Isabella the Catholic (1451–1504) of Castille. Citizenship, needless to say, was not in that period what it is today. The same applies to missionaries and merchants in the Far East. Francis Xavier (1506–52), from Navarre, then part of France, placed himself under the protection of the Portuguese crown, while Will Adams (1564–1620), an Englishman, was employed as a pilot aboard a Dutch vessel, the *Erasmus*. Similarly, many of the so-called 'Dutch' who later were able to establish a small factory in the island of Dejima, which was maintained until the mid-nineteenth century, were not Dutch at all, but Swedes, Hessians, and so on.

Francis Xavier met a Japanese migrant in Goa by the name of Yajiro, who through his extended residence there spoke fluent Portuguese and was asked by Francis to accompany him and two other Jesuits to Japan, which they reached in 1549. Francis Xavier stayed for some two years, before returning to Goa, where he died. Others followed, until the Jesuit missions became quite sizeable and established an impact, if not always an actual presence, in most of Japan. Conversions were numerous. It has often been alleged, however, that such conversions were spurious and motivated simply for commercial or political advantages. There can be little doubt that there was an element of opportunism – something which invariably occurs whenever there are mass conversions anywhere – but to write off the Japanese Christians of this period in such a manner is misleading. It must be remembered that courageously, indeed heroically, many Japanese Christians faced martyrdom, rather than apostatise. Also, in spite of most effective means employed by the Tokugawa shogunate to completely eradicate Christianity from Japan during a period of more than two centuries, when in the 1860s Christian missionaries were once again allowed to come to Japan (albeit restricted in their activities to three ports), it transpired that a good number of members of fishing communities had kept their faith in secret throughout these centuries; they were known as the *kakure kirishitan* (crypto-Christians).

Although successful to begin with, as the century progressed the Jesuits incurred difficulties, some of which were attributable not to the Japanese but to missionaries operating from the Philippines. It will be recalled that in 1580

Spain and Portugal were joined under the single crown of Philip II. With Philip's consent however Pope Gregory XIII (1502–85) had decreed in his *Ex pastolari officio* of 28 January 1585 that Japan was to remain a preserve of the Jesuits; Franciscans, Dominicans and Augustinians in the Philippines, however, resented and increasingly ignored the papal instructions and began sending their own missionaries to Japan, until Pope Paul V (1552–1621) in his *Sedis Apostolicae Providentia* of 11 June 1608 revoked the ban and permitted both Jesuits and mendicants to propagate the gospel in Japan. The incessant feuding between the Jesuits and the mendicant orders was by no means the sole cause of the eventual eclipse of Catholic missionary enterprise in Japan, but it certainly contributed to it.

By the late sixteenth century a number of anti-Christian edicts were passed and persecutions begun. The missionaries were made to understand that their presence was no longer welcome. They persisted. Finally in 1614 the conclusive edict banning Christianity was promulgated and all remaining missionaries expelled. Japanese Christians either abjured their foreign faith, or chose martyrdom, or, in some cases as pointed out above, went into hiding, while a number managed to go into exile, some to the Philippines, others to Macao, where in fact it was Japanese Christians who built the magnificent cathedral of St Paul, of which only the impressive façade remains today.

Before leaving this subject, two events are worth mentioning. The first is that the Jesuits were instrumental in encouraging two pioneering Japanese missions to visit Europe. The first of these, under the auspices of the Christian daimyo Omura Sumitada (1532–87), Arima Yoshisada (1531–88) and Otomo Yoshishige (1530–87), consisting of four young men, sailed from Nagasaki in 1582; the route was Nagasaki–Macao–the straits of Malacca–Goa–Cochin–round the Cape of Good Hope and hence to Lisbon. They were received in Madrid by Philip II and in Rome, with splendid pageantry, by Gregory XIII; they returned to Japan in 1590, after a trip of eight years' duration. The second mission was carried out under the orders of the formidable daimyo of Mutsu, in north-eastern Japan, Date Masamune (1566–1636), and entrusted to Hasekura Tsunenaga (1561–1622) of Sendai. Hasekura left in 1613 and travelled to Spain by way of Mexico; he arrived in Madrid a year later, was baptised in the presence of Philip III (1578–1621) and was also received with great pomp in Rome by Pope Paul V. Hasekura returned to Sendai in 1620, seven years following his departure, to find that the policy in regard to Christianity had undergone a significant metamorphosis. In spite of Masamune's order to apostatise, Hasekura refused; his life was spared, though his son, also a Christian, did become a martyr.

Martyrdom, therefore, was fairly rife in Japan of the late sixteenth and early seventeenth centuries. Initially, the missionaries were simply told to leave; martyred, however, were those who either refused or sought to return. There is in this context an interesting point to be raised. As suggested above, the Christian convictions of a good number of the Japanese converts were firm. In its attempt to root out what came to be officially labelled as the *jashumon* (which could be translated as 'the evil or pernicious heretical faith'), the new Edo bakufu was prepared to resort to whatever means possible. One of the most effective in suppressing the alien faith was Inoue Chikugo, himself an apostate, who was appointed the first head of the Inquisition Office. It came to be realised by Inoue particularly, but also by others, that the martyrdom of the foreign missionaries had the effect of serving as models for the native Christians and gave them greater resolution in their faith. Therefore another ploy was resorted to. It was thought that if the missionaries could be made to apostatise themselves, then this might prove much more effectual in terms of sapping the morale of the indigenous Christians and also in terms of ridiculing the practitioners of the evil sect. A number of such 'conversions', carried out by means of torture, were brought about. Such was the case of Giuseppe Chiara (1606–85), who married and took the Japanese name of Okamoto Sanemon, and of Christovão Ferreira (1580–1654), who took the name of Sawano Chuan and assisted Inoue in the work of the inquisition. (Ferreira is also the subject of two works by a best-selling contemporary Japanese novelist, Endo Shusaku, born in 1923, both available in English translation: a novel, *Silence*, and a play, *The Golden Country*.) There was one final great Christian uprising: the Shimabara rebellion of 1637–8 led by Amakusa Tokisada (and the ostensible immediate pretext for the policy of *sakoku* adopted the following year), in which rebellious peasants were spurred on by quasi-messianic hopes. By and large, however, and with the exception of the *kakure kirishitan*, Japan from the late 1630s to the mid-nineteenth century was rid of both missionaries and indigenous Christians. In 1709 an Italian Jesuit, Giovanni Batista Sidotti (1668–1715), sought to smuggle himself inside the country; he was caught, interrogated and ultimately put to death. He must have been a man of a singularly persuasive character, for among other things he managed to convince his chief interrogator, Arai Hakuseki (1657–1725), one of Edo Japan's leading intellectuals, that the Christian religion was not necessarily as injurious to the country's interests as the authorities wished to make out.

Two very different points can perhaps be derived from the events narrated above. First, traditionally the atmosphere in Japan has generally been reasonably tolerant in regard to religious matters. In early-seventeenth-century Japan, however, Christianity was perceived by the authorities not so much as a religion but as an ideology; this ideology was held to be inimical and subversive to the interests of the state, of what could be described as the nascent Tokugawa body-politic, and hence had to be rooted out. Without wishing to stretch comparisons too far, there is nevertheless a certain similarity here between the way the Tokugawa authorities viewed Christianity and the way in which, three hundred years later, the military regimes of the 1930s perceived Marxism: both were condemned as not only evil, but pernicious and dangerous and just as the Tokugawa authorities sought in due course to stamp out heresy by forced conversions to orthodoxy, so did the government of the 1930s prefer conversion to execution.

Secondly, what occurred in Japan also corresponds to a fairly universal pattern. A characteristic of the period lasting from roughly the late sixteenth to the early eighteenth centuries was the rise of absolutist monarchies – this was happening in the Ottoman Empire, also in Russia with the consolidation of Romanov rule, especially under Peter I (1672–1725), in France under a succession of Bourbon kings from Henry IV (1553–1610) to Louis XIV (1638–1715), in Mughal India under Akbar (1556–1605), in the foundations of the Ch'ing Empire in China, and so on.

The establishment of the Tokugawa dynasty by Ieyasu (1542–1616) was a Japanese variant of this fairly universal phenomenon. The advent of these absolutist monarchies in many parts of Europe and Asia was due to a multiplicity of factors, notably, for example, the changing technology of warfare and particularly the introduction and proliferation of firearms. At the same time, these absolutist monarchies required supportive ideologies. Thus, whereas the literature on Japan in the late sixteenth/early seventeenth centuries will inevitably mention the persecutions of Christians, it must not be forgotten that the Christians in their own territories were carrying out a good deal of persecution themselves. For the Iberians it was the age of the Inquisition. In England at this time the climate was not particularly healthy for Catholics. In France Huguenots were being persecuted or forced into exile; many of these chose England and with their skills and ethic thereby contributed to the first industrial revolution taking place in England rather than France. The point then is that the consolidation of monarchical rule anywhere also required the consolidation of orthodox ideology; or, to put it another way, an absolutist monarchy required an absolutist doctrine. What was taking place in Japan was not in nature any different from what was happening in many other parts of the world undergoing similar political developments.

Apart from Christianity, the Portuguese introduced the Japanese to a good number of things. Among these one should not forget to include bread, the Japanese word for which to this day remains *pan*, borrowed from the Portuguese, as indeed is the case with *tabako* (tobacco), and they taught the Japanese how to fry fish in batter, leading to the national dish called *tenpura*.

Gunpowder and the printing press, as every schoolchild knows, were Chinese inventions, but for reasons uncertain, having invented them, the Chinese then forgot about them, with the result that both were re-introduced into the Far East by the Iberians. There were other consequences of the Portuguese arrival which deserve attention.

In terms of shaping the destiny of Japanese history, and especially the unification of the country which was achieved by the end of the sixteenth century and thus terminated the era of civil war, the greatest Portuguese contribution was the introduction of firearms. Given the raging wars, needless to say, these came to be in considerable demand. First introduced in 1543, within two years the Japanese were manufacturing their own and urban centres such as Sakai and Yokkaichi became famous for their production. Firearms were responsible for the consolidation of power into fewer hands and ultimately for the rise to power of the famous trio, in succession Oda Nobunaga (1534–82), Toyotomi Hideyoshi (1536–98) and ultimately Tokugawa Ieyasu.

Originally samurai battles consisted not so much of a general mêlée, but of a whole series of individual combats; the samurai would announce his pedigree, his motivation in engaging in battle and his intention after victory – though often waiting for chroniclers to arrive before bothering with any of these. By the fourteenth century, as there developed a more sophisticated knowledge of the use of the horse in warfare, battles became more co-ordinated, especially in their greater reliance on cavalry charges. The samurai then was a mounted archer and indeed the way of the samurai was referred to as the way of the bow and the horse. The introduction of firearms and the use of cannon by the last quarter of the sixteenth century led to a metamorphosis both in combat and fortification. Huge stone castles were built, hence leading to the establishment of castle-towns throughout Japan. In terms of tactics and organisation, firearms led to the abandonment of close combat in favour of long-range fighting, of the cavalry being replaced in favour of the infantry, and of rearrangements of units within the army, leading to larger armies under central command. Changes of course also occurred in armour. What all this meant, among other things, was the increasing professionalisation of the warrior and consequently a greater differentiation between warrior and peasant.

The last major battle of the *sengoku* era was that of Sekigahara in 1600, although a number of serious engagements did occur in 1614 and in the Shimabara rebellion mentioned above. By the end of the third decade of the seventeenth century, however, Japan was for all intents and purposes at peace. The firearm fell into disuse. In that sense, its impact can be said to have been of relatively short duration, albeit powerful at the time. The distinctive mark and symbol of the samurai in the course of the peaceful Edo era was the sword. The great aura attached to the sword, therefore – with army and navy officers even in the Second World War carrying them at their side – is a comparatively recent phenomenon. Certainly when in the second half of the nineteenth century the Westerners returned, the Japanese were making very little use of firearms, while the sword appeared to be omnipresent.

In the sixteenth century the scientific gap between Europe and East Asia was by no means as substantial as it was to be in the mid-nineteenth. Nevertheless the Europeans were able to teach the Japanese a few things; the printing press and the manufacture and use of firearms have already been mentioned, but one should also add that under European guidance significant strides were made in naval construction and navigation, including the use of the compass and developments in cartography.

Even in the first decade of the seventeenth century Ieyasu was seeking to obtain from the Spanish Governor General of the Philippines skilled carpenters in order to assist the Edo *bakufu* in the construction of ships. This request was not acted upon immediately, on the ostensible grounds that the Governor General had to obtain approval for such a venture from the Viceroy of Mexico, under whose jurisdiction the Philippines were placed, though the real reason may have been the Spaniards' belief that their security against the Japanese lay in the latter's relative ignorance of naval construction. The Iberians, however, had also instructed the Japanese in more sophisticated methods of mining and in the refining of certain metals, especially silver. The Japanese were also taught techniques in Western painting, with quite a number of Japanese Christian paintings surviving to this day. Perhaps the most significant work of the Jesuits, however, lay in the field of medicine, both in the sense of medical science and that of medical care. To this Christovão Ferreira contributed a great deal, as did a devout merchant by the name of Luis de Almeida (1525–84). Some of the more impressive medico-pastoral work carried out was that catering to the needs of orphans and especially to lepers.

The Japanese followed Chinese nomenclature for the Portuguese, namely by referring to them as the *nanban-jin* (barbarians from the south), hence the sciences which they imported into Japan were referred to as *nanban-gaku* (*gaku* meaning studies or school). The concrete contribution of the Jesuits here must not be exaggerated, partly because their own knowledge was limited and the atmosphere in Catholic kingdoms at the time was not particularly conducive to scientific inquiry. Also in the chauvinistic hysteria which led to the policy of *sakoku*, progress in Western studies was limited; in fact one could probably speak in terms of regress. Nevertheless, *nanban-gaku* was the first in a series of Japanese accumulation and assimilation of (mainly) scientific knowledge from the West – to be followed in the eighteenth and early nineteenth centuries by *Rangaku* (Dutch Studies) and in the second half of the nineteenth century by *Yogaku* (Western Studies) – which in due course permitted the country to experience her own, albeit borrowed, scientific revolution so that by the early twentieth century Japan had by and large 'caught up' with the West. In other words, the reception of *nanban-gaku* is a reflection of the Japanese spirit of intellectual curiosity and scientific enterprise.

It should be understood that in its inception the policy of exclusion, *sakoku*, was directed primarily against the Iberians. It should also be remembered that as far as Japan's neighbours, Korea and China, were concerned, it was they who by severing relations with Japan in the mid-fifteenth century – a policy further strengthened by Hideyoshi's abortive attempt to conquer both towards the end of the century – were isolating themselves from the Japanese, not vice versa. The Dutch, whose first vessel, *de Liefde,* reached Japan in 1600, were not expelled from Japan, although they were severely restricted in their movements in the country. The English did make a brief appearance in the decade 1613–23, but it was they who chose to leave, not the Japanese who forced them out. The fact that when the English tried to return to Nagasaki in 1673 and resume trading relations they were in fact rebuffed is a separate matter, though part of the reason for the Japanese refusal was the Dutch informing them of the marriage between Charles II (1630–85) and the Portuguese Catholic princess Catherine of Braganza (1638–1705).

European commercial rivalries and warfare were pursued, or at the very least reflected in both Asia and the New World. From the point of view of the Dutch it was not so much a question of the royal marriage as the fact that England and the Netherlands were at war with each other. This reflection of European rivalries can also be seen in the fact that the Dutch assisted the Japanese in the siege of Shimabara, where there were a number of Portuguese Jesuits. *Sakoku*, it must be emphasised, was originally an essentially anti-Christian edict, directed almost exclusively at the Iberians: Christian in the ideological sense referred to above, but also against the kingdom of Philip II and his descendants because of the proximity of their colony in the Philippines. The Dutch were also, of course, Christians but whereas the Portuguese revered both God and Mammon, in their East Asian activities at least, the Dutch were prepared to content themselves with the latter. The *predikanten* (Dutch Calvinist missionaries) simply did not play the role in Dutch commercial and territorial expansionism that missionaries played in Catholic kingdoms, initially Spain and Portugal and subsequently France. Nor must it be believed that Tokugawa fear of militant Christianity was purely illusory; the Shimabara rebellion has already been alluded to, but also in the Osaka campaigns waged by the Tokugawa against Hideyoshi's son and presumptive heir, Hideyori (1593–1615), Christian samurai had swelled the ranks of the enemy and they advanced into battle carrying crosses and the names of Jesus and Santiago (the patron saint of Spain) inscribed as martial insignia. European rivalries, therefore, persisted in Japan, a phenomenon the Japanese were able to benefit from, and such was the case especially in the area of trade – a complex matter, a general outline of which we should now consider.

FOREIGN TRADE, CIVIL WAR AND ISOLATION

In the mid-sixteenth century, as we have seen, China and Korea severed all relations, including commercial ones, with Japan. It is true that an indirect trade with the two could still be maintained, partly via the Ryukyu (L'iu-ch'eou in Chinese) islands, which the Satsuma *han* (fief – hereafter not italicised) annexed as a tributary state in the early seventeenth century, and partly via the increasing number of Chinese immigrant merchants who set themselves up in most ports of South-East Asia. Japan's main import requirements were raw silks, silk goods, metals and sugar. With the arrival of the Portuguese these requirements significantly expanded; although the Japanese, as pointed out earlier, began manufacturing firearms themselves, there was a constant demand for imports as well, not only of firearms but also of a variety of commodities needed for warfare. The daimyo of the *sengoku* era, for obvious reasons, became very active in foreign trade. In order to pay for imports there occurred a frantic development in mining of gold and silver, especially the latter which was the medium of exchange in foreign trade.

The Portuguese increasingly became the lynch-pin of Japan's overseas commercial activities. The *sengoku* daimyo welcomed Portuguese ships and competed in luring them to the ports in their domains. Portugal's Eastern operations were triangular in nature: chartered ships left Goa annually for Macao carrying mainly silver bullion and spices; with the proceeds obtained from the sale they purchased raw silk, silk goods and gold which were added to their stock of firearms and gunpowder, with which they sailed to Japan; these were then exchanged for silver with which the Portuguese ships returned to Goa. By the late sixteenth century the Portuguese had come to monopolise most of Japan's foreign trade and they were thereby able to maintain profit rates of 70 to 80 per cent, at times even more than 100 per cent. Portugal's control of Japan's trade was clearly detrimental to the latter's economic interests.

The central government sought to remedy this situation by two measures: the first was to obtain government monopoly on mining and foreign trade, the second was to play the Portuguese against the Dutch and ultimately to force the former out. The city of Nagasaki was the centre of foreign trade. The city had in fact been quite simply donated to the Portuguese missionaries by the

Christian daimyo Omura Sumitada (1532–87); Hideyoshi confiscated the city and its surroundings and placed the whole territory under the jurisdiction of his administration. Hideyoshi, as we will see, had dissipated his energies and his coffers in two fruitless campaigns on the mainland. Ieyasu, forsaking foreign military adventures, sought to consolidate the economic foundations of his bakufu by profiting from foreign trade. He encouraged commercial transactions with foreign countries and sought to establish cordial relations with China and Korea and with the Spanish government in the Philippines. One of the very first steps which followed the establishment of his regime was to promulgate an ordinance on the conduct of the silk trade. Thus a quasi-governmental monopoly was established in the shape of the *itowappu*, whereby the merchants of the major commercial centres, Kyoto, Sakai and Nagasaki, subsequently including Edo and Osaka, were forced to form an association for the import of raw silk goods; the bakufu required priority of purchase, the remainder being distributed for marketing in the rest of the country. The *itowappu* (*ito* means silk, *wappu* quota) was subsequently broadened in order to include commodities other than silk.

By the early seventeenth century trade between Japan and China resumed – and indeed grew initially, though it came to be interrupted owing to the wars raging between the Ming and the invading Manchus – and Ieyasu was able to increase trade with the English and the Dutch at the expense of the Portuguese. Ieyasu then proceeded to establish a bakufu monopoly in merchant shipping overseas. He sent personal letters to the various rulers of South-East Asian countries informing them that hereafter only those Japanese ships which carried his official red seal permits (*shuinjo*) should be allowed to carry out trade on Japan's behalf. The 'red seal ships' (*shuinsen*) proliferated with the result that in the three decades preceding *sakoku* close to 400 ships navigated in East and South-East Asia. Japan's exports still consisted mainly of metals (essentially silver, copper and iron), while imports continued to be dominated by raw silk and silk goods, though deer-skins and shark-skins (for sword hilts) were also an important commodity. It is clear then that at this stage the bakufu was moving in the same general direction of governments such as those of Spain, Portugal, the Netherlands, England, France and Denmark, namely the establishment of monopolies (in the case of European countries via the founding of the East India Companies) over foreign trade.

Why then did Japan suddenly alter course and revert completely from a policy of commercial expansionism to one of isolationism? This is, needless to say, a much-debated subject among historians. The answer, we believe, is to be found more in political than in economic developments. *Sakoku* in terms of trade was more illusory than real. First, one needs to consider Japanese trade with China and Korea. Trade with Korea continued at an admittedly uneven but generally uninterrupted pace through the intermediary of the So daimyo family of Tsushima island who maintained a factory in the Korean port of Pusan – an arrangement which lasted well into the latter part of the nineteenth century and which the Koreans were loath to abandon. In regard to China, official relations were not re-established until China and Japan signed a European-style treaty in 1871, but trade between the two was vigorous.

It was in 1635, four years before *sakoku*, that the ban on Japanese leaving the country was imposed and subsequently naval construction for seafaring, as opposed to purely coastal navigation, was prohibited. Chinese ships, however, frequently visited the port of Nagasaki; in the first half of the seventeenth century the number of Chinese ships averaged about sixty per annum; in the years of the Ming-Ch'ing wars in the sixties and seventies there was a substantial decline, though by the end of the seventeenth century the number increased to close to 200 per annum. The nature of the trade, the commodities bought and sold, remained substantially the same, and it was also the Chinese who imported into Japan goods from South-East Asia, including rhinoceros horns – the powder of which, according to universal belief, has powerful aphrodisiac effects.

The loss of the Japanese trade, immensely valuable in terms of its ratio of world silver transactions, was a contributory cause to the decline of the Lusitanian empire. The Portuguese loss was a Dutch gain and they subsequently jealously guarded the monopoly, among European powers, which they came to have over Japanese trade. The Dutch exported from Japan mainly silver and copper – the latter especially played a vital role in the Netherlands' international trade and balance of payments throughout the seventeenth and eighteenth centuries – but also lacquer-ware and porcelains; Persia, for example, is said to have imported annually thousands of Japanese teacups bought from Dutch ships.

In the course of the eighteenth century the turnover of foreign trade in Nagasaki diminished. There were essentially two reasons for this. One is that, as shall be seen later, Japan's population (which following the *sengoku* era increased dramatically within the first 120 years or so of the Edo era from an estimated fifteen million to somewhere in the region of thirty million), by the second quarter of the eighteenth century ceased to grow and remained virtually stagnant for over a century. Thus the domestic market for imports reached a demographic ceiling.

Secondly, it will have been noticed that in all discussions on trade so far, raw silk and silk goods always figured prominently in Japan's imports. Throughout the late sixteenth and seventeenth centuries Japan consistently suffered from a considerable and indeed very harmful balance of payments deficit. Thus, it will also have been noticed that Japan's exports consisted primarily of precious metals, especially silver. Japan, therefore, was experiencing a drain of specie for the purchase of silk. The bakufu became aware of and increasingly alarmed at this situation, and began to resort to various measures. One was what in contemporary terms would be called selective import controls, in other words the importation of certain products was banned or limited quotas were imposed. Another more productive measure was, wherever possible, to encourage domestic production. The most important and fruitful area in which this policy was pursued was in sericulture. It must be stressed that throughout the Muromachi, *sengoku* and early Edo eras Japan had been completely dependent on the import of both raw silk and silk fabrics. With an assiduity comparable to that of the second half of the nineteenth century when the Japanese set about learning Western technology, Chinese treatises on sericulture were brought into Japan, studied, and Japanese works on the subject also written and distributed. Mulberry trees were grown, silkworms reared, and in due course the entire process of the silk industry, from rearing worms to finished products, was established throughout most of the country. In the short term this of course meant that Japan became self-sufficient in the product which hitherto she had been most dependent on obtaining from abroad, which, inevitably, in turn meant that her balance of payments benefited considerably. In the long term, however, though no one could have divined this at the time, the domestic production of silk was to have much more far-reaching consequences, in that when Japan was re-opened to international trade in the mid-nineteenth century it was raw silk initially, and subsequently silk products as well, which became Japan's major item of export to Europe and thereby subsidised the country's programme of industrialisation.

PACIFICATION AND UNIFICATION

We must now turn our attention briefly to the process of pacification and unification which brought the *sengoku* era to an end. The reunification of Japan may be said to have started when Oda Nobunaga entered Kyoto with Yoshiaki (1537–97), the last Ashikaga shogun; Nobunaga had already achieved the pacification and control over the central provinces from Owari to the Kinai region. Nobunaga was from a small daimyo family in the province of Owari. As he was not a descendant of the Minamoto he could not claim the shogunal throne; initially, therefore, he allowed Yoshiaki to remain shogun while he set himself up in the position of *shikken* (regent). Upon his death the mantle of pacification was taken over by Hideyoshi. Nobunaga had succeeded in controlling the central provinces of Japan, but the north and Kyushu still eluded his grasp. In 1587 Hideyoshi dealt a severe defeat on the Shimazu daimyo, whose power had extended through most of the island, and forced him back to the confines of the southern domain of Kagoshima. Three years later, with Hideyoshi's victory at Odawara, the eight provinces of the Kanto area, hitherto controlled by the Hojo, were brought to submission and placed under the supervision of Tokugawa Ieyasu. Date Masamune, recognising *force majeure*, submitted to Hideyoshi and thus was the unification of Japan achieved.

Arising out of a predilection on the part of some to find Western counterparts to major Japanese historical figures – such as Admiral Togo Heihachiro the 'Nelson of Japan', Okubo Toshimichi the 'Bismarck of Japan', etc. – Hideyoshi is sometimes referred to as the 'Napoleon of Japan'. Whereas the Corsican was of petty nobility, Hideyoshi's origins were far more modest. Both, however, were complete parvenus on the political scene, both rose to prominence because of their impressive records in warfare, both were first-class generals but poor admirals, both waged war, but also carried out extensive internal reforms which had radical and long-lasting effects. Hideyoshi's nerve, in every literal and figurative sense of the term, was amazing. He fraudulently claimed to be of Fujiwara descent and thereby in 1585 received the investiture from the tenno Ogimachi (1516–93) as *kanpaku*. The fiction is less important than the fact. The tenno Ogimachi – as was also the case with his grandson Go-Yozei who was forced to recognise Ieyasu's fraudulent claim to Minamoto pedigree and thereby invested in him and his descendants the office of shogun – was in one sense impotent, in that he could not counter Hideyoshi's military strength, but he retained supreme legitimacy. The imperial court in the course of the *sengoku* era had fallen in material terms in possibly the worst condition of its existence. Hideyoshi revived imperial finances and imperial prestige, while securing his own prestige and power. The very act of seeking imperial sanctification sanctified, once again, the tenno; Hideyoshi, therefore, and Ieyasu subsequently, paved the way for the Imperial Restoration which was to occur three centuries later.

Hideyoshi was the architect, Ieyasu the builder – albeit inserting a few modifications in the original blueprint. There is, however, one major difference between the policies of the two. Ieyasu, as we have seen, believed in the benefits of international commerce and international intercourse, but he did not, however, favour territorial expansion. Hideyoshi's internal policies will be looked at shortly; first, however, we must ask why Hideyoshi sought to embark on a policy of expansionism and how it was implemented.

The second question is easier to resolve than the first. In regard to Hideyoshi's motivation, one can do little more than hypothesise. As has been pointed out above, marauding by Japanese pirates on the coasts of China and Korea had occurred in the fourteenth century and was resumed with greater force in the mid-sixteenth. Hideyoshi had put a stop to the activities of these latter-day *wako*, but China still refused to re-establish relations with Japan. One factor, therefore, was a sense of pique on Hideyoshi's part for being rebuffed by the Ming – a sentiment no doubt aggravated by the contempt in which the Japanese were held by the Chinese. There is, it would seem, another element. Warfare, except perhaps in cases where the result is complete defeat, does not appear to drain warriors' energies, but to fuel them. In 1590 domestic peace was achieved. The atmosphere, however, remained militantly warlike, thus providing circumstances under which a good foreign campaign would be welcome. Also a foreign campaign was a means of dissipating the attention and energies of potential foes. Victory would no doubt have also resulted in substantial economic gains; Japan would then control all the wealth and trade of the Far East and South-East of Asia, and indeed Hideyoshi's vision stretched as far as India. It is possible also, though there is no way to prove it, that Hideyoshi was moved by Spain's example. Finally, no doubt one of the most vital factors was quite simply Hideyoshi's megalomania.

Hideyoshi had originally hoped for, if not Korean alliance, at least acquiescence in his planned invasion of China. Due to a degree of recalcitrance and procrastination on the part of the Korean kingdom, in May 1592 an army of just under 200,000 landed at Pusan. The whole campaign, including intermittent periods of armistice and peace negotiations, lasted six and a half years, ending shortly after Hideyoshi's death and indeed at his dying request. Initially the Japanese were highly successful and soon occupied all of Korea and reached as far as south-eastern Manchuria. Spectacular though their initial victories may have been, they were still far from Peking. In fact they never progressed any further and when the Japanese troops were withdrawn, a stalemate had been reached; the Japanese, it is true, suffered little, but Korea was left devastated.

Although the Ming response to Korea's plea for aid was initially weak, it subsequently increased significantly; and although the Japanese were far superior both in arms and tactics on land, the Koreans, especially under the brilliant admiral Yi Sun-sin (1545–98), mastered the sea and therefore cut off Japan's supplies; the severe Korean winter caused sickness and demoralisation in the Japanese camps; the Japanese were constantly harassed by Korean guerrilla-type bands, known as the *uigan* (righteous armies). Thus ended Japan's first concerted attempt at imperialism. One footnote perhaps can be added: the comparison with Napoleon, precarious in any case, ceases in that Hideyoshi, unlike the Corsican, did not lead his own troops into battle, but sought to orchestrate the campaign from Japan – in spite of repeated announcements that he was shortly to depart.

REFORMS AND A NEW SOCIAL ORDER

The background of the *sengoku* era must be clearly understood in order to appreciate the numerous intensive and extensive reforms which occurred, first under Hideyoshi and then subsequently under Ieyasu and his early successors, in the last decade or so of the sixteenth century and the first four of the seventeenth. Japan in the *sengoku* decades did not suffer merely from political anarchy and the ravages of warfare. The country can be said to have been inflicted with a moral cancer – which is no doubt one of the (admittedly many) reasons why Christianity should have proved appealing in this atmosphere of depravation. The most hedonistic forms of licentiousness were rife and in battle savagery and treachery prevailed. Among the numerous reforms passed, therefore, one of the major elements which must be constantly borne in mind is that the new rulers of Japan were strongly motivated by a desire to impose a moral order. This will be seen in various areas, though to show the extent to which they went, one example is worth citing.

Prostitution, needless to say, had been rife; following an edict enacted in 1617 under Ieyasu's heir, Hidetada (1579–1632), a cleaning-up operation was undertaken. Hereafter the profession was allowed to be exercised only in designated areas on the periphery of the cities, in areas which came to be referred to as *yukaku* ('pleasure enclosures') – thereby adopting a policy, albeit of course unwittingly, pioneered in Europe by the sixth-century BC Athenian statesman Solon, who had established houses of prostitution in certain quarters of the outskirts of Athens and declared them a state monopoly. It must of course be pointed out that, as in the case with Solon, Hidetada's motivations may not have been exclusively moral, but economic as well: licensed prostitution = taxed prostitution.

The Edo bakufu also sought to limit the extent of concubinage. Strictly speaking Japan was a monogamy in that a man had only one wife, but the system of concubinage was well established. According to rules passed in 1615, in theory daimyo were limited to eight concubines, high functionaries to five, samurai to two, while commoners should have none. As with all moral legislation anywhere, such proscriptions had only a very limited effect.

In regard to economic and political reforms, the overriding concern of Hideyoshi and subsequently the early Tokugawa shogun was to achieve the maximum degree of national unification, a necessary precondition of which was to ensure the weakening of the daimyo. (The abolition of the daimyo at this stage was militarily impossible.) In social terms the concern was to restore order, to restore feudal hierarchical relations and thereby to prevent the sort of social chaos which had prevailed – and which, ironically, Hideyoshi himself had benefited from – in the *sengoku* era. The ideology which was used to buttress the regime was a rigid form of Confucianism, which, as indicated briefly in the earlier chapter, perceived society in hierarchical terms and alleged that chaos did ensue when the hierarchical order broke down.

In economic terms we have already seen how Hideyoshi imposed a monopoly on mining. Subsequently a central monopoly was also enforced in regard to minting of coins. It was also during this period that the standardisation of weights and measures was carried out. We have also seen how Hideyoshi sought to establish a monopoly over foreign trade and how this policy was pursued with effect by Ieyasu, including the retention of Nagasaki as a bakufu-administered port. Further steps were taken to achieve greater national economic consolidation. Since the Nara era customs barriers (*sekisho*) had been erected and in the course of the Ashikaga shogunate these multiplied; in 1568 Nobunaga began to abolish the *sekisho*, a policy continued by Hideyoshi, while under the Tokugawa the private construction of *sekisho* was prohibited and those which existed no longer performed an economic function, but a purely policing exercise.

Perhaps Hideyoshi's greatest achievement was the land survey which he had carried out from 1582 to 1598 – known as the *taiko-kenchi, kenchi* meaning land surveying. The land survey was carried out in a manner according to which the village (*mura*) was the basic unit; from the assessment of the yield of each individual plot, the total was calculated in the form of the *muradaka*, namely the agricultural yield of the village. On this basis taxes were to be paid; thus the responsibility for the payment of taxes was not an individual, but a collective matter, it being up to the village administrators (*mura-yakunin*), usually elected from among the farmers, to ensure that each household contributed its due and the total reached, as indeed it was also their responsibility to control irrigation and generally maintain order. The *taiko-kenchi*, therefore, recognised the right of cultivation of the farmers on their plots; but at the same time peasant migration and the buying or selling of land were strictly prohibited.

The social order which came to be imposed on Japan was derived from Confucianist principles. In the Chinese scheme of things, society was divided into (in descending order), literati, peasants, artisans and the merchants; because they were not directly engaged in production and labour, but benefited from that of others, merchants were relegated to the bottom rung of the ladder. The settlement in Edo Japan consisted of replacing the literati with the samurai. There is, however, an important distinction which made the Japanese system far more rigid. In China any male, irrespective of how lowly his birth, could aspire to the top rung of the ladder, assuming he passed the competitive civil service examinations. China, therefore, in social philosophy remained a meritocracy and admitted social mobility. Japan, on the other hand, was an aristocracy, the only determining factor being that of birth.

The process of social differentiation between the peasantry and the samurai was accelerated by Hideyoshi's *katana-gari* (sword hunt) of 1588, whereby weapons were confiscated from peasants; it should be noted, however, that although this policy may have been couched in ideological terms, it had also been motivated by strong pragmatic considerations, namely to try to bring to an end the numerous and constant peasant rebellions which had become endemic in the *sengoku* era. The process of differentiation between samurai and peasants was furthered by the policy of removing all samurai from the land and installing them in the castle-towns (*joka-machi*). This measure was also aimed at securing the feudal bonds between lord and retainers; by placing the latter in firm allegiance to the former, it was hoped that the practice of *gekokujo* would be brought to an end.

The establishment of this network of relationships was of a social, political, but also economic character. For the sake of simplicity, we shall ignore here merchants and artisans. The basic social and judicial unit was the household (*ie*). The institution and concept of the *ie* is one to which we shall be frequently referring in this work. It is at the same time one of the most important and complex phenomena in Japanese history and society. Sometimes translated as 'family', preference here is given to 'household', in that the *ie* included all those physically attached to the household and not necessarily by ties of kinship – for example, servants, apprentices, adopted sons and daughters, with wives belonging to their husbands' *ie* but not to that of their parents – while family members, brothers, sisters, aunts, uncles, etc., would probably belong to separate *ie*. Inside the *ie*, according to Confucianist precepts, a strict hierarchy was supposed to be observed, in that all owed allegiance to the head of the household, while younger brothers were subservient to the eldest brother, sisters to their brothers, and so forth. The individual *ie* was part of that greater collective, the *mura* (village), and each owed obeisance and paid taxes to the *mura-yakunin*. They in turn paid homage and the taxes to the samurai administrators, who passed on the latter into the daimyo's coffers, and, of course, owed the daimyo complete and absolute allegiance.

The samurai were forbidden – in keeping with the strict social segregation – from engaging in remuneratory activities; their income consisted of fixed stipends, determined by their rank, which they received from their daimyo. The daimyo, therefore, had the exclusive right of taxation and jurisdiction in their han (fiefs). They were not responsible for direct taxation to the bakufu, but they could be, and frequently were, called upon to contribute to public works. The daimyo, who were also ranked in hierarchical order, owed allegiance to the shogun (or to the *kanpaku* at the time of Hideyoshi). While the shogun (or *kanpaku*) owed absolute allegiance to the tenno, from whom his legitimacy was derived, the shogun was also responsible for the economic welfare of the imperial court. The system was one of decentralised unification; this may appear to be a contradiction in terms, but would be, nevertheless, a reasonable translation of what in the Edo era is referred to as the *baku-han-sei* (bakufu-han system).

The daimyo – the number of which varied, but was generally during the Edo era in the region of 270, though their revenue, territory, power and status differed enormously as well – remained, therefore, in theory autonomous. For peace and unification to be achieved, however, the absolute prerequisite was to secure the submission of the daimyo. What Hideyoshi did was to deprive all existing daimyo of their estates. Those he was militarily strong enough to crush, he abolished; the others he enfeoffed anew, either in their former estates, or in different ones, or in smaller segments of their former estates. This practice was carried on by the Tokugawa shoguns, with indeed the most extensive reorganisation of daimyo taking place following the decisive Tokugawa victory in the battle of Sekigahara in 1600 – in which Ieyasu's power was challenged by the daimyo who remained faithful to the house of Toyotomi and the person of the young Hideyori. This policy pursued by both Hideyoshi and Ieyasu was aimed not only at weakening foes, but also at rewarding allies. The han given by the shogun to the daimyo – and the same applied to the shogun's direct retainers, of which there were two categories, *hatamoto* (bannermen) and *go-kenin* (personal attendants) – were personal gifts to the individuals concerned, not to their descendants. What generally happened, though not invariably, especially in the early years of the Edo bakufu, was that once a daimyo died, his heir was re-invested with jurisdiction over his fief. Similarly, when a shogun died the relationship was renewed.

The battle of Sekigahara was undoubtedly a landmark and it was this victory which enabled Ieyasu, three years later, to proclaim himself shogun, establish the Tokugawa dynasty and a bakufu in the eastern city of Edo. In spite of this success, however, Ieyasu's position remained somewhat precarious: he had both former foes and ambitious allies to fear, and while Hideyori remained alive his claim to legitimacy was jealously and resolutely fostered by his heroically courageous and legendary mother, Yodogimi (1569–1615). The Toyotomi family ceased to pose a danger in 1615, for the simple reason that it ceased to exist altogether following the Tokugawa siege and destruction of Osaka castle in that year and the suicide of both Yodogimi and Hideyori. Ieyasu died the following year.

Ieyasu's heirs, notably the second and third shoguns, Hidetada (1579–1632) and Iemitsu (1603–51), further consolidated the Edo bakufu's military, economic, and political power, thereby weakening that of the daimyo, until in the mid-seventeenth century it could be claimed without any exaggeration that the Tokugawa house had established what amounted to an absolute monarchy in a fashion comparable, in many respects, to that of Louis XIV in France – with the important difference, however, that Hidetada, Iemitsu and their successors did not drain the treasury by engaging in foreign wars. It remains, therefore, in the final pages of this chapter to describe the Tokugawa settlement as it was formed in the course of the seventeenth century and, *mutatis mutandis*, remained in essence until 1862 (the year in which the *sankin-kotai*, the system of alternative residence of daimyo in Edo, was abandoned).

FOUNDATIONS OF THE TOKUGAWA BAKUFU

Obviously one of the more important pillars of the Tokugawa edifice had to rest on wealth. Already under Hideyoshi, the Tokugawa domains had been substantially increased, with the result, in fact, that their value – calculated in terms of yields of rice, the normal unit being the *koku*, equivalent to 4·96 bushels – was by far the greatest in Japan, in fact more than double the second largest han. In the rearrangements which occurred under Ieyasu and his successors, these holdings were increased; in fact the *tenryo* (shogunal domains) came to account for about a quarter of the Japanese territory. We have already seen how the bakufu maintained a monopoly on foreign trade, mining and minting. The Tokugawa administration also took under its control most of Japan's major commercial urban centres, including Nagasaki, Kyoto, Sakai, Hyogo, Niigata, Hakodate and Osaka. Thus the bakufu enjoyed substantial revenues from agricultural taxation, commerce and mining. Furthermore, the bakufu obtained considerable contributions in both kind and labour from a number of daimyo for public works, which included the Tokugawa's own castles, such as the Edo castle, the newly constructed Nijo in Kyoto, and so on.

The enrichment of the bakufu was accompanied, by and large, by the impoverishment, in relative terms, of the daimyo. Daimyo, under the Tokugawa settlement, were ranked according to two, non-corresponding, methods. Thus a daimyo's power could be measured in terms of the number of *koku* of rice at which his domain was valued. In terms, however, of status and proximity to the shogunal throne, there was another form of division, namely the *shinpan*, *fudai* and *tozama*. The *shinpan* were collateral branches of the main Tokugawa family; they had close access to the shogun, and in cases of the ruling shogun dying without an heir, a successor might be chosen from one of three families (collectively known as the *go-sanke*), the Owari, Kii and Mito. The *fudai* were those who had allied themselves to the Tokugawa prior to the battle of Sekigahara, while the *tozama* were those who submitted themselves to Ieyasu in the course of or immediately after the battle. The *tozama*, who included such powerful daimyo as those of Shimazu (Satsuma han), Maeda (Kaga), Date (Sendai) and Mori (Choshu), were in many cases wealthy, but were perceived by the Tokugawa with suspicion and throughout the Edo era they were generally without any influence or notable presence at the shogunal court. The *fudai*, on the other hand, usually had far more meagre revenues, but they could hold influential positions within the shogunal court, and indeed it was from their number that the *roju* (councillors, generally a body of about six members) were appointed.

Following the death of Hideyori and at a time when Tokugawa power was clearly in an uncontested ascendant, the bakufu issued the *buke sho-hatto* and the *kuge sho-hatto* in 1615; these were the rules which were to govern the conduct of *buke* and *kuge* affairs. They were the most extensive codes to be published in Japan since the *ritsu-ryo* of the Heian era and provided the bakufu with the cornerstone of its legal institutions. Nevertheless, the daimyo did not always prove as submissive to these laws as was intended, and their recalcitrance provided the bakufu with further need to discipline and rearrangements of han; in the first half-century of the Edo bakufu's existence, daimyo were removed from one part of the country to another on something like 300 occasions. So far as the *kuge* were concerned, of which there were about 140 families, the rules which governed their conduct consisted essentially of ensuring that they remain in their residences in the *gyoen* (imperial park), ministering to the needs of the most exalted prisoner of all, the tenno. The *sho-hatto* could be modified according to circumstances or indeed according to the whims of succeeding shogun.

In 1635, as the most devastating means of weakening the power of the daimyo, shogun Iemitsu instituted the system of *sankin-kotai* – *kotai* means to alternate, while the term *sankin* can be roughly translated as 'reporting for audience'. Under this system daimyo were required to travel to Edo and, though there were variations, generally to spend one year in two in personal attendance at the shogunal court. We have here a good illustration of the methods used by an absolute monarchy – the principles and indeed the means are comparable to those lying behind Louis XIV's building of Versailles. The expenses incurred by the daimyo were enormous: as a result of *sankin-kotai*, daimyo had to maintain at least two residences, one in their fief capital, another in Edo – indeed some daimyo maintained as many as five *yashiki* (mansions) in Edo alone; to and from Edo the daimyo could not travel light, *noblesse oblige*, but needed to be escorted by huge retinues of retainers, servants and so on. The *sankin-kotai*, therefore, was the most effective means of weakening the daimyo's economic base. The daimyo's wife and children were forced to reside in Edo, hence hostages to the bakufu in case of rebellion. The long periods of attendance at Edo also had the effect of weakening the daimyo's links with his han. The national repercussions of the *sankin-kotai*, albeit indirectly, contributed more than any other measure in ultimately laying the foundations for modern Japan and hence the ultimate overthrow of the Tokugawa regime.

The Tokugawa system was moving towards crystallisation. Another measure taken in this period, already frequently referred to, was *sakoku* (closing the country). Four years before its formal and final implementation, in 1639, the Edo bakufu had already banned the travel abroad of Japanese subjects. The reason for this policy, as that of *sakoku* in general, was primarily political. There had already been a number of serious uprisings; it was believed, no doubt correctly, that the Iberians would not hesitate in forming an alliance with a party hostile to the Tokugawa regime. By prohibiting Japanese to travel abroad, for example to Macao or the Philippines, the bakufu was seeking to ensure that there would be no intrigues likely to result in Iberian assistance or alliance with potential rebels.

While the bakufu was consolidating its military, economic and political base, it was also establishing one national orthodox ideology. Christianity, the *jashumon*, was proscribed and numerous measures, apart from persecution, were taken in order to ensure that the evil, heterodox sect was in fact rooted out; these included, for example, *fumi-e*, the practice of treading on sacred Christian images which people had to carry out, usually at the time of the census, in order to prove they did not belong to the proscribed faith. To insist, however, on the persecution of Christians and the proscription of their faith is perhaps to perceive Japanese history from an excessively europocentric point of view, for the simple reason that it was not only Christians who suffered. Nobunaga, for example, had ruthlessly crushed certain Buddhist centres, especially those of the Ikko sect – including the burning to ashes of the temples of Mount Hiei in 1571 and the forced submission of the bonzes of Mount Koya in 1581. In the Edo era for the most part Buddhism was tolerated, but only as a religion, not as a secular force.

Ieyasu, Hidetada and Iemitsu had taken considerable personal control of affairs. Although Ieyasu built on foundations laid by Hideyoshi and his successors continued erecting an edifice generally along the lines of Ieyasu's intentions, it nevertheless remains the case that the first three Tokugawa shoguns were undoubtedly dynamic innovators. The fourth shogun, Ietsuna (1639–80), inherited his father's throne when he was twelve. It was under his reign that the practice of *junshi* (self-immolation) was abolished; otherwise, Ietsuna followed a policy of severe censorship, imprisoning many writers, and it was he who carried *sakoku* much further by imposing a strict ban on the importation of foreign books (including Chinese translations of Western books or even Chinese works which dealt with Western sciences). His brother, Tsunayoshi (1646–1709), had a degree of innovatory impulse, but is perhaps chiefly remembered for his veneration of dogs – he was born in the Year of the Dog – and for forcing the population to follow his example, whereby not only must no dogs be injured, but also they should be respectfully addressed as *O-Inu-sama* (Venerable Master Dog). Tsunayoshi died at the age of sixty-three, stabbed by his wife.

Thus the institutionalisation of the office of shogun had also begun. Although there was an occasional enlightened despot among them, for example the eighth shogun Yoshimune (1677–1751), by and large the later shogun were undistinguished, often ascending to the throne when still children, until certainly by the latter part of the eighteenth century the authority of the shogun was no more than nominal. The last shogun, Yoshinobu (1837–1913), was an immensely dynamic and innovative leader, but by then it was too late.

The policies of Nobunaga, Hideyoshi, Ieyasu and his two immediate successors were in great part motivated by a desire to bring *gekokujo* to an end. In fact by the latter part of the seventeenth century, both at bakufu and individual han levels, *gekokujo* reasserted itself. There are occasional exceptions – there were a few masterful daimyo for example – but *mutatis mutandis* the picture to be drawn here has widespread application.

Although originating as an absolutist monarchy, in the course of time the major feature of Edo Japan was its bureaucratic nature. Daimyo were virtually incapable of undertaking the affairs of their domains in view of the amount of time they had to spend – mainly doing nothing but engaging in conspicuous consumption – in Edo; administrative responsibility, therefore, was entrusted to their retainers. At this stage, however, it should be stressed that the bureaucracy, both at bakufu and han levels, was based on an aristocratic, not meritocratic principle: most offices were either hereditary or limited to persons of certain rank within the samurai hierarchy. Certainly at bakufu level, also at least among the larger han, administrative affairs became both more numerous and more complex and required an adequate machinery.

At the apex of the bakufu pyramid stood the shogun. The immediate Tokugawa relations (the *go-sanke*) and the shogun's female relatives, wife and concubines, residing in the *ooku* (grand interior) had direct access to the person of the shogun, but in both cases their influence was generally limited to choosing an heir to the throne when circumstances required it. The chief official counsellors to the shogun were the *roju* (council of elders), who were recruited exclusively from the *fudai* daimyo. From their number a *tairo* (chief elder) might be appointed. Below the *roju* came the *waka-doshiyori* (junior elders). Both *roju* and *waka-doshiyori* were changed at regular intervals, the number in both groups generally in the region of five. Another office was that of *ometsuke* (great censors), again numbering about five, who reported to the *roju*, mainly on the activities of the daimyo; the *ometsuke* were recruited from the *hatamoto* (bannermen, the shogun's direct retainers). Lower down were the *metsuke* (censors) who reported to the *waka-doshiyori* on the conduct of the *hatamoto*. Parallel to these posts were other offices. The *Edo-machi bugyo* (Edo magistrate) was in charge of all administrative and police matters of the city of Edo – whose population was huge as a result of *sankin-kotai* – and was assisted by officials and constables numbering about 150. The other cities under bakufu control also had their *bugyo* and administrative apparatus. The *jisha bugyo* (commissioners of temples and shrines) kept an eye on the activities of monks and bonzes. One of the more important offices was that of *kanjo bugyo* (administrator of finance) who was responsible for the finances and general matters pertaining to the fiefs under the direct jurisdiction of the bakufu. The *kanjo bugyo* was assisted by a number of deputies (*gundai* or *daikan*), who in turn relied on the service of *tezuke* (clerks). At the bottom of the bureaucracy were the *mura-yakunin* (village administrators).

In this apparently byzantine administrative machinery a most sophisticated system of checks and balances was in operation: to put it another way, everyone was spying on someone else and simultaneously being spied upon. Edo Japan, it is no exaggeration to say, was a highly effective police state. It should also be clear that although high offices were named, administrative responsibility devolved to lower echelons. Official bureaucratic power was absolute in Japan, a phenomenon well illustrated in the slogan of the time, *Kanson-minpi*, 'revere officials – despise the people'. Also, it will be recalled that samurai or bushi were warriors; on the other hand, fighting, apart from peasant rebellions, had been eradicated.

Increasingly in the course of the Edo era, the civil branch of both bakufu and han bureaucracy (*yakukata*), which took charge of administration, finance, justice and so forth, became increasingly appealing to samurai and an important aspect of their society and outlook. *Kanryo-shugi* (bureaucratism), which has undoubtedly been *the* most marked feature of modern Japanese society and remains so to this day, was born and developed in the Edo era. This is not to say that bureaucracies had not existed beforehand, and certainly a fairly elaborate bureaucracy existed, for example, under the old *ritsu-ryo* system. But it was in the Edo era that it became all-pervasive, that Japan moved away from a martial to a bureaucratic society. Finally, though the nature of this phenomenon remains to be explained in the following chapters, one can at this stage already indicate that the revolution which overthrew the Edo bakufu and 'restored' the tenno in 1868 was in fact a bureaucratic revolution.

PART 2

PRELUDE TO MODERNITY: THE EDO ERA

Introduction

Writers of Japanese history in the second half of the nineteenth and early twentieth centuries tended to subscribe to what has since been somewhat derisorily called 'the Sleeping Beauty Theory'; namely, that upon entering the period of *sakoku* Japan fell fast asleep, remained unchanged, until the Western powers arrived and all of a sudden everything happened. This view of history was, to a certain extent, compatible with contemporary Japanese perceptions: the light of the new era of civilisation and enlightenment – *bunmei-kaika*, the slogan of the 1870s – contrasted sharply with the feudal obscurity of the past.

An impressive amount of research, especially in the last three decades or so, has revealed numerous elements of dynamism in Edo society. Even apart from empirical observation, however, from a purely speculative point of view it is simply illogical that Edo Japan should, so to speak, have gone into hibernation: the remarkable changes which occurred in the latter part of the nineteenth century must have had their roots somewhere.

The chronological evolution of the Edo era from the period with which we concluded the former chapter, the late 1630s, until the beginning of the nineteenth century will not be dealt with in any detail here. Rather we will be concerned in investigating certain prominent features of the Edo era and identifying trends; this exercise will be carried out thematically rather than chronologically. A general periodisation, however, may not be out of place.

The three most important determinants of the evolution of Japanese society in the Edo era were peace, *sakoku* and *sankin-kotai*. The establishment of peace led to the stabilisation of economic life; which, in turn, resulted in a substantial growth in population on the one hand and more land under cultivation on the other. *Sakoku* also meant an increase in domestic production and obviously far greater self-reliance. *Sankin-kotai* led to a substantial movement of goods, techniques, and ideas throughout the country. This resulted in a number of significant economic developments: transportation and communications were much improved, agricultural techniques became more sophisticated and there was a greater variation in crops. The separation of peasants and samurai, the forced migration of the latter into the *joka-machi* (castle-towns), and the inevitable increase in the population of Edo because of *sankin–kotai* led to a marked degree of urbanisation. This development gave rise to substantial urban consumer demand, not only for clothes, food, drink and other essentials, but also for luxuries – ceramics, silk-ware, lacquer-ware, swords, and so on. All this movement and demand motivated agricultural diversification, which led to the erosion of subsistence agriculture in favour of cash crops. Cash crops, in turn, necessarily involved the monetisation of the economy. Monetisation requires money-lenders, brokers, and so forth. Money-lending and the need for transporting and storing goods, as well as providing services and retailing, inevitably resulted in the rise of merchants. The consolidation of a national market also brought about a degree of regional specialisation and agricultural diversification, which led to an expanding rural entrepreneurial group. This is the general picture, details of which will be looked at shortly.

Historiographical orthodoxy has been that, whereas the seventeenth century, culminating in the brilliance of the Genroku era (1688 – 1703), experienced growth and increasing prosperity, the eighteenth century witnessed stagnation. As inevitably happens with orthodoxy, revisionism has crept in, the latter tendency insisting that the eighteenth century also experienced evolution and economic development. One's appreciation of Edo society would depend on whether it is viewed macroscopically or microscopically. The overall impression obtained from the seventeenth century is that of a significant degree of dynamism, innovation, movement at practically all levels. For example, in spite of *sakoku*, the rapidly growing population managed to feed itself. The most startling fact, by any standard, is that Japan's population in the eighteenth century simply ceased to grow. No doubt *sakoku* was responsible for this state of affairs. The interdiction on Japanese going abroad meant that at times of famine there were no means of obtaining external sources of food-stuff; also, the generally limited nature of contact with the outside world imposed serious restrictions on technological developments. This must be contrasted with the significant amount of geographic mobility occurring in Europe, where societies were able to capitalise on the inventions and innovations of others.

There are other indices of decline: official corruption in the bakufu, for example, assumed alarming proportions. Also, whereas city merchants in the seventeenth century had proved to be enterprising and innovative, in the eighteenth century they were little more than usurious. Population control seems to have been achieved largely as a result of infanticide (the current idiom being *mabiki*, 'thinning out'). It was noted in the former chapter that one of the major motivations for Hideyoshi's *katana-gari* (sword hunt) was to bring an end to peasant revolts. The peasants went on revolting, but the number of uprisings increased in geometric proportions in the course of the era: during the seventeenth century there was approximately one uprising per annum, jumping to three a year in the first four decades of the eighteenth century, five in mid-century, followed by six for the remaining part of the Edo era. It has been suggested that the combination of infanticide and peasant uprisings need not be interpreted as manifestations of decline, but rather as an illustration of rising expectations resulting from higher standards of living. This is not necessarily an implausible explanation. The point is, however, that current perceptions in Japan at the time – whether rebellious peasants, moralists, reformers or critical intellectuals – were that both the economy and society were in a parlous state. On the surface, even with the proverbial benefit of hindsight, this certainly appeared to be the case.

Indices, indicating either progression or regression, could be invoked. The point requiring emphasis, however, is that at a general societal level the country was in a state of stagnation, indeed decline. Upon closer examination, however, it becomes clear that there were areas of growth and development, though these tended to be scattered. This two-dimensional picture helps to explain two things. If everyone had been happy with the general state of affairs, it goes without saying that the revolution would not have occurred. If, on the other hand, the situation had been one of utter stagnation and collapse, Japan's remarkable and rapid modernisation could not have taken place.

3 Society in the Edo Era

Japanese society was organised according to a strict hierarchy of basically four estates, namely the *shi-no-ko-sho* – samurai, peasants, artisans and merchants. Here a very important point has to be made. These four groups, or estates, must not be confused with classes. Class, in fact, is not a useful analytical concept in terms of the early part of the Edo era. It is as a result of a number of forces which evolved in the course of this period that classes, along with class interest and class conflict, began to emerge; but the process of differentiation which occurred took place mainly *within* the four estates. When one comes to consider the disintegration of the Tokugawa regime and the nature of the revolution, to speak in terms of a peasant, merchant or samurai class is misleading, in fact meaningless. The variations within these estates were far too substantial to allow any sense of homogeneity or solidarity, in spite of occasional rhetoric to the contrary.

THE PEASANTRY

The *shi-no-ko-sho* aspect of the Edo settlement was motivated partly by ideological considerations, but it was also economic. Tokugawa economic philosophy was quintessentially physiocratic. It is for this reason that the peasants were allotted the second rung in the social order and that Edo moralists engaged in platitudinous incantations about the virtues of agriculture and of the peasant existence. It should be emphasised that irrespective of changes taking place within the economy, notably the dominant role of merchant wealth, the basic social ethic of Edo Japan remained constant and was never, unlike the rise of the capitalist ideology in north-west Europe and the United States, effectively challenged in the course of the Edo era.

Leaving ideology aside, the major contribution of the peasantry as envisaged by the Tokugawa order was two-fold: to feed the ruling orders and pay taxes. The peasants constituted the vast bulk of society, even towards the end of the period corresponding to approximately 80 per cent of the population. They were the backbone of the economy and neither bakufu nor han governments hesitated in extracting from the peasantry as much as was materially possible, in fact in some cases more than was materially possible. The basic theory of the Edo agrarian economy was quite simple. Peasants paid

64

taxes into the coffers of the han or bakufu treasuries – that is, to whatever government had jurisdiction and rights of taxation over them. Taxes were paid in kind, while daimyo or shogun paid stipends, also in kind, to their retainers. The peasant should be allowed to live, or simply, perhaps, survive; agriculture, as envisaged by the Tokugawa settlement, therefore was at a subsistence level.

In fact, there was considerable agricultural development, especially in the course of the seventeenth century. This was obviously necessary in order to allow for the significant demographic increase, already noted, to take place. The population was able to grow, partly due to an increase in agricultural productivity, but mainly due to a considerable territorial expansion by means of land reclamation; the area of land under cultivation was about doubled in the period 1600 to 1720. Agriculture throughout the Edo era, it must be emphasised, remained labour-intensive; very little use was made of capital equipment and those technological improvements which did occur were only of marginal significance – Japanese agriculture was not really mechanised until after the Second World War.

The actual yield per acre remained low, very much in accordance with other Asian cultivators. By the early eighteenth century agricultural development had reached a ceiling: given existing conditions there was no more food to cater to a further increase in population. The secondary and tertiary sectors developed, but not to a sufficient degree to absorb large numbers of surplus rural population, nor, owing to *sakoku*, could surplus population be channelled into emigration – as occurred, for example, in the British Isles and Ireland with surplus population being exported to the colonies of settlement. Population had to be controlled, therefore, by a number of Malthusian checks – other than war, in view of the Pax Tokugawa – which consisted primarily of infanticide in the rural areas and abortions in the cities, as well as a number of famines which occurred at fairly frequent and regular intervals especially during the latter part of the eighteenth century.

Riziculture in Edo Japan was labour-intensive. The cities, especially Osaka, developed as significant centres of commerce and services, but *not* manufacture. The manufacturing sector established itself where the labour supply could be found, namely the rural areas, where there was the opportunity of recruiting seasonal labour – in fact more often females from the farms. A contrast was drawn, therefore, between the affluent cities and the deprived villages. The popular rural perceptions of this contrast amounted more to caricatures of reality than reality itself; there was urban deprivation in Japan, as indeed there was village affluence. But it remains a significant feature of Japanese history until the conclusion of the Second World War – or, more precisely, the 1946 Land Reform carried out by the American

Occupation authorities – that these perceptions remained steadfast. The peasantry were exploited in order to subsidise urban life – symbolised, among other things, by the recruitment of peasant girls to service the urban brothels. If one fails to grasp this tension between rural and urban areas as a leitmotiv of pre-modern and modern Japanese history, then one will misunderstand the nature of the evolution of Japanese society; the Japan Communist Party of the inter-war period, rigidly and blindly dogmatic, failed to understand this phenomenon which, in turn, partly explains why its success in terms of recruitment was minimal and hardly to be found outside university circles.

By no means, however, should the nature of Edo agricultural society be viewed as static. Several points need to be clarified. The first was that significant urbanisation in quantitative terms did take place, qualitatively consisting essentially of samurai and merchants. Consumer demand in the urban areas was inevitably going to have significant repercussions on the rural economy. In short, from a subsistence economy, there occurred a definite trend towards the development of cash crops and diversification. Another point to be borne in mind regards taxation. The percentage of output siphoned off for taxes varied according to region and circumstance – much lower, for example, in the case of reclaimed land – but at a macro level would probably average out at about 50 per cent. Generally speaking the amount to be given up in the form of taxes was fixed; in other words, it was determined on the basis of the yield calculated at the time of Hideyoshi's land survey or other surveys which occasionally, but infrequently, occurred in the course of the Edo era. Taxation, therefore, took account of potential yield, not actual yield, on an annual basis; fluctuations resulting from climatic, technological or other factors did not figure in the registers. Peasants obviously stood to lose a great deal, especially in bad years, but they could also benefit, possibly quite substantially, were a bumper crop to occur.

Conditions, adverse or favourable, obviously did not affect all peasants throughout Japan equally at the same time. For example, the topographically and climatically better endowed south-west had far better chances of prospering than was the case in the harsher climate of the north-east – which is, in fact, what happened. The Kansai region particularly improved, partly because of a more benign climate, also because of its proximity to the huge market of Osaka. There developed in the course of the Tokugawa era, therefore, a geographical differentiation between, in relative terms, a rich south-west and a poor north-east. This is another feature of Japanese history which remained reasonably constant until fairly recently.

Even within the same region, however, significant differences between the peasantry developed. Farming in Edo Japan was definitely a precarious form of existence; nonetheless opportunities, given a degree of luck and a good dosage of initiative, did exist and could be exploited. In view of a number of developments taking place in the course of the Edo era, and especially the rise in urban consumer demand, the forces of a market economy were in operation. The astute – and lucky – peasant could judge the requirements that the market demanded and the opportunities it offered. Having been successful, for example, in generating a small surplus after taxes had been paid and mouths fed, there were a number of things he could do. He might invest in the purchase of some implement or raw material necessary for diversification; he might extend his land by reclamation; he might also extend his control, if not actual proprietorship, over his less fortunate neighbour's land. This last point is important and merits brief consideration. The unsuccessful, unlucky peasant would have difficulties paying taxes and feeding himself and his family. In order to meet both demands he might resort to borrowing from a more affluent peasant. The selling and buying of land, as was noted earlier, was forbidden but nevertheless the poor peasant might offer his land as collateral, in other words he mortgaged it. In view of the law regarding selling and leaving one's land, but more significantly in view of the continued labour-intensive nature of riziculture, the poor peasant would not be forced off his land, but would remain and pay rent to his creditor. This provided yet another potential source of revenue for the richer peasants.

Thus, in the course of the Edo era, a rural surplus was generated, the forces of the market economy resulted in diversification, inter-han trade, regional specialisation, cottage industry and small-scale manufacture – most notably in sericulture – and, inevitably, social differentiation occurred *within* the peasant estate. By the latter part of the Edo period, therefore, the social composition of the peasantry would include substantial rural landlords – who might also be engaged in some trade and manufacture – at one end of the scale, poor tenant farmers at the other end, with in between various groups including single farm families and share-croppers.

What all this amounts to is that in fact Japanese agriculture had become capitalistic, albeit in a somewhat primitive form. It was also invariably from the richer peasants that the *mura-yakunin* (village officials) were chosen; and generally from among that number the richest would be appointed village headman (*nanushi* or *shoya*). As social turmoil increased in the latter part of the Edo era and hence both bakufu and han had to rely extensively on the services of the headmen to keep peace in the villages and ensure the steady flow of taxes, as a reward they might be granted the right to adopt a surname and even to carry a sword, both theoretically privileges exclusively reserved to the samurai. Similarly, the position of headman became increasingly hereditary. A significant blurring of distinctions between samurai and rich peasant (*gono*) was taking place. In the Edo era, therefore, a landlord *class* was emerging, combining wealth with social prestige and political influence – yet another feature of Japanese society which was, *mutatis mutandis*, to remain constant until the end of the Second World War. In analytical terms, it would not be too far off the mark to suggest that the richer peasants of the later Edo era represented the rural wing of the bourgeoisie. They contributed, by means of payment, to the revolution of the mid-nineteenth century; in turn, they were amply rewarded in that one of the early acts of the new regime was to lift the ban on the buying and selling of land.

If a Japanese agriculture was developing, in economic terms, in the direction of capitalism, leading to the emergence of classes, it does not necessarily follow that rural society, that is, the superstructure in terms of values and mores, is to be perceived in the same way. The social history of rural Japan can by no means be written simply in terms of class conflict. One might suggest that it was one of the contradictions of Edo society – as it was, indeed, of the subsequent decades of modernisation – that whereas the economy was evolving along a basic capitalist line, society retained certain marked 'feudal' traits. Major affinities among the rural populations, especially the poorer segments, tended to remain geographic rather than social in character. This arose mainly out of the diffuseness of the rural population, which was scattered among thousands of villages, generally inhabited by small numbers, without much communication existing between them. This, in turn, accounts for the fact that although Japan in the course of the Edo and Meiji eras witnessed numerous peasant rebellions, she never experienced anything approaching a peasant revolution. Furthermore, landlords in general exercised a form of paternalistic authoritarianism which was not necessarily unenlightened. The fairly widespread phenomenon of the 'absentee landlord' did not arise in Japan until the 1920s. Thus the entrepreneurial landlords can be said to have exercised social control.

There was undoubtedly a good deal of suffering among the poorer peasants of Edo Japan; there was also a great deal of injustice. Poor peasants were exploited. Nevertheless, from a purely economic perspective, enterprising landlords, by accumulating capital and investing it in a variety of ventures, contributed significantly to the economic vitality of Edo Japan and thereby laid the foundations for the industrialisation of the later nineteenth century. This point can be made even more emphatically. As will be seen, although city merchants flourished and proved daringly innovative in the course of the early Edo period, by the late eighteenth century their productive and innovative capacities had seriously diminished. In many cases, rural entrepreneurs combined agricultural exploitation with trading and manufacturing. While not necessarily in the way the Tokugawa had intended, nevertheless the peasantry, or elements of it, did ultimately prove able to provide a strong backbone for the Edo economy.

MERCHANTS

The social philosophy of the Edo era in regard to the merchants might be introduced, indeed summed up, by the slogan *Kikoku-senkin*: 'revere grain – despise money'. It is one of the contradictions of Edo society that money, albeit perhaps despised in essence, was much appreciated in concrete terms and came to pervade all sectors of society. In spite of the official physiocratic ideology, the Edo economy became thoroughly monetised and the axis of economic life centred on the cities, mainly Osaka, Kyoto and Edo. The city merchants laid the foundations for the economic life of Edo Japan and lubricated its machinery for more than two centuries. By the end of the Edo era they ceased to perform any useful function, indeed arguably they had become parasitic. Even, however, if it can be claimed that their contribution was no longer constructive, it was and certainly had been destructive in terms of hastening to its end the Tokugawa regime and all that it stood for.

By the latter part of the nineteenth century Japan industrialised according to essentially capitalist lines – namely, private control of capital and the means of production. The nature of Japanese capitalism, however, differed from that of its Western counterparts. Many of the institutions and values which came to be associated with Japanese capitalism – some of which survive to this day and will doubtless continue to survive in future – have their roots in the Edo era and more specially in developments within the merchant estate. It is these patterns which we shall seek to isolate here.

In terms of modern Japan one can suggest that there have been three periods of conspicuous nation-wide entrepreneurial dynamism and genius: the seventeenth century, the second half of the nineteenth and the two decades or so which followed the end of the Second World War. In all three periods there was an element of *tabula rasa*, while at the same time certain benefits accumulated from the past were exploited. The seventeenth century witnessed the definitive end of the *sengoku* wars and the establishment of peace, the mid-nineteenth heralded the abandonment of past official restrictive laws and practices, while the years following 1945 also experienced the re-establishment of peace. In all three periods great fortunes were made and enterprises either revitalised or born completely anew. All three periods set a high premium on initiative, ingenuity and intrepidness. So far as the individual entrepreneurs were concerned, in all three cases, to use current jargon, there were both 'push and pull' factors; in other words there were forces which motivated individuals to abandon their existing stations on the one hand, while on the other there were forces attracting these individuals to new ventures. We will be concerned in this chapter with only the first of the three periods; the point we wished to emphasise was that in the seventeenth century, as in the other two periods, there was a national climate which was favourable to entrepreneurship.

The factors responsible for the new climate of early Edo Japan, apart from peace, were the side-effects of *sankin-kotai*, the growth of the market economy and inter-regional trade, urbanisation and the tremendous amount of construction which was undertaken, the creation of sizeable consumer markets, especially Edo, the significant improvements in communications, and in due course the increasing dependence of the ruling orders on credit facilities. The major pull factor, therefore, was that early Edo Japan, to put it quite simply, provided opportunities for making a quick profit. Characteristics subsequently associated with the Japanese firm, for example, collective, enterprise-centred motivations and methods, do not apply here; rather, on the whole, this was a period of rugged individualism with material reward as the goal.

Tokugawa legislation on the separation of the estates and official moral incantations, such as *mi no hodo wo shire* ('know your place'), were singularly ineffective. The city merchants originated from three sources: merchants of the *sengoku* period, peasants who downed farm tools and samurai who preferred financial remuneration to social prestige. The push factors, therefore, were a combination of the demographic increase, resulting in some surplus rural population, and the straitened circumstances of samurai whose stipends were fixed at the lower end of the scale, the latter including the founders of such enterprise, later to become empires, as Mitsui, Sumitomo and Konoike.

Edo, which in the eighteenth century reached a population approaching one million, was mainly a consumption centre. Initially, the great hustle and bustle of economic life gravitated in Osaka. A quick glance at a map of Japan will establish the geographical significance of that city. Situated at the north-eastern end of the Inland Sea, all movement, whether by land or sea, from Kyushu, Shikoku and the south-western part of Honshu towards Edo passed through Osaka, and the same applied to the western coast of northern Honshu. Osaka, therefore, became the major geographical centre of the *sankin-kotai*, a position from which it developed in order to become the commercial and financial centre of Edo Japan. The payment of taxes and stipends in kind, the development of inter-han trade and the consumption requirements while in residence in Edo all combined in making Osaka the great entrepôt of Japan. One of Osaka's major functions, therefore, was in wholesale transactions. The wholesalers (*tonya*) handled all large transactions, especially rice, but also other commodities, such as cotton and silk goods, oil, paper, straw matting (*tatami*), and so on.

Osaka, it will be recalled, was a bakufu city; daimyo were not permitted to own land there; hence they resorted to renting warehouses from local merchants. Originally daimyo entrusted samurai to supervise their Osaka affairs, though increasingly these were effectively in the hands of merchant administrators (*kuramoto*), while the financial agents (*kakeya*) were also merchants. The importance of *kuramoto* and *kakeya* and the increasing reliance of the daimyo on them led in certain cases to their assuming family names and carrying swords; therefore, as in the case of village headmen mentioned earlier, the distinction between samurai and merchant became blurred. The monetisation of the economy obviously meant the need to convert goods in kind into specie, bank notes or bills of exchange, all of which were in circulation during the Edo era; similarly, for reasons it is unnecessary to go into here, fluctuations existed between gold (used primarily in Edo), silver (more current in Osaka) and copper (in the provinces). The complexities of the Edo monetary system – a complexity which was to assume labyrinthine proportions – gave rise to the need for a professional service of money exchangers, again the major group of which came to settle and operate in Osaka (called *ryogaeya*). The *kuramoto, kakeya, ryogaeya* and *tonya* composed the *crème de la crème* of the Osaka merchant establishment. Besides the activities already mentioned, wealthy Osaka merchants also became the chief creditors of the bakufu, the daimyo and the samurai.

The activities just mentioned, albeit among the more remunerative, were by no means the only outlets for individuals with initiative and the requisite capital for entrepreneurship. Thus the retail trade, given the sizeable consumption market especially of Edo, was another potential source for making profits. Here lies, for example, the genesis of the Mitsui fortune, when Hachirobei Takatoshi (1622–94) established his shop, the Echigoya (direct ancestor of the Mitsukoshi Department Store), in Edo. Hachirobei's entrepreneurial talent is well reflected in occasional daring innovations, such as the institution in 1689 of a system of cash on demand, instead of credit, in return for which customers would have cloth cut to suit their requirements, rather than having to buy it in bulk.

The seventeenth century, then, was a period of initiative and innovation. Surplus capital obtained from an enterprise was either reinvested in the same enterprise, for example by setting up branches in the same city as did the Mitsui in Edo or in various parts of the country, or channelled into completely new ventures, such as textiles, *sake* brewing, the lumber industry, and so on. Alternatively capital could be used for purchasing reclaimed land, an investment frequently resorted to by merchants, hence blurring the merchant/peasant distinction. Profits could also be channelled into finance capital, namely lending money with interest to daimyo and samurai; this, as will be seen, became the chief characteristic of the city merchants in the latter part of the Edo era. Of course it was also possible that capital might quite simply be drained away in extravagant living. No doubt instances of profligacy did occur among the merchant community, but the disincentives for such a course of action were considerable: there were a whole series of regulations governing the conduct of the city merchants (collectively known as *chonin*, city dwellers), including, for example, the prohibition on the use of silk garments; thus conspicuous consumption involved risks of official reprobation, a number of rather spectacular cases of which occurred in the Edo era *pour encourager les autres*.

If the merchants resisted the temptations of extravagance, such was not necessarily the case among the bakufu or the han. As with political control, bakufu finances under the first three Tokugawa shogun were carefully administered. Under the fifth shogun Tsunayoshi, who presided over the brilliant Genroku era, all fiscal caution vanished. Conspicuous consumption and the construction of palaces for prestige were indulged in by both shogunate and daimyo. Reliance on merchant administrative expertise and finance increased until it reached endemic proportions; in other words, from the early eighteenth century until the end of the Edo era bakufu and many daimyo were more or less permanently in debt to the merchants; hence the latter consolidated their economic strength.

More or less simultaneously with the establishment of the definitive economic preponderance of the city merchants, other events and trends occurred which led to a major transformation in the spirit and operations of urban economic life. Notwithstanding the limitations imposed by the Tokugawa regime, the seventeenth-century economic setting was one of relative free enterprise. As firms flourished, however, the main objective became to secure the advantages gained rather than attempt to reap new ones.

In the *sengoku* era urban commercial life had been regulated by a system of guilds, but these had been abolished. In the course of the late seventeenth and early eighteenth centuries there were considerable pressures to re-establish them. In 1651 a minor concession had been made in favour of bath-house keepers (*furoya*). Under shogun Yoshimune, however, guilds (*kabu nakama*) received official sanction. The advantage as far as the merchants were concerned was that the monopolistic guild system provided them with protection, especially from potential interlopers. From the perspective of the bakufu the advantages were two-fold. The system made the urban commercial landscape better organised and hence easier to control. Secondly, under the original Tokugawa settlement taxation was based exclusively on land, hence merchant wealth remained untapped; the guild system, therefore, was of economic benefit in that charter fees (*unjo-kin*) and regular contributions (*myoga-kin*, literally 'protection money') were paid into the Bakufu treasury – it was the *tairo* (chief elder) Tanuma Okitsugu (1719–88) who originated another method for collecting from merchants, which was to be resorted to increasingly frequently in the late Edo era and also in the beginning of the Meiji era: the *goyo-kin*, or forced loan extracted from merchants on an *ad hoc* and arbitrary basis. The guilds were monopolistic and generally individually confined to a single product or single line of activity. The guilds were ultimately abolished in 1843 by the *tairo* Mizuno Tadakuni (1794–1851) as part of his ill-fated Tenpo reforms, but the bakufu economy was in such a desperate state, indeed aggravated by Mizuno's reforms, that the effects were nil.

It was noted earlier that the chief characteristics of the seventeenth century included innovation and diversification. The establishment of the guild system effectively brought both to an end so far as the general climate of city commerce was concerned. Significant surpluses continued to be accumulated, but increasingly these were channelled almost exclusively into usury capital, namely loans to the bakufu and daimyo at very high interest rates. It became the easiest and generally safest way of making money; it did not, however, require particular skill – it was an exercise conspicuously lacking in intellectual stimulation. The city merchants were able to settle comfortably into an entrepreneurial climate of at least semi-paralysis owing to the protection which they enjoyed internally, the guilds, and externally, due to *sakoku*. By the time the guilds were abolished and more importantly when Japan was open to foreign trade, paralysis had set in to many of the city merchants to such an extent that they were completely incapable of moving in the new direction of the times. The city merchants had become completely rooted in the Tokugawa regime; when it was overthrown, so were they.

Earlier it was suggested that the rural landowners and provincial merchants might constructively be viewed as the rural wing of the bourgeoisie; the city merchants, as an entity, that is allowing for individual exceptions, could perhaps best be termed the urban wing of the feudal order. From there, however, it should not be inferred that theirs was necessarily a comfortably insulated existence. Throughout the Edo era the atmosphere in which the merchants operated was one of insecurity. There are elements of comparison between the rise of seventeenth-century Japanese entrepreneurs and their English counterparts. The latter however were not protected by a comparable policy of *sakoku*, but on the contrary were able to capitalise on England's growing foreign trade and all the ancillary industries it gave rise to. More significantly, English entrepreneurs were able to enjoy the benefits of judicial protection and identity, an ideology, especially for example in Calvinism, that gave moral justification to their pursuits and consequently both a degree of social prestige and political influence. The Japanese merchants were denied all of those things. The merchants might be creditors to daimyo and samurai, but they had no legal redress against them should the latter default on their debts. The *shi-no-ko-sho* classification was judicial as well as social. A samurai could not be held justiciable for a crime committed against a commoner – indeed there existed the phenomenon of *kirisute-gomen*, 'slay and take leave', illustrating the samurai's ability and not unusual proclivity to hack to pieces some commoner whom he found objectionable and then leave without further ceremony or fear of punishment.

There were differences between Osaka and Edo merchants and indeed between these two and the provincial merchants. Yet it is possible to trace a fairly general picture of the emerging merchant ideology both in regard to the nation as a whole and to individual firms in particular. Let us first look at the national climate of opinion in regard to merchants. The atmosphere emanating from all layers of society can easily be summarised in one word: hostility. Everyone – bakufu official, daimyo, samurai and peasant – was in debt to the merchants. Scholars inveighed against them, notably, for example, some of the most prominent thinkers of Edo Japan: Kumazawa Banzan (1619–91), Ogyu Sorai (1666–1728) and Miura Baien (1725–89); merchants were portrayed as a cancerous growth within society, responsible for its economic ills, which in the later Edo period were assuming very alarming proportions, hence moralists generally preached a return to the physiocratic ideal.

Social mobility between the four estates did occur and, indeed, in spite of official prohibitions to the contrary, merchants, apart from obtaining samurai rank in their own right, were also successful in penetrating the bushi estate via marriage and adoption – and in fact some of the leading scholars of the Edo era issued from merchant stock. This was the case of one of the towering and ultimately most influential figures of the Edo era, Motoori Norinaga (1730–1801). Motoori and other scholars of merchant background, however, did nothing to provide ideological justification for merchant entrepreneurship; on the contrary they generally adhered to the principles of *kikoku-senkin* ('revere grain – despise money'). An exception is sometimes made of *shingaku* ('heart or mind learning'), founded by another scholar of merchant birth, Ishida Baigan (1685–1744). The anthropologist Robert Bellah (*Tokugawa Religion: The Values of Pre-Industrial Japan*, 1957) sees in *shingaku* the closest Japanese equivalent to the Weberian model of the Protestant ethic; although there are undoubtedly certain similarities, for example the emphasis on frugality and hard work, nevertheless implicit in the concept of the Protestant ethic is an outlook which is assertive, indeed defiant – elements totally lacking in *shingaku*. To the extent that *shingaku* may be said to correspond to a merchant ideology, it was primarily presented in a defensive manner, in fact it sought to exonerate merchants from the evils commonly attributed to them and rather insisted on their perfect compatibility *within* the feudal order.

As Japan witnessed the decline of the semi-feudal regime of the Tokugawa settlement and entered into the modern age, the economic base of which became essentially capitalist, what she lacked was a coherent, articulated bourgeois ideology. It was not really until Japan's most recent revolution, which occurred following 1945, that entrepreneurship and capitalism gained widespread respectability. In the course of the decades following the revolution of 1868, the ideological response of the new capitalist entrepreneurs was meek, subdued, consistently defensive; the general climate of opinion and especially the attitudes of political propagandists remained hostile. In the modern age Japan's capitalist ideology failed to develop adequately, mainly because it lacked roots.

From the lower echelons of society the merchants were also despised and not infrequently attacked. Peasant rebellions, if not necessarily always directed against merchants, nevertheless involved looting of warehouses and other merchant possessions and indeed attacks on their persons. The most spectacular of these was led by the samurai scholar Oshio Heihachiro (1793–1837), who was moved to extreme sympathy for the plight of the poor peasantry in years of famine, which ultimately terminated in the near destruction and looting of the merchant quarters of Osaka in February 1837. (Oshio Heihachiro remained a legendary figure in the popular Japanese pantheon.) Similarly, in the decades following 1868 and perhaps especially in the turbulent thirties – when *nohonshugi*, agrarianism, appeared as a modern variant of the principle of *kikoku-senkin* – ideologically motivated attacks on entrepreneurs continued and increased, with the leaders of the big cartels (*zaibatsu*) having to pay right-wing organisations protection money.

As we have seen, Edo Japan did witness a degree of social mobility between merchant and samurai; throughout the period, however, this remained illegal and in any case, compared with, say, English entrepreneurs joining the gentry, limited. The ordinary merchant was unlikely to aspire to, and even less gain, entry into the bushi estate. On the whole, therefore, merchant capital remained within the enterprise; it was not squandered in pursuit of a social ideal. What is interesting, however, and of great significance in terms of understanding the roots of modern Japan, is that the ideology and organisation of individual firms came to be modelled on the way of the samurai, the *bushido*.

It was stated earlier that the seventeenth century was essentially one of individualistic entrepreneurship. Although the system we shall describe here had certain antecedents in the early Edo period and indeed before, on the whole the model became mainly a product of the eighteenth century. This model, therefore, emerged at a time when other forces were at work, including the establishment of the guilds.

The first point to note is that the turn of the century witnessed the steady erosion of individualism in entrepreneurship and the rise of collectivism. The individual firm (referred to as the *ie*) came to adopt many of the characteristics and values of the han, relationships within the enterprise corresponding to those between daimyo and samurai. This pattern will be studied shortly. Here it might be appropriate to insert a parenthesis in regard to terminology frequently used in reference to Japanese history and indeed contemporary society.

The institution and concept of the *ie* is perhaps one of the most distinctive characteristics of Japanese social and economic history, among other things because of its remarkable resilience in surviving the vagaries of revolution and industrialisation. It was pointed out earlier that *ie* has frequently been translated into English as 'family', and reservations were expressed. One of the major reservations is that this translation may be partly responsible for the use in Western literature on Japan of the term 'familism'. In the following section comment will be made on the nature and evolution of the Japanese family; it will be argued that the ideal of the Japanese family was also modelled on the daimyo – samurai relationship, not vice versa. All ideal social relationships in Japan came to be based on the tenets of *bushido*. In the *bushido* scheme of things the family, in terms of consanguinity, was of only subordinate significance. The relationship between the samurai and his lord was much more important than that between him and his wife, children or parents. In Confucianist moral philosophy two major virtues were highly prized: filial piety (*ko*) and loyalty (*chu*); but whereas the former was supreme in China, in Japan it was the latter. The ideal of the *ie*, therefore, was based on the ideal of the han; in other words, the latter did not develop as a macrocosm of the former, but the *ie* became a microcosm of the latter. In due course, after 1868, the han disappeared while the *ie* remained. Though familism may be a term favoured by some writers, feudalism is adopted by others. Feudalism, as an operative analytical definition of Japanese society in the modern era, is also misleading for a whole variety of reasons, but mainly because the term 'feudal' implies something pejorative and regressive. The institution and concept of the *ie* are by no means necessarily regressive; in certain circumstances, as is arguably the case in Japanese industrial relations today, it can be a most progressive, indeed dynamic, force. Having discarded both familism and feudalism, what is left? Only to describe the phenomenon as '*ie*-ism', with apologies for the infelicity of the term. If, however, it is difficult to define the *ie*, it can at least be described.

In general, allowing for individual variations, the commercial *ie* combined all or most of the following characteristics. The employment – and often adoption (*yoshi*) – of apprentices (*deshi*) was widespread and the system of apprenticeship became rigorously institutionalised. On the recommendation of colleagues, friends or relatives, a young boy was introduced into the *ie* and began his apprenticeship. If he proved unsatisfactory he would be sacked without further ado and his referees could be held responsible for some form of compensation payment. The apprentice did not receive any wage, but was given free board and lodging and, depending on the humour of his employer, might on festive occasions receive a small gift. The rules applied to *deshi* were very strict; they had virtually no freedom whatsoever, in fact to all intents and purposes they became the property of the *ie*. In exchange, however, an apprentice learned a craft or a trade and by virtue of having secured entry into an *ie*, he was also assured of membership and protection of the guild. The period of apprenticeship varied, but could easily last as much as a decade, indeed even more. After having satisfactorily served his period as an apprentice and when coming of age (usually at about eighteen), the *deshi* would be promoted to the position of *tedai* (journeyman). The next and ultimate stage up the ladder within the *ie* was to be appointed *banto* (manager). A *banto* could become head of the *ie* if he were adopted as the heir, in which case he would marry a daughter of the *ie* if there were one available; alternatively a good *banto* might be given a capital sum with which he would establish a *bekke* (branch *ie*) from the *honke* (main *ie*).

Two features of the *ie* system should be noted. The first is that it was rigidly hierarchical, the lines between the head of the *ie*, the *banto*, the *tedai* and the *deshi* being clearly defined. The second is that the *ie* head exercised full authority over all members and expected to receive complete loyalty and obedience from them; in return, however, he guaranteed them security for life, for once the probationary period of the *deshi* was over, only as a result of a very serious infringement of the *ie*'s rules would an employee be sacked. Thus, as suggested earlier, the relationship between the head of the *ie* and its hierarchically organised members, in both structure and values, came to reflect the daimyo–samurai ideal.

The *ie* then, both as structure and ideology, became the pattern and model of the Japanese enterprise in later Tokugawa times. Two more features of the *ie* deserve brief mention. Only members of the bushi estate had the right to surnames. What happened among the merchants is that the name of the firm came to be used as the chief means for designating individuals within the *ie*, whether head, *banto*, *tedai* or *deshi*. The custom whereby Japanese to this day will commonly introduce themselves by prefacing the name of the organisation they work for (as in Fuji Ginko no Hattori, Fuji Bank's Hattori) has its roots in the *ie* system of the Japanese enterprise, which in turn was modelled on the han, as samurai always prefixed their surnames by the han to which they belonged. The *ie* in this way gained both an identity and a sense of corporate solidarity. Both identity and solidarity were further elaborated by yet another feature, also patterned after the han: the codification of house rules. In the case of Mitsui, for example, the code was derived from the will of Hachirobei in 1694 and formally promulgated in 1722. Most *ie* had their own regulations codified; the general tenor of all of these, however, varied little, consisting mainly of exhorting members of the *ie* to virtues of loyalty, diligence, probity, respect for hierarchy, and so on. These codes can collectively be termed *chonindo* (way of the townsman/merchant), the basic message of which is hardly distinguishable from *bushido*, after which it was modelled.

The codification of *ie* regulations resulted in the institutionalisation of the *ie*. Along with the establishment of the guilds, the conservative investment of capital into money-lending, the institutionalisation of the *ie* also contributed towards the stagnation of the urban economy. Founding fathers became the *ie* deities (*kami*) and their bequeathed legacy, in the form of the codified rules, holy writ. The general atmosphere pervading the *ie* came to be backward rather than forward looking; the underlying ethic was a strict and unimaginative obedience to ancestral precepts.

In the course of the latter part of the eighteenth century and first few decades of the nineteenth the bakufu economy deteriorated seriously; the various attempts at reform, including the more protracted Kansei reforms (1784–1801) and the Tenpo reforms (1830–43), provided either negligible results or indeed aggravated the situation. There is one element of Mizuno Tadakuni's Tenpo reforms worth noting, partly because of its relevance to the Tokugawa era, also however because of its association with more contemporary trends in other parts of East Asia outside Japan. As indicated earlier the principles of *kikoku-senkin* remained official doctrine, in spite of everything, throughout the Edo era: urban merchant money was evil, rural peasant produce was good. The cancer afflicting Edo society, scholars asserted, could be remedied by a return to physiocratic principles. Mizuno actually sought to implement such a policy, known as *hitogaeshi* ('sending people back', by implication to the country), whereby a forced migration from the cities to the villages was to be undertaken. Mizuno's *hitogaeshi* was never able to develop extensively; he himself was dismissed from offices in 1843, and shortly afterwards his programme was abandoned in its entirety. The principles lying behind *hitogaeshi* of 'feudal' Japan are certainly reminiscent of the programme of *hsia-fang* ('going down to the villages') in Maoist China, whereby cadres and intellectuals were sent into the countryside in order to be purified from the polluting corruption of the cities, and, of course, the comparable measure adopted by the Vietnamese communist regime and with tragic consequences by the Khmer Rouge in Cambodia.

The fact that in the last half-century or more of the Edo era the bakufu economy was in dire straits cannot by any means be entirely attributed to the city merchants. The bakufu administration was itself responsible, mainly because of its incapacity to resolve a fiscal situation which was chaotic and a currency system which had degenerated into anarchy. In its attempts to improve the economy, however, the bakufu was not able to rely on the support of the *chonin*, apart, that is, from the *goyo-kin*. When in its final convulsions the bakufu sought to innovate and introduce modern industries and technology, in the 1860s, it had to depend on its own enterprising human resources and not on the paralysed merchants, as was also, in fact, the case in some of the han. In other words, capital could be extracted from the merchants, but not the genius and foresight of talented entrepreneurship.

This is the situation which the Meiji government inherited and, in the early stages at least of its regime, perpetuated: the human capital of the established commercial enterprises had by and large dried up. Innovatory ideas and practices had to be extracted from elsewhere, and in lieu of fertile entrepreneurship outside the new bureaucracy, and in anticipation of the emergence of new entrepreneurs, the government was willy-nilly forced to go it alone.

The preceding chapter ended on the introduction of the concept and pattern of *kanryo-shugi* (bureaucratism) in Japan as part of the early Tokugawa settlement. *Kanryo-shugi* developed and broadened; ultimately the samurai/bureaucrats of the Edo era extended their scope and control to hitherto despised merchant activities. By the end of the Edo era the samurai/bureaucrats were forced to assume the role of capitalist entrepreneurs. A new entrepreneurial class did eventually emerge in Meiji Japan and the bureaucratic quasi-monopoly of the new sectors of industry ceased. Between bureaucrat and entrepreneur, however, the separation never amounted to a total divorce. The close relationship between the bureaucracy in contemporary Japan and the business community is also, therefore, a phenomenon – and one which has no exact comparison in other so-called free economies – which has its roots in the Edo era.

THE SAMURAI

The *katana-gari*, the development of the *joka-machi* and the officially enforced hierarchy of *shi-no-ko-sho* were all policies designed to segregate the samurai socially, functionally and to a degree geographically from the *heimin* (commoners). Samurai were forbidden to marry into the other estates, as indeed inter-marriage between all estates was forbidden. The Tokugawa settlement sought to freeze society; in other words, whereas in the past men had been able to rise and penetrate into samurai ranks, in theory, according to Tokugawa law, this was impossible. It was not difficult to distinguish a samurai in a crowd: only samurai were able to bear swords, generally two, one short, one long, carried on the side. They enjoyed other exclusive privileges, for example that of having a surname (*myoji*) and also the exclusive right to commit *seppuku* (disembowelment, more generally known in the West as *hara-kiri*).

The first point to establish in regard to samurai is that there were a great many of them. The samurai estate is generally estimated to have corresponded to approximately 6 per cent of the population; assuming a total population in the later Edo period of about thirty million, this means that the samurai estate totalled not much less than two million. It is important to stress the large number of samurai for three reasons. The first is economic. Generally speaking, samurai were not supposed to engage in any form of productive or commercial activity – to put it another way, they were not supposed to 'make' (as opposed to receive) money. What percentage of the bakufu's or a han's budget was allocated to paying the samurai their stipends (*horoku*) is virtually impossible to determine; it stands to reason, however, that this must have been a substantial amount, all of which was borne by the peasantry through taxation. Samurai were, among many other things, an expensive luxury.

Secondly, the comparatively large number of samurai tells us something about the social composition of Tokugawa Japan and distinguishes her from European feudal societies where the percentage of the upper feudal orders was very much smaller. Similarly, as has already been suggested earlier and will be stressed here again, in the course of the Edo era many samurai came to perform some form of bureaucratic function; the *kanryo-shugi* (bureaucratism) phenomenon can be gauged to some extent quantitatively as well as qualitatively.

Thirdly, the large number of samurai must qualify certain misconceptions regarding the nature of the mid-nineteenth-century revolution and the decades which followed it. There has been a somewhat unfortunate tendency in the literature on Japanese history to refer to the Restoration and the early programme of modernisation as having been carried out by 'the' samurai. As has already been pointed out, in fact the distinction between samurai and the better-off peasants and some successful merchants came to be blurred; a number of the so-called samurai leaders of the early Meiji years were not fully pedigreed samurai, but recent parvenus into that estate. Seen in numerical terms, it also follows that the article 'the' is misleading, hence inappropriate. Even excluding women and children from the samurai estate, one is still left with an estimated figure of not much less than half a million adult samurai. Thus the operative qualifier would have to be 'some', not 'the', so far as samurai leadership of early Meiji Japan is concerned. There occurred in the course of the latter part of the Edo and early Meiji eras a process of selection within the samurai estate; a differentiation between a select, talented, progressive group on the one hand, with on the other a larger mass once described as a lumpen-aristocracy. It was, needless to say, the first group which spearheaded the process of modernisation, while the latter, albeit in occasionally somewhat raucous manner, faded away into historical oblivion.

The samurai estate was by no means a homogeneous group. There were variations from han to han and obviously the larger the han the more samurai there were and the more complex their organisation, this being particularly true of a number of the *tozama* han, notably Satsuma and Choshu. Generally, however, one can speak of upper, middle and lower samurai, though within each major category there might be a further grading of as many as five or six subdivisions. Rank was determined by revenue, the source of which was either a fief (*chigyo*), or more commonly an allotted stipend (*horoku*). The essential principle here was hereditary: a samurai's status was defined at birth. Elaborate rules were devised to govern social intercourse among samurai and their ceremonial functions. In certain circumstances the rules of *apartheid* could be as strict within the samurai estate as between samurai and *heimin*. Thus, for example, marriage between upper samurai (*joshi*) and lower samurai (*kashi*) was forbidden, as indeed was adultery, though not unlike a great deal of Tokugawa legislation this rule was obviously difficult to enforce.

The bureaucratic machinery of the bakufu was described in the preceding chapter. In many respects han administration was a smaller replica of the bakufu. At the top of the scale were the daimyo's chief retainers (*karo*, literally house elders), who performed advisory functions comparable to those of the *roju* at bakufu level. While the *karo* acted as councillors to the daimyo and were generally responsible for the overall administration of the han, the more detailed and defined civil and military offices were placed as the responsibility of the middle samurai, *hirazamurai*, comparable in status, though not always in revenue, to the bakufu's *hatamoto*. These included finance, liaison with the bakufu, administration of the castle-towns or of the rural areas, collection of taxes, the daimyo's household affairs, education, administration of shrines and temples, security, military procurements, supervision of the han guard, and so on. Some offices were simply hereditary, while others, though not strictly hereditary, were limited to samurai of a particular rank. The system was in principle, therefore, strongly aristocratic.

At the lower end of the scale the situation was, if anything, more complex. One might simply mention here two categories, though once again there were considerable variations of status and income among these. One was the *ashigaru* (foot soldiers), in fact somewhat on the periphery of the samurai estate, whose name indicates their military function, while their civil responsibilities consisted mainly of acting in subordinate positions in the various offices administered by the *hirazamurai*. Another category was that of the *goshi* (rustic samurai), especially prevalent in Satsuma, who varied somewhat from the general pattern of the Edo era in that they lived in villages rather than the *joka-machi*, and engaged in agriculture.

A samurai's rank determined his relationship with the daimyo. The *karo* were his close advisers, *hirazamurai* had the right of audience, lower samurai did not. Protocol in Edo society was sacrosanct and minute in detail. In the shogun's palace, for example, different reception rooms, in greater or lesser proximity to his living quarters, were used depending on the quality of the visitor; the same kind of ceremony applied to the daimyo's entourage. Caste distinctions were equally reflected in income: a *hirazamurai* might receive an annual stipend of as much as 500 *koku* of rice per annum, an *ashigaru* as little as fifteen. The *grands seigneurs* of the Edo and han courts lived in splendour, while at the bottom of the scale the poorer samurai had great difficulty living on their meagre income.

To simplify a complex historical development, one might postulate the following. The Edo era witnessed the erosion, ultimately the disintegration of the han; there were, it is true, a number of han uprisings in the post Meiji Restoration years, such as the Saga (1874) and Satsuma (1877) rebellions, but although their immediate impact was considerable, seen from a longer historical perspective, their significance is negligible. At the same time as the disintegration of the han was taking place – though it must be stressed that this was a very slow, evolutionary and by no means nationally uniform movement – a process of unification, albeit imperceptible at first, was taking place, ultimately leading to the creation of the Japanese nation under the political legitimacy of the tenno. The basic structures and values of the han ideal, however, were eventually retained at the levels of enterprise, village and family. The heads of all three enjoyed an authority over their constituent members, comparable to that of the daimyo over his vassals, and the organisation within the three tended to be hierarchically organised; also, whereas the head expected absolute loyalty from his subordinates, he was in turn morally obliged to look after their welfare in a generally authoritarian paternalistic manner. What is being postulated here is a model, and therefore readily admits of variations whether in regions, types of organisation and indeed time. The tenno reigned not really over so many individuals, but over a large number of units all basically derived from the han and eventually metamorphosed into more manageable entities, generally referred to as the *ie*. This pattern has remained to this day and accounts for what is termed the verticality of Japanese society. The process to be studied now could be described as the rise and fall of the han in terms of the ideal daimyo–samurai relationship.

The daimyo was surrounded by his samurai, generally geographically isolated in the *joka-machi*. With the exception of a small and constantly dwindling number of upper samurai who were permitted to maintain their own sub-fiefs and the peasant samurai (*goshi*) of some han, the vast majority of the samurai derived their livelihood exclusively from the stipends which they received from the daimyo's treasury. The first point to establish in this daimyo–samurai relationship, therefore, is that it was an economic one, and indeed one which involved the samurai's complete economic dependence on his lord. It is important to bear this in mind, for the erosion of the daimyo–samurai relationship was to be partly caused by economic forces.

All samurai swore an oath of allegiance to the daimyo. The relationship between daimyo and samurai, however, was not contractual, but moral. This is a phenomenon of absolutely crucial significance, both in terms of Edo society and for an understanding of the nature of certain facets of Japan's subsequent modernisation and indeed of her contemporary society. It was stressed in the former chapter that a constant leitmotiv of the early Tokugawa settlement was the determination to restore a *moral* order to society. In the course of the preceding pages reference has occasionally been made to the terms law, rules, regulations, and so forth. Among the differences between Western civilisation and East Asian civilisation (namely those areas coming under Chinese influence), perhaps one of the most significant lay in two radically different approaches to the concept of law. The ancient Greeks appointed Themis as goddess of justice and to this day we still find her represented all over the Western world, invariably clutching on to her scales. In the course of European history law, both as a concept and as a system, has been in a position of paramountcy. Practically all forms of social intercourse came to be legally defined and in the course of time individual legal rights were recognised. Although there were variations in both content and philosophy, between natural and positive law, civil and canon law, and so on, law in the European tradition was a recognisable, supreme and guiding principle – leaving aside economic and other factors of causation, the French revolution, mainly carried out by lawyers, can be said to have originated in a jurisprudential dispute.

The contrast with East Asian civilisation is striking. There existed, it is true, a legalist tradition in China, namely in the *Fa chia* school, which maintained that good government should be based on a fixed code of law instead of on moral precepts. Always in somewhat of a heterodox position, however, by the time of the Sung dynasty (960–1280) Confucianism was in a period of full renaissance. The Confucianist tradition by no means negates the necessity of laws, but relegates the science and codification of law to a minor branch of ethics. In other words, the greatest emphasis in the social order is placed on morality and especially on virtuous conduct. Within this scheme of things the individual had no rights (indeed no term existed in the Chinese or Japanese languages to correspond to 'rights' and had to be invented in the mid-nineteenth century), but was responsible to a host of various obligations, words for which abound in Japanese. It was this reinvigorated, highly moral Sung Confucianism, seen especially in the writings of Chu Hsi (1130–1200), that the Tokugawa founding fathers were to impose as the ideological orthodoxy of Edo society. The Chu Hsi school of Confucianism did not, by any means, enjoy a complete monopoly during the centuries of Pax Tokugawa. The point is that the other schools as well all stressed the supremacy of virtue as the fundamental essence necessary for the preservation of the moral, hence social, order.

The principles of *bushido* are not solely derived from Confucianism, but rather represent an amalgam of various Japanese traditions, whether wholly indigenous or imported. The fact that it was termed the way of the bushi is a recognition of the role of the samurai in the last five centuries or so of Japanese history and of his paramount position in society – a striking contrast to China where the man of arms was always inferior to the man of letters. And, of course, the bushi were the top layer of society, far removed in every respect from the *heimin*, hence theirs was the responsibility of moral example. *Bushido's* emphasis on the futility or evanescence of human existence was largely a product of Buddhism. The moral principles of *bushido*, however, were Confucianist. Although the moral code of the *bushido* was treated in numerous and lengthy treatises, its essence can be summed up fairly simply. Society was organised hierarchically according to the five basic relationships (*go-rin*), described in Chapter 2; whereas it was incumbent on the inferior to be absolutely loyal to his superior, the superior was expected to show benevolence to his inferior. These two virtues, loyalty (*chu*) and benevolence (*jen*), were the very essence of the moral code of the *bushido*. The pattern established in the daimyo–samurai relationship devolved into other sectors of society; thus a wife was expected to show complete loyalty to her husband, an apprentice to his master, a tenant to his landlord, while they in turn should treat their own dependants benevolently.

So far as the samurai were concerned, however, it must be made clear that *bushido*, elaborated by a whole series of moralists in the Edo period, but notably initiated by Yamaga Soko (1622–85), was not a recognition, far less a description, of reality, but an exhortation to an ideal. This is not to say that samurai were not loyal to their daimyo. There are numerous instances of acts of absolute and fearless loyalty in the Edo era – notably in the incidents occurring in 1701–2 from which was derived the heroic epic of *Chushingura*, the story of the forty-seven *ronin*, whose graves in the Senkakuji in the Takanawa district of Tokyo are still the venue of annual pilgrimages. The fact remains, however, that for this ideology to remain operative, certain objective conditions within the han were necessary, which, especially in the latter part of the Edo era, were either absent or limited.

In any case, apart from the supreme virtue of loyalty, there were other moral injunctions in *bushido* which do not appear to have been conspicuously practised. A samurai was supposed to lead a life of austerity, but many lived in opulence; samurai were supposed to be sexually reserved, whereas both heterosexual and homosexual relationships appear to have been frequently indulged in – including visits to the *yukaku*, theoretically off-limits to samurai. It is not the intention here to deny the existence of *bushido* or to denigrate its influence in samurai society during the Edo era. The concept of loyalty remained in a predominant position and ultimately it was loyalty – albeit to the tenno – that was the moral justification for the overthrow of the *ancien régime*. Nevertheless, so far as samurai society during the Edo era is concerned, *bushido* should be recognised as what it was: an ideal. The moral bond between daimyo and samurai weakened because increasingly contradictions arose between reality and the ideal.

The objective conditions which came to weaken the daimyo–samurai relationship were both economic and political. There was the increasing indebtedness of both daimyo and samurai to the merchants, which arose out of a number of factors. The expenses of *sankin-kotai* borne by the daimyo were exceedingly onerous; as much as 70–80 per cent of a han's cash outlay was necessary to meet the requirements of *sankin-kotai*. Extravagant life in Edo really got under way during the reign of the shogun Tsunayoshi, with the daimyo in general feeling it incumbent upon them to emulate his example. The number of *yashiki* (mansions) maintained by the daimyo in Edo increased, the total number surpassing 600 in due course; this obviously involved expenses of construction, maintenance, repair, staffing, and so on. The income of the daimyo consisted essentially of that part of the tax in kind which could be converted into cash; generally speaking, therefore, income was fixed, especially by the eighteenth century when the earlier process of land reclamation had reached an end and technological improvements were not of a nature to increase significantly output per acre. While income, therefore, was limited, requirements for expenditure were not.

In order to make revenue and expenditure meet, the daimyo could contemplate five alternatives. One was to cut down on expenses. Although this was occasionally resorted to, frugality went against the grain of the prevailing Edo atmosphere, especially since wealth indicated power and importance – and it is perhaps a fairly universal phenomenon that economising is held in contempt by any ruling élite, and at worst is contemplated as a last resort. A second alternative was to seek other sources of revenue. This alternative was engaged in by a few han, some with considerable success. A third alternative was to raise taxes; this was not often resorted to because of endemic peasant uprisings. Although one, two, or all three of these alternatives may have been occasionally adopted, the most common were the last two. The fourth alternative, then, was simply to borrow more money from the *chonin*; the majority of the daimyo by the end of the Tokugawa era were hopelessly in debt, which partly accounts for the meekness with which they accepted the new order and their own demise, especially since the new government was thoughtful enough to cover their debts. The fifth alternative was to renege on the payment of the samurai's stipends. Generally this took the form of samurai being informed that their stipends would be temporarily forfeited. Loyalty also has its price. One of the features of the later Edo era was that the economic link between daimyo and samurai, if not necessarily completely severed, was nonetheless seriously jeopardised, especially at a time when samurai too were facing serious economic difficulties.

The samurai's economic difficulties can be largely ascribed to three major causes. The first is that the samurai, in wishing to emulate their lords, also engaged in a life of extravagance. The second is a consequence of the fifth daimyo alternative indicated above, namely that they were not being regularly paid. The third is that their income, when they received it, was also fixed and in kind; the monetisation of the economy meant that samurai had to exchange their stipends for specie, while the exchange rate fluctuated significantly, with samurai invariably coming worse off. Their economic plight, therefore, was of considerable proportions. The samurai too had a number of alternatives when trying to alleviate their financial distress. They could seek to economise, although for samurai at the bottom of the stipendiary scale this was virtually impossible, for a mere subsistence existence does not allow scope for saving. Although both bakufu and han occasionally attempted major fiscal reforms, there was a constantly recurring assumption and insistence that the economic plight of the samurai estate was essentially caused by a moral decline. The Kyoho reforms of Yoshimune, the Kansei reforms of Matsudaira Sadanobu and the Tenpo reforms of Mizuno Tadakuni all laid great emphasis on the need for the samurai to return to practising the moral values of sobriety and frugality; the arrest of economic decline could be achieved only through moral regeneration.

Another means of meeting expenses, albeit illegal, was for samurai to obtain capital from *chonin* either by marriage or adoption. Alternatively, and equally illegal, samurai might simply abandon their status and enter the commercial field or turn to agriculture.'Another method, as with the daimyo frequently indulged in, was to go further into debt by borrowing from the *chonin*. Finally, however, samurai could also seek alternative sources of income and at the same time maintain their samurai status.

This last alternative requires some elaboration. One of the most significant features of Tokugawa society was the development of education, to be looked at in more detail in Chapter 4. The point here, however, is that if the supply of educational facilities grew, so did the demand. Thus talented samurai, irrespective of birth, who had achieved a high standard of education and were able to establish an academic reputation, might find themselves either employed in the proliferating bakufu or han schools or indeed set up their own academies. At the same time, as both bakufu and han affairs became increasingly complex and required adequate human resources to staff the various offices, a demand for able administrators also developed. Most of these offices, it is true, remained open only to samurai from certain ranks; within these ranks, however, selection was increasingly made on the basis of ability and educational achievement. In some cases, rank qualifications might be dispensed with, for example by giving a truly promising samurai incremental stipends (*tashidaka*), thus enabling him to rise in the samurai social scale.

Along with the economic deterioration of the samurai estate, this development was to be of fundamental significance. The Tokugawa settlement in its inception, it was stressed, was based on a rigid aristocratic principle: status, function and income were determined by birth. What was taking place within the samurai estate, however, albeit in evolutionary and initially imperceptible manner, was the introduction of the meritocratic principle into the aristocracy. In Japanese the operative term became *jinzai* (men of talent), ultimately leading to a doctrine of *jinzaishugi* (which can be translated as meritocracy).

In other words, we have here the reassertion of the laws of *gekokujo*. The *gekokujo* of the *sengoku* period witnessed the ascendance of talented warriors; by and large the *gekokujo* of the mid-nineteenth century consisted primarily of the ascendance of talented bureaucrats. The reforms which followed the Meiji Restoration could be summed up in terms of opening careers to talents, even though initially talent was to be recruited almost exclusively from samurai. The educated, talented, progressive, meritocratic samurai in the latter part of the Edo era were objectively still members of the samurai estate; subjectively, however, their attitudes differed radically from the bulk of their oafish, parasitic, backward-looking fellows. It was in this sense that within the samurai estate a revolutionary class developed.

The daimyo–samurai particularistic bond, therefore, was weakened by economic forces. There were other negative forces. The fact that owing to *sankin-kotai* the daimyo had to spend a considerable amount of time in Edo meant that his links, if only geographic, with those samurai who stayed behind were significantly weakened, especially in the cases of those daimyo who for economic reasons tended to stay on in Edo for much longer periods than was required. The emergence and proliferation of *ronin* (lordless samurai) also led to an erosion of the daimyo–samurai relationship.

A samurai might become a *ronin* as a result of a number of possible causes. For example, he might be sent into exile from his han because of an offence; alternatively he might decide to abscond and seek fortune elsewhere of his free will, possibly because his daimyo was not paying him at all, or not paying him enough and the attraction of greener grass elsewhere proved too alluring; or because he was invited by another han to join in some capacity due to the good reputation he had been successful in establishing. The latter part of the Edo era witnessed a spiralling increase in the number of *ronin*, a phenomenon related to the rise of the meritocratic samurai. Thus a talented samurai in a progressive and sizeable han would find an outlet for his intelligence and energy. A talented samurai in a retrograde or very small han would have no such opportunity; he might on the other hand find a suitable occupation elsewhere.

The samurai enjoyed considerable freedom of movement in Edo society. Geographic mobility of the samurai, therefore, was a prominent feature of their estate during the Edo era. By travelling, or by being billeted in Edo during their daimyo's period of attendance, samurai of one han got to know samurai of other han; they were able to exchange ideas and impressions and the more educated among them would find kindred spirits with whom to discuss all manner of things. This paved the way intellectually and politically for the national unification and centralisation which were to be achieved with such remarkable speed in the years immediately following the Restoration.

A distinguishing characteristic of these educated, meritocratic samurai was that they were pragmatists and not ideologists. This does not mean that they lacked principles or indeed that the tenets of *bushido* were abandoned; but *bushido* as originally conceived, with its emphasis on the daimyo–samurai relationship, was certainly jettisoned. It must be stressed that here one is identifying trends. The major factor which was to result in these various trends coalescing was going to be an external one, namely the impact and menace of the Western powers. The process described here was how the evolution within the samurai estate had occurred. Those samurai who emerged as the leaders of modernising Japan were in most respects, intellectually, socially and politically, very different kettles of fish from their forebears and indeed from the majority of their kinsmen. In other words, as in the peasant and merchant estates, from *within* the samurai estate the Edo era witnessed a new élite in the process of formation.

WOMEN

In terms of social status samurai were the most privileged group within Edo society while the female sex, taken *in toto*, were the least significant. Perhaps for that reason it is quite common for books on Japanese history to ignore them, or simply to mention (and more often dismiss) them *en passant*.

The status of women in Japan presents something of an anomaly. Compared to most non-European societies, Japanese women have suffered neither physical disgrace nor impairment: there was no female circumcision in Japan, no binding of feet, widows were not burnt at the pyre of their deceased husbands, nor were they forced to cover their faces with a veil. There were a few customs associated with the female sex, though none of these were of a particularly barbarous nature. In the Edo era women of the higher orders shaved their eyebrows and blackened their teeth with a thick paste; whereas the origins of the former are unknown, the latter was clearly for preservative purposes. The pigeon-toed gait, commonly associated with Japanese women today, seems to have been of comparatively recent origin; early Edo paintings of Japanese females show them with their feet in a parallel position, whereas by the Genroku era the more familiar inward inclination of the toes appears. Widows were not forced to accompany their husbands to the grave, the practice of *junshi*, as we saw earlier, being limited to male retainers. A woman of the samurai estate might, under certain circumstances, follow her husband in suicide, though she would not disembowel herself (*seppuku*), but thrust her own small dirk (*kaiken*) into the jugular vein. Court ladies, wives, concubines and so on, whether in Kyoto or Edo, were kept segregated from the rest of the household and were not to be visited by strangers.

Although there are a few formidable female figures in the Nara era, generally the more recent political history of Japan can be written while excluding women altogether, or perhaps with the occasional insertion of a forceful mother or wife. In terms of post-Heian history this can no doubt be explained by the martial nature of Japanese society. Another factor, however, which may have accounted for the insignificance of females is that they did not bring large domains with them; there were political marriages, but although these might serve to cement an alliance, they did not as such alter the domainal geography of Japan. Women's role was in the interior; the degree of an individual's influence would presumably be dependent on the force, or otherwise, of her own personality and that of her husband, lover or son, as the case might be.

The subordination of women in Japanese society was part of a general East Asian pattern. The fact remains, however, that while rare, even in Confucianist China it was possible for a woman to play an influential political role – the modern history of China could hardly be written without frequent reference to the Empress Dowager Ts'u-hsi (1835–1908). Similarly, other contemporary Asian societies have produced their female political figures, notably in the cases of Sirimavo Bandaranaike (b. 1916) and Indira Gandhi (b. 1917). In Japan the anomaly to some extent continues; although, in fact and as things stand at present, the percentage of women in the Diet (the Japanese parliament) is higher than that of the House of Commons, it is for the time being inconceivable that there should be a female prime minister in Japan, nor has a woman ever been a member of Cabinet. The alleged inferiority of women in Japan, however, is more apparent than real; in fact women do wield a considerable amount of power, not in the limelight, but from the concealed confines of the interior. The historical roots of the status of women in contemporary Japanese society are complex; some of these can be isolated here, while the more modern nineteenth-century transformations, or lack of them, of the female condition will be looked at in a subsequent chapter.

It has been suggested in this chapter that whereas the daimyo–samurai relationship disintegrated in the course of the Edo era, a number of *bushido* ideals inherent in this relationship were absorbed and ultimately rooted into other types of organisation, namely the village and the firm (*ie*). The model samurai family incorporated both *bushido* and the official Confucianist ideology (including the *go-rin*, five basic relationships, according to which woman was clearly man's absolute inferior). In the course of the Edo era *bushido*, the daimyo–samurai relationship and the model of the samurai marriage gradually came to be absorbed into the upper layers of the other estates. Historians have spoken of the social development of the Meiji years as one where a process of 'samurai-isation' took place. It is in the second decade or so of the Meiji era, the 1880s, that this process gathered momentum; it had however already begun in the course of the later Edo era.

Two things should be made clear at the outset. First, an analysis of this kind inevitably involves one in an element of generalisation. Thus, if we say that samurai women did not work, that their position was clearly relegated to the interior, there will, of course, be exceptions. It is more than likely that the wives and daughters of the poorer *goshi* (rustic samurai) participated in farming. It is also known that especially in the latter part of the Edo era some poor samurai sought to find remunerative activity for their females, albeit perhaps clandestinely; certainly in the north-east of Japan (the Tohoku region), poor samurai females worked in textiles and a number of regional products, notably the *Sendai-hira* or *Yonezawa shoku*, were produced by samurai female labour. Samurai girls of destitute families joined the ranks of the labour force in the Meiji era. This point also serves to illustrate the social differentiation taking place within the estates: that poorer peasant and merchant women, like their samurai sisters, worked, while richer peasant and merchant women along with better-off samurai females did not.

Secondly, it will also be clear that the evolution of the economic function of women in Japanese society, *mutatis mutandis*, does not vary significantly from more universal patterns. A woman's role and status in society, however, is a function of both economic conditions and ideology; when poverty is the rule, then ideology must accommodate itself. Thus the distinction between poor Japanese women and poor Western women will be only marginal; with affluence, however, the separation may intensify, simply because of prevailing ideologies.

Japan was theoretically a monogamy, though the practice of concubinage was accepted, indeed institutionalised. Thus, the tenno took one principal wife, called the *kogo*, generally chosen from the highest ranking *kuge* families, though, as we have seen, occasionally, whether willingly or not (in fact will had very little to do in these arrangements) he might marry a relative of the shogun. In the early Edo era the *kogo* seem to have served the purpose of producing an heir, but most of the later ones were childless. In spite of the relative national obscurity and impotence of the imperial court, conjugal politics and intrigue nonetheless continued; the tenno's marriage was a political marriage, but given that his heir need not be his wife's offspring, consummation of the marriage was unnecessary. The tenno had a large entourage of female attendants, some official mistresses, others serving other purposes, most of whom were lodged in separate apartments within the palace grounds. The *kogo*, who lived in her own palace, the *Higyo-sha*, had a number of ceremonial duties to perform, while the rest of the tenno's women did not appear in public.

The same pattern applied on the whole to the shogun's court and to the daimyo, though obviously there would be a variation in the number of females depending on the daimyo's wealth. The function of these women was to provide progeniture and otherwise cater to their lords' needs and whims. The main shogunal palace was estimated to have a female staff of somewhere in the region of 250. It goes without saying that by no means were all of these expected to perform sexual services; in fact in many cases the shogun is unlikely even to have cast his eyes, concupiscent or otherwise, upon them. If one adds to the shogunal palace the numerous *yashiki* of daimyo and *hatamoto*, it is clear that the demand for women reached the thousands.

The shogun's and the daimyo's chief consorts and official concubines would be recruited from certain specific social groups and indeed families. Other female attendants, however, and ones who could become unofficial mistresses, would be provided from a variety of different groups. For the Edo *chonin* it was a matter of some ambition to place a daughter in a daimyo's household. The girl might, if pleasant and lucky enough, bear the daimyo's child, or alternatively be offered by the daimyo to one of his samurai; in either case the *chonin* family's prestige and standing would improve. Most of these women, however, were segregated in their own quarters in the palaces and could not freely engage in court social life; a Madame de Pompadour (1721-64) was an inconceivable phenomenon in Edo court society.

Tenno, shogun and daimyo would, presumably, find within their harems enough (or more than enough) to satisfy their sexual appetites. In any case, however, their freedom of movement was limited; even had they wished to venture outside this would have been virtually impossible. As for the samurai and *chonin* of Edo, three brief points need to be made here. First, the social etiquette governing court ladies applied to all women who aspired to follow the general guidelines of *bushido*. Secondly, family life in Edo Japan was a microcosm of the total society, hence involving strict hierarchy and ceremony in every respect: place, speech, and so on. Thirdly, although higher samurai may well have kept women in both their *joka-machi* and Edo, this was clearly impossible financially for the lower samurai, for example the *ashigaru*, who also had to accompany their lords on *sankin-kotai* to Edo and would have to leave their wives behind. These reasons (with the exception of the third in regard to *chonin*) explain the great popularity and proliferation of the *yukaku*. As these were such a prominent feature of Edo society and also as to some extent they help give an historical explanation for the continued practice of 'professional' female entertainers (which by no means need be synonymous with prostitute), a brief description of the *yukaku* institution and the role they came to play is called for.

The *yukaku*, as pointed out, were districts in the cities, usually on the outskirts, where legalised prostitution could be exercised: the most famous of the *yukaku* was the Yoshiwara situated in the northern boundaries of Edo. The atmosphere here was by no means seedy, but colourful, indeed flamboyant. The brothels were interspersed with restaurants, tea-houses, theatres, and so on. The *yukaku* were designed to provide pleasure for all the senses, while inside the various establishments the emphasis was above all placed on a mood of relaxation. The *yukaku* were, therefore, a refuge from the highly status-conscious, rigidly formal society of Edo Japan, which pervaded all levels, whether the council of the daimyo's government or the home. In the *yukaku*, flippancy could be engaged in, idle chatter with the inmates, as well as other activities, while enjoying a good meal and *sake*. The inmates of the *yukaku* were, therefore, much more than just prostitutes. The reputation of the various establishments was based not simply on the beauty of their women, but on the sophistication of their discourse, the skill of their repartee, the quantity and quality of their gossip – for, needless to say, the *yukaku* became notorious centres of intrigue – and their artistic accomplishments. The girls were expected to be versatile not only in the arts of love, but also in dancing, singing and playing musical instruments, especially the *shamisen*, a balalaika-type instrument originating from the Ryukyu islands and imported into Japan towards the end of the sixteenth century. These facts help to provide an explanation for a linguistic phenomenon, namely the use of the term *geisha*. The generic term for prostitute in Japanese is *joro*, though there were numerous other appellations meant to indicate both type and status of the different *joro*. *Geisha* literally means 'artistic or talented person' and originally applied to the Kyoto court male musicians and other professional male entertainers. As in the *yukaku* the function of the inmate became more sophisticated and she was expected to show artistic talent in various fields, the term *geisha* came to be applied; hence the use of the word *geisha* for a female professional entertainer dates from the seventeenth century.

A number of rather disparate points regarding the *yukaku* and *geisha* can be made. The relaxed atmosphere provided by the entertainers of the *yukaku* – who, incidentally, were not only women but also included males, generally called *taikomochi* or *hokan* – fulfilled, to use contemporary jargon, a role of 'tension management'; here the stiff etiquette of society and the family could be left behind. This function of 'tension management' provided by Japanese professional female (and male) entertainers remains not only among *geisha*, but also among the thousands and thousands of bar-hostesses.

Although we have spoken here of the *yukaku*, it should also be clear that, in spite of official regulations to the contrary, prostitution was practised in areas outside the licensed quarters. The inns at the relay stations (*shukueki*) along the routes of the *sankin-kotai* were almost invariably staffed with girls who would act as both servants and prostitutes. The proliferation of prostitution in the Edo era was not simply a reflection of men's lust, but also of the economic conditions of the time. Recruitment of girls to service the various inns, brothels, tea-houses, and so on was carried out in the rural districts, a poor peasant receiving a payment in cash in exchange for the sale of his daughter, who left her village never to return. The recruitment of girls from poor rural districts, again especially the Tohoku region, continued in the decades following the Restoration and indeed reached a peak during the Depression years of the 1930s.

The profession of prostitution and the brothel came to reflect certain characteristics of the Edo era. Although the visitor might bathe in an atmosphere of insouciance, the organisation within the profession was rigidly hierachical, the prostitutes being accorded ranks which determined both the fees they received for their services and the social prestige they enjoyed within the *yukaku* society. Normally a girl would be introduced into a brothel at a very young age, about five or six years old. She would then serve an apprenticeship, learning to dance, sing and play musical instruments, while generally helping in a number of menial capacities, for example carrying messages. She was the property of the brothel and could only be released if she were bought from the establishment by another one – in a manner perhaps comparable to football players today – or by someone who wished either to marry her or set her up as a concubine for his exclusive use. On the whole, however, once she entered a particular brothel, this was for 'life-time employment'; having served her apprenticeship, depending on the degree of her versatility, she would rise up the ranks.

Prostitution existed (exists) in all societies, but in comparison with Western societies of the same period there were a few commendable features in the Japanese system. First, Japanese prostitutes did not suffer the social disgrace which was the fate of their Western sisters. Secondly, given the fact that the *geisha* at least was sought after not only for her physical charm but also for her artistic and social talents, ageing was less of a problem, indeed the disaster, that is was in the West. As the years passed, perhaps less called upon for copulation, she continued to fulfil an important and esteemed role as entertainer and tutor, namely in educating the new recruits. The life-long employment, the hierarchical ranking, the association of belonging to the brothel and, so far as one knows, the degree of benevolence (*jen*) exercised by the proprietor in looking after the well-being of the inmates, all attest to the brothel's quality as another example of the *ie*.

One final point needs to be made in regard to the *yukaku*. In view of all the facts cited so far in regard not only to the *yukaku* but also the condition of upper-stratum women in general, it is hardly surprising that the *yukaku* became a centre of the cultural scene of Edo Japan. The beauties portrayed in the *ukiyo-e* (coloured wood-block prints of the 'floating world') were from the *yukaku*, while many plays, usually romantic tragedies, centred round the amorous intrigues and accompanying emotions of the *yukaku* inmates, perhaps the most famous being *The Love Suicides at Sonezaki* by Chikamatsu Monzaemon (1653–1725), first performed in 1703. In the closed society that was Edo Japan and the restrictions imposed on women in accordance with the minatory prescriptions of *bushido*, there was relatively little outside the *yukaku* which could serve as inspiration for romantic stories.

Apart from prostitutes, concubines and domestic servants, women in Edo

Japan were, needless to say, engaged in other activities. There were, for example, women employed in various capacities in the Shinto shrines and staffing the Buddhist nunneries: here again the principle of birth often operated, the headship of certain nunneries in Kyoto, for example, being restricted to females of prescribed *kuge* families. Education proliferated considerably during the Edo era and although the main beneficiaries were men, some girls were also exposed to learning. In the samurai estate those girls who did receive an education would concentrate on Japanese letters (*wafu no narai*), rather than the more demanding, 'masculine' Chinese studies. Education opened the doors to a number of (albeit very limited) possibilities, including the writing of poetry and prose, teaching, and so on. Again the phenomenon of private, rather than public, scholarship may have been operative in a few instances, it being suspected, for example, that the *Onna Daigaku* ('Greater Learning for Women', of which more shall be said shortly), attributed to the Confucianist moral scholar, Kaibara Ekken (1630–1714), was in fact written by his wife. Among the merchant estate, women participated in a number of activities, including book-keeping, retailing, and so on, hence a knowledge of the three Rs would be an advantage in a merchant's prospective bride.

It is, however, of course especially in the primary sector that women were most numerous and economically most functional. In fishing, for example, it was women who were the fishmongers and it was also females who dived for seaweed; patterns of continuity can be seen here in that since diving was traditionally a female activity, when Mikimoto Kokichi (1858–1954) founded his cultured pearl empire women were employed as divers (*ama*) – generally not the case in other pearl-diving communities, for example in India, the Persian Gulf and Mexico – and this remains the case to this day. In agriculture there were also a number of activities generally carried out solely by women, the hulling and milling of grain and the annual transplantation of rice shoots being two examples. Sericulture was almost exclusively a female domain and treatises were written in the course of the Edo era giving advice to women on how best to breed worms, and so on; the advice, some of it scientifically advanced, some of it not, went into considerable detail, including for example warnings about talking too loudly when in the presence of worms and staying clear from them during periods of menstruation, the main reason for this presumably being the association in Shinto of menstruation with uncleanness (*tsumi*). In the cottage industry which proliferated in the Edo era, women played an important role, especially in spinning and weaving; and in the primitive types of textile factories which began emerging in the later Edo era it was generally farm girls who were employed as operatives.

In view of the fact that peasant women represented the overwhelming majority of the female population, a brief, fairly general description of their way of life is called for; partly also in order to illustrate the point made earlier – the evolutionary process of the 'samurai-isation' of society which occurred in the course of the later Edo and Meiji eras.

If one ignores the poorer tenants on a subsistence or indeed below subsistence existence, the richer landlords whose women would experience the same fate as those of the samurai estate, and if one excludes periods of obvious hardship, such as famines, it is reasonable to conjecture that peasant women must have led a much happier, more fulfilled, freer existence than their samurai counterparts. The ordinary peasant, it goes without saying, could not afford to keep concubines, hence sexual relations would be generally limited to the couple; similarly, the ordinary peasant, tied to his land, would have neither the resources nor the opportunity to visit the *yukaku*, which presumably also meant that venereal disease – a scourge of vast proportions in urban Japan – would be far less common in rural districts. Women worked side by side with their men and though certain customs might have been observed in the household, for example in seating arrangements, peasant women were obviously on a plane of far greater equality with their men. Nor were women excluded from the village celebrations and festivals, so peasant females could have an easy-going, entertaining social life, denied to females of the upper strata.

Thus, during the Edo era the strict ideological code in regard to women, as manifested in the concept of *danson-johi* ('revere man – despise woman'), or illustrated in the pages of the *Onna Daigaku*, in fact affected only women of samurai and quasi-samurai standing. The so-called 'traditional' Japanese marriage of more contemporary society was derived from samurai custom and did not affect the general community until much later, as a fairly widespread phenomenon perhaps not until the Showa era (1926–   ). Real traditional conjugal relations among commoners were of a very different order. Though practices varied considerably from region to region, traditional marriages included the following characteristics.

Both courtship and pre-marital sexual relations were the norm. One found, for example, the custom of *yobai* (literally 'night crawling'), whereby a suitor would go at night to sleep at the house of an eligible girl. Though there were regional variations, generally speaking what this implied was that when a girl became of marriageable age she would be left to make her bedding in some easily accessible and reasonably private part of the house. A young man would come to sleep with her; if he decided he wished to marry her, he would stay till morning to be 'discovered' by the girl's parents. If he decided against betrothal, he would abscond in the night. More informal methods of courtship also took place. In fact it is reasonable to assume that a lad would have secured the girl's permission before the *yobai*. Thus sampling and selection of mates took place and the decision whether or not to marry was left mainly to the two individuals concerned.

In the case of the ideal samurai marriage, neither courtship nor pre-marital sex took place, the bride was chosen by the family in consultation with and through the help of an officially appointed go-between (*nakodo*) and the marriage was not so much a contract between individuals as between families; thus personal choice, of either groom or bride, had very little to do in the matter, nor, needless to say, did love. Japan was of course by no means exceptional in this respect and in spite of certain differences in structure and ceremony the same general pattern would apply to European upper-class families, especially in the sense that marriage was an affair more between families than between the individuals concerned; among the various differences, however, one should point out that although in both societies pre-marital sex was not the norm, in Europe extra-marital sex on the part of both partners was, if not the rule, at least not exceptional, whereas in Japan it was generally the exclusive prerogative of the male.

A second feature of traditional marriages among the peasantry in contrast with the samurai had to do with the ceremony itself. In weddings of the bushi estate, the bride was brought to the groom's family home (*yome-iri*, literally 'bringing in the bride'), and the ceremony and the consummation of the marriage were held under the roof of the husband's parental home; henceforth the bride belonged to the same *ie* as the husband, a property to be used, abused or disposed of virtually at will, and her functions included not only those of mother and wife, but also daughter-in-law; in fact her ministrations in early marriage, apart from the sexual act, were more likely to be at the behest of her mother-in-law than her husband, until she herself became a mother-in-law. Among the peasantry, in some regions it was the practice to have the wedding ceremony in the groom's home, in others in the bride's (*muko-iri*, 'bringing in the groom'). In some cases the groom might remain in his wife's *ie* for periods ranging from one to five years; he would subsequently return to his father's *ie* sometimes with his wife, sometimes without her. In fact it was not uncommon for peasant girls to join their husbands only once they had set up their own *ie*. In other regions, after the marriage the husband would work for his *ie*, the wife for hers, with the husband only joining her at nights; they would come and live and work together once they had set themselves up independently. In all of these cases, apart from the partnership being both far more egalitarian and relaxed, the emphasis was on the conjugal, rather than the lineage, relationship.

In the course of the modern era, European marriages of the lower orders have tended to follow a process of *embourgeoisement*, while in Japan it has tended to be one of *ensamouraisation*. The fact that the *femme bourgeoise* has been able to maintain a greater degree of independence – albeit in very relative terms – than her Japanese homologue is partly due to ideology, partly to custom, but also partly to economics. If the development of *yome-iri* has taken place in a consistently evolutionary manner and without significant resistance, this is, among a number of factors, due to the general absence in Japan of the dowry. The Japanese bride, irrespective of which estate she belonged to, rarely took with her more than items of purely personal use, such as clothing, a chest of drawers (*tansu*), which contained her cosmetics, and even if she took a sum of money (*jisankin*), the amount was minimal. A more substantial dowry would normally figure only in cases of *chonin* girls marrying into samurai families. The general practice of primogeniture, whereby the eldest son was left everything, plus the fact that when a bride entered her husband's *ie* the links with her parents' *ie* were severed, also meant that she had nothing to expect following the death of her parents. Wives, therefore, were a very cheap commodity; they had practically no economic value of their own, hence the proprietary rights exerted by the husband's *ie* over them.

Among the peasantry, therefore, women in the household were freer and more equal to their husbands. This resulted from the fact that peasant women had a higher economic value, in terms of labour, and from the remoteness of the villages from the more urban-centred official Confucianist ideology. As peasants rose in the social and economic scale and as Confucianist moral teaching spread in rural areas – a process begun in the Edo era and subsequently continued with far greater effect in the Meiji period – the peasant *ie* came to follow the example of the samurai. Samurai women, apart from the economic factor already mentioned, were in a very subordinate position because of both ideology and certain institutions inherent in the family system. The latter included the widely recognised practice of concubinage, the absorption of the wife into the husband's *ie* (*yome-iri*) and the husband's virtually absolute power of divorce – causes for which could include not only failure to produce offspring, contraction of disease (including venereal ones which the husband was likely to have passed on to the wife following a bout in the *yukaku*) and disrespect shown to his parents, but also a fairly general heading of talking too much and thereby disturbing the peace of the *ie* – without the need for financial compensation. In its essentials this system remained operative in Japan until the reforms imposed by the American occupying forces following defeat in the Second World War; these included the wife's right to divorce, which in turn led to the not surprising result that the majority of divorce suits filed in the immediate post-war years were by wives.

In terms of ideology Japanese women were relegated to a very inferior position, partly as a result of the martial values inherent in *bushido* and the emphasis which it placed on the daimyo–samurai relationship to the practical exclusion of all else. This was reinforced by the highly phallocratic Confucianist social doctrines. The numerous moral tracts written for women in the Edo era in some respects did not differ markedly from, say, their Victorian counterparts in the West, stressing as they did sobriety, propriety in demeanour, and so forth. One difference which can be noted is that in regard to attitudes towards sex. As is well known, the Victorian ideology regarding sex for women was that it was an evil necessary for the sake of procreation, an intolerable burden for girls whose best course of action was 'to close their eyes and think of England'. Traditionally in Japan there were practically no sexual taboos (apart from incest); adultery on the part of the wife or pre-marital sex on the part of the samurai girl were proscribed not so much because of laws of chastity, but because of laws of property – in other words a girl belonged, literally, to her father before marriage, to her husband after marriage and to her son in widowhood, hence her body was not hers to offer of her free will, but a commodity which was the property of the *ie* in which she lived. Under the proper circumstances, however, there was no shame attached to sexuality and indeed part of the education of young girls was that they should be properly instructed in the art of love and to that end were given *makura-zoshi* (pillow books consisting mainly of illustrations) as part of their pre-nuptial training – not, however, it should be emphasised, in order to secure their enjoyment, but that of their husband.

The most famous of the moral tracts for women of the Edo era was Kaibara Ekken's *Onna Daigaku*. It may be appropriate to close this section with two selections from this work. The first quotation will illustrate the point made about the absorption of daimyo–samurai relationship within the marriage; while the second will provide a reasonably colourful impression of the esteem with which women were held according to the prevailing ideology.

> A woman has no particular lord. She must look to her husband as her lord, and must serve him with all worship and reverence, not despising or thinking lightly of him. The great life-long duty of a woman is obedience . . . When the husband issues his instructions, the wife must never disobey him . . . A woman should look on her husband as if he were Heaven itself, and never weary of thinking how she may yield to her husband, and thus escape celestial castigation.

> The five worst maladies that afflict the female mind are: indocility, discontent, slander, jealousy, and silliness. Without any doubt, these five maladies infest seven or eight out of every ten women, and it is from these

that arises the inferiority of women to men . . . The worst of them all, and
the parent of the other four, is silliness.

ETA AND *HININ*

If women receive only cursory mention in most general histories of Japan,
generally the *eta* and *hinin* receive none at all. To say that this is the equivalent
of writing the history of the United States without the Blacks or of Germany
without the Jews would be a considerable exaggeration; the *eta* were neither
enslaved nor were they exterminated in concentration camps. Nor were their
numbers comparable in percentage terms to more widely known
discriminated minorities in other societies. When the legal distinction between
outcast groups and other commoners was abolished in 1871 it was estimated
according to the census – and hitherto outcasts had not figured in Edo
censuses – that there were approximately 400,000 *eta* and a further 750,000 or
so other types of outcast. Another reason why the problem of *eta* may not have
received attention is that they are not an international group: Blacks exist not
only in Africa, but in both American continents and, of course, more recently
in some countries of Western Europe, while the Jewish diaspora is a well-
known phenomenon; whereas *eta*, on the other hand, exist only in Japan. The
eta and other outcasts can hardly be labelled a powerful force in Japanese
history and although the last century or so has witnessed a number of
emancipation movements, no *eta* leading figure has attracted international
attention to warrant, for example as in the case of Martin Luther King
(1929–68), the award of the Nobel Peace Prize. So far as modern Japan is
concerned, however, the *eta* remain a social and political problem; although
the roots of this problem lie as far back as the Nara period, they were given a
further twist in the course of the Edo era.

In the pre-Edo era all outcast groups (*senmin*, literally 'despised people') had
been lumped together. While they were discriminated against, society was not
particularly ordered (in the *sengoku* era far from it), so they enjoyed a
considerable degree of freedom of movement and financial remuneration
since, as we have seen, in the period of civil wars demand for leather goods
was significant. Edo legislation, however, drew a distinction between the *eta*
and the *hinin* (non-human), mainly along occupational lines. The *eta*
slaughtered animals and manufactured leather products; they were also the
only group in Japan at the time to eat meat. Apart from leather work, they
made *zori* (sandals), *geta* (wooden clogs) and other goods. The *hinin* consisted
of a variety of mendicant groups, acrobats, strolling minstrels, actors, and so
forth. Although there were different responsibilities accorded to *eta* and *hinin*,
generally both were engaged in the various jobs associated with criminals: as
prison wardens, torturers, executioners, whether by transfixing with spears

those who were crucified (normally Christians) or sawing off heads in decapitation.

A whole series of minatory rules were issued regarding their way of living. *Eta* were forbidden to marry or to have sexual intercourse with non-*eta*; they were forbidden employment by commoners as servants; they were not permitted to reside outside designated *eta* villages or ghettoes – hence the current terminology for *eta*, *burakumin*, literally 'village people'; nor were they permitted to cross the threshold of non-*eta* or *hinin* houses, or to sit, eat or smoke in the company of ordinary citizens. Although, as pointed out above, *eta* and *hinin* did not figure in the census, if they had to be counted the numeral form for animals was used. (In the Japanese language different numerical forms are used depending on the objects being counted; hence one, two, three human beings will be *hitori*, *futari*, *sannin*, while one, two, three animals will be *ippiki*, *nihiki*, *sanbiki*; *eta* and *hinin* were counted according to the latter rather than the former.) It is probable that it is as a result of these extreme forms of both segregation and discrimination that popular beliefs regarding the habits and physical peculiarities of the *eta* arose, the latter including the myths that they are born with only four fingers and that they are not capable of urinating and defecating simultaneously.

The *eta* and *hinin* had their own rulers and administration, though needless to say these were answerable to the bakufu. The chief of the *eta* of the Kanto area was always called Danzaemon and he had his residence and offices in the Asakusa district of Tokyo. Danzaemon's legitimacy was partly based on the claim that he was the direct descendant of Minamoto no Yoritomo (1147–99), founder of the Kamakura bakufu, and a peasant girl; although this lineage appears to have been bogus. Danzaemon was nevertheless permitted to carry two swords. Danzaemon and leaders of the other regions were responsible for law and order among the *eta* and *hinin*; their ranks could swell as criminals and fallen samurai (that is, from the grace of their lord) could be placed temporarily or permanently (in the latter case this would also affect all their descendants), in the outcast group. Otherwise, the bakufu undertook to protect *eta* monopoly, in a manner comparable to the guilds, over their traditional activities; this practice has also survived to the contemporary age in that to the annoyance of countries such as Italy, Spain and France that export manufactured leather goods, the Japanese government imposes strict import controls on leather goods in order to protect this still traditional *eta* activity and, owing to continued discrimination, one of the few remunerative areas open to them.

The *sengoku* era, as we have seen, was one in which the *eta* were able, relatively speaking, to prosper. In the early Edo period their economic standing appears to have been quite reasonable and indeed a number of them were wealthy. As the years and decades passed, however, and mainly as a result of the falling demand for leather goods, poverty increasingly became the lot of the *eta*. To social discrimination and popular abuse, therefore, was added precipitous economic decline – a fate which, generally speaking, remains the case for the *burakumin* in the 1980s.

RYUKYUANS AND AINU

Among the advantages Japan enjoyed in the development of a nation-state indicated in Chapter 1 were the internal and external recognition of what constituted the territory of Japan and the ethnic homogeneity of the inhabitants. While these remarks remain true, qualifications need to be made in order to illustrate certain trends of the Edo era, which were accelerated in the ensuing Meiji period. Thus, whereas today no one would deny that the Ryukyus and Hokkaido are part of Japan, such was not necessarily the case in the Edo era.

There are certain ethnic and linguistic differences between the people of the Ryukyus and the Japanese, but these are not of great significance. The differences which do exist are more marked in regard to the lower orders of the Ryukyus and far less so in the case of the ruling élites. The ancient Ryukyuan monarchy also claimed divine ancestry, namely in Tinsunshi (Grandson of Heaven), though, unlike the Japanese imperial institution, it was not 'unbroken for ages eternal': a dynastical change occurred in the late twelfth century with the new king, Shunten, being a Minamoto offspring. The Chinese had been visiting, occasionally invading, the Ryukyus since the early part of the seventh century at least, but it was not until the latter part of the fourteenth that they obtained from the Ryukyu monarchy the recognition of supremacy and henceforth the Ryukyus were included in the Chinese sphere of tributary states.

The Ryukyus, in view of their strategic geographic position and also especially at a time when official relations between China and Japan had been suspended by the former, played a pivotal role in Sino-Japanese trading relations. Tension developed between Japan and the Ryukyus when the king at Shuri (the capital) refused to assist in Hideyoshi's continental campaigns. Not surprisingly, in view of their geographic proximity, Ryukyuan affairs were mainly of interest to the Shimazu daimyo of Satsuma. In 1609 Satsuma invaded the main island of Okinawa and kidnapped the king, bringing him to Kagoshima. Although he was eventually allowed to return to Shuri and his throne, this was on condition that he should recognise Satsuma suzerainty and pay tribute. The Ryukyuan monarchy, therefore, for over 250 years found itself having two masters and having to pay tribute to both of them. The Ryukyus served the Satsuma han well, both in terms of trade and in terms of gathering intelligence on events in the outside world. Although the Ryukyus were formally – and unilaterally – absorbed into Japan in 1879, when they were renamed and reorganised as the Okinawa prefecture, in the course of the Edo era these islands can be said to have been part of a Japanese 'informal empire', albeit administered by the Satsuma han.

In the north, the area which used to be called Ezo, now Hokkaido, the situation was completely different. The northernmost han of Edo Japan was that of Matsumae which was situated on the southernmost tip of Ezo. The founding daimyo of this han was Matsumae (alias Kakizaki) Yoshihiro (1550–1618) whose great-great-grandfather had originally settled there in the mid-fifteenth century. Under the Tokugawa settlement the Matsumae han was responsible for Ezo affairs, in a manner somewhat analogous to the So daimyo of the Tsushima island han being responsible for Korean affairs and Satsuma for the Ryukyus. So far as the rest of Ezo was concerned, this was wilderness inhabited by the aboriginal barbarians. They were generally referred to by the Japanese as *ebisu*, the Chinese character for *ebisu* being the same as the '*i*' in *sei-i-tai-shogun*, 'barbarian-repressing generalissimo', and, for that matter, the same as the '*i*' of *joi*, 'expel the barbarians', the xenophobic slogan of the mid-nineteenth century and intended to summarise and direct the policy which the bakufu should adopt in regard to the recently arrived Westerners.

The *ebisu*, however, called themselves Ainu which in their language simply means 'man'. We shall not dwell here on the numerous interpretations given to the possible origins of the Ainu people – including, inevitably, the theory of their being one of the lost tribes of Israel; suffice it to say, however, that they differ from the Japanese in practically every respect. The Ainu economy was based almost exclusively on hunting and fishing. There was a link with the Japanese and especially with Shinto in that the Ainu worshipped nature and the term for a deity is *kamui* – Shinto pronounced differently but with the same characters becomes *Kami-michi*, the way of the deities, though it is not known whether *kami* comes from *kamui*, or vice versa. Apart from the sun, the wind, the ocean, and so forth, the Ainu also worshipped the bear, although unlike, say, the Hindus with the sacred cows, Ainu ate bears, albeit ceremoniously, in essence comparable to the Christian custom of communion and other similar fairly universal religious traditions, though the rite itself was perhaps more reminiscent of the Spanish *corrida de toros*.

The Ainu are the most hirsute of any known human racial species, while their women had the custom of tattooing, not simply by painting but also by carving, moustaches on to their upper lips. There are other interesting contrasts. For example, as Western sailors and others discovered when relations with Japan were established, the Japanese did not engage in kissing – not surprisingly, therefore, the Japanese vocabulary for the word 'kiss' is somewhat limited, in fact today generally the term used is *kissu* (that is, a loan word from English). Among the Ainu, however, not only kissing, but indeed nibbling, constituted an important part of affectionate or sexual demonstrations and the Ainu vocabulary is rich in this area: *chopchopse-kara, chopohopse-kara, echopnure, chokchokse-kara, nankotukte* and *charonunnun* all refer to the action of kissing, though the last might be more exactly translated as to suck the lips (see J. Batchelor, *An Ainu–English–Japanese Dictionary*, 1926). In spite of considerable intermarriage between Ainu and Japanese in the past, the Japanese, as the dominant culture, do not seem to have adopted the Ainu custom of kissing/nibbling, but the integrated Ainu seem to have abandoned it. Apart from intermarriage, a considerable amount of mutual influences obviously occurred over the centuries, that is, when the aboriginal tribes still resided in parts of the main islands; and a number of toponyms are derived from the Ainu language: notably the mountain Fuji, *Fuji* in Ainu meaning fire.

During the first 150 years or so of the Edo era nothing of much consequence occurred in Ezo. By the second half of the eighteenth century, however, bakufu interest in these northern areas awoke and developed. The motivations for this new direction were essentially two-fold, albeit somewhat contradictory. The latter part of the eighteenth century, as has been seen, was a period of stagnation, occasional famines and general economic decay. A small number of officials and scholars, but most notably Honda Toshiaki (1744–1821), believed that Japan's economic ills might be partly cured by developing foreign trade and to that end argued in favour of establishing trade links with Russia via the northern territories of Ezo and Sakhalin. The second motivation was the fear generated by reports of Russian visits, incursions and indeed occasional invasions of parts of these northern territories. Interest in Ezo, therefore, was prompted by both economic and strategic considerations.

The first major fact-finding mission occurred in 1785 under the orders of the *roju* Tanuma Okitsugu (1719–88). For the next thirty-five years, although no clearly defined and consistent policy regarding either what to do with the Ainu or establishing control over Ezo can be identified (partly because of the fairly frequent changes in the Bakufu, Okitsugu, for example being forced out of office in 1787 and replaced by Matsudaira whose views on Ezo differed), nevertheless bakufu activity in the area was considerable. Surveying expeditions occurred at frequent intervals, especially those of two intrepid explorers, Mogami Tokunai (1754–1836) and Mamiya Rinzo (1775–1844), leading to occasional armed confrontations between Russians and Japanese. These events in turn led to a revived interest in, and numerous publications on, economics, geography, maritime affairs and military science, Honda being one of the most prolific writers, but equally influential was the scholar Hayashi Shihei of Sendai (1738–93), whose work *Kaikoku Heidan* ('Military Talks for a Maritime Nation') represents a major milestone in Japanese expansionist thought.

The importance attached to Ezo and Edo's suspicions regarding the efficacy of Matsumae's administration – in fact the bakufu sent espionage teams to Matsumae to gather intelligence on their operations – in due course led to the bakufu taking over direct control of Ezo and the surrounding territories; in 1799 the southern half of Ezo was placed under bakufu administration, and in 1807 this was extended to include all of Ezo and Sakhalin. In 1821 the bakufu lost interest, and Russia in the intervening period was more absorbed with affairs in the West and in particular with the Ottoman Empire. Japanese colonisation of Ezo did not begin in earnest until after the Meiji Restoration, when the island was renamed Hokkaido.

The general area of Ezo, Sakhalin and the Kuriles, all of which were inhabited, though sparsely, by Ainu, constituted in the eighteenth and nineteenth centuries what one might term open frontier country. The Russians, it will be recalled, were expanding in Siberia and, following the explorations and discoveries of the Dane Vitus Behring (1681–1741), had begun settling in Alaska by the mid-eighteenth century – where they remained until it was sold to the United States in 1867. Sakhalin, the Kuriles, ultimately Ezo, were further routes for possible expansion. Russian expansion was forestalled owing to a variety of factors, including Japanese resistance, but also the lack of adequate relaying facilities on the mainland and Russia's increasing absorption and ultimately confrontation over peripheral areas of the Ottoman Empire. The element of Japanese resistance during this period, however, must not be exaggerated; for all the forcefulness of the arguments of Honda, Hayashi and others, scepticism – indeed, outright hostility – towards northern expansion also had influential and no less forceful advocates in bakufu circles, who were at an advantage in that expansionism was certainly anathema to the *sakoku* ideology and mentality.

One thing is certain, however, and that is that the destiny of these areas was not going to be shaped by the wishes or activities of the inhabitants – the Ainu. The Ainu might prove resistant in certain circumstances, and indeed rebellious, as was the case in 1789 when a sizeable Ainu rebellion occurred on the island of Kunashiri (today one of the disputed islands between Japan and the USSR), while under other circumstances they might prove more amenable. They were, however, little more than pawns in the Russo-Japanese confrontation. As the British or the French might, through various means, incite Indian tribes in the North American continent to join with one against the other, so both the Russians and the Japanese used the Ainu, with alternative policies of intimidation, brute force and indoctrination to win the natives over to their side and have them comply with their demands. The Russians appear to have relied exclusively on force. So far as the Japanese were concerned, the situation varied considerably. Under the Matsumae han's administration the Ainu were treated with ruthless, exploitative contempt; and indeed Mogami had got into trouble with Matsumae officials when it was discovered that he had taught an Ainu how to read and write the Japanese syllabary, *kana*. Some Edo scholars and notably Honda, however, had argued that Ainu too were descendants of the gods (*kami*) and hence to be treated as Japanese. Whether out of ideological or strategic considerations, when the bakufu took over control of Ezo it issued an edict according to which a programme of japanisation of the Ainu was to take place. In other words, the bakufu carried out a policy of assimilation, Ainu being encouraged to take Japanese names, learn to speak, read and write the Japanese language, wear Japanese clothes and indeed miscegenation was positively encouraged, while certain customs, including the ritual killing and eating of the bear, were proscribed. Mogami, whose interest in the Ainu people was genuine and humane – in fact, in view of his study and knowledge of the Ainu people, he could be described not only as an explorer and geographer but also as an early anthropologist – was opposed to this policy, realising that by destroying the Ainu sense of identity, the result would be alienation, rather than assimilation. In the short term Mogami's reservations proved correct, with many Ainu absconding to Russian-held territory, presumably preferring the brutality of the Russians to the civilising efforts of the Japanese. In the long term, the Ainu were doomed.

It is impossible to know what was the Ainu population of the Edo era. According to census taken during the Meiji period they would appear to have numbered somewhere in the region of seventeen and a half thousand, while today they are reckoned to be about sixteen thousand out of a total population in Hokkaido of some five and a quarter millions. Thus whereas the total population of Japan from the end of the Edo era to the present has almost quadrupled, the Ainu population has decreased, or at the very least remained stationary. In the Darwinian scheme of things, the Ainu race was not one to emerge among the fitter for the struggle for survival. It is true, as indeed has been briefly mentioned in these pages, that the Ainu were for a while at the mercy of conflicting marauding groups of Russians and Japanese and thereby suffered the consequences. However, nothing remotely comparable to genocide occurred at any time. The colonisation of Hokkaido in the Meiji era would appear to have been conducted by reasonably peaceful and indeed comparatively humanitarian methods; the Ainu were certainly better treated than, say, the Indians in North America. The apparent stagnation in their numbers is largely to be explained by the process of assimilation, originally conceived in the Edo era, but systematically carried out in the Meiji period: in other words, the Ainu were increasingly absorbed into the Japanese population, leading to half-breeds, quarter-breeds, and so on. Of course the disappearance of any of the species of humanity is bound to be a matter of regret; but on the other hand there was here an element of inevitability. It would be a mistake to construe an idyllic existence for the hunting–fishing, bear-worshipping Ainu of the pre-modern era. The Ainu race was already in demographic decline in the course of the Edo era; polygamy, and possibly polyandry were practised, while on the other hand endogamy was the rule, exogamy a very rare exception. This situation resulted not only in sterility, but also obviously in all the usual consequences of excessive in-breeding.

Objectively there can be little doubt that Meiji Japan's colonisation of the northern territories and the japanisation of their populations probably accelerated the movement towards near extinction. Ainu were taught Japanese, indeed they were given schools and educated in the same manner as the Japanese, the young men were recruited into the army, and, as already pointed out, there was considerable intermarriage with the Japanese. On the other hand, some, whether by intention or accident, remained true to their race and their customs; today those who still remain can be visited in certain specified 'Ainu villages', where, as one guide-book puts it, 'these primitive people may be seen in their native surroundings'. Between exhibition and extinction, perhaps the latter is preferable if it occurs in a reasonably peaceful and dignified manner.

SOCIAL ROOTS OF MODERNITY

In the course of the Edo era a protracted evolutionary process had taken place which laid the foundations for the revolution which occurred in the mid-nineteenth century. It will be made clear, however, that in spite of the very perceptible and rapid changes which occurred as a result of the revolution, namely the modernisation of Japan, in fact a good deal of it could be described as a 'cleaning-up operation'. In the eleven decades or so following the revolution, a number of major transformations have taken place; the greatest stimulant was undoubtedly provided by the West.

By the end of the Edo era, society had been significantly modernised. One must be cautious here not to exaggerate, not to be too wise after the event. Not only in the course of the decades immediately following the Restoration, but indeed throughout the first half of the twentieth century there were major obstacles and antagonisms to the transformations inherent in a process of modernisation. Nevertheless, in laying the roots for modernity the achievements of the Edo era are significant, impressive, and probably unique outside the Western world. It remains, by way of conclusion, simply to summarise these.

Sankin-kotai resulted in considerable political centralisation and geographic mobility. These in turn led to a definitive trend towards national unity; fief particularism was being eroded in favour of the creation of a nation-state. Not only was this true of the three main islands of Honshu, Shikoku and Kyushu, but, as has been seen, the process of including Hokkaido and the Ryukyus was well under way.

Economically Japan had emerged as a national market; major centres, primarily Osaka, acted as the axes of economic life; there developed a significant amount of inter-regional trade, diversification, regional specialisation, improvements in transportation and so on. This is not to say that geographic disparities in terms of distribution of wealth disappeared. On the contrary, it is probable that the Edo era witnessed an intensification of geographic differentiation; economic distress and a tendency to political extremism remained a feature of the poorer districts of Japan, notably southern Kyushu and the Tohoku (north-east) area, well into the twentieth century. But geographic differentiation, like social differentiation, has been a characteristic of all industrialising societies.

The social differentiation which took place in the course of the Edo era resulted in the emergence of so-called middle sectors. The high feudal orders and their allies, the big city merchants, were swept away in the transformations of the latter part of the nineteenth century. The new groups of meritocratic samurai bureaucrats, rural landlords and innovative merchants in due course coalesced as the ruling class.

Finally, the basic social unit of Japan, the *ie*, had been to a considerable extent institutionalised in the course of the Edo era. It came under attack in the early Meiji years and in the ensuing decades it experienced a number of alterations. No moral value should be attached to the *ie*; it can, depending on the wider national circumstances, be a force for progress, as it can lead to regression. It is perhaps in contemporary Japan that it can be seen in its most favourable light. From the late Edo era on, however, it was undoubtedly the *ie* which provided the social basis for Japan's modernisation.

4 Intellect in the Edo Era

The term 'intellectual' is used here in its broadest sense: we are interested in developments which affected the mentality and the outlook of the Japanese people during this prelude to modernity. It is, needless to say, a vast subject. It will be impossible to treat it either extensively or indeed intensively. The major concern will be to identify those trends which ultimately contributed to and influenced the course of modern Japanese history.

In regard to the general cultural climate of Edo Japan, no doubt the most negative factor was the policy of *sakoku*. Even here, however, certain areas can be singled out where *sakoku* may have had positive side-effects, at least in the years leading up to the Genroku era. Peace, relative prosperity in some quarters, urbanisation and the exchange of ideas facilitated by *sankin-kotai* contributed greatly to artistic and intellectual activities and these in turn may have benefited, possibly stimulated by a period of contemplative seclusion.

Certainly there was a veritable boom in artistic productions of all kinds. In regard to ceramics, for which Japan was to acquire an international reputation, one finds an interesting blend of expansionism at the end of the *sengoku* era and isolationism in the Edo era contributing towards the development and refinement of this art in Japan. When Hideyoshi's troops invaded Korea, the Japanese were impressed by the exquisiteness of Korean porcelain and faience products. A number of daimyo brought Korean artisans back with them to their han and there set them to work both to produce and to instruct native artisans. For example, the much-sought-after Imari ware dates from this period, being first produced in Hizen han in north-west Kyushu in about 1600.

Merchant wealth, in Edo Japan as in Renaissance Italy, greatly facilitated the expansion of artistic productions. Also *chonin*, not restricted by samurai ceremony and supposed asceticism, were able to indulge their purses and fancies in new, more flamboyant forms, perhaps especially visible in the colourful décor of Kabuki theatre in contrast to the austerity of Noh. There was a tremendous proliferation in publications of all sorts – poems, prose stories, moral tracts, historical essays, legends, religious pamphlets and a great deal of pornography. Printing on a movable type, originally introduced by the Portuguese, was an activity of quasi-febrile dimensions in Edo Japan and one characteristic of the period was the booklets and their vendors widely dispersed throughout the cities.

Culture as such was by no means new to Edo Japan, indeed Japan's cultural legacy stretched back at least a millennium. It was, however, only in the Edo era that Japan can be said to have acquired a reasonably popular culture; in other words, aesthetic experiences whether of the mind or the senses were not limited to a narrow court élite or to the more richly endowed temples. It was, it is true, an urban phenomenon of the Edo era, hence not touching the vast majority of the population, but in the urban areas popular culture proliferated and gradually encompassed most groups irrespective of estate; samurai, albeit surreptitiously, attended Kabuki performances. On the eve of modernisation the urban population had, *mutatis mutandis*, a common cultural base. Secondly, it will be seen that in the course of the early Meiji years one of the chief characteristics of the period was the seemingly insatiable appetite with which the citizens devoured all kinds of literature: the press proliferated, new journals were constantly appearing and translations of Western works were rife. Indeed the urban Japanese of the early Meiji years could be described as indiscriminate culture vultures – a quality that contributed to the nature and pace of modernisation. The avidity for reading, thereby widening the national cultural horizons, could not have been possible unless its roots had been firmly planted in the Edo era. In terms of shaping the intellectual outlook which Edo Japan bequeathed to the modern era, attention will be focused primarily on religion and morality, education, and the development of Western studies.

RELIGION AND MORALITY

During the Edo era numerous temples were built, expanded, or simply spruced up. The whole of the Nikko ensemble, for example, with its highly ornate temples and bridges and *torii*, where the remains of the Tokugawa shogun were laid in mausolea, dates from this period. Buddhist temples also benefited from the custom of shogun and daimyo to retire from the world of mundane matters to the sacerdotal for a life of sophistication and indeed some grandeur; generally speaking, the emphasis was hardly on frugality and chastity, but more on art, the tea ceremony and literature. Buddhist monks were also able to take advantage of the peace which reigned and the availability of printing material in order to compile and systematise various doctrinal *magna opera* of their respective sects.

Buddhist affairs came under the jurisdiction of the bakufu office of *jisha-bugyo* (commissioner of temples and shrines, hence also responsible for Shinto affairs). The Buddhists, who in the *sengoku* era had to contend with and confront the doctrines of the Christians, enjoyed considerable privileges and protection under the Tokugawa settlement. It was, for example, the responsibility of the temples to compile the census and to ensure that there were no concealed Christians. During the Edo era, at least in theory, the Buddhists enjoyed what amounted to a monopoly over metaphysics. Partly no doubt because of this religious nationalisation, in no period of Japanese history since the introduction of Buddhism in the Nara era was that faith in a more parlous state: the general image being comparable to that of pre-Reformation Christianity. The Buddhist clergy appear on the one hand to have sought indulgence in all manner of sensual pleasures, while on the other the various sects engaged in petty doctrinal squabbles. The image is of course, both in regard to Edo Buddhism and pre-Reformation Christianity, somewhat of a caricature and just as in the case of the latter it is derived from the ecclesiastical hierarchy, so it is probably the case that what applied to the more imposing and well endowed temples in Kyoto and elsewhere need not represent reality at the lower levels. The point is, however, that in the Edo era the Buddhist clergy neither earned nor obtained the respect of the intellectuals.

The religious picture of Edo Japan is complex and we shall try here to disentangle some of the difficulties. So far as the spiritual life of the Japanese people are concerned, it is in fact misleading to isolate one of the faiths. Indeed the Edo era witnessed a considerable degree of eclecticism. *Bushido*, as already pointed out, was derived from a variety of sources, but included certainly both Confucianism and Buddhism. As to the Shinto revival, which will be looked at more closely in the next chapter, it too was by no means solely a reproduction from its own sources.

On a more popular level, one may note the eclecticism of the *shingaku* movement of Ishida Baigan and its appeal to the *chonin*, already mentioned, as well as the *hotoku* movement (literally indebtedness or recompense) which spread among the peasantry and was founded by Ninomiya Sontoku (1787–1856). These are two of the better known of a fairly large number of 'new' faiths or sects which sprouted in the Edo era and were generally founded on the teachings of a particular individual. In general, however, while these sects catered to certain emotional needs, they can hardly be deemed theologically sophisticated.

It would be incorrect to view the Edo era as irreligious, and one could certainly not call it ungodly; on the contrary there was an abundance of gods. The point would seem to be that in metaphysical terms, in terms of beliefs and faith, religion in Edo Japan (with the exception of Christianity, which was proscribed) was a private affair. In villages ritual observances, whether at Buddhist temples or Shinto shrines, were encouraged, indeed the norm, partly because this is a universal feature of village life – as is the case, for example, in rural Roman Catholic areas with their village saints and the ceremonies and fun engaged in by all on the occasion of the saint's feast day. The temples served as meeting places for the villagers, the feasts and rituals as a means of strengthening the bonds between the families, and the gods were prayed to for clement weather and abundant crops. The line between 'religion' and 'superstition' here, as in all comparable rural societies, is, needless to say, a thin one, but it is not necessary to enter theological or semantic discussions in order simply to ascertain the fact that in terms of religious observances the rural Japanese of the Edo era tended to correspond to fairly universal patterns. Nor would it by any means be the intention to denigrate the role, the general joyfulness, indeed heartiness of these religious observances to state that the kind of faith one is talking about is of a primitive nature. This is a pattern which has been on the whole preserved in the course of modern Japan. The Japanese, it is often avowed, are not religious, but this is missing the point; rather one should say that in general cultural terms religion caters almost exclusively to an emotional rather than intellectual need, hence it is not that traditionally the Japanese are irreligious, but that they are not metaphysically inclined – the distinction is an important one.

This general gaiety, earthiness – indeed one could almost say irreverence – of popular Japanese religion in the latter part of the nineteenth century was to incur the severe censure of some Westerners, especially missionaries, but equally the admiration of others, notably Lafcadio Hearn (1850–1904). The absence of a national religious orthodoxy, the relegation of matters of faith to the individual, resulted among other things in a high and possibly incomparable degree of religious tolerance. Religious fanaticism, a characteristic at some stage or other even in the modern era of practically all societies, is conspicuous by its absence in more recent Japanese history. The lifting of the ban on Christianity in 1873 led neither to mass conversions nor to popular fanatical anti-Christian movements, in contrast to, say, the fanatical, millenarian proto-Christian Taiping rebels (1851–64) or equally fanatical anti-Christian Boxers (1898–1901) in China. It was not, needless to say, the absence of anti-Christian movements or persecutions which upset the missionaries, but rather the perhaps inevitable converse of the absence of religious fanaticism, namely that in terms of the general cultural atmosphere religion is not a subject which is taken desperately seriously.

There was, however, an important countervailing development which mainly originated in the Edo era and a pattern was established which, in spite of a number of permutations, remained constant until 1945. This phenomenon might at the outset best be described by contrasting it with the European and Islamic traditions. In the European tradition the role of the state was generally limited to collecting taxes, administering justice and waging war. Morality was within the jurisdiction of the Church. Thus

Europeans were governed by a form of diarchy, generally following Jesus's prescription of rendering unto Caesar what is Caesar's and unto God what is God's. Of course, jurisdictional battles did occasionally occur; at times the Church sought to expand its temporal power, while the state might occasionally resort to invading the spiritual domain. All things being equal, however, this duality was recognised and persists to this day. In the European tradition, therefore, legality and morality are by no means necessarily equated; for example, in most European countries today contraception and abortion are legal, yet according to the precepts of the Catholic Church both are immoral, indeed sinful. The same general pattern can be discerned in Islamic societies. Thus in the Ottoman Empire whereas the Caliph exercised spiritual power over the world of Islam, the Sultan was vested with temporal power over the affairs of the Empire. Both in Islamic and Christian states, even when these have been secularised, the power of the clergy and the moral authority which they enjoy have remained considerable. It must be stressed, therefore, that in both Christian and Islamic traditions – which together account for a fair percentage of the world's population – there is at the very least a potential conflict within the individual as well as within society at large between the legal order, namely the government, and the moral order. A 'good' Christian or a 'good' Muslim may feel that according to his conscience and spiritual beliefs it is incumbent upon him to seek to overthrow a godless state. The most recent illustration of this phenomenon is obviously the so-called Islamic Revolution which occurred in Iran in 1979; while in the Christian world perhaps the best recent example is that of the support of the clergy in the overthrow of the Spanish Republican regime and the consequent spiritual justification given to the putsch and subsequent government of Franco (1892–1975).

If some time has been spent on this tangent it is in order to give the greatest possible emphasis to the contrast with Japan. In writing about Japan of the immediate pre-Second World War period, Professor Maruyama Masao (*Thought and Behaviour in Modern Japanese Politics*, 1963) elucidated the power of the state in the following manner:

> In Japan we are faced with a situation in which national sovereignty involves both spiritual and political power. The standard according to which the nation's actions are judged as right or wrong lies within itself (that is, in the 'national polity'), and what the nation does, whether within its own borders or beyond them, is not subject to any moral code that supersedes the nation.

The reasons for the development of this form of *étatisme* or what one could almost call, in spite of the apparent contradiction in terms, a secular theocracy are various. Firstly, one might point out that no religious body or set of beliefs ever enjoyed a complete monopoly in Japan in the manner of Christianity and Islam. Thus Buddhism may have occasionally been in the ascendant, as was the case in the Edo era, but at no stage in Japanese history would it be possible to identify the country as Buddhist, as would be the case for example of Thailand, Laos, or Cambodia prior to the revolution. Secondly, the process of the secularisation of the nation was established and developed by various means by Ieyasu, his predecessors and successors. Thus Oda Nobunaga, as we have seen, ruthlessly suppressed the Buddhist clergy and destroyed some of their temples. We also return to the point made earlier, that Ieyasu and his successors sought to establish a moral order as part of the Tokugawa settlement. Apart from officiating at ceremonies, both private and public, the clergy in Japan of whatever denomination has not since the end of the sengoku era played any significant role or exercised any power. In the so-called Shinto revival of the latter part of the Edo era, or in the Shintoist legitimacy bestowed on the spiritual and temporal power of the tenno, or indeed in the development of State Shinto (as opposed to Shrine Shinto) which reached its apogee in the 1930s and early 1940s, the Shinto clergy itself was little more than the instrument, if that at all, of lay scholars or government officials.

The development of *bushido* as at least a quasi-official code of ethics and the Tokugawa adoption of Neo-Confucianism as the social ideology meant that the state bestowed upon itself the legitimate power to exercise moral authority over its subjects. What applied to the general social order could also be found, with minor variations in emphasis, in more particular groups, such as han or *ie*. Thus the famous *Hagakure* (Hidden Among Leaves), a fairly extreme version of the *bushido* propounding a rather morbid fascination with death, originated in Hizen han and was a particular code to be followed primarily by the samurai of that domain. Similarly the Mitsui Constitution of 1722 was meant, among other things, to be a moral guide for the members of the Mitsui *ie*. Religious beliefs, namely whether one believes in a god or not and which one, are purely personal matters. Moral conduct, however, is a public – country, han or *ie* – matter, leading to what Professor Maruyama has called the 'exteriorization of morality in Japan'. Thus, if we return to the point made earlier in regard to Europe, that what is legal is not necessarily moral – and in Europe generally morality, obviously within certain limits, is a matter for the individual to decide – in Japan one can say that what is legal, namely what is within the rules, is moral by definition.

The term 'legality' here should be understood in a very broad sense; one is not necessarily referring to written laws, but rather to official ideologies and codes of conduct. Edo Japan, therefore, developed and systematised public morality, to which it was incumbent upon every individual to adhere, both at a national level and at the level of various organisations and groups. So far as the state was concerned, this basic pattern remained operative until Japan's defeat in 1945. Public morality in the form of codes, however, has been retained as a characteristic of most Japanese institutions, whether businesses, schools, factories, and so on. One may add a footnote here. The Westerner arriving in contemporary Japan may express surprise, amusement, scepticism or derision upon discovering that Japanese companies, for example, have their own moral codes, along with mottoes, songs, and so forth. The point to remember is this. Whereas the European may (or may not) go to Sunday service and receive in the form of a sermon moral injunctions and sing that he intends to walk in the path of righteousness, the Japanese will probably receive moral guidance from his section chief or company president and sing that he too will walk in the path of righteousness, but in his place of work rather than in a church.

If one were writing about intellectual developments in Christian, Islamic, Hindu or Buddhist societies, a great deal of space would have to be accorded to religious thought. The intellectuals of these cultures will, of course, concern themselves with matters of this world, but generally in relation to the domain of God. Politics and the social order in all of these cultures were subordinate considerations to theology. It is, by contrast, the absence of theological thought which is striking in Japan and the consequent evaluation of social and political considerations to a level of absolute primacy. It is for this reason that the development of philosophy in Edo Japan will not be looked at in this section, but will be reserved for consideration in the chapter dealing with politics.

EDUCATION

In regard to education three points can be made by way of introduction. First, the development of education in the Edo era further underlines the emphasis in regard to the secularisation of Tokugawa society. In Europe, until fairly recently, education was almost exclusively the prerogative of the clergy and educational institutions were ecclesiastical establishments; a similar pattern would be found in Buddhist South-East Asia, and so forth. From the early decades of Edo Japan responsibility for education at practically all levels was taken away from the bonzes and placed in the hands of Confucianist scholars; thus village schools for the *heimin* continued to be called *terakoya* (literally, temple school), but their links with the temples were in fact severed.

Secondly, we noted earlier that in Japan's early absorption of Chinese culture, one element which was lacking was that of a civil service chosen by competitive examination. The point was made that whereas in theory China's administrative system was that of a meritocratic bureaucracy, Japan's was an aristocracy. In reality, however, whereas in the course of the Ch'ing dynasty China's administration increasingly became rigid and confined to a closed self-preserving élite, in the course of the Edo era Japan's administrative apparatus became increasingly open to talent, hence evolving in the direction of a meritocracy.

The third point is essentially a derivation of the second. Japan today is probably the most meritocratic society; in fact the Japanese themselves have come to label it the *gaku-reki shakai* (literally, 'school record society'). It is one of the major features and forces of the Japanese revolution and of the modernisation which ensued that merit by educational standards replaced privilege of birth; this transformation having been achieved far more radically than is the case in Western societies. As suggested in the pages dealing with the evolution of the samurai estate, this too is a phenomenon which finds its roots in the Edo period; not only in regard to the meritocratic principle in general, but also to a number of more particular features of the education system. Thus, education in Japan, certainly from the late nineteenth century to 1945 and especially at primary level, placed great emphasis on moral teaching; this was the case in the Edo period. Furthermore, however, critics of the contemporary education system – and there are many – complain that it is entirely geared towards passing examinations, that there is excessive stress on rote learning at the expense of innovatory and imaginative thinking, that consequently the pupil is more of a jug pedagogically filled than a candle intellectually lit. The typical product of the system, therefore, possesses, once he has been processed, a number of qualities, including perhaps above all that of sheer perseverance, but is lacking in others, notably that of originality. Although this criticism would be valid only with a number of serious reservations, it is nevertheless the case that here again there is a significant legacy from the Edo era.

So far as the development of education in Edo Japan is concerned, the first point to make is that the general atmosphere was conducive to learning, at least among the upper ranks of the samurai estate. Learning in this context, however, should be understood in terms of a reasonably leisurely pursuit: one does not have here the mad rush to acquire knowledge which was a characteristic of the early decades of the Meiji era. The peace which enshrouded Edo Japan enabled samurai to metamorphose from rustic warriors to urban and urbane men of letters. The transformation was certainly significant. In the early Edo period probably very few samurai could even read or write; by the end of the era many had acquired the attributes of the literati. It has been noted that the climate of Edo Japan, certainly in its first century or so, was one which facilitated, indeed encouraged, initiative in many diverse enterprises. This equally holds true of the realm of the intellect. Similarly, although stagnation may have developed in certain areas of economic activity, for example among urban merchants, dynamism emerged in others, as in the case of provincial landlord–entrepreneurs, the same generally applies to education in that while the more orthodox avenues may have become intellectually limited, others grew up and proliferated. Edo Japan, therefore, witnessed significant intellectual development, though a shift is discernible in terms of the more fertile environments.

It is important to perceive the establishment of education not simply, by any means, as the initiative of officialdom, but as a response on the part of the authorities to a growing demand among the samurai to spend their time usefully and to improve themselves, while the same generally applies to the upper strata of the common population. To that end the bakufu established schools, as did a good number of han, increasing in proportion throughout the Edo era until towards the end practically all han had an official school and in some cases two (or more), namely one in Edo and one in the domainal capital.

Formal education was officially endorsed, indeed encouraged, for a number of reasons. At least in respect to samurai, the ethic of learning was part of the official ideology. Here again, therefore, the influence of Confucianism was significant. Thus Buddhism stresses enlightenment (*satori*) as a desirable end to be achieved primarily by contemplative means; reading is not necessarily altogether shunned, but it is certainly subordinate to pure meditation which aims at purging the mind rather than filling it. Buddhist exercises – for example, *zazen* which involves sitting in a single, rigid position for hours on end – are certainly more physical than they are intellectual. Confucianism, on the other hand, places great emphasis on the acquisition of wisdom, one of the cardinal virtues; in the manner interpreted by the Sung Confucianists and adapted by Japan in the Edo era, Confucianist intellectualism, it is true, is not characterised by innovatory thinking, for truth is to be found in the writings of the Sages. It is in that respect backward rather than forward looking. Nevertheless a great deal of reading was demanded both of the classical texts themselves and of later exegetical writings.

Secondly, and especially in view of the intensive input of moral teaching, education was deemed an important means of maintaining the peace of the realm. This view certainly held sway in regard to samurai education, but was also gradually accepted as an argument in favour of education for commoners, the general desirability of which was by no means initially recognised for fear that learning might encourage them to develop ideas above their station. Thirdly, again especially in regard to samurai, the purpose of education was also to secure more able and better qualified administrators. The Edo era, therefore, was marked by a desire to learn for a variety of reasons among increasingly wider sectors of the population and the opportunities to fulfil these aspirations were by and large provided.

Ronald Dore (*Education in Tokugawa Japan*, 1965) has estimated that by the end of the Edo era approximately 40 per cent of boys and 10 per cent of girls had received some form of formal education outside the home. The literacy rate was undoubtedly higher, for it is reasonable to assume that different categories of people would have received some form of basic education in the *ie*: samurai girls, for example, are more likely to have been tutored at home, apprentices will have received instruction in basic numeracy and literacy in their work-place, and so on. While it is impossible to establish figures with any degree of scientific accuracy, it is nevertheless safe to assume that on the eve of modernisation probably about half the Japanese population knew how to read. As Dore has pointed out, this is, on the whole, a far higher average than is the case in many developing countries today and indeed at least equal to, perhaps even higher than, the more advanced European states of the period. It is a generally accepted axiom that reasonably extensive literacy and education are prerequisites to successful development. Having assessed the quantitative side of Japanese education in the Edo era, however, a few words on the qualitative side are called for.

For this exercise one has to distinguish between the various types of institution which existed. The curriculum of the *terakoya*, namely those schools catering for commoners, included the three Rs along with a heavy dose of moral instruction. The system here was conservative, seeking to preserve peace and rectitude among the commoners; by no means, therefore, was it progressive and it was most certainly not the intention that the *terakoya* should serve as the base for a meritocratic pyramid. The search for *jinzai* (men of talent) was intentionally restricted to the samurai and indeed generally to those above low rank. Towards the end of the Edo era, however, a few fief schools were opening their doors, albeit only slightly, to commoners.

As far as samurai education was concerned, the majority would have received their instruction from the bakufu or han official schools. By the end of the Edo era most samurai boys above the rank of *ashigaru* would have spent a few years in these institutions. Generally, the schools did not deviate from the patterns of wider social hierarchy; where one sat in the classroom, the number of attendants one was permitted to have accompany one to school, and so on were all fixed by regulation according to one's rank. The teacher was invariably a *jusha* (Confucian scholar) and generally the position was hereditary. The curriculum consisted essentially of the following: reading of the Chinese classics, calligraphy, a little arithmetic, ethics and the martial arts. In respect to the last element, it must be remembered that samurai were, after all, warriors and therefore proficiency in military skills received a high premium; these included archery, riding, swimming, *kendo*, *judo*, and so on. Physical and intellectual efforts were combined according to a *mens sana in corpore sano* philosophy. Indeed, the combination of rigorous orthodox intellectual exercise, emphasis on physical training, a strict moral code and the inherent assumption that this was the training of the élite all contributed to a system which might perhaps be labelled proto-jesuitical.

Although the point has already been made, it must nevertheless once again be stressed that the pedagogy was highly conservative. Memorising was certainly more at a premium than thinking; exams, introduced by the bakufu and some fiefs in the late eighteenth century, essentially tested one's ability to regurgitate the classics and received knowledge. Another point to emphasise is that relationships within the school were not primarily institutional and horizontal, but personal and vertical: the key relationship was that between master (*sensei*) and disciple (*deshi*), thus we see here once again the adoption of the basic daimyo–samurai relationship as the operative one in education as in other spheres. Devotion, dedication, loyalty were directed towards a person, not an idea; this basic general pattern continues to apply to Japanese academe to this day.

The purpose of the official schools was to train the ruling élite to be good rulers. The basic assumption was that such training could only adequately be provided by sticking closely to the orthodoxy of Neo-Confucianism. Morality, it must once again be stressed, was the predominating concern: the good ruler was he who possessed virtue (*jin*) and virtuous rulers could cure all social ills, whether corruption, economic stagnation, and so on. This idealism did have its critics, most notably perhaps Ogyu Sorai (1666–1728) who preached a much more realistic gospel and who indeed has been compared by Maruyama (*Studies in the Intellectual History of Tokugawa Japan*, 1974) to Niccolo Machiavelli (1469–1527). The establishment and development of heterodox schools by Ogyu, his disciples and many other prominent scholars of the Edo era led to considerable intellectual debate, centred mainly in Edo, and no doubt significantly contributed to a certain scholastic dynamism. The bakufu did, however, occasionally retaliate; Matsudaira Sadanobu's reforms, for example, included virulent attacks on heterodoxy.

It was suggested earlier that developments in the field of education paralleled to some degree developments in the economic life of Edo Japan. Once the urban merchants established themselves, were protected by guilds and succeeding generations guided by precepts of the founding fathers, institutionalisation set in which in turn led to stagnation. The same pattern can be discerned in education. The bakufu and fief schools no doubt served a useful purpose in the early stages of the Edo era. With the passage of time, however, both their pedagogical orthodoxy and their strict enforcement of hierarchical principles, their emphasis on respect for the sages and opposition to critical thinking, made them increasingly parasitical institutions. Apart perhaps from keeping young samurai boys off the streets, their function came to be more negative than positive; the ruling administrative élite was inculcated with a mentality which when applied to real problems probably resulted in the exacerbation, rather than alleviation, of these.

The dynamic element in Japan's pre-modern intellectual life is not to be found in the official institutions as in other areas. First, reputed scholars set up their own private academies, or simply surrounded themselves with disciples in a quasi-socratic manner. The more stimulating thinkers of the late Edo era tended to be found outside the established system and it is they who were primarily responsible for the intellectual maturation of the men who subsequently became leaders of the Meiji era of modernisation. Secondly, however, although Sung Confucianism continued to predominate throughout the Edo era, a number of other trends of deviant or possibly eclectic nature developed. In the latter category can be found the emergence of *kokugaku* (national learning) which, although generally associated with the Shinto revival, embraced both nativist and various strands of classical Chinese thought. Although *kokugaku* in its inception was undoubtedly academic, in the course of time its significance came to be primarily political, hence we shall look at it in the following chapter. A very different sort of intellectual exercise was the proliferation of *Rangaku* (Dutch studies) which took off in the early part of the eighteenth century and which also contributed significantly to the education and outlook of the Meiji leaders.

Before turning to *Rangaku*, however, one might draw up a preliminary balance sheet on the legacy of general Tokugawa education. The Confucianist nature of education, albeit hardly progressive, nonetheless ensured that mental concentration centred round matters of this world rather than speculative metaphysical thinking. In the period of modernisation a difference in direction was called for, as well as a shift in the optic, from the past to the future and from China to the West, but the emphasis on the overall pragmatism of education, namely how society should be administered, was by no means a radical departure from the past. The intellectual activities and occasional controversies and debates also ensured that spirits were not dormant. The official schools may not have catered satisfactorily to those with an avid intellectual curiosity, but other institutions developed to satisfy these needs. The desire to learn and to set learning to good use for overall social improvement became a tradition in Japan, not something, as is the case in many developing countries today, to be created *ex nihilo*.

If one adds that widespread literacy facilitates the acquisition of technical skills and the employment of a reasonably talented work-force and also, as we shall see, that in the course of the Edo era advances were made in various scientific domains, then it is clear that one important legacy of the education of the Edo era was to help lay the infrastructure for subsequent modernisation. All these points can be written up on the credit side of the balance sheet. There is also, however, the debit side. One might suggest the proposition that whereas the Tokugawa education system perhaps enabled enlightenment to be attained by the very few, so far as the vast majority were concerned the excessively official moral content of the syllabus resulted in indoctrination rather than education. This duality remained on the whole the basic pattern of education for the Japanese until 1945.

To the extent that education is a means of buttressing the current ideological and political order then its function lies primarily in the superstructure. It follows, therefore, that governments will seek to ensure that the education system is compatible with their ideology; this is a universal phenomenon though there are, needless to say, significant variations in degree. The cohesiveness of Japanese society in the mid-nineteenth century was achieved as a result of a number of objective factors, frequently mentioned in this book, but also as a result of subjective political and ideological pressures which were widely disseminated throughout society. If there was a period of mild educational anarchy in the 1870s and early 1880s, by the latter part of that decade orthodoxy had been re-established and the purpose of schools, at least at the lower levels, was not to enlighten the masses but to indoctrinate them. The Meiji government was successful in its educational policies of imposing orthodoxy, partly because all that needed to be done was to re-orientate slightly an already existing pattern: the Japanese were accustomed to schools telling them what they should think, how they should behave, and above all that they should obey. Modernising Japan was constituted from many parts.

WESTERN STUDIES

Certainly another significant element in the process of Japanese modernisation was the general receptivity to ideas and techniques from the West; these were comprehended and applied within a short space of time. It must be emphasised that it is not the comprehension among certain individuals that makes the case of Japan, among non-Western societies, unique, but the degree to which comprehension was translated into fairly extensive application. The remainder of this chapter, therefore, will be devoted to a brief study of the role and impact of the Netherlands in Edo Japan.

The islet of Dejima at the head of Nagasaki bay (today attached to the mainland) was claimed from the sea in 1634 and served as the residence for the

Portuguese prior to their final expulsion. Initially the Dutch maintained their factory on the larger island of Hirado lying off the western coast of Kyushu. In 1641 the Dutch were transferred from Hirado to the much more claustrophobic Dejima. Dejima (or Deshima as it is sometimes spelled) arouses certain connotations in the imagination when projected on to Japanese history, being, for example, fairly frequently referred to as 'Japan's small window on the West'. The general impression, therefore, is that throughout Japan's isolationist 'dark ages', a small beacon of science and rationality flickered off Nagasaki bay to where Japanese scholars wishing to find Western enlightenment might turn. It is important to get reality into proper perspective.

For the first eight decades or so of the Edo era the most that can be said about Dutch Studies (*Rangaku*) is that there were practically none. This was partly due to official censorship. It was also due, however, to the fact that the appointed interpreters of the Dutch language were, as was customary in Edo Japan, hereditary offices, hence by no means reflecting individual linguistic ability; and, according to contemporary accounts, what ability there was was indeed limited. Intercourse between the Dutch and the Japanese was severely curtailed by a plethora of regulations and an equal number of policemen who kept an eye on what was going on in Dejima and prevented their curious compatriots from venturing over the bridge which linked the islet to the mainland.

The Dutch factors in Dejima, like their counterparts elsewhere, tended towards the boorish and philistine, rather than the refined and cultivated. It has already been pointed out that the Dutch were forbidden to be accompanied by their wives or to allow any *predikanten* to reside on the island. In the early period they did enjoy the right to keep their Ambionese slaves – a Japanese print of the late seventeenth century depicts Dutch factors being entertained with a chamber music recital by a slave orchestra – but this practice gradually disappeared. The number of European residents was generally limited to eleven. Japanese servants might attend during the day, but they had to leave at sunset. This rule did not apply to prostitutes who were permitted to remain in order to minister to the factors' needs. The children of such union, however, were taken away from their fathers at an early age. For most of the time, life in Dejima appears to have been excruciatingly monotonous, the day being taken up mainly in drinking and smoking. Intellectual life in Dejima was far more likely to be characterised by vapidity rather than stimulation.

Relief from boredom might be obtained, at least for the director of the factory and one or two assistants, at the time of the annual visit to Edo. It was a bakufu regulation that every year the *opperhoofd* (chief factor) should come to

Edo, present tribute in kind and provide an annual report (*fusetsugaki*). The original intention behind the submission of these *fusetsugaki* was for the Netherlanders to inform the bakufu on the activities of the Iberians. With the passage of time, however, the scope of the reports was significantly widened, namely to the affairs of Europe in general. The information contained in the *fusetsugaki*, however, was not widely diffused, but on the contrary made available to only a very small number of bakufu officials, mainly the *roju*. These reports served a useful purpose, to the extent that they were actually read rather than simply filed away, and the journey to Edo might well provide diversion from the sedentary life of Dejima. On the other hand, generally the reception at Edo could hardly be described as cordial, let alone flattering. The Dutch factor came to attend upon the shogun's court and was to obey his command – including occasions when the *opperhoofd* and assistants were asked to dance together and generally move about for the distraction of the shogun and his court. Generally speaking, therefore, the Dutch were treated with crushing contempt.

A major motivation lying behind *sakoku*, it will be recalled, was to purge Japan from the *jashumon*, the evil craft of Christianity. As part of this exercise the bakufu in 1630 imposed a near-total embargo on the importation of Chinese books which treated Western topics. Interestingly, though perhaps not surprisingly, it was China which served as the source for the reintroduction of Western learning into Japan, although the process was by no means rapid. The early Edo period in Japan corresponded to the last stages of the Ming dynasty and the golden age of the early Ch'ing dynasty in China. This period of Chinese history witnessed intense cultural activity; many books were compiled and published and a number of them were shipped to Nagasaki. It was also during the early part of this period that the Italian Jesuit Matteo Ricci (1552–1610) exerted a significant influence on the development of science in China.

Ricci had first reached China in 1583 and after numerous and strenuous efforts on his part, he was finally able to take up residence in Peking in 1601 where he remained until his death. It is arguable that no single European until Marx (whom the Chinese first read in Japanese translation) has had as much influence in China as did Ricci, who is better known in China under his Chinese name, Li Ma-Tou. Ricci wrote numerous works in Chinese himself, but also under his supervision or that of other Jesuits, their Chinese disciples compiled extensive treatises on mathematics, astronomy and the calendar, geography and so on.

The paranoia of official bakufu censorship was such, however, that not only books mentioning Christianity were banned, but indeed any book making even the slightest reference to Li Ma-Tou. This state of affairs remained operative until the third decade of the eighteenth century and the advent to the shogunal throne of Yoshimune. As we shall see shortly, Yoshimune's personal initiative was responsible for the reintroduction and ultimate proliferation of Western studies in Japan. There is, however, an interesting point worth noting in passing. As has already been indicated the atmosphere in Peking in the late Ming and early Ch'ing period was receptive to the absorption of Western knowledge, in particular the sciences, indeed especially under the patronage of the second Ch'ing Emperor, K'ang-hsi (1654–1722), who, among other things, was responsible for the compilation of some ten thousand volumes known as the *Ku-Chin T'u-shu Chi-Ch'eng* (Collection of Books Old and New). Following K'ang-hsi's death, however, the Jesuit order was banned in China; although subsequently relations were resumed for a brief period – until in fact the Jesuit order was suppressed by the Vatican of Clement XIV (1705–74) in 1773 mainly because of a dispute over the propriety of allowing Confucianist flavouring in the practice of the Catholic mass in China – no publishing activities comparable to what had been undertaken previously were resumed. Western scientific studies in China, therefore, began to wane precisely at the time that they began to pick up in Japan. In the early eighteenth century Western knowledge was transmitted from China to Japan, where it established a fairly secure base with the result that in the late nineteenth and early twentieth centuries much Western knowledge was transmitted to Chinese scholars from Japanese works and Japanese translations.

Western scientific studies in the *sengoku* era, as we have seen, fell under the general label of *nanban-gaku*, studies of the southern barbarians – the Iberians. In the Edo era Western studies are normally referred to as *Rangaku*, namely Dutch studies, the '*ran*' being the middle syllable of the Japanese word for Holland, Oranda. The initial source of Western scientific studies, however, came not from the Netherlands so much as from Chinese works. The reason for this is quite simply a linguistic one. The official interpreters of Dutch were, as we have seen, by and large next to useless and in any case it was not until the end of the eighteenth century that the first Japanese–Dutch dictionary was compiled. Nor were the Netherlanders avid to teach or indeed to learn about Japan, barring a few notable exceptions. In due course their services and their books were to be used, but their role was more passive than active. This, generally speaking, with the possible exception of the American occupation in the years 1945 to 1952, has corresponded to the basic pattern of Japanese absorption of Western knowledge. In other words, at certain periods in Japanese history, such as the mid/late sixteenth, the late eighteenth/early nineteenth and later nineteenth centuries, the Japanese have sought Western instruction as an official or at least semi-official policy. Although there were in all of these periods a number of very capable European tutors, invariably these have filled roles, rather than created them.

The significant shift in regard to Western sciences which occurred in the 1720s resulted from Yoshimune's concern over general economic and social decline and his attempt, visible in the so-called Kyoho reforms, to reverse the situation. Four years after ascending the shogunal throne in 1716, the first partial lifting on the book-banning policy dating from 1630 occurred. The motivation behind Yoshimune's reversal of official policy was his desire to promote *jitsugaku*. Literally *jitsugaku* means the study of real things; in this context *jitsugaku* was mainly applied to the necessity of carrying out revisions in the calendar system and generally the application of science and mathematics to practical use. Although knowledge of the Dutch language was circumscribed, indeed practically non-existent, reading of Chinese was, of course, widespread. Yoshimune's reforms initially resulted in a very large-scale acquisition of the Chinese texts prepared by Ricci, his colleagues, and their disciples. Thus Euclidean geometry, for example, was introduced into eighteenth-century Japan through a Chinese treatise, the *Chi-ho Yuan-pen*, on the subject. Furthermore, however, and in the longer term, Yoshimune's reforms can be said to have had two major consequences. The first was that *Rangaku* was emancipated from its narrow Nagasaki environment and imported to Edo, in due course to spread throughout most of the country. Secondly, it is possible to translate *jitsugaku* more figuratively by suggesting that it corresponds, to some degree at least, to empiricism. In intellectual terms this constituted a major revolution in Japanese history: *jitsugaku* is perhaps the vital link in the chain of modernisation which extends from the early Edo era onwards.

Confucianism was orientated to this world, rather than metaphysical. On the other hand, the doctrinaire approach of the Sung Confucianists and their Japanese followers resulted in recognising the classics as nothing less than holy writ. In the field of medicine, for example, in keeping with Confucianist dogma Edo Japan's orthodox anatomical sciences were based on the theory of *gozo roppu*; literally this means 'the five viscera and six entrails', but more generally illustrates the classical Chinese view of human activities and human organs, namely that every bodily function had an exact correspondence in external nature. Anatomy, therefore, was not an empirical science, but a basically philosophical and rather speculative view of man's place in the universe.

In the mid-eighteenth century, however, it came to the notice of a Kyoto physician, Yamawaki Toyo (1705–62), when gazing upon the dissected corpse of a criminal, that his insides varied somewhat from what they were supposed to be according to Chinese anatomical theory; moved by his discovery he proceeded to compile a brief work, which he entitled *Zoshi* (Reflections on Entrails) and published in 1759. A further major landmark was achieved in early March 1771 when two men, who subsequently became perhaps the chief pioneers of *Rangaku*, Maeno Ryotaku (1723–1803) and Sugita Genpaku (1733–1817), received bakufu permission to carry out a dissection themselves on the corpse of a female criminal at Senju Kotsukahara, the Edo execution grounds. Maeno and Sugita carried with them a Dutch translation of *Tabulae anatomicae in quibus corporis humani*, written by the Silesian anatomist Johan Adam Kulmus (1689–1745) and published in 1733; the woman's interiors, they discovered, corresponded neatly to Kulmus's charts. Maeno undertook the supervision of the translation into Japanese of the Dutch translation, entitled *Ontleedkundige Tafelen*, of Kulmus's work and in 1774 published it as *Kaitai Shinsho* (New Treatise on the Understanding of the Human Body). From this point onwards *Rangaku* took off.

In 1788 another *Rangaku-sha*, Otsuki Gentaku (1757–1827) published his two-volume *Rangaku Kaitei* (An Introduction to Dutch Learning) and in the following year set up one of the more famous academies of *Rangaku* in Japan, namely the Shirando in Edo. One of his pupils, Imamura Sanpaku (1759–1811), published the first Japanese–Dutch dictionary in 1796. This, however, represented the culmination of decades of work undertaken by a number of men; the 1796 dictionary was in fact a Japanese adaptation of a French–Dutch dictionary, the *Woordenboek der Nederduitsche en Fransche Taalen*, edited by François Halma (1652–1722) in 1710.

The early development of Rangaku may have been slow, painful, indeed tortuous. By the late eighteenth century, however, it flourished. Following Otsuki Gentaku's founding of the Shirando, a number of other centres of Rangaku excellence were established, notably the Shosendo of Ito Genboku (1800–71) and the Teki-Teki-Sai of Ogata Koan (1810–63). By the early part of the nineteenth century, not only had the Nagasaki monopoly been broken, not only were there *Rangaku* research and educational institutions, but indeed approximately sixty han created *Rangaku* schools. Needless to say, the increase in the number of establishments resulted in a proliferation of the number of scholars.

Although originally *Rangaku* was mainly concerned with medicine and a few of the applied sciences, in the course of time painting also became a favourite activity of *Rangaku-sha*, especially in the cases of Hiraga Gennai (1729–80) and the perhaps better known Shiba Kokan (1747–1818). The appeal of the Western form of painting was not simply the pursuit of an aesthetic ideal – it was equally prized for its practical value; that is to say the major distinction between Japanese and Western painting was that the latter involved realism – things are painted as they are. One point which should be made about these *Rangaku-sha* is that their field of interests was markedly catholic: the works of any given individual might include treatises on anatomy, medicine, philology, geography, painting, and indeed navigation, gunnery and Western military strategy.

These men were the pioneers and indeed protagonists of Western culture in Japan. Their praise of Western sciences struck a reasonably receptive chord among those who were getting somewhat tired of the excessive sinophilism of the age and were not displeased to find alternative areas to study and at the same time to use these as a stick to beat the doctrinaire Neo-Confucianists. At the same time, one also sees a phenomenon which here in embryonic form was to achieve full flowering in the decade or so immediately following the Restoration: an uncritical, highly adulatory Western mania. Respectable scholars adopted Dutch *noms de plume*, wrote to each other in Dutch, and so forth. This was known as *ranpeki* (Dutch mania), though it covered the West in general, many aspects of which were praised to ludicrous extents – in a manner perhaps reminiscent of the Western adulation for Maoist China in the late 1960s and early 1970s. Indeed, Western monarchs had fanatical admirers in Japan, though they could hardly have been conscious of the fact; Honda Toshiaki, for example, adored Catherine the Great of Russia (1729–96), while Rai San-yo was so upset upon hearing of the defeat of Napoleon (1769–1821) at Waterloo that he was moved to write a eulogistic poem in his honour.

The development and significance of *Rangaku* were certainly considerable, but certain points need be made in order to keep the general picture in perspective. In spite of the *ranpeki* of the late eighteenth century, it nevertheless remained the case that the Edo atmosphere remained highly volatile; *Rangaku-sha* might enjoy encouragement, indeed patronage, under certain circumstances, in certain domains at certain times, but they might equally find persecution, indeed execution, at other times. Again, one finds here striking analogies with more contemporary totalitarian states: a hundred Dutch tulips might be allowed to bloom for a while, only to be nipped in the bud shortly afterwards. Secondly, and again in spite of *ranpeki*, although it gradually came to be agreed that Western science was no doubt superior to that of the East, the spirit of the East should not be altered for that reason. Indeed, in the immediate pre-modern era scholars, such as Sakuma Shozan (1811–64) or Hashimoto Sanai (1834–59), one finds the attempt to blend the spirit of Western scientific enquiry with the spirit of Eastern ethical mentality. The approach, therefore, at this stage at least, remained firmly ensconced in a Confucianist framework; while for some of the more nationalist or 'japanist' thinkers, namely those of the *kokugaku*, such as Hirata Atsutane (1776–1843), Western science was perceived as a means of achieving a sort of millenarian Japanist dream. Finally, in spite of the considerable achievements to the credit of the *Rangaku-sha* – including, for example, experimenting with electricity – it goes without saying that their knowledge remained limited when compared to Western scientists' and that it was derived mainly from books rather than practical experience.

Nevertheless, *Rangaku* in the very broad sense of the term was a vital factor in preparing Japan for her heady course of modernisation which followed in the later nineteenth century. The academies of Dutch studies counted among their pupils some of the leading figures in numerous domains of the post-Meiji era. The 'father' of the Japanese navy, Katsu Kaishu (1823–1900), Nishi Amane (1829–97), one of the men most responsible for introducing Western administrative and jurisprudential practices into Japan, and Fukuzawa Yukichi (1835–1901), the intellectual and educator *par excellence* of the Meiji era, to mention only three out of many, were all pupils of *Rangaku* academies. When facing the Western menace fully, the bakufu was able to set up an institute in 1856, the *Bansho Torishirabesho* (Office for the Study of Barbarian Writings), which was ably staffed and enabled the government to avoid pitfalls more rapidly than was the case with Ch'ing China's homologous institution, the *Tsungli Yamen*, established in 1860; in other words, the bakufu and some of the han had at their disposal a reservoir of human resources skilled in the knowledge of the West which was conspicuously lacking in other countries of the East. The speed with which the Japanese were able to learn from the more advanced Western countries, Britain, France, Germany, would hardly have been possible without the preliminary Dutch tuition.

The annual visits of the *opperhoofd* to Edo and his *fusetsugaki* enabled the bakufu to keep reasonably abreast of events in Europe, certainly more so than was the case in China – the Portuguese in Macao were only given a commercial role and were not called upon to visit Peking to submit reports. *Rangaku* itself, though encompassing diverse fields, also played a significant role in instructing the Japanese in Western military technologies such as gunnery, navigation, strategy, and so forth. Although the academic knowledge of these subjects hardly sufficed to gain them the wherewithal to defy the Western powers, it did nevertheless enable them to appreciate their own military inferiority – a notable achievement and advantage.

It will be recalled that we have stressed the conflicting centrifugal and centripetal forces in Japanese history. By liberating *Rangaku* from its Nagasaki enclave and having it spread throughout the country, the result was that in almost all areas of Japan there was at the very least an awareness of the nature and advance of Western science. Furthermore, *Rangakusha* from Sendai, Kagoshima, Edo, Osaka, Kanazawa and so on came to know each other, study together, and therefore this coterie of intellectuals also came to provide a national intellectual élite. *Rangaku*, in that sense, was a centripetal force.

INTELLECTUAL ROOTS OF MODERNITY

Intellectual developments also, therefore, contributed towards the unification of the country into a nation-state and laid certain foundations for subsequent modernisation. Among the more marked characteristics of this period one would include the following.

First, a high degree of secularisation was achieved. The Japanese were not to be plagued by religious shibboleths or annoyed, possibly pilloried, by fanatical monks with national prestige and influence. Secondly, there was a widespread development in education, resulting in both a broad basic literate base and a reasonably enlightened élite. There developed a respect for knowledge, a recognition of the advantages of education for the administration of human affairs, hence the incursion of a meritocracy within a hitherto aristocratic framework. Thirdly, the importation of Chinese books on Western science, the discovery of the inadequacy of Chinese medical theory, the subsequent proliferation of *Rangaku*, all helped to accelerate the emphasis on a rational, empirical approach to the physical world.

These features represent a good deal and help to explain the pace with which the Japanese were able to modernise in the later nineteenth century. The picture, however, must not be excessively embellished. In terms of progress, there were also a number of regressive elements, some of which have been indicated in the preceding pages. Having looked at how Edo Japan became increasingly unified in social, economic and intellectual terms, it now remains to study the political ideology and movement which ultimately gave birth to the modern Japanese state.

5 Ideology, Politics and Revolution

GENESIS OF A NATIONAL IDEOLOGY

The Edo era witnessed significant economic, social and intellectual developments. The forces at work, in all these fields, were mainly of a centripetal character. In objective terms it is clear that national unification was in the process of formation. In order to weld these forces together, however, two further conditions were necessary: a national ideology and external pressure. Both of these emerged in the latter part of the Edo era. The element of hostility from the outside, real or perceived, is a *sine qua non* for the reinforcement of the sense of a common identity, namely Ibn Khaldoun's concept of *'asabiyya*. Internal differences diminish significantly in proportion when the interior is under siege. The crucial factor in being able to resist external pressure, however, is that of timing. If the external threat is not properly perceived and especially if there is no consensus on the means to be used for withstanding it, then the forces of coalescence will be dispersed and possibly counter-productive. In a word, this is what happened in China under the impact of the West; China possessed a cultural ideology, not a national one. Japan's remarkably rapid response to the West was greatly facilitated by the fact that the national ideology had been evolved, it was there, it was simply a question of effectively projecting it.

In terms of understanding the evolution of the national ideology, several points regarding the general background need to be stressed. In the first place as was indicated in the former chapter, education and learning had developed significantly in the course of the Edo era. It was difficult for a samurai to be an active man of arms, for there was no fighting, but it was possible for him to become a man of letters. Although stress was still placed on the *bu* (the martial character), the way of the warrior also recognised, indeed elevated, the importance of *bun* (letters). The atmosphere, therefore, was conducive to learning and to research. Secondly, although it is true that official orthodoxy was rather dogmatically attached to the Chu-Hsi school of Confucianism, it is nevertheless the case that a number of heterodox schools emerged. These were not necessarily met with favour, indeed at times attempts were made to suppress them; in 1790, for example, Matsudaira Sadanobu (1758–1829) had an ordinance issued whereby only orthodox Chu-Hsi scholars should receive administrative and academic posts both at bakufu and han levels. Nonetheless, heterodox thought continued to afflict the Tokugawa regime. Thirdly, isolation leads to contemplation; it is not surprising, therefore, that the Edo era witnessed among certain scholars an awareness of their past and a desire to study and interpret it.

In the atmosphere of intellectual dissent which existed in Tokugawa times, a few general features of the more prominent heterodox schools are worth noting. One of the earlier manifestations of ideological dissidence can be found in the creation of the so-called O Yomei school of Confucianism – O Yomei is the Japanese reading for the Chinese Wang Yang-ming, founder of a school of Confucianism which flourished in China in the late fifteenth and early sixteenth centuries. In Japan *Yomei-gaku* was introduced by Nakae Toju (1608–48). Basically Nakae's contention was that whereas the Chu-Hsi scholars preached the Way, not sufficient emphasis was placed on the actual practising of the Way. *Yomei-gaku*, therefore, came to reduce the significance of scholasticism, while praising the value of moral intuition and action. In regard to the former, *Yomei-gaku* can be said to place greater emphasis on the heart than on the mind; while the latter indicated that simple contemplation was not sufficient, that thought should be more readily translated into deed. Nakae Toju counted a number of prominent disciples, including Kumazawa Banzan (1619–91), a major and active reformer of the Tokugawa era. The inspiration derived from Nakae's and his disciples' doctrines moved some of Japan's more remarkable and influential heroes. Oshio Heihachiro (1792–1837), profoundly affected by the plight of the needy and the ills of society ultimately to the point of seeking to destroy the city of Osaka, was a *Yomei* scholar. Similarly, the *Yomei* emphasis on *acta non verba* was a major influence in the life of Yoshida Shoin (1831–60), the outstanding tutor of early Meiji Japan's leadership, whose martyrdom and heroic death moved Robert Louis Stevenson (1850–94) to include a chapter on him in his *Familiar Studies of Men and Books*, where Yoshida found himself in such distinguished company as that of Victor Hugo, Robert Burns, Walt Whitman, François Villon and Samuel Pepys. *Yomei-gaku*, therefore, with its insistence on moral intuition and the need for action to ensue, significantly influenced both the motivation and indeed the designation of Japan's activist patriotic zealots of the mid-nineteenth century, namely the men called *shishi*, men of sincere will.

Both the Chu-Hsi and Yomei schools were derived from the exegetical works of Neo-Confucianists. Another influential school, generally labelled the *kogaku* (ancient school), reacted against the exegesis of both Chu-Hsi and

Yomei and, as its appellation implies, preached the need to return to the original sources. Originally founded by Yamaga Soko (1622–85) and Ito Jinsai (1627–1705), perhaps this school's most erudite and critical scholar was Ogyu Sorai (1666–1728). The ultimate purpose of the Way was to achieve peace and harmony; Ogyu, while by no means dissenting with this cardinal principle, argued that the end justified the means. In other words, political manipulation is necessary for ensuring the realisation of the end; in that sense, Ogyu's espousal of what amounts to a doctrine of *realpolitik* ranks him, in Maruyama's words, as the 'discoverer of politics' in Tokugawa Japan. Politics could, indeed should, be used to alter a social system which did not lend itself to the achievement of the Way. Ogyu Sorai was deeply critical of the manner in which Japan was being governed, namely by an aristocracy of birth. Among other things, he asserted that the richer and higher ranked samurai were probably not suited for the administration of affairs of state in that from earliest childhood onwards they had been accustomed to lead a life of comfort and self-indulgence, as a result of which they became indolent. Nothing, Sorai insisted, forms the character and the mind like adversity: one must struggle to achieve virtue and merit. Ogyu Sorai's thought came to have wide implications for the nation as a whole, in its struggle for survival against an external menace, and, of course, for the individuals whose destiny it was, or so they believed, to lead the struggle.

The *kogaku* revived the study of the Chinese classics as opposed to later interpretative works. The study of the past was not to be limited to China's. Already by the second half of the seventeenth century the second daimyo of the Mito han, Tokugawa Mitsukuni (1628–1701), established in his domain an academy primarily concerned with historical scholarship and to that end historians were organised into a body which came to be called the *Mito-gaku*. In academic terms the main claim to fame of the Mito school was its compilation, over a period lasting from the 1650s to the second decade of the eighteenth century, of a voluminous history of Japan from the foundation of the imperial dynasty to the late fourteenth century, resulting in a work known as the *Dai Nihon Shi*. It is clear that a study of the Japanese past was bound to include analysis of the imperial institution, which in turn led to a reappraisal of the tenno's position within the body politic, which ultimately led to the development of loyalism, that is, loyalty to the imperial throne and the ideology of restoring the tenno to his rightful place. For it must be remembered that all of these schools, no matter how heterodox from the bakufu's perspective, remained nonetheless essentially Confucianist in outlook. In the Confucianist scheme of things, the ideal is the past, not the future; hence in calamitous circumstances, the need, indeed the urgency, was to *return* to the Way and *restore* the former order. It must be stressed, however, that prior to the tumultuous years leading up to the actual Restoration itself, the major tenor of all these schools, including Mito, was academic and not political: measures were perhaps indicated to seek to improve the present system, certainly not to replace it with something else.

This last point also applies to the emergence of another school, that of *kokugaku*, national learning. Whereas the *kogaku* scholars advocated a revival of the ancient Chinese texts, *kokugaku* scholars sought to revive and reinterpret the Japanese classics. This was of some revolutionary significance, for the atmosphere in Edo Japan was intellectually highly sinophile. Japanese writing was held to be all right for women; men must rise to the challenge of the more demanding Chinese. Initially, therefore, the major contribution of *kokugaku* lay in fields such as literary criticism, philology, religion, not political thought. One of the instigators of the *kokugaku* movement, Kamo Mabuchi (1697–1769), resurrected the *manyoshu*, an anthology of Japanese poetry compiled in the eighth century, and sought to illustrate how it vividly evoked the sentiments of the Japanese of antiquity. The *Genji Monogatari* was another work which, among *kokugaku* scholars, enjoyed a return to the literary limelight. Motoori Norinaga (1730–1801), generally reckoned as the chief luminary of the *kokugaku* movement, devoted his scholarly energies primarily to the study of the *Kojiki*, the record of antiquity which begins with the creation of Japan and ends with the reign of Suiko (554–628). In the course of their studies of the ancient texts, the *kokugaku* scholars came across the concept of *sai-sei-itchi*; this term might be translated as 'the unity of rights and office', which can – and ultimately was – interpreted as signifying that both spiritual and temporal power should reside in the person of the tenno. It will be recalled that traditionally the main function of the tenno was to act in a spiritual capacity as an intermediary with the gods, from whom he was descended. In this sense his function was a sacerdotal one. The concept of *sai-sei-itchi*, however, seemed to indicate that no distinction should be made between sacerdotal ministration to the divinities and administrative guidance over the affairs of men, that both responsibilities should reside in the person of the tenno. Motoori and other *kokugaku* scholars of the period, it should be stressed, advocated nothing of the kind. Theirs was an academic exercise, devoid of any political message. It is clear, however, that the academic exercise could be exploited for political pursuits – which is precisely what happened subsequently. Later writers of *kokugaku* persuasion used the findings of their predecessors to argue that Japan's national salvation lay in *osei fukko*, namely a return to the ancient system of monarchic rule, for that is what the gods had ordained.

Kokugaku paved the way for an increasingly greater emphasis in some quarters to a nativist reaction against excessive sinophilism. This can be illustrated in one of the sequels of early *kokugaku*, namely the emergence of what has been termed the Shinto revival. The most forceful exponent of Shinto was Hirata Atsutane (1776–1843). While Motoori may be said to have preached respect for the indigenous past and native traditions, including Shinto, Hirata went a significant step further by expressing contempt for Japan's extraneous influences, namely Buddhism and Confucianism. Although Hirata clearly indicated strands of rabid nativism, paradoxically he was by no means opposed to Western science and was even somewhat ambivalent over Christianity. This stand was no doubt derived from a greater awareness of the outside world. At the time of Motoori's death in 1801, although Western ships had already begun to appear on the horizon, they remained distant. In the course of Hirata's lifetime the Western presence in East Asia was increasingly felt, indeed by the time of his death the Opium war had already been fought and China defeated. Hirata's fairly voluminous writings, undoubtedly polemical in nature, contributed significantly to the development of a national consciousness in Japan.

Apart from Hirata, the later eighteenth and early nineteenth century witnessed the emergence of more scholars, some of whom were still operating from the academy of Mito, such as Aizawa Seishisai (1782–1863) and Fujita Toko (1806–55), the basic tenor of whose message included the proclamation of Japan as the land of the gods, the need to preserve it from external pollution, namely to withstand Western encroachments, and that in the deliberation of the national policy greater reverence should be paid to the tenno. Here lies the genesis of the two terms which characterised early political movements in the years following Perry's arrival: *sonno*, 'revere the emperor', and *joi*, 'expel the barbarians'. Two things, however, should be noted. First, in its inception the concept of *sonno* did not signify the overthrow of the bakufu, but that rather by achieving closer co-ordination with the tenno the shogun would be strengthened. Secondly, although there was significant commitment in most quarters of the late Edo intelligentsia that Westerners must not be permitted into Japan, there was nevertheless a recognition that perhaps some of the ways of the West should properly be employed to help the country withstand the West. Hirata, in spite of his strident nativism, was not averse to advocating the study of Western techniques. Takashima Shuhan (1798–1866), Yokoi Shonan (1809–69) and Sakuma Shozan (1811–64) openly favoured the adoption of Western technology for the purposes of national self-preservation. In the irrational atmosphere which pervaded late Edo Japan and the xenophobia which flourished, the advocacy of rational compromises with the Western reality was dangerous; indeed both Sakuma and Yokoi met violent deaths at the hands of extremist xenophobes for the views they held.

From what has been described above, it is clear that a national ideology and a sense of identity did not have to be desperately sought and formulated rapidly in the face of the Western menace. In a manner comparable to the social and economic forces, the development of a national ideology had occurred in an evolutionary manner. The major features of the ideology were derived from various sources, pointed in various directions, but together produced a reasonable sense of unity. *Chu-Hsi-gaku* stressed morality and order and the usual Confucian virtues; *Yomei-gaku* advocated that intuitive morality should be translated into action; *kogaku*, by insisting on the need to return to the original sources, provided an important turning-point in Japanese intellectual history; for *kogaku* facilitated the emergence of *kokugaku*, the study of the Japanese tradition and identity, which encapsulated the concept of the divine legitimacy of the tenno and in the Shinto revival the special attributions of the Japanese land and its people. The fact that scholars and subsequently activists were both samurai, or at the very least men who entirely subscribed to samurai values as prescribed in the tenets of *bushido*, also resulted in a continued insistence on the virtue of loyalty as supreme. In order to save the nation and return to the traditional and legitimate policy of the country, a comparatively simple operation had to be carried out: the transference of loyalty. In other words, loyalty remained the supreme virtue, but under the misguided rule of the past it had been improperly channelled, to daimyo and shogun, whereas *sonno* ('revere the emperor') clearly called on all pure-hearted men of action (*shishi*) to rally, with body and soul, round the greatest symbol and reality of the Japanese empire – the tenno. Again, however, it must be emphasised that although the trend was towards national unification and a body of literature indicated the direction under which unification should be brought about, the ultimate force of crystallisation came from the outside.

THE WESTERN IMPACT

European expansion towards the East had been embarked upon with renewed vigour in the course of the second half of the eighteenth century. The old seaborne empires, especially the Portuguese and the Spanish had not made a nuisance of themselves in Japanese waters for some time. The new or rejuvenated imperial powers – the British, the French, the Russians – however, began making more frequent appearances. Temporarily diverted by the Napoleonic wars, though, the pressure from Europe failed to reach endemic proportions until the second quarter of the nineteenth century. From the Japanese perspective, nevertheless, what was subsequently labelled the *seiryoku-tozen*, the eastern advance of Western power, came to acquire a quality of inexorability. From a European perspective, although there was clearly a push towards the East, the attention paid to Japan must be placed in its proper context, albeit briefly. The quality of European interest in Japan *per se* can be defined in one word: minimal. This is partly because European attention in East Asia was primarily focused on China; it is also, however, due to the fact that there were numerous other preoccupations and needs for further consolidation of acquired gains which diverted European interest away from Japan. For the British, the French and the Russians, the second quarter of the nineteenth century was mainly taken up by concentration on questions relating to the Ottoman Empire, ultimately resulting in the Crimean War (1854–6). The British also had to contend with the Indian Mutiny (1857) and were joined by the French in the so-called second Opium War in China (1856–60). Apart from their activities in Asia, the British and the French also had African affairs to attend to, while the French included a brief foray into Mexico. Japan figured in the European horizon, but very far in the distance, no more than a speck; it can and indeed should be categorically stated that at no time did either London or Paris seriously entertain the idea of colonising Japan.

It is also in the second quarter of the nineteenth century, however, that a newcomer appeared on the scene. The Americans, after having successfully overthrown the yoke of the English empire, came to be gripped by the spirit of Manifest Destiny: trekking in southerly, westerly and northerly directions, they purchased land here, massacred Amerindians there, and put the Mexicans firmly back in their (diminished) place. The major ambition on the part of both Americans and Europeans in regard to Japan was quite simply to make use of Japanese ports in order to allow refuelling and obtaining victuals, to be able to repair ships and provide a temporary safe haven for shipwrecked sailors. Among the groups with the most immediate grievances with the Japanese was the American whaling industry: whaling was very much part of the American scene in the early nineteenth century, and it was whalers who provided the most vociferous lobby for the opening of Japan. Clio, the muse of history, delights in providing ironical twists to all her tales, but surely few can rival the modern history of Japan whereby as a result of the pressure of American whalers Japan was opened in 1854 in the sacred name of free trade, only to find herself 120 years later having to face American protectionism and a hysterical outburst against her whaling activities.

In any case, as pressure mounted in the United States for Japan to be opened, it was Commodore Matthew 'Old Bruin" Perry (1794–1858) who offered his services to carry out this civilising mission. Perry's notoriety as a staunch disciplinarian, namely in the advocacy of and frequent reliance on flogging, may have partly inspired the composite character of Captain Claret of the *Neversink*, created by Herman Melville (1819–91) in *White Jacket* (1850). Perry was also a brilliant example and exponent of manifest destiny imperialism, having played a prominent role in the Mexican war of 1846; when in sober mood he contented himself with pressing for American colonisation of the Isthmus of Tehuantepec, while at times of greater exuberance he advocated nothing less than grabbing the whole of Mexico and all of Central America as well. Upon embarking on his mission to Japan, he had proposed that the US should seize the island of Okinawa in order to demonstrate American power. Perry was aloof, arrogant, self-righteous. It is tempting to seek to draw parallels between Perry and General Douglas MacArthur (1880–1964). Suffice it to be remarked here that, whereas Perry defeated Japanese isolationism in 1854, MacArthur in 1945 brought to an end Japanese expansionism; both events heralded major transformations in Japanese society and politics, and both individuals, Perry and MacArthur, are probably better known today in Japan than in their own country.

Perry first arrived off Japanese shores in 1853 and, after having successfully insisted that his letters from President Fillmore (1800–74) be received by an official Japanese delegation, he departed, announcing he would return within a year. Fillmore's request was that Japan should open her doors, join the civilised world, and sign a treaty of friendship and commerce with the United States. The Japanese reaction could be summed up in one word: panic. The Japanese had a saying at the time that in order to waken from peaceful dreams one should drink a superior brand of tea, but that if one had four cups of the brew, then one would not be able to sleep at night. The tea in question was called *jokisen*, which, although written in different Chinese characters, is the same word for 'steamship'. With the arrival of Perry's four *jokisen* (steamships), not only were the Japanese rudely awakened from peaceful slumber, but they would sleep no more. Perry was successful in extracting a convention from the Japanese in 1854. There was, however, considerable scope for misunderstanding. The *lingua franca* was Dutch, hence negotiations and memoranda were translated from English into Dutch into Japanese and vice versa.

Two years after Perry had come and gone, and while furious debate continued to rage in the country over what to do about Westerners, the first Western diplomat to Japan, the American Townsend Harris (1804–78), arrived on the scene. Harris was determined to set up, in spite of Japanese resistance, a permanent residence for the American consulate in Japan. A popular legend developed regarding Harris's alleged affair with his maid, Okichi-san, culminating in the novel by Robert Payne, *The Barbarian and the Geisha* (New York, 1958). It is difficult to imagine a greater contrast between the fictional account and reality. Harris, during most of his stay in Japan, was sick and exceedingly lonely, the loneliness exacerbated by the fact that he was completely forgotten by Washington to the extent that he had to borrow money from the Japanese authorities in order to pay his servants and meet his daily needs. Okichi-san existed, though it is unlikely she became Harris's mistress; in fact Harris dismissed her from his service because of a skin ailment (possibly a sign of venereal disease).

In spite of official harassment and procrastination and in spite of the danger in which he lived – and in 1861 the murder of his trusted adviser and companion, Henry Heusken – Harris resolutely stood his ground. In this respect, he paved the way of other foreign diplomats to arrive on the scene, though the obstacles remained for the time being formidable. The United States, however, after having opened Japan, lost interest; preoccupations now centred almost exclusively on domestic matters as the nation advanced towards civil war which finally broke out in 1861. Although the United States still played a role in Japanese affairs, compared to the British especially and also the French and the Germans, in the next few decades it was a secondary one.

Following the Americans the other major Western powers came to Japan and concluded treaties – though extracted might be a more correct description of the transaction. The question of the Japanese reaction to the treaties will be looked at shortly. It is appropriate here to consider briefly the nature of the relationship between Japan and the Western powers. The mid-nineteenth century was not, on the whole, a period of significant European colonial aggrandisement; the expansionism which did take place was, in theory at least, based on the principles of free trade. Markets had to be opened to European manufactured goods and access granted to sources of raw material. Force might occasionally be needed, usually in the shape of gunboat diplomacy, to convince recalcitrant governments of the benefits and moral value of free trade; generally, however, it was felt that economic pursuits need not be accompanied by political control.

The European conception of international relations, namely the principle of the equality of states, differed significantly from that which had operated in East Asia, namely the tributary system. Japan was not, as has been pointed out, strictly speaking in a tributary relationship with China. China's, however, was the only system of international relations she knew and which to some extent she emulated; the annual visits to Edo by the Dutch factors of Dejima, bearing tribute and paying homage, corresponded to some degree to a Chinese pattern. There were significant discrepancies between the European and East Asian systems of international relations. The first fifteen years or so of relations between Europeans and the Japanese could largely be written in terms of the Europeans seeking, ultimately successfully, to impose their views and system on the Japanese, as they had had to do previously in China, and it is worth noting that a number of the European diplomats coming to Japan had served an apprenticeship in China. For example, the idea of a permanent legation residing in the capital (Edo or Peking) was anathema to East Asian tradition whereby diplomacy was conducted simply on the basis of an occasional visit. Allied to this was the European institution of the right of audience of a diplomatic agent before the head of state in order to present his credentials. A great deal of Harris's time was taken up with trying to persuade bakufu officials that he should be introduced to the Shogun; his European colleagues faced similar difficulties. Problems of protocol also arose, thus even when an audience might have been reluctantly granted, interminable negotiations ensued over questions of etiquette.

While Europeans were busy tutoring their hosts in the ways of European international relations, they also ensured that certain modifications to the system as it operated between Europeans were introduced in order to protect themselves and guarantee certain advantages. European international law is based on the concept of the equality of states; principle, however, might have to be qualified by the recognition of reality and that reality from a Western perspective was quite simply that not all states were equal. The system which was elaborated had its origins in the sixteenth century when the Ottoman Sultan, Sulaiman the Magnificent (1494–1566), accepted the Capitulations to the French and English monarchs; in fact this amounted to the French and English extending their jurisdiction and jurisprudence over Christians inhabiting the Ottoman Empire so that they would not be subjected to Islamic law. (There was, needless to say, no reciprocity, but then there were not many Muslims living in France or England at the time.) In due course, and especially from the late eighteenth to the mid-nineteenth centuries, the system derived from the Capitulations extended from Tunisia, through Egypt, the Persian Empire and eastwards to China and Japan.

The major motivation lying behind this arrangement was based on law. Differences between Western and Eastern jurisprudence, both in philosophical and practical terms, were significant. Europeans were concerned that they should not have to find themselves justiciable to what they perceived as inferior, indeed barbarous, Eastern jurisprudence. In some cases, in China for example but not in Japan, Western jurisdiction might be extended also to natives having adopted the Christian faith. The operative term here is that of extra-territoriality, namely that Westerners accused of a crime would be brought before their own consular courts only and also that litigation between a European and a native would fall under the jurisdiction of the European's consular court. This was an important safeguard which the Westerners inserted into their treaties with Japan. There were, however, others. One was the most-favoured-nation clause, whereby any advantage, for example the opening of another port, granted to one nation would automatically accrue to all the others; under this system no Western nation could be in a disadvantageous position by comparison with the others. While these measures were of a mainly juridical nature, some were economic. For example, the Western nations arrogated on to themselves the right of cabotage, that is, to carry on coastal trade and passenger traffic by sea aboard their own ships; in Europe cabotage was always exclusively the right of the nationals of the state. Not surprisingly in the age of free trade, the Europeans also forbade the Japanese the sovereign right to determine unilaterally their own tariff levels. Tariffs were a matter included in separate conventions and, needless to say, they were kept down to a minimum.

Until 1854 Japan was a 'closed country'. When it is stated that Perry opened Japan, this is not strictly speaking correct; Japan, as such, was not really fully opened until 1899. What Perry and subsequent Western diplomats succeeded in obtaining was the opening of a few ports. In these treaty ports Westerners were permitted to carry on trade, buy land, build houses, establish churches and cemeteries, practise their faith. None of these things, however, they were to do outside the treaty ports. The interior of Japan remained closed, though occasionally special passes might be granted to travel; under special circumstances, for example, an offer to a Westerner of a teaching post in a provincial town, permission might be granted for temporary residence.

Something should be said about the general atmosphere pervading the treaty ports. The Westerners who lived there were, for the most part, the only Westerners with whom the Japanese were likely to come into contact. The Western community was composed of merchants, missionaries, diplomats, soldiers and sailors, visiting globe-trotters, writers, painters and so on. It follows that this was a heterogeneous community and that any generalisation regarding it is bound to be somewhat sweeping in character. Nevertheless, certain of the more flagrant features of European treaty-port life can be singled out. Regarding the merchant community, for example, although some serious and well-established firms did set up agencies in Japan, many individual traders were simply out to make a quick profit; their methods were unscrupulous, and they remained all the more confident in that they were protected by extra-territoriality. What has been said about merchants in regard to a quick profit would apply in general terms to sailors, soldiers, globe-trotters in their attitude to Japanese women: enter Madame Butterfly. The European community was very self-centred. Following the well-known adage of 'when in Rome, do as you would at home', clubs for the exclusive use of Europeans were set up where such exotic activities as cricket (or baseball), shooting, racing, whist, ballroom dancing, and so on took place. In general terms, personal relations between the European community and the Japanese were either distant or purely on a superior-inferior basis; Europeans kept

Japanese servants, unskilled employees and mistresses. In the age of social-Darwinism, quite clearly the Japanese could neither be treated nor even considered as equals. This applied to all domains, even including the athletic – for example, it took Tokyo's First High School (Ichiko) baseball team five years of painful persuasion before they managed to get the Yokohama Athletic Club American baseball team to condescend to have a match (in 1896); much to the intense embarrassment of the Western community, the Americans were routed by 29 to 4. More will be said in due course regarding Western attitudes towards the Japanese and Japanese reactions. It remains the case, however, that in spite of a number of very close personal relationships – including, for example, that between Herbert Spencer (1820–1903) and Kaneko Kentaro (1853–1942) – Westerners tended to remain distant and arrogant.

JAPANESE REACTION

The most remarkable thing about the opening of Japan is that it took place so peacefully. This was rarely the case elsewhere. From Morocco to China the Western nations generally had to rely on the use of force. Japan, then, in her essentially peaceful response to the West was quite exceptional. Why?

Part of the answer to this question certainly lies with the information the bakufu was able to obtain from the Dutch factors regarding developments abroad and the might of the Western powers; indeed in 1844 the bakufu received, unsolicited, a letter from King William II (1792–1849) of the Netherlands, informing Edo of the course of the Opium War and, more to the point, the motivations behind it and thereby putting forward the case that it would be in Japan's own interest to anticipate developments by widening her doors to European trade. From this first point, two others immediately follow. The bakufu, needless to say, had not needed the information provided by William II to learn the outcome of the Opium War. If mighty China could thus be defeated, indeed humiliated, Japan's chances of successful resistance were clearly circumscribed. Events in China, therefore, introduced an influential element of caution in Japan's nascent *Weltanschauung*. The information obtained by the Dutch, whether orally or through literature, was accumulated and assessed by the *Rangaku* scholars and filtered out to other sectors of society. Also there were those who advocated that it was indispensable for Japan to obtain Western technology and greater expertise in making use of it in order to defend the nation. As the Western fleets approached, one constant leitmotiv in the exhortations to action was that the improvement of coastal defences required urgent attention. Thus it is important in this context to emphasise that the *joi* movement ('expel the barbarians') was by no means monolithic, but contained disparate tendencies:

whereas some advocated immediate and uncompromising resistance, others argued that Japan should bow to the reality of her weakness, accumulate Western technology and strengthen the fighting forces and *then* proceed to expel the barbarians. Another significant contributory factor to the lack of Japanese resistance was due to the fact that in the 1850s there was a lack of central, united control; in other words, the bakufu was weak, but there was, as yet, no other serious rival to exercise power. Resistance, therefore, was muted partly because of indecisiveness.

In preceding chapters – it has been perhaps the whole tenor of the book so far – it was argued that the prevailing forces at work within Japanese society were clearly in the direction of uniting the nation. This, undoubtedly, is the picture when Japanese history is viewed from a reasonable distance. Upon closer examination, however, it also becomes apparent that there were other forces pulling in completely the opposite direction. This greater degree of scrutiny by no means invalidates the more general panorama; it does serve to show, however, that the process of unification, albeit ineluctable, nonetheless incurred significant opposition. In regard to the *bakumatsu* (end of bakufu) years, the most significant political phenomenon is the dispersal of power and authority away from Edo.

In order to comprehend this phenomenon, it is important to bear in mind the gravity of the economic situation of late Edo Japan and the general administrative chaos of the *baku-han* system. In attempting to recoup some of the expenses necessary for *sankin-kotai* and in reaction to the stagnating stranglehold of the bakufu economy, a number of daimyo had turned quite simply to cultivating their own gardens. This gave rise to a system described as that of han monopolies. Daimyo sought to develop a degree of economic autonomy and to generate wealth by stimulating agricultural, commercial and industrial development within their own han and impose on these a reasonable amount of control so that the emoluments derived would be deposited into han treasuries. By the latter part of the Edo era about 20 per cent of the han had such monopolies, though some were far more successful and sophisticated than others. Whereas in the north han monopolies tended to be restricted to the produce of riziculture, in the south and west of Japan a significant degree of diversification and some embryonic industrialisation occurred. This was true particularly among some of the larger *tozama* han; Satsuma and Choshu, for example, the two han most actively engaged in the politics of Restoration Japan, were able to operate effectively thanks to a comparatively firm economic base. The operation of these monopolies, albeit generally administered by samurai, also involved close collaboration with the provincial merchants, who, as was seen in Chapter 3, were far more dynamic and innovative than their city counterparts. In due course the revenue obtained from the lucrative monopolies would permit the han to purchase ships, arms, machinery and foreign expertise, and to despatch some of their men to the West either to study or lobby the various foreign ministries; indeed Satsuma even sought to set up its own pavilion, separate from the bakufu's, at the Paris World Exposition of 1867. All of these activities had to be carried out surreptitiously, for the bakufu still monopolised the authority to treat with the foreign representatives and their respective ministries and permission to leave Japan could only be granted by Edo. Some of the rebellious han were able to obtain Western allies and intermediaries, the most famous of these being the Aberdonian Thomas Glover (1838–1911), whose house on a hill overlooking Nagasaki bay still stands and is well worth the visit. Ultimately, one of the motivations behind the overthrow of the bakufu was resentment at the monopoly it enjoyed over foreign trade, in that the ports open to the West were all under their jurisdiction. This rapid review of economic affairs, indicating *en passant* that a degree of economic particularism undoubtedly did occur, must be seen in the context of political developments. The purpose here, however, was to show that the political and military devolution of power in the *bakumatsu* years was not taking place in an economic vacuum: among the reasons for the prominent position which Satsuma and Choshu came to enjoy, a degree of economic strength and autonomy was an imperative one.

As the Western menace was appearing more clearly on the diminishing horizon, the bakufu accepted that a greater degree of consultation was a prerequisite to the formulation of national policy. Who, however, should be consulted? Traditionally, the supporters and councillors of the Tokugawa house were the *fudai* daimyo, while the *tozama*, as their title implies, were to be kept outside the councils of deliberation. Ironically, it was one of the shogun's own relatives, the daimyo of Mito Tokugawa Nariaki (1800–60), who argued that the council of some of the *tozama* daimyo should be sought, impressed as he was, among other reasons, by their success in handling their domestic han affairs. The *roju* Abe Masahiro (1819–57) acknowledged the strength of Nariaki's argument and began, albeit secretly, to meet with a number of *tozama* daimyo, including those of Satsuma, Tosa and Echizen. All this had been occurring prior to Perry's arrival. With his visit in 1853, however, all precedent was broken when Abe proceeded to solicit the advice of all of the daimyo. If he had hoped for some form of consensus, he was to be severely disappointed, for none emerged; on the contrary there were absolute divisions among the daimyo as to which course should be followed. The vitally significant element which was introduced here, however, was that almost at one stroke Abe Masahiro undid what Ieyasu and his early successors had been so painstakingly active in undertaking and ensuring: the weakening of the feudal lords. The inevitable sequence of the consultative process is best illustrated by the abolition of mandatory *sankin-kotai* in 1862. Initially, therefore, the Japanese revolution began by a revolt of the old order, either the daimyo themselves or those (in *gekokujo* manner) acting on their behalf.

Reference has already been made to the emergence of a universal political ideology. What needs to be stressed here is that initially the main impetus of the political movement of late Edo Japan was not in the direction of greater universalism, but on the contrary in that of greater particularism. What the activist samurai, especially from the more substantial domains, envisaged was a sort of confederation of han; initially it was accepted that the shogun might have some form of presidential power over such a confederation, while subsequently it was believed that the tenno would not actually rule, but simply reign over the semi-independent domains. There certainly were voices arguing in favour of complete unification. In general, however, this was not an important element in pre-Restoration rhetoric. It is important to bear this point in mind, for when following the Restoration sweeping reforms towards centralisation occurred, han loyalists, notably Saigo Takamori (1828–77), could well be excused for feeling a bitter sense of betrayal. It is here, however, as indicated in the first paragraph of this chapter, that the West played a determining role; it became clear to the new leaders – as indeed it had been clear to the last shogun, Tokugawa Keiki (1837–1913) – that strength lay in unity.

At the same time another element was introduced in the course of the early crisis years at the time of Perry's arrival. One argument espoused with tenacity, indeed fanaticism, not the least by Nariaki, was that the policy of *sakoku* was an enactment of imperial command, issued from the sacred institution of the tenno. In fact, there was no substance whatsoever to this view, in that the policy of *sakoku* had had nothing to do with Kyoto, but had been unilaterally formulated and imposed by the Tokugawa house. The only credibility which could be given to the argument was that inherent in the title of the shogun, *sei-i-tai-shogun* ('general in charge of suppressing barbarians'). In due course the name of the tenno could be invoked as an attack on those policies of the bakufu which seemed to run counter to the imperial will. The tenno, it will be recalled, was for all practical purposes a prisoner in his Kyoto fortress. By the second decade of the nineteenth century some relaxation in bakufu control over the imperial court had been obtained. Kokaku (1771–1840), for example, had been permitted to leave the palace gates and visit Kyoto following his abdication (in 1817). That, however, was quite a step removed from Abe, again breaking with precedent, seeking to obtain advice from the imperial court over the Western demands. Ineluctably, therefore, just as power was eluding Edo in the direction of some of the provincial centres, so was it shifting from Edo to Kyoto. This phenomenon was illustrated in a number of developments. Abe's seeking court approval was one. The proposal to marry shogun Iemochi (1846–66) to the tenno's sister, Kazunomiya (1846–77), in order to consolidate Kyoto–Edo ties and especially to enhance the prestige of the shogun by imperial betrothal was another; negotiations for the wedding began in 1858, with the marriage taking place in 1862, producing, however, no heir. In spite of the shogun's temporal power in theory being invested on to him from the tenno, in fact since 1634 not a single shogun had visited Kyoto.

From 1863 onwards, however, succeeding shogun Iemochi and Keiki spent more time in Kyoto than in Edo. Also in 1863 another precedent was set, when for the first time since the establishment of the Tokugawa dynasty a reigning tenno, Komei (1831–66), left the precincts of the palace in order to visit the Kamo shrine where he prayed for the expulsion of the foreigners from Japan.

For in 1858 the court in Kyoto had unequivocably adopted the policy of *joi* as its own. Court policy does not necessarily reflect the views of the tenno himself. In Kyoto at the time various groups were in rivalry in order to proclaim the tenno's wishes. Intensely xenophobic Choshu loyalists were in the ascendant in Kyoto until September 1863 when they were ousted by more moderate Satsuma samurai. Thus, in regard to modern Japanese history in general, it would be inaccurate to equate national policy with the imperial will. Nevertheless, in this particular instance it would appear to be the case that Komei was personally committed to the policy of *joi* – it is partly because of this intense personal commitment that suspicions have arisen that in fact he may have been killed by poison in 1866, for the emerging leadership, having radically altered its views on how to cope with the West, felt that he might become an embarrassment and that his young son Mutsuhito (1852–1912) would be much easier to manipulate. It is also, however, for this reason that the initially quite distinct ideologies of *sonno* and *joi* came to be linked.

Joi, therefore, came to be espoused as a holy cause. As a movement it was both xenophobic and millenarian. The *shishi* in adopting measures to expel the foreigners were manifestly expressing the imperial will. Although *joi* was primarily political and highly emotional, there was also an economic *raison d'être* for the espousal of this policy. Initially, the effects of foreign trade on the late Edo economy had very negative results; due to Japan's gold–silver ratio being at variance with the outside world (gold was cheaper in Japan), one of the most lucrative activities for foreign merchants was to purchase Japanese gold, sell it in Shanghai for silver, return to Japan with the silver and buy more gold, which obviously resulted in a significant outflow of specie. Although the bakufu soon stopped this particular gold rush by changing the silver–gold ratio and fixing it in accordance with the international standard, other deleterious economic effects, including a high rate of inflation, continued to cause havoc to the national economy and suffering among the people, with the exception of course of those who profited from the foreign trade.

The Kyoto court insisted with the bakufu that it should not only adopt but indeed implement the policy of *joi*. The bakufu prevaricated. *Shishi* emotions swelled into a fury of passionate indignation. Action was undoubtedly called for. The *shishi*, however, were a very disparate group, consisting essentially of coteries of bushi from the various han; in other words, at this stage there was no concerted plan or action. Their activities mainly took the form of acts of terrorism, these being directed either against the foreigners themselves or against those officials in the bakufu whom the *shishi* perceived as collaborators. The most spectacular coup was the assassination of the *tairo* Ii Naosuke (1815–60) in March 1860 by *shishi* of Mito who were enraged at Ii for having signed the 1858 treaties (with the United States, Great Britain and France) and by his numerous purges, including the house-incarceration of Tokugawa Nariaki. Yoshida Shoin (1831–60) also sought to deflect bakufu policy by intimidation in his plan to assassinate Manabe Akikatsu (1804–84) on the occasion of the latter's trip to Kyoto as emissary of Ii in an attempt to obtain the court's consent for the treaties. Shoin's plan aborted and he was beheaded.

During the early years of the foreign presence in Japan there was not much of an opportunity given to Westerners to study and discover the various movements and intrigues of domestic politics. It was believed that the bakufu was at the very least sympathetic to those who were perpetrating acts of terrorism against the foreigners. A number of incidents had occurred, the murder of Henry Heusken, a very popular figure among the foreign community, already having been mentioned; there were other attacks, including for example the assassination of the Chinese cook attached to the French legation. In July 1861 a group of *shishi* broke into the British legation with the intention of murdering all who were there. Among the staff at the legation was Laurence Oliphant (1829–88) who had previously served as secretary to Lord Elgin (1811–63) when the latter acted as envoy extraordinary in East Asia and signed Britain's treaty with Japan; Oliphant's published record of these events, *Narrative of the Earl of Elgin's Mission to China and Japan* (1859) remains a masterpiece, providing among other things one of the most fascinating first-hand accounts of British gunboat diplomacy. On the occasion of the attack on the legation, Oliphant suffered a wound on the side of his head, from which he never totally recovered. Returning to Britain, he joined the Liberal Party, and in 1865 became MP for the Stirling burghs; in 1867 he was converted to an American spiritualist sect, later he proposed the Jewish colonisation of Palestine, albeit not Jewish himself, and in 1882 went to settle in Haifa.

Although Oliphant escaped death, such was not the fate of another Englishman, Lennox Richardson, in September 1862. On the 14th of that month the daimyo of Satsuma, Shimazu Hisamitsu (1817-87), was on his way with his cortège from Edo to Kyoto along the famous Tokaido. Richardson, along with three companions, including one English woman, were on a riding expedition when they came across the procession; instead of dismounting, as was not only custom but indeed law, they continued on their horses. A number of samurai, incensed at the rudeness of the foreigners to their lord, drew out their swords; Richardson was killed, while the other three managed to escape back to the treaty port of Yokohama. This was the proverbial straw so far as the European community was concerned. Already quite a number of foreigners had been arguing, and lobbying, that the only means to enlighten the Japanese on the benefits of free trade and to induce them to proper and civilised behaviour was to teach them a lesson; in other words, force had to be resorted to. The official British representative, attempting to retain a degree of coolness in the heated demand for vengeance, demanded of the bakufu that, in compensation for the murder of Richardson, it should pay an indemnity, so should the Satsuma han and the criminals arrested and brought to trial. The bakufu complied, in due course, with the first request, but protested its inability to carry out the latter two, owing to the fact that these were Satsuma matters over which it had no jurisdiction. Attempts to obtain satisfaction directly from Satsuma failed. In August of 1863 a British fleet under the command of Rear-Admiral Augustus Kuper (1809-85) bombarded the Satsuma capital of Kago-shima. This was the first use made of gunboat diplomacy in Japan. To his eternal credit, the Liberal MP for Maidstone, Charles Buxton (1823-71) – who had earlier advocated clemency for the Indian mutineers of 1857 to roars of self-righteous indignation in the House – protested vociferously, both in the House and in a moving letter to *The Times* (of 4 November 1863), against the wanton destruction of innocent lives.

It is indeed interesting, however, that this British action – and in spite of the fact that Satsuma put up a good fight – resulted in a significant change in the attitude of Satsuma to the West; as indeed was the case with Choshu when the Europeans bombarded Shimonoseki a year later. Following these two Western attacks, *joi* was abandoned, though not necessarily in rhetoric, as a viable policy; indeed, shortly afterwards Satsuma entered into close relations with some of the Westerners, namely, Thomas Glover and, more significantly, the master of intrigue, the British legation's second secretary Ernest Satow (1843-1929), who sought to influence his chief, Sir Harry Parkes (1828-85), in favour of the Satsuma cause. Ivan Morris (*The Nobility of Failure*, 1975) has made an interesting comparison between the bombardment of

Kagoshima and a more notorious and devastating bombardment eighty-two years later in terms of the consequences they had not just on Japanese policies, but indeed on Japanese attitudes: 'In much the same way, America's near destruction of Japan, culminating in the atomic bombardment of August 1945, far from turning Japan away from the West and its values, inaugurated the most intense period of westernization and adulation of all things foreign since the early Meiji decades.' Leaving aside all moral considerations regarding these punitive measures, if the intention had been to teach the Japanese a lesson, a lesson indeed was learned.

In the meantime, however, Kyoto had remained adamant in its position that the bakufu should proceed to expel the Westerners. Ultimately, as a *quid pro quo* for the marriage between Iemochi and Kazunomiya, the bakufu was compelled to agree not only to the general policy of *joi*, but that implementation of it should begin in June 1863. Having acquiesced to the imperial will, the bakufu nevertheless proceeded with its usual *modus operandi*, namely procrastination. Choshu, however, opted for more decisive action. The date having been arrived at, Choshu cannon began firing on foreign vessels which happened to pass the straits of Shimonoseki – the usual route for the southern Chinese ports and Hong Kong. The Western representatives, that is, the British, French, Dutch and Americans, consulted each other and as a result ordered their respective fleets to take part in another gunboat expedition.

As the preparations for the operation were in progress, a revealing incident regarding the transformation of late Tokugawa politics occurred. One of the bakufu officials for foreign affairs (*gaikoku-bugyo*), Takemoto Masao, called on the French and British heads of legation, Léon Roches (1809–1901) and Rutherford Alcock. As a result of two official missions to the West, the bakufu was very much aware of the fact that the European powers had no intention of withdrawing from Japan. The pressure within the country to take decisive action, however, was overwhelming; although instructions emanated from Kyoto, the real motivating force came from Choshu. So when Takemoto paid his visit to Roches and Alcock, ostensibly as a step in the direction of asking them to depart from Japan, he was informed by the diplomats that not only had they no intention of leaving, but that they were about to castigate Choshu. Takemoto let it be known that, since such was their intention and that they were obviously going to carry it out, the bakufu would not necessarily view this action without some satisfaction and indeed relief.

It is at this stage that for the first time European representatives were able to gauge to some degree the cleavages which were occurring in Japanese politics. By the third or fourth year of the sixties, Westerners were in a far better position to appreciate the rival forces, their support and ambitions; generally, however, this did not result in a marked change in European policies towards Japan. Two individuals did become personally committed to one or other of the parties: Roches in unconditional support for the bakufu and Satow in equally intense support for Satsuma. Some historians have mistakenly attributed these rival personal involvements to Anglo-French imperial rivalry. In fact the chief British representative, Parkes, held on to a mainly neutral line, while Roches's policies were not orchestrated by Paris, but resulted from his own creative, albeit misguided, intuition; while Satow, though betting on a winning horse, was not being guided by instructions from Whitehall. At this period there was no Anglo-French rivalry in the Far East. The fact, however, that the Europeans were, at the very least, able to gather more reliable intelligence arose quite simply out of a sudden change in the Japanese climate, namely that rival groups actually started talking to the Westerners and providing them with information.

The Western allied fleet proceeded to Shimonoseki, with the bakufu's surreptitious blessing, and in September 1864 carried out a successful amphibious operation. Two Choshu men, Ito Hirobumi (1841–1909) and Inoue Kaoru (1836–1915), who had spent some time in England, had sought to urge their han not to engage in hostilities with the Europeans. Although unable to prevent the confrontation, their dire warnings regarding the actual might of Europe ultimately led to a reversal in Choshu policy, though only after civil war within the han; the contending sides might perhaps be labelled as the romantics versus the realists, and the latter won.

Growing European awareness of the Japanese political situation led the diplomatic agents to the realisation of what was the cause of all their difficulties, namely the imperial condemnation of the treaties. Hitherto Europeans had, quite understandably, been rather mystified by the apparent diarchy of the Japanese constitutional system. Generally, however, they had opted for recognising the shogun – who at the time was referred to as the Tycoon, after the Japanese appellation, Taikun, meaning great lord – as the monarch responsible for temporal matters, while the tenno, whom they called the Mikado, they dismissed as some form of Lama. Having had the opportunity given them by more forthcoming communication from a variety of Japanese sources of reappraising the situation and understanding the conundrum facing the bakufu, fresh from their Shimonoseki success, they sailed off to Osaka and simply waited for their naval display of force to result in obtaining imperial ratification of the treaties. This was granted on 22 November 1865.

From that moment *joi* was a dead letter and indeed both bakufu and some of the han, again especially Satsuma and Choshu, engaged in a mad scramble for westernisation. With the abandonment of *joi*, *sonno* came to be associated now with *tobaku*, 'overthrow the bakufu'. A movement which originally sought to expel the barbarians now altered course and instead sought to expel the ruling shogunal dynasty. Why? Perhaps the simplest reason is that put forward by Walter Rostow as a universal phenomenon: 'As a matter of historical fact, nationalism has been the most important motive force in the transition from traditional to modern societies – vastly more important than the profit motive. Men have been willing to uproot traditional societies primarily not to make more money, but because the traditional society failed, or threatened to fail, to protect them from humiliation by foreigners' (quoted in *The Economist*, 15 August 1959). Louis XVI (1754–93), after all, was guillotined mainly because it was discovered, following his abortive flight to Varennes, that he was seeking foreign intervention to quell the forces of the Revolution. The Ch'ing Empire in China had its fate finally and irrevocably sealed following the humiliating defeat at the hands of the Japanese in 1895; the Romanovs proved incapable of defeating the Japanese in 1905 and things were not faring any better in the course of the 1914–18 war; and so on. The Tokugawa bakufu had clearly failed in adequately protecting Japan against the external threat: the Tokugawa bakufu had to go.

There were other reasons. One, already indicated, was the rise of han patriotism in some quarters. Satsuma and Choshu activists were undoubtedly concerned about the fate of the wider Japan, but they were equally strongly motivated by their particularistic brand of patriotism. As *tozama* han, they had been humiliatingly kept outside the important affairs of state for too long, and now was their chance to assert themselves. These perceptions of Satsuma and Choshu ascendancy were equally resented by other han, especially Aizu who felt they were losing out and therefore fanatically resisted the transformation Satsuma and Choshu sought to impose – not just out of loyalty to the bakufu, but also because of its own han patriotism. Perhaps the strongest and most rational motivation, however, was the realisation that in spite of vestiges of emotional attachment to one's han, survival for the han individually and hence the nation collectively could only be brought about if the country could be effectively unified and government policy co-ordinated and centralised. Indeed, the last shogun, Keiki, recognised as much himself; he had elaborated an ambitious and far-reaching programme of centralisation, but recognised that the Tokugawa bakufu would be incapable of carrying it out; hence his abdication in late 1867.

At an earlier stage it had been hoped in certain quarters that Japan might strengthen her policy by achieving a closer union between Edo and Kyoto, in a movement known as *kobu-gattai* (amalgamation of civil and military power). This compromise, however, had proved unsatisfactory. By late 1865 the need for a complete break, *tobaku*, was not only recognised, it became urgent. It is in this sense that the Western powers, albeit indirectly, came to precipitate the overthrow of the old order. In preceding years both bakufu and the belligerent han had been actively engaged in the purchase of Western arms. With the abandonment of *joi*, however, both also sought to obtain the services of Western experts. In 1866 the bakufu enlisted a military mission from France to help form a modern army, the British Royal Navy was called upon for similar services in regard to the navy, while Western engineers were employed for the purpose of laying an industrial infrastructure to support military development. While the han might seek similar arrangements, owing to the fact that the bakufu was the only government recognised by the Western powers, they were at a serious disadvantage; London, for example, would not approve the dispatch of a team from the Royal Navy to assist Satsuma unless such a measure was granted bakufu approval, which, needless to say, was highly unlikely. To put it in simple terms, the opposing han had to act quickly before the bakufu was allowed to become too strong.

And the bakufu was indeed militarily weak. It sought to crush Choshu in 1866, but failed. To resist bakufu invasion of Choshu territory was one thing; to succeed in actually ousting the bakufu from power was quite another. No han could do this alone. As pointed out earlier, the *shishi* by no means operated on a co-ordinated plan; on the contrary their actions arose from anarchic, disparate policies, indeed often in violent rivalry between themselves. Some of the more perceptive *shishi* realised that as long as they were acting unilaterally they had no chance of success, and especially while Satsuma and Choshu continued to view each other with hostility. They therefore set about urging the two to join, none more painstakingly, and ultimately successfully, than Sakamoto Ryoma (1836–67) of the Tosa han. Once the reconciliation between Satsuma and Choshu had been achieved, in 1866, the bakufu was doomed. Keiki attempted to rejuvenate and reinvigorate the bakufu; but, as one of the very few rulers of a dying dynasty to have had the perception of reading and paying attention to what was written on the wall, he resigned. A brief civil war ensued. In early 1868, however, the restoration of the young tenno was proclaimed, a new order was announced, a new era embarked upon, namely that of Meiji, or enlightened government.

THE REVOLUTION

Was the Meiji Restoration, as the events culminating in 1868 are called, a revolution? The question is raised partly because in the ordinary Western individual's consciousness the existence of a Japanese revolution figuring among the 'great' revolutions, such as the French, the Russian and the Chinese, is not generally recognised. Indeed, especially in the 1950s and early 1960s it used to be advocated that Japan had succeeded in industrialising without having undergone a revolution. One might proceed here by assessing the events of 1868 according to the usual criteria applied to revolutions and some of their more overt manifestations.

If one were to begin with the more trivial, one might point out that all revolutions have been highly romantic affairs. These are times propitious for heroes and heroines to dazzle the world of the imagination and to engage in heroic, quasi-supernatural acts – the Long March is an evocative example. Revolutions also provide inspiration for great literature: *A Tale of Two Cities*, for the French, *Doctor Zhivago*, for the Russian, to mention only two examples. Heroic figures of revolutions assume legendary proportions, with Emiliano Zapata (1879–1919) one of the more colourful cases. The events of 1868 lacked none of these qualities. The idealistic passion of Yoshida Shoin, the bravado of Saigo Takamori, the furtive intrigues of Sakamoto Ryoma, the tortured sincerity of Katsu Kaishu and many others provide vivid illustrations of the heady revolutionary days and ample material for the imagination of novelists and dramatists. Also, in the struggles of the *bakumatsu* period daring women participated in a number of different ways, though perhaps mainly by providing clandestine shelter, protection and comfort to the *shishi*. The poetess and *kokugaku* scholar, Nomura Botoni, offered a haven to the Choshu *shishi* Takasugi Shinsaku, as a result of which she incurred the punishment of the bakufu and was exiled to Himeshima (princess island); while another poetess of equally intrepid character, Matsuo Taseko, joined the *shishi* in Kyoto where she acted as spy and delivered messages. Nor must one forget the heroic fighting of the women's squadron in the defence of Aizu, with those either too young or too old to fight resorting to suicide when the battle was lost. The events of 1868, therefore, were, like all other great revolutions, highly dramatic and romantic.

Another characteristic of revolutions is that these have invariably been rather bloody affairs. Summary justice, executions, violent attacks and equally fearsome reprisals have all figured prominently. Here the Japanese are somewhat exceptional. Although a civil war did break out and some of the fighting was particularly sanguinary, it was much more short-lived than the battles which ensued and raged in the course of the French, Mexican, Russian, Turkish, Chinese and Cuban revolutions. Far less blood flowed. The same applies not only in terms of quantity, but in terms of quality. A distinguishing feature of most revolutions is that the heads and representatives of the old order are eliminated, either publicly, as was the case for Louis XVI and his spouse, or furtively, as was the case with Nicholas II (1868–1918) and his family. The new Meiji government did execute a number of former bakufu officials, Oguri Tadamasa (1827–68) being one example on the grounds that he actively sought French military assistance to quell the *sonno* forces. But

Keiki was not killed; on the contrary, he was subsequently rehabilitated and granted a hereditary title under the new peerage system. The final resistance to the new government was led by Enomoto Takeaki (1836–1908), a brilliant naval strategist, who sought to establish an independent republic in the island of Hokkaido; overwhelmed by government forces, he finally surrendered in the summer of 1869, yet within three years he was pardoned and proceeded to lead a distinguished career in the new navy and subsequently in diplomacy.

Why should Japan have been different in this respect? The answer lies in two major preoccupations which the government had to face. The first is that the new leaders were above all concerned at strengthening the country, not weakening it. Excessive retaliation would result in exacerbated dissensions which in turn would inevitably have caused further fighting. With the aim of uniting the country, it was not so much the vestiges of the past which needed to be destroyed, but foundations for the future to be solidly laid. If Japan were to engage in protracted civil war, the likelihood of Western intervention would become all the more real. The second is that if the new leadership were to succeed in strengthening the country against what were overwhelming odds, then use must be made of human talent wherever it could be found.

Another fairly universal pattern of revolutions which Japan did not experience was that of large-scale emigration. The loyalist Americans went off to Canada, the French nobility to wherever they could find refuge, White Russians poured into Western Europe, the United States – a few even went to Japan – Chinese fugitives from the revolution were able to establish a Republic of China in Taiwan, and so on. Why did the Japanese variant in this respect deviate from a more universal pattern? The first answer no doubt derives from the point raised above; the refugees of the other revolutions were not simply motivated by ideological considerations, but were in many cases literally fleeing for their lives. Another important element in regard to the Japanese, however, is that they had nowhere to go. The French, Russian and Chinese refugees had relatives and friends who could help them, provide them with temporary shelter, indeed even attempt to collect funds to raise anti-revolutionary movements in the hope of returning victorious to the fatherland. The Japanese had no such international contacts. There may also be a psychological factor here: the legacy of *sakoku* in terms of attitudes to the outside world. Throughout modern Japanese history, even in the course of the thirties, there have in fact been very few Japanese political refugees seeking asylum abroad. A notable exception is Katayama Sen (1859–1933), one of Japan's leading socialists, later communist, who exiled himself, lived in Moscow where he died and is buried in the Kremlin wall. There is a sad story in the plight of an earlier refugee, Baba Tatsui (1850–88), who sought to awaken the Western world to the evil despotism of the Meiji government, but found such lack of interest in his cause that he died of a broken heart in Philadelphia.

Of three characteristic features of great revolutions, it would appear that only one, the romance, fits the Japanese case. What other ingredient is there? Presumably revolutions are supposed to change the order of things, as is implicit in the very etymology of the word. Thomas C. Smith, in describing events following the Restoration ('Japan's Aristocratic Revolution' in *The Yale Review*, spring 1961), has made the following claim: 'I believe, though of course I cannot prove, that these decades brought greater changes to Japan than did the Great Revolution of 1789 to France.' It is primarily in that sense that the events of 1868 deserve the label of a revolution and that indeed the Japanese revolution should figure among the great revolutions of modern history. The changes which did occur will be the subject of the following chapters of this book. There is, however, one important consideration that needs attention before the nature of the Japanese revolution is assessed: the distinction between motivation and causation.

It may well be objected that one of the most profound characteristics of the other great revolutions has been so far completely neglected: the espousal of a universal revolutionary ideology. The American revolutionaries held that what was true for them, the pursuit of freedom and happiness, should equally apply to all men. The French believed that the Declaration of the Rights of Man and of the Citizen should extend to all mankind, while the Russian revolution urged the workers of the world to unite. For these reasons, not surprisingly, the revolutions mentioned above – and subsequently the Chinese and the Cuban – had wide universal appeal; or, alternatively, wide universal condemnation. One does not need, however, too strong a dose of cynicism to point out that, for example, it was going to take quite a while before American Negroes would be permitted to pursue freedom, let alone happiness; that the Declaration of the Rights of Man and of the Citizen, when properly scrutinised, in fact included such restrictions and qualifications that the extent of its application was bound to be rather narrowly circumscribed; that the Russian revolution resulted more in the dictatorship of the apparatchniks than in that of the proletariat. Japan's revolution in that sense was lacking in the rhetoric of a universal ideology; this did not, however, prevent the subsequent social upheaval which ensued to have been at least as substantial as that of the more notorious revolutions, indeed, as T. C. Smith suggested, possibly more so.

To say that Japan's revolution lacked a universal ideology purporting to appeal to all men is not to say that it lacked an ideology. Although individually men may be prepared to fight and die for love or for profit, collectively they need to be inspired by a cause. A cause needs to be articulated. And that is what, in its bare essence, is termed an ideology. It is the ideology which motivates men to action. So far as the motivation of the Japanese revolution is concerned, it consisted of two elements: nationalism and tenno-ism.

In the face of the foreign threat it became increasingly apparent that the solitary han had little relevance and certainly little power. In actual contact with the West, either through the communities in the treaty ports, or travel to the West, or simply contemplating the spectre which it evoked, the realisation dawned upon the disparate members of the various han that they were *Japanese* – in other words, not simply sons of Satsuma, Kanazawa, Sendai, and so on. This intuitive awakening found articulation in the writings of a number of ideologues. Sakuma Shozan warned that military defence was called for and that this could be best achieved by a concerted political effort of all the nation that would transcend han sectionalism. Yoshida Shoin appealed for the united action of what he termed the *somo no shishi* (unattached patriots) who would throw off the shackles of parochialism and struggle for the survival of the nation.

It is important to define what is meant by nationalism as an ideology. First, as the term implies, it is an ideology which extends to the whole nation, not just sections of it. Secondly, nationalism is modern in that it is concerned with building for the future glory of the nation. Nationalism was born in Japan when *joi* was discarded. The significance here is by no means simply a semantic one. *Joi* was not nationalism, it was sheer xenophobia. *Joi* was an obscure and irrational expression of a desire to retain what was perceived as an idyllic existence: the seclusion of Japan from the outside world and its corrupting influences. *Joi*, in other words, sought to maintain the *status quo* as far as the country's relations with the West were concerned. Perceiving that the bakufu was incapable of protecting that particular cocoon, *sonno*, in its inception, illustrated a romantic desire to return to an illusory historical womb. If the old monarchical system of past glory could be restored, the gods would be pleased and Japan would be saved. This is what was meant by *osei-fukko*. The nascent political leaders of Japan, however, especially after the thrashings of Kagoshima and Shimonoseki, realised that this was a dream which would too easily metamorphose into a nightmare. In order for the nation to be saved, indeed to become strong and powerful, reality had to be accepted and compromises made. And this is also what is implied by nationalism, as opposed to xenophobia: the ideal of national survival and strength is the end that transcends all others; in order to achieve it all means are justified. *Joi* sought to expel Westerners; after 1865 both bakufu and progressive han were inviting them in. The West, it was realised, could and should be used for the purpose of strengthening Japan.

The distinction between modern nationalism and obscurantist xenophobia is vital. In China, for example, the Boxer movement of 1900 was not nationalistic, but xenophobic; with the May Fourth movement of 1919 modern Chinese nationalism was forcefully articulated, for it was directed against the imperialism of the West (and Japan), but not those elements of external culture which could be imported into China in order to strengthen the nation. Numerous other examples could be cited. The point to emphasise here, however, is that Japan was the first of the non-Western societies to comprehend and adopt modern nationalism as an ideology. The shift is equally perceptible in the vocabulary of the revolution. *Osei-fukko* came to be discarded in favour of *ishin*. *Ishin* is composed of two Chinese characters, the second of which (*shin*) means new. The political leaders of Meiji Japan sought to *restore* the tenno, but primarily in order to *renovate* society.

What has been said above, however, requires qualifications. The new leaders of Japan, those who ultimately steered the ship of state, were modern and enlightened men. The broad base of the society in which they were operating, however, was neither modern nor particularly enlightened. It has also been pointed out that the perceived threat from the West resulted in a highly emotional response. What is emotional is rarely rational. The leadership, therefore, was faced with a conundrum. In view of Japan's backwardness in relation to the advanced Western powers, a great leap forward was called for. This would undoubtedly involve heavy sacrifices. It is in this sense that nationalism as such was too vague a concept; it needed a concrete symbol and that was to be the tenno and all that the institution stood for. In fact, the person of the tenno had little significance, it was rather what he was held to represent. And what the tenno represented above all was the past, the continuity of Japanese history, the beacon of its civilisation. As far as the essential spiritual ingredient of nationalism as a popular ideology was concerned, it was in the tenno that it could be found. In real terms what happened is that with great pomp and circumstance the tenno was taken from his imprisonment in Kyoto to a new prison in Tokyo, alias Edo. Hereafter, however, decrees, edicts and sundry exhortations would be issued in his divine name. For him the people of Japan would be prepared to accept whatever sacrifice, whether hard work in the fields or factories or death at the front; just as in other societies it may be incumbent on men and women to offer themselves unhesitatingly for Christ or Allah. Not to put too fine a point on it, it was essential, or so the leadership believed, that the people should be duped.

The motivation of the Japanese revolutionaries, therefore, was undoubtedly nationalistic. The manner in which it was expressed was the formulation of tenno-ism. The term which in fact came into circulation was that of *kokutai*; *kokutai* is derived from two Chinese characters, the first (*koku*) meaning nation, the second (*tai*) meaning body or substance. In spite of the concrete implication in the latter, however, the substance was of ethereal nature. The term was intended to connote everything which the spirit of Japan encapsulated. The whole body rested on the legitimacy and infallibility of the tenno. The terms *kokutai* and tenno-ism, or *tenno-sei* in Japanese, are interchangeable. The motivation explains how the superstructure of Japanese society developed. Motivation, however, does not determine how the base will evolve. For an understanding of the nature of Japanese economic development, the causation of the revolution needs to be assessed. As will be seen, the tragedy of the Japanese revolution and the society to which it gave birth was that there was an antagonism, a contradiction, between the superstructure and the base. This contradiction, albeit more attenuated at certain times than at others, plagued the people of Japan until they were finally liberated after 1945.

In attempting to define more precisely a revolution the question to be asked is not only who was it who led the revolution, but what are the groups which ultimately benefited most from it. The French Revolution was a bourgeois–capitalist revolution primarily because the society which subsequently emerged was bourgeois operating on a capitalist system of production. This is not to say that this was a perceptible phenomenon which occurred suddenly at a specific date. Rather, in defining the revolution in these terms, one is mainly indicating historical trends.

The Japanese revolution of 1868 was carried out by men who claimed, fraudulently or otherwise, samurai or *kuge* status. This does not mean, however, that consequently the revolution should be described as aristocratic. It is difficult, indeed misleading, to seek to label the whole of the *buke/kuge* estates as an aristocracy; mainly because, in the Greek derivation of the term, the last two syllables indicate power or government: while some samurai exercised a degree of power, others had none at all. Also the revolution did not significantly benefit the samurai estate as an entirety. On the contrary, their privileges were steadily eroded.

Needless to say, the Japanese revolution was not a proletarian revolution for the simple reason, among others, that there was no proletariat. Was it a peasant revolution? That is a more difficult question to answer. There can be no doubt that the numerous peasant rebellions which occurred, especially from the latter part of the eighteenth century onwards, significantly contributed to the gradual demolition of the old regime until it finally collapsed. That in itself is by no means an indication that it was a peasant revolution, however, for it does not explain whether or not the peasantry reaped advantages from the revolution. The problem here, however, relates back to that of definition raised earlier. Although the Tokugawa order had defined, indeed delimited, a peasant estate, there was most certainly not the degree of homogeneity within the estate to merit the application of the term 'class'; also, even the Tokugawa delimitation incorporated certain grey areas, such as the *goshi* (rustic samurai). The rich peasants undoubtedly benefited from the revolution, mainly in the sense that one of the first government acts consisted of granting peasants the legal right to buy and sell land: this was primarily of value to those peasants who had accumulated sufficient capital in order to carry out these transactions. It is true that in the initial period of industrialisation land taxes were onerous; this was mainly, however, due to the fact that the government had no other readily available source of revenue. In any case this was a temporary measure and in the course of the Meiji period rich peasants got richer and more powerful and influential.

In regard to the merchant estate, the final death blow to the big city merchants was the opening of the country to foreign trade. It is true that some did survive, notably Mitsui. Mitsui, however, was saved by the appointment of a complete outsider as manager, Minomura Rizaemon (1821–77). Minomura, originally of poor peasant stock, illustrates another characteristic of revolutions, namely that the chaos which occurs permits a vertiginous degree of social mobility generally not found in times of quietude. Also, the new economic situation of Japan offered opportunities for a new class of entrepreneurs to emerge. The city merchants, for reasons indicated in Chapter 3, were incapable of seeing or grasping the opportunity. The more dynamic and visionary provincial merchants and rural landlords, however, did respond, some of them subsequently becoming the leaders of the private sector of industry: Shibusawa Eiichi (1840–1931), an industrial pioneer *par excellence* of modern Japan, was from rich peasant stock, while Iwasaki Yataro (1835–85), founder of the Mitsubishi industrial empire, was a *goshi*. It was the revolution of 1868 which paved the way for these men to rise to influential economic, social and ultimately political positions. It was for this reason that a number of them, perceiving that such might well be the case, had been prepared to contribute funds to the anti-Tokugawa cause.

The most significant element in the revolution were the meritocratic samurai bureaucrats. The process of differentiation within the samurai estate, although beginning well before the *bakumatsu* years, was nevertheless precipitated following the arrival of the Western powers. In facing the Western menace new offices had to be created. In view of the sophisticated knowledge required in administering these new posts and the urgency of the situation, it was no longer possible, as tradition would have it, to appoint men simply on the basis of heredity; a much wider meritocratic net had to be cast. And it was these talented officials, mainly though not exclusively samurai, who overthrew the old order and carried the nation into the modern age.

The civil bureaucracy, the rural landlords/manufacturers, the new urban industrialists came to constitute the post-revolution ruling class. The members of all these groups had one common feature: they represented Japan's new bourgeoisie. Also, although the economy initially was a form of state capitalism, by the third decade after the'revolution the means of production were mainly in the private sector. Does all this lead to the irrefutable conclusion that 1868 marked a bourgeois–capitalist revolution?

While contemporary Japan can undoubtedly be described as a nation founded on a capitalist system of production and with a bourgeois superstructure, this combination is of relatively recent vintage, in fact not more than about three decades old. In the earlier period, however, although industrial capitalism did develop, Japan remained an overwhelmingly agrarian nation. Also, the bourgeoisie, until recent decades, was far too narrow an élite. The distance, whether in terms of wealth, culture, education, values, travel – most of the rural population stayed in their villages throughout their lives, the exceptions being military service for boys and factory work for girls – between the bourgeoisie and the rest of society remained vast. In fact, as will be seen in following chapters, the Japanese revolution, in social terms, resulted not so much in an *embourgeoisement* as in a *samurai-isation* of the lower echelons of society. For reasons of internal development and defence against perceived external pressures the government required docile and well-disciplined peasants, workers, soldiers and sailors: to achieve that end, it was best not to instil in the hearts and minds of the populace liberal bourgeois values, but rather those samurai virtues of loyalty and obedience. It is also in this sense that the obscurantist tenno-ist ideology could be used to advantage. Finally, it must also be noted that while the civil bureaucracy, rural landlord/manufacturers and urban industrialists were three of the elements in the composition of the ruling order, there was a fourth: the military officer corps. These, as will be seen, tended to perceive themselves as ferocious guardians of the tenno ideology.

There had occurred a number of remarkably modern developments in the Edo era. Nevertheless it remained a comparatively immature society and an immature economy for all the transformations which Japan was suddenly to experience. The speed with which Japan was absorbed into the international economy, the great leaps necessary to develop a system which could cope, and the threat, real or illusory, of the Western powers all combined to cause serious dislocations in both economy and society. The year 1868 was a major step in the direction of a bourgeois–capitalist revolution; it was to take several decades, however, before this revolution could come to fruition.

PART 3

TRANSFORMATION TO MODERNITY: THE MEIJI ERA

Introduction

Until very recently most analyses of modern Japanese historical development tended to differentiate between 'tradition' on the one hand and 'modernity' on the other. A corollary to this dualistic view, either explicitly or by implication, was to associate tradition with what was indigenous and the modern with extraneous Western importations. This perception in turn legitimised the theory of convergence: as nations industrialise their social patterns converge into a common model. Modernisation was held to be reasonably synonymous with westernisation. Both Marxist and liberal historiography adhered to variants of this particular theme. For Marx, European imperialism in Asia was progressive in that it would destroy the Asiatic mode of production. For Thomas Macaulay (1800–59) the mission of the British empire in India was to ensure that the native would emerge as an Englishman in every sense except colour.

These Western conceptions, or preconceptions, survived the vagaries of time. For the New Deal idealists who were initially instrumental in seeking to reshape Japanese society under the aegis of the US occupying forces following Japan's defeat in the Second World War, both their motivations and the ends they aspired to were formulated on comparable principles: traditional Japan must be uprooted and in its place seeds of Americanisation would ensure the growth of a healthy, liberal, peaceful society. Once not only the nation's economy, but also its basic political and legal structures were modelled on the West, then the only thing which would distinguish Japan from her mentors would be the people's physical appearance and such incidentals as diet, art forms, and so on.

The convergence theory has had to be discredited. In recent decades Japan has emerged as an economic superpower. Her basic political structures are in almost every respect comparable to those of Western democracies. Yet in societal terms Japan is different. While in the last decade or so the West has been astonished, indeed frightened, by Japan's successful economic performance, increasingly, albeit reluctantly, the West has also had to come to terms with Japan's no less remarkable social success. In spite of a common economic system, Japan's success, perhaps, lay in the fact that her pattern of social behaviour and relationships had evolved along non-Western lines. As the oil shock seriously shook the Western economies, leading to spiralling unemployment, massive and endemic strikes, a degree of political extremism and violence, Japan weathered the storm. Interest in Japan intensified. In the last two years a significant turnabout has been achieved in that now Japan is being held up as a model for Western societies to emulate. Ezra Vogel illustrated this phenomenon in his publication *Japan as Number One* (1979). Today Western study missions and official delegations arrive at Narita airport as thick as flies in a seemingly unending flow. For the historian, this is an engaging event. One would wish that Japan's Western instructors of the mid/late nineteenth century could be here to witness the scene.

The economic determinism of yesterday, ideological pillar of the convergence theory, has, however, metamorphosed into a radically different phenomenon: that of cultural determinism. Japan, it is argued in many quarters, cannot be emulated for the society that exists is the reflection of a particular culture which cannot be transplanted into a different environment. This perception gives rise to a view of Japanese culture as being static, or at least constant. Claude Lévi-Strauss has recently added his own distinguished voice to this chorus by putting forward the proposition that 'Japan is the only country which has succeeded in modernising without betraying its origins' (*Le Matin Magazine*, 25/26 October, 1980). This note is emphatically discordant with a hitherto far more familiar leitmotiv in regard to Japan, one which began in the mid/late nineteenth century and has only gone into abeyance very recently, namely that Japan had undergone a thorough process of occidentalisation – hence, it was argued, her success. Western perceptions of Japan reflect self-perceptions. The confusion prevalent in the Western hemisphere in this last quarter of the twentieth century prevents Westerners from feeling confident in their own model.

A study of Japan's historical setting, of her prelude to modernity and of society's transformation to modernity should, it would seem, provide a few answers to these problems. First, the opposition between tradition and modernity is a non-tenable proposition so far as Japan's modern history is concerned. Or, to put it another way, the alleged conflict between tradition and modernity in Japan has as much meaning as it would to any society, including advanced Western countries. Secondly, however, the theory that Japan has somehow managed to survive the transition to modernity without altering the basic fabric of her cultural and social values or traditions is not acceptable by any empirical standard. Cultures do change. Japanese social and cultural values have undergone a thorough process of transformation. Japan's modern history is a dialectical process between the economic base and the cultural superstructure. This dialectic is a far more instructive manner of approaching modern Japanese history than seeking to isolate opposing tendencies of tradition and modernity.

The cultural change experienced by Japan was more radical than was the case for Western industrialised societies. The major determining factor here was that of time. Once the new government of Meiji Japan decided to adopt a no-holds-barred programme of intensive modernisation, it was recognised that the efforts necessary to achieve this end would be immense. Japan was far behind; Japan was a late-developer. The industrial revolution in Britain and other Western European countries – Russia's is obviously a different problem and a different model – occurred in a far more evolutionary manner. Japan's was indeed revolutionary. The title of Part 3, 'Transformation to Modernity', therefore, appears appropriate in that Japan in the course of the late nineteenth and early twentieth century was not subjected to a long-term course of medical treatment, but rather underwent a major, and sudden, surgical operation. That the body was able to survive, that the major organs not only remained intact, but indeed fully operative, is due to the strength and resilience which had been developed in the period of Tokugawa incubation. Not only did Japan have roots, she had roots which were well suited for modern growth. This distinguishes Japan from China, from the Persian Empire, from the various component parts of the Ottoman Empire, from the host of Latin American republics, and so on. Major surgical operations, however, inevitably have certain debilitating effects. The operation is traumatic. The imbalance which resulted in the Japanese metabolism was, ultimately, to have tragic consequences.

6 The Challenge of Modernity: The Japanese Response

I

The determinant force in Japan's transformation to modernity was her absorption into the world economy and the international relations which evolved in the course of the latter part of the nineteenth and early twentieth centuries. Japan was wrenched from the quiescence of *sakoku*, even from the comparative tranquillity of the traditional East Asian order, into the turbulence of the European-dominated international setting. In the period 1870 to 1914 there occurred the most significant and momentous changes which the world had ever witnessed.

Western economic development was well fortified by numerous revolutionary advances in science. Scientific supremacy and technological applications in transportation, communication and, of course, armaments led to the continents of Asia, Africa and Latin America being carved up into colonies or spheres of influence by the major Western powers. Europe and the United States expanded in all directions. Traditional peasant economies were either uprooted or made to serve the economic needs and interests of the metropolitan powers: beef from the Argentine, cocoa from Ghana, silk from China were ferried in bulk to Marseille, Liverpool, Rotterdam, New York. In order to secure readier access to sources of raw materials and markets for manufactured goods, greater political, military and financial control was exerted by the industrialised powers over the rest of the world.

Following the Treaty of Vienna internal European peace was maintained for a century, in spite of the occasional hiccup, as in the Crimean and Franco-Prussian wars. European rivalry was projected on to the continents of imperial expansion. While the geography of the non-European world was changing and various degrees of external sovereignty imposed, the balance of power in the West, however, was equally shifting in perceptible fashion. The supremacy of Britain was being challenged economically, militarily and in terms of international influence. The newly unified Germany particularly was accelerating the pace of change and the shift in the centre of gravity.

While this was an age of nationalism and imperialism, it was also an age in which the European political order was being militantly challenged by the dissemination of revolutionary ideas and the resort to means of direct action: socialism, communism, syndicalism, anarchism counted vociferous apostles and an increasing number of disciples. Indeed the prologue to this period was the Commune, its epilogue the October Revolution.

While political orthodoxy was being undermined, so were hitherto accepted social and cultural values. The growth of feminism is one illustration of this phenomenon. While movements such as the suffragettes may have been primarily concerned with achieving political ends, others were concerned with a radical re-evaluation of prevailing European sexual mores. Both birth control and free love were passionately advocated in certain quarters. In the arts radicalism featured prominently. The drama of Henrik Ibsen (1828–1906) evoked contemporary philosophical and social themes in direct challenge to the bourgeois conscience. Claude Monet (1840–1926) launched the school of Impressionism with his painting 'Impression, soleil levant' (1874). The naturalism of Emile Zola (1840–1902) created a powerful genre whose influence spread throughout Europe and beyond. Claude Debussy (1862–1918) caused a furore in musical circles. These new tendencies, to cite only a few of the more obvious examples, illustrated the cultural revolution which Europe was in the process of experiencing – while the gyrations of Isadora Duncan (1878–1927) vividly reflected a mood of hedonistic escapism.

Japan's absorption into the European-dominated world meant that not only was she heavily influenced, indeed motivated to action, by the major economic and imperialistic trends of the time, but she was also subjected to the whole range of Western intellectual, political, social, cultural and sexual contemporary ideas. In the Meiji era (1868–1912) Japan experienced and expressed nationalism and imperialism, but she was also penetrated by socialism, syndicalism, anarchism, feminism; advocates of birth control and free love could also be found in Meiji Japan. All aspects of Japanese culture were deeply impregnated by Western art forms and thought.

The only area in which European influence, albeit present, was not fundamental was religion. There is no doubt that Western missionaries did their best to achieve conversion and it is also true that for a while at least they did strike a responsive chord; ultimately, however, their efforts reaped a meagre harvest. It is perhaps somewhat of an irony that Japan, the most advanced, thus hitherto designated as occidentalised, nation of the modern era, was one of the least christianised countries. There are many reasons for this phenomenon. One, however, refers back to the European scene in the modern age. While on the one hand Pope Pius IX (1792–1878) proclaimed papal infallibility, on the other Europe witnessed the growth and indeed ascendancy of secularism, anti-clericalism and atheism. The power and influence of the established Churches were among the many orthodoxies being undermined in the Europe of the modern age.

Japan's absorption into the modern world, however, was not limited to the West. For the purposes of the period under review here, Africa, Latin America and the Middle East need not figure prominently. Africa, in fact, can be totally ignored. Latin America seemed to provide in certain cases possible areas for Japanese colonisation, in terms of exporting surplus population. While, so far as the Middle East was concerned, and especially Egypt, the Japanese found here a situation which they must endeavour to avoid. It is instructive that as early as the 1870s Japanese government officials were analysing the dangers confronting Japan in relation to the Western powers by making references to developments occurring in that part of the world. Although China was a more obvious negative model, the internationalisation of the official Japanese outlook on world affairs is well illustrated by this phenomenon.

Among the features which radically altered the international landscape in the late nineteenth and twentieth centuries was the emergence of newly industrialised, internationally influential powers. As indicated earlier, Britain's paramountcy, with France in second place, was challenged not only by Germany but also by the United States and Japan. By the early part of the twentieth century Japan had joined the exclusive club of the world powers: Britain, France, Germany, the United States, Russia. Yet while Japan was achieving this exalted status, there was also an ambivalence in her international position – one which, to a degree, has been retained to this day: although Japan came to be with Europe, she was not part of Europe. Japan's ambivalent position in the international setting, namely that of a world power associated with the West in one sense, but situated in East Asia, racially and culturally part of East Asia, created a confusion, indeed a contradiction which gave rise to tensions and frustrations. This ambivalence remained a constant source of perplexity, indeed anxiety, throughout the course of Japan's transformation to modernity. It heavily influenced the direction of Japan's relations both with the Western powers and her East Asian neighbours and indeed had a significant impact on more underlying socio-psychological factors, all of which can perhaps be subsumed under modern Japan's quest for a national identity.

In terms of an understanding of Japan's transformation to modernity it is, therefore, essential that the context of Japan's relations with the West be properly understood. This exercise involves far more than simply economic or diplomatic relations. All of this will be looked at in greater detail in Chapter 9. Here we are not so much interested in the chronological development of these relations as in their more general characteristics. This context must be perceived from two angles: that of the West and that of Japan. While this may appear to be stating the obvious, it is important that the two perspectives be properly appreciated for an understanding of the propelling forces of Japan's transformation to modernity.

In terms of the Japanese perspective, the first point which needs to be stressed is that Japan was obsessed with the West; the West was by no means obsessed with Japan. Indeed, apart from the odd occasion when Japan would temporarily figure prominently on the international scene, as in her wars against China in 1894–5 and against Russia in 1904–5, generally speaking there was only marginal Western interest in Japan. From the start, therefore, there existed a significant imbalance. Japan's obsession with the West operated at different levels. Throughout the period of transformation to modernity what may rather loosely be termed the superiority of the West was recognised by the Japanese. This superiority was clearly manifested in economic, technological, scientific, generally political and military terms and, of course, in the West's predominant position in the world. The West was feared. The Japanese had only to look round them to see what the West was capable of. All of Asia, apart from China and Thailand, was colonised and China was in a Western stranglehold. While Western power and the arrogance which it bred were undoubtedly resented, much of Western civilisation tended to be respected, admired and emulated.

The respect, admiration and desire to emulate were particularly strong in the seventies and eighties. By the nineties, for a variety of reasons, the adulation of the earlier period waned. The national mood was more assertive, more defiant. This was partly due to the fact that by this time Japan after all could boast not insignificant successes on both the economic and military fronts, partly due to the fact that the treaties, especially the more injurious clauses of extra-territoriality, had been revised. A major turning point, however, as will be seen in Chapter 9, was the Triple Intervention of 1895, whereby three Western powers – Russia, Germany and France – ganged up on Japan in order to deprive her of her fruits of victory in the war against China.

In the preceding decades, however, the internal and external policies of the Japanese government were completely dominated by the country's relations with and position *vis-à-vis* the West. In fact, the early part of Japan's transformation to modernity could be written in two words: treaty revision. It is not simply that in order to try to convince the West that Japan was achieving 'civilised status', that is by Western standards, that the whole indigenous jurisprudential system had to be radically overhauled and developed along

Western lines, but that even such innocuous customs as mixed bathing were officially frowned upon in order to cater to Western susceptibilities. As the West played the tune, Japan danced. The fact that it became increasingly apparent that the melody was frequently made to change in order to suit Western tastes not unnaturally led to bitterness.

So far as general European policies and attitudes towards Japan are concerned, a few factors need to be borne in mind. Policies were elaborated, needless to say, by considerations of economic and geopolitical factors. European resistance to treaty revision, for example, was motivated not simply by pig-headedness, but because Europeans perceived that their economic interests were better served by maintaining a relationship based on inequality. The Triple Intervention, so injurious to both Japanese interests and susceptibilities, was determined by geopolitical strategies. The policies of the various Western powers towards Japan were established and developed according to contemporary rationality in the field of international affairs. An addendum to this general proposition is that if Japan perceived the Western powers as a monolithic force, this was not necessarily a misconception.

There were, of course, intense rivalries between the occidental powers. In the Far East, however, all efforts were directed towards minimising these, though in the case of Russia not necessarily successfully. The operative system of Western international relations in the Far East throughout most of the nineteenth century was what was called the Concert of Powers. The intention was that the Western powers should share in a common, reasonably harmonious, exploitation of the opportunities afforded by Far Eastern markets and sources of raw materials. The most-favoured-nation clause was an important instrument devised to achieve this end. Although as the century advanced, European imperialistic rivalries in diverse parts of the world, though initially mainly over the disintegrating Ottoman Empire, came to be reflected in the Far East, it was in fact Japan's defeat of China which shattered the Concert of Powers; it was occasionally resurrected, such as in the allied intervention in China at the time of the Boxer uprising (1900–01) – with, however, Japan as one of the allies – but in real terms it was moribund. Japan's defeat of China (1895), the German-initiated 'slicing of the Chinese melon' (1897–8) – whereby the Western powers appropriated to themselves spheres of influence in China in a manner reminiscent of the earlier partition of Africa – the US victory over Spain and the former's acquisition of the Philippines (1899), the Anglo-Japanese alliance (1902) and the spectacular victory of Japan over Russia (1905) heralded an entirely new age of international relations in the East Asian sector of the globe. Following 1905 the Concert of Powers was until the 1914–18 war briefly reduced to a quartet and, following Germany's exit from the scene, to a trio composed of Japan,

Great Birtain and the United States; that particular age in the history of East Asia came to an end in 1945.

While Western policies towards Japan may have had their own internal logic, based, as has been stated, on economic and geopolitical considerations, there were also other factors, less tangible perhaps but no less important, which were influential in terms of both European actions and Japanese reactions. Among the various 'isms' mentioned earlier in regard to Europe of the late nineteenth/early twentieth centuries another very important one needs to be added: racism. It is of course true that European racism was by no means a feature solely of this period; it is, needless to say, still very much with us today. The point is, however, that racism in this period of European history enjoyed philosophical and scientific respectability. It was a subject about which biologists, ethnologists, anthropologists, philosophers and all manner of literary amateurs did not hesitate to pontificate. On the continent of Europe the major figure was undoubtedly Joseph-Arthur de Gobineau (1816–82), whose four-volume work, *Essai sur l'Inégalité des Races Humaines*, was translated into numerous languages and heavily influenced scores of writers on the subject. In the Anglo-Saxon world the predominant theory of race was found in that rather loose body of doctrine known as Social-Darwinism, namely the application of Darwin's biological theories to ethnology and anthropology, with as its most articulate and prolific exponent Herbert Spencer (1820–1903).

The use of the term 'racism', however, implies a degree of ideological conformity which was markedly not in evidence. Rather, perhaps, one should speak of 'racisms'. For while racial theories ran rampant throughout the West, there were not just a few self-contradictory elements in this particular period piece. For the purposes of Japanese history only two need to be noted. On the one hand, social theories derived from Darwinism postulated that the inferior species were doomed either, in an extreme case, to extinction, or, alternatively, to a perpetual status of absolute inferiority. The races were inherently unequal. Nothing could be done to alter this situation, or indeed this truism. On the other hand, consciousness of the European's superiority dictated in some quarters a responsibility for educating, and elevating to the standards at least approximating those of the West, the inferior peoples. There was, therefore, a paternalistic quality evident in a great deal of Euopean rhetoric and indeed policy. This applied mainly to Christian missionaries. The sense of a civilising mission, of the proverbial white man's burden, however, was by no means exclusively limited to missionaries, but motivated many men and women of diverse persuasions to bring enlightenment to the unenlightened. In her period of transformation to modernity, especially the early decades following the revolution of 1868, Japan by no means lacked advice from these do-gooders. These Europeans, however, whether Christian or atheist, with very few exceptions, never questioned, indeed accepted as axiomatic, the inherent and eternal superiority of the West. A paternalistic attitude necessarily implies that others are perceived as children. Herein lies a second contradiction of European racism, dramatically visible as it was projected on to Japan in the early part of the twentieth century. That is, while the non-European races were held to be inferior, once they did manage to challenge, indeed contradict, this proposition, then they became threatening. In the course of her transformation to modernity, especially when a measure of success, on both economic and military fronts, was at hand, Japan became the victim of European racial discrimination.

Racism as an important element in modern Japanese history cannot be underestimated. As Japan was increasingly opened to the West, as contacts between Japanese and Europeans, both in Japan and in Europe, as Japanese officials, the press, and hence the populace, came to a greater appreciation of the nature and motivations and underlying tenets of Western policy, the Japanese became not only aware, but indeed acutely conscious of European racism.

While realisation of this phenomenon and resentment against it began developing in the course of the earlier decades, the crunch undoubtedly came with the Triple Intervention of 1895. The national mood changed. The conversion of hitherto pro-Western ideologies from liberalism to social-Darwinism, in certain cases *à outrance*, is testimony of the Japanese reaction to Western racism. Japanese people came to accept the principles of the struggle of survival, something which only the fittest would achieve. In spite of numerous vagaries in the course of subsequent Japanese political, social and cultural history, this perception, indeed obsession, of a potential racial conflict certain to be translated into actuality in the future remained a significant and increasingly loud leitmotiv in the ensuing decades of the twentieth century. Counter-factual speculation is not a particularly fruitful exercise. In all probability, however, the course of modern Japanese political and military history would have been substantially different had the Japanese not been repeatedly faced with, and humiliated by, European racist barriers. Western racism has a lot to answer for; its eradication is perhaps the greatest challenge in this twilight of the twentieth century.

Having noted this leitmotiv of Western racism and Japanese consciousness of and reaction to it, it should be made clear that by no means was it the only theme in Japan's transformation to modernity. Similarly, while Japanese nationalism developed, and indeed was fuelled by success, atavistic xenophobia remained in certain quarters, but very much in the background. Japanese reaction towards the West tended to be positive in that throughout the period of transformation the West continued to be perceived as a model which should be emulated, not necessarily in lock-stock-and-barrel fashion, but by careful selection and adaptation, though that too frequently proceeded on a trial and error basis.

II

Earlier it was stated that Japan's transformation to modernity took place under Western domination. The question which may be asked is: what does this mean? Alternatively, what was the role of the West in the course of Japan's modernisation? First, as was made clear in the former chapter, the West was initially perceived above all else as a menace – a menace to Japanese sovereignty. This perception induced fear, and fear concentrates the mind. In that sense the West acted as a catalyst. Political and administrative centralisation, military modernisation, concentration and rationalisation of the means of production, the widespread diffusion of literacy and numeracy by means of a national education system, scientific research, importation and integration of modern technology in the mode of production, broadening of the national intellectual horizon, were all policies or pursuits embarked upon out of a sense of necessity, indeed urgency, in the face of the Western peril. All of these measures were implemented with a reasonable degree of success and ultimately popular approval because of the rising tide of Japanese nationalism. Japanese nationalism, generally credited with providing the motive force of modernisation, was the offspring of the Western challenge. The roots, as seen in earlier sections, were there; the West provided the impetus to grow.

In the manner described above, the role of the West can be defined as impersonal and indirect. Japan's transformation, however, also occurred under more direct Western tutelage. On the part of the Japanese there was undoubtedly a strong desire that their society should be transformed to the extent of reaching Western standards. Desire, however, albeit representing a great deal, was not everything; the necessary extra input was the material wherewithal.

Capital is one obvious, indeed essential, element in the recipe for modern transformation. The Japanese case in terms of industrialisation and foreign investment of capital is generally presented as exceptional in that Japan is credited with having been successful in generating her own capital; in other words she was not dependent on foreign loans. This is not an altogether acceptable view of Japanese economic development. A certain chronological sequence must be borne in mind. In the period covering roughly the three decades following the 1868 revolution, no foreign loan capital was imported into Japan with the exception of five million yen borrowed from Britain in 1871 in order to construct the railway between Tokyo and Yokohama. This was a track of some eighteen miles; the fact that two decades later railway track mileage had expanded more than a hundred times is an indication of what the Japanese were capable of doing without foreign capital investment – and certainly a stark contrast with the situation in China (and in Russia for that matter) where railway construction was almost exclusively financed by foreign capital. In so far as these decades are concerned, however, three factors need to be borne in mind. First, Japan was not a particularly attractive market to Western financiers; China was much more interesting and perceived as far more lucrative. Secondly, the Japanese government's decision not to depend on foreign capital was taken mainly for political, rather than economic, reasons. As has been repeatedly pointed out, the Japanese were not only acutely conscious of what was happening in China in terms of spiralling foreign indebtedness, but more than dimly aware of comparable developments in places such as Egypt and Turkey. Thirdly, however, a good deal of Japanese initial industrial capital was fiduciary. For that reason, among others, although industrialisation was undoubtedly taking place and proceeding at an accelerating pace, its fiscal foundations were far from sound.

Japan's take-off into sustained modern economic growth occurred in the final years of the nineteenth century and the first decade or so of the twentieth. It was precisely during this period that external capital flowed into Japan. A good deal of it, admittedly, came from China; the reparations imposed following the victory of 1895 and the Japanese share of the Boxer indemnity provided a welcome fillip to industrial development and the further laying of the social infrastructure necessary for industrialisation – for example, part of the Boxer settlement was invested in education. At the same time, however, Western capital began pouring into Japan. The Japanese government required external funds in order to pursue military ventures, particularly against Russia. The country's obvious economic success and viability made it a more attractive market for Western financial investment. Similarly, from the Japanese government's viewpoint, the country's military and diplomatic (thanks to the Anglo-Japanese Alliance) security of the early twentieth century meant that borrowing from the West involved far fewer risks than had been the case when Japan was in a more vulnerable position. Foreign capital, therefore, undoubtedly played a significant role; indeed as the First World War broke out foreign capital represented a quarter of the country's GNP. The importation of foreign capital is one thing, the intelligent absorption and application of it is a different matter; in the latter sense, the Japanese were eminently skilful in a way that the Argentines, the Brazilians, the Egyptians, the Chinese were not.

Another vital element of the material wherewithal for industrialisation was modern technology. Throughout the period of transformation, and indeed until recently, Japan was almost totally dependent on Western technology. All industrialising societies, not excluding Britain, have depended on imports of foreign technology. Between the various Western European countries and the United States, however, there was a greater degree of reciprocity in terms of exchange of inventions. Also, migration patterns within the Western hemisphere disguised the degree of foreign dependence, thereby giving an impression of greater national self-reliance. It remains the case, however, that throughout her period of transformation to modernity Japan was a beneficiary rather than a benefactor of major scientific and technological inventions.

This phenomenon can be explained by a number of factors. First, there is the element here of the latecomer, perforce reliant on the pioneering efforts and advances of others. Secondly, Japan's geographical situation must be borne in mind. In Western Europe not only was there a tradition of scientific enquiry which had existed for centuries, but the short geographical distances and close intellectual affinities between the centres of learning and those who were actively engaged in the pursuit of knowledge provided a European-wide atmosphere conducive to fruitful research. This atmosphere was completely lacking in East Asia. Thirdly, in spite of significant advances when compared to other non-European societies, Japan remained, as has already occasionally been pointed out but needs to be frequently emphasised, backward by comparison with Western Europe and the United States. In adopting an ambitious policy of modernisation, the Japanese government was in effect attempting a great leap forward. Emphasis had to be placed on a rapid achievement of ends rather than in a patient pursuit of causes.

A third prerequisite in terms of material wherewithal for industrialisation was that of expertise. It is undoubtedly here that Japan's initiatives are the most impressive. By the end of the century the country possessed a highly capable, efficient, modern élite. Japanese medical doctors, professors of the various disciplines, school teachers, technicians and scientists, foremen of skilled workers, bureaucrats, army and navy officers, industrial managers and financiers provided the high-quality human resources necessary for the country's development and self-reliance. This, needless to say, did not occur overnight. Here again the debt to the West was substantial. While a trickle of Japanese had gone abroad to study in the *bakumatsu* period, following 1868 this temporary academic migration to the West assumed the proportion of a steady flow – never that of a flood, emphasis generally being placed more on the quality of the expatriate students rather than the quantity. Also, whereas, as we have seen in the former chapter, the bakufu had inaugurated the policy of importing Western expertise, the Meiji government not only continued, but indeed significantly increased, the allocation of national revenue to this (expensive) exercise. Experts were invited mainly from Britain, Germany, France and the United States, but also from other countries, such as the

Netherlands, Italy, Switzerland, Belgium, Russia, Sweden, Austria, Canada, and so forth. Throughout the first two decades of the Meiji era there was an average of approximately one thousand Western experts per annum engaged either by the government or by the private sector. While the emphasis was not unnaturally placed in areas of greatest national relevance in terms of industrial and military development, even more erudite activities such as painting and music were not deprived of foreign tutelage.

On the surface Western nations would appear to have been most generous in terms of provision of expertise. Both on the part of the governments and the individuals concerned there undoubtedly was a certain element of altruism. This motivation was very much in keeping with the consciousness of Europe's civilising mission mentioned above. This in turn – as is made clear from the memoirs of those foreign experts who chose to bequeath their thoughts to contemporaries and posterity – provided those individuals with a sense of moral self-satisfaction. They were, after all, not only providing enlightenment but were also highly respected, indeed flattered, for doing so. In Europe their intellectual capacities would not necessarily gain the degree of recognition and admiration that they were able to command in Japan. These comments should not be interpreted as belittling the qualities of the individuals concerned; there were inevitably a number of charlatans, of self-seekers, but there were also many men of integrity and dedication, indeed a few of whom associated themselves strongly with Japan's endeavours at modernisation and obtaining respectability in Western eyes, including, for example, advocating the revision of the treaties. To paraphrase Cecil Rhodes, however, while altruism may be fine, altruism plus 5 per cent is even better. There was also a not insignificant financial incentive. As far as the individual Western experts were concerned, they were very handsomely paid. For the governments the provision of expertise also had economic implications in that it was hoped that the Japanese would purchase capital goods and technology from the countries of origin of the experts.

As was indicated in the case of the importation of foreign capital, similarly in that of foreign expertise, it is not the importation which is significant, but the use made of it. Japan succeeded in forming an indigenous élite capable of leading and sustaining the country's progress to modernisation in a manner of which the Argentinians, Brazilians, Egyptians, Turks, Siamese and Chinese were incapable. Why?

It cannot be the purpose here to analyse the problems which the various nations listed above encountered in terms of creating a modern indigenous élite. Certain features specific to the Japanese experience, however, should serve the purpose of indicating those contrasts which did exist. Perhaps the most fundamental element is that in the new society which began emerging in the course of the first decade or so following 1868 there were no major contending élites in Japan. In other words, certainly by the early 1880s, the élite was almost entirely composed of the modern sectors of society: the bureaucrats staffing the new ministries, military officers, the liberal professions, managers of industry, financiers, scientists. Increasingly in the course of the period of transformation, a common element among all these components of the élite was that they had obtained a modern, Western-inspired education. Japan, in spite of being a late developer, nevertheless quite quickly entered into at least an embryonic form of the age of the technocrat. In the early period of transformation, Japanese landlords provided a local élite, not a national one. This situation changed, much to the country's detriment, but the important point to note for the present is that in this initial spurt towards modernisation the élite was concentrated, reasonably homogeneous, educated and modern-orientated. In most other societies, including those mentioned above, the élite was still closely associated with and indeed derived from the possession of land and/or religious station: bishops and latifundists in Latin America, nawabs and mullahs in the Ottoman empire, the Confucianist Chinese scholar–gentry, all retained privileged and highly influential positions in all domains of society for which there were no Japanese counterparts. There were progressive doctors of medicine, skilled scientists, modern military officers – *hic nascent* the Young Turks – etc., in all of these countries, but their status was inferior to traditional élites and in many cases their livelihood insecure. Japan is not rich in natural resources, nor, as we have seen, was she endowed with capital at this stage of her history. Her economic development had a great deal to do with the skilful exploitation of the capital she had at her disposal or that she fabricated. Workers and peasants, as will be seen in the following chapter, were exploited; the former provided cheap labour, the latter a high percentage of government revenue in the form of taxes. The élite, on the other hand, tended to be well remunerated. Narrow national income differentials, a prominent and indeed highly admirable feature of contemporary Japan, represent a very recent development. Material incentives, therefore, undoubtedly played a significant role among Japan's modern élite.

For all that, however, and again in stark contrast with the other societies mentioned above, it is the comparative absence of conspicuous consumption among the Japanese élite that represents a marked feature of this period of transformation to modernity. Profits and savings were reinvested into production. The samurai ethic of frugality may have had something to do with this, but that particular proposition should not be pushed too far; there cannot be many 'ethics' which actually encourage profligacy. The behaviour of the Japanese élite can be attributed – even if it cannot be satisfactorily explained – to the national atmosphere, however intangible such variables may be, one which in the early stages of modernisation was expressive of a national will to achieve ambitious ends irrespective of the sacrifices. In terms of motivation, therefore, once again, one turns to nationalism, but a nationalism which encapsulated a high degree of determination and singularity of purpose among the élite; that element was lacking in the other would-be modernising nations.

III

The remainder of this book will assess the developments which occurred in the course of Japan's transformation to modernity. These will be presented, as in the preceding section, along thematic lines: social developments, politics, and finally the origins, nature and impact of the Japanese empire. While these themes have been separately identified for analytical purposes, it goes without saying that they must not be seen in isolation. The nature of the exercise inevitably involves a degree of arbitrariness. By proceeding in this manner, however, it is hoped that some of the aspects of the transformation to modernity will be penetrated more deeply. Delimitation of the dates of the transformation to modernity is also somewhat arbitrary. While the general period under consideration corresponds on the whole to the years of the reign of the Meiji tenno, no specific dates are too closely adhered to. The purpose of the remaining section of this book is to identify major trends; these cannot be too narrowly circumscribed by exact chronology.

It would appear appropriate at the outset to clear up a few possible misunderstandings regarding the nature of the transformation under study. While the period 1868–1912 is referred to as the Meiji era, it should be stressed from the start that the actual individual tenno had little direct impact on the process of transformation. At the time that he was 'restored' to power the tenno was fifteen years old. The new post-1868 leadership at the time of the Restoration and in the ensuing decades placed great emphasis on the alleged historical and sacrosanct tradition of imperial rule. This was, however, mainly a device for ensuring that the government's policies, and indeed the government itself, would receive the degree of legitimacy which the bakufu in its final reforming stages had failed to achieve. This is not necessarily to say that the tenno should be perceived as no more than a cardboard figure, a puppet adroitly moved upon the national political stage; he undoubtedly had his views, his personality, and his influence in certain areas was not altogether negligible. In historical terms, however, the Meiji tenno should most definitely not be presented as an enlightened monarchic despot. In fact, albeit accepting that these things are difficult to measure, it would nevertheless appear reasonably accurate to state that the sacrosanct Meiji tenno had less influence on the affairs of state than the constitutional monarchs Queen Victoria (1819–1901) or Edward VII (1841–1910).

It would also seem appropriate at this stage to define more specifically what is meant by the 'new leadership'. As far as the control of the reins of government is concerned, throughout most of the period of transformation these tended to be concentrated in the hands of what came to be termed the 'Sat-Cho oligarchy'. The revolution of 1868, as has been seen, was carried out mainly by the sons of the Satsuma and Choshu fiefs. When they assumed power they were, for the most part, young men. While a major split occurred in 1873 and a brief civil war erupted in 1877, originating from disenchanted elements of Satsuma, by the mid-seventies the government contained a unity of purpose and vision. The leaders were determined to see their programme through. This monopoly of power was resented by the sons of other fiefs. To that extent, han particularism did survive into modern Japan. By the end of the period of transformation, however, although vestiges of han particularism were still visible – notably, for example, in the armed services – this was nevertheless a phenomenon nearing extinction.

While throughout most of the Meiji period the Sat-Cho government not only held the reins of power, but indeed kept a tight grip on them, nevertheless there emerged in the course of the decades of transformation what can be termed the ruling classes: it was these who ultimately inherited the power to govern. It is in this context that another important matter of some ambiguity should be cleared up. In the course of the decades following 1868 many of the new élite in most sectors of society – entrepreneurs, army officers, bureaucrats, intellectuals, etc. – either came from or claimed samurai background. Undoubtedly samurai status still conveyed a degree of social prestige. Also, it is no doubt the case, as was seen in Chapter 3, that many samurai had received a good preparation for leadership roles. The samurai ethic of public service provided an ideological stimulus to national enterprise. While all this is important, it should not be exaggerated. Indeed one of the aspects of Japan's passage to modernity is that a significant social transformation occurred. While the new national ethic derived from samurai ideology, actual samurai status as such was of little significance. Belonging to a samurai family in late-nineteenth–early-nineteenth-century Japan had less social significance than being able to prefix one's name with a 'de' in France or 'von' in Germany. For one thing, apart from major daimyo families, it was more difficult to distinguish a samurai simply by name from the ordinary mortals. Although one's registration papers made a distinction between *shizoku* (samurai background), *heimin* (commoner, namely the three lower rungs of the Edo social ladder) and *shin-heimin* (new commoners, mainly *eta*), the new government had decreed early on that henceforth all Japanese citizens should possess a surname; for the most part there was not much in a Japanese name that could indicate social origins. Another important facet of the social transformation of Meiji Japan is that while some samurai undoubtedly enjoyed successful careers in the new society, many others faded away – albeit in some cases rather noisily. Similarly, as will be seen, education increasingly became the determinant factor in social mobility: it was far more prestigious and far more influential in terms of career prospects to be a graduate of Tokyo Imperial University, irrespective of social background, than to be able to claim that one's grandfather was of a distinguished samurai family. For these reasons, not too much should be made of the alleged role of the samurai. It seems preferable to refer simply to a new élite, or the ruling classes, accepting that in the period of social turmoil which existed in post-1868 Japan these tended to be derived from various social backgrounds. Their backgrounds were less important than the activities they engaged in and the values they espoused.

While the new élite may have been motivated to achieving impressive national ambitions and society may have been concurrently transformed, at least to a degree, nevertheless both the causation of the transformation to modernity and the sole reliable index for success can only be gauged by economic performance. In economic terms, therefore, what is meant by Japan's transformation to modernity?

So far as demographic factors are concerned, Japan's population increased substantially: from an estimated thirty million at the time of the revolution, by the 1914–18 war it had surpassed fifty million. This, in turn, indicates that the Japanese were capable of feeding themselves, either by domestic production or imports – in fact, by 1894 and for the ensuing decades up to the end of the Second World War Japan was a net importer of rice.

A factor which will be stressed in greater detail in the following chapter, but which needs to be mentioned from the start, however, is that Japan's transformation to modernity did not result in a dramatic redistribution of the population. Industrialisation took place within an overwhelmingly agrarian context. Thus, at the dawn of the twentieth century, while approximately 10 per cent of the population can be defined as urban (namely, living in units of 100,000 or more), 80 per cent continued to be villagers living in units of 10,000 or less. In terms of the distribution of the working population, the following pattern emerges: 1872: primary sector – 85 per cent, secondary – 5 per cent, tertiary – 8 per cent; 1895: primary – 73·5 per cent, secondary – 11·5 per cent, tertiary – 13 per cent; 1913: primary – 62 per cent, secondary – 17 per cent, tertiary – 18·5 per cent. The point to be stressed here, however, is that while there is a relative decline in the primary sector and a corresponding increase in the secondary and tertiary, in absolute terms the primary sector experienced a significant increase. In other words, in the years 1872–1913 the overall population had increased by more than 50 per cent, a figure far greater than the rise in the secondary and tertiary sectors. Furthermore, throughout the period of transformation the percentage of the population in the manufacturing sector was overwhelmingly (never falling below 80 per cent) in textiles and other light industries. Many of these industries were situated not in the major urban centres, but scattered in provincial towns.

Japan's transformation, therefore, included all the characteristics of a dual economy: on the one hand a relatively backward, over-populated, labour-intensive agrarian sector, and on the other an advanced, capital-intensive urban industrial sector. It should be noted that this remained a constant pattern in modern Japan until recently. In 1950 approximately half the population still lived in villages of less than 10,000 population, while the industrial distribution of the labour force consisted of about 50 per cent in the primary sector, 20 per cent in the secondary and 30 per cent in the tertiary. Japan's second industrial and social revolution is not much more than a quarter-century old.

Japan, therefore, remained essentially a nation of peasants. In terms of economic development, however, other indices indicate the degree to which industrialisation was occurring. In the period 1870–1914, among the major industrial powers – the UK, Germany, France, the USA and Japan – Japan's annual rate of growth was second only to that of the United States. In terms of transport, the increase in railway track mileage has already been noted, while a similar spectacular development was witnessed in the gross tonnage of steamships; iron, steel and coal production, and shipbuilding were other areas which experienced prodigious increases in output. Not only the volume, but especially the structure of the import–export trade further indicate the changing nature of Japan's position in the international economy. While in the first couple of decades of the Meiji period just under half of Japan's import trade consisted of finished manufactured goods, by the end of the period these represented less than a quarter; in terms of exports, in the initial stages about 50 per cent were raw materials (including foodstuff), decreasing to 20 per cent by the first decade of the twentieth century, while exports of finished manufactured goods rose from 2 per cent in the early 1870s to over 30 per cent by the time the Meiji tenno died. While Japan was absorbed into the world economy, therefore, she emerged not simply as a client to the major industrial powers, but indeed as a major competitor.

IV

In 1872 there were eighteen miles of railway track. This was a line between

Tokyo and Yokohama. Its opening was a major historical event. The twenty-year-old tenno presided over the ceremony, attired in traditional (and highly cumbersome) court dress – it was only later that he was to take to Western-style military uniforms. The occasion marked a truly innovative step in Japan's direction towards progress. In his sixtieth year the tenno died. Japan then possessed some seven thousand miles of railway track. In 1872 the Iwakura mission was putting out a few tentative feelers, which were brusquely rebuffed, in Western capitals regarding the possibility of revising the treaties. While the official Japanese embassy, yet again exotically dressed, caused a certain amount of excited curiosity – indeed its passage through New York moved Walt Whitman (1819–92) to compose a poem on the occasion, 'A Broadway Pageant' – once the parade was over, little significance was attached to the event. In 1902 Japan became Britain's partner in a military alliance of equals. In 1868 the political fate of Japan still seemed to reside in the hands of excitable, two-sworded samurai, rushing about and hacking opponents to pieces with impunity. By the last decade of the nineteenth century, Japan was endowed with a constitution, a parliament, a limited franchise, parties and other modern political paraphernalia. In every respect, therefore, this period is one of rapid, substantial and perceptible change. While it may have been felt more in certain quarters than in others, for example in the urban as opposed to the rural sectors, nevertheless the whole nation was engulfed in what amounted to a near national metamorphosis. Before proceeding to the more thematic considerations, therefore, a rapid chronological overview, indicating *en route* the major landmarks, should prove useful.

The coalition which came to power in 1868 consisted of samurai mainly from the Satsuma and Choshu han, along with representatives from Tosa and Hizen – two other fiefs whose sons had figured prominently in the events leading up to 1868 – and a sprinkling of *kuge*. They established themselves in Edo and took over the bakufu's administration and offices. Edo was renamed Tokyo. This change in nomenclature entailed a symbolic significance: traditionally the two major centres of East Asian civilisation were associated with the cities of Peking and Nanking, the former meaning capital of the north, the latter capital of the south, while Tokyo, capital of the east, was indicative of the new leadership's determination to create a new centre of civilisation. Since the establishment of the shogunal system in the twelfth century, whereas the bakufu might establish its quarters on the eastern seaboard, for example, Kamakura or Edo, the imperial family never left its precincts in Kyoto. One of the first acts of the new government was to have the tenno move from Kyoto to Tokyo – a shock to Kyotoites from which they have yet to recover. The tenno's move was also symbolic, in that it served to illustrate the fiction that temporal power, namely the administration of the affairs of state, was being restored to him.

The new leaders were young men, generally in their early/mid thirties, the doyen of the group, the *kuge* Iwakura Tomomi (1825–83) being only forty-three at the time of the revolution. Some had already been to the West, most had been involved at some stage of their career in Western studies. Satsuma and Choshu, as noted in the preceding chapter, were the only han to have had direct experience of the might of Western arms. While they by no means, at this stage, possessed a blueprint for achieving their ends of modernisation, there were certain immediate imperatives which they recognised.

The issue of greatest priority was to destroy the horizontal barriers to modernising the Japanese nation-state. The establishment of both the tenno and his government to Tokyo was the first step towards the urgent policy of centralisation. And indeed it can be noted here that although, as pointed out earlier, residual han particularism lingered on among the government throughout most of the Meiji period, namely in the so-called Sat-Cho oligarchy, this form of fief favouritism only included a narrow circle of the élite and did not extend to the territories of the former han or their inhabitants. The former area of Satsuma, for example, became one of the poorest regions of Japan and remains so to this day. The crisis facing Japan permitted no sentimental regional patriotism. It was essential that a national policy be devised and that all affairs of state be orchestrated by the central government. Kido Koin (1833–77) took the initiative in instituting the policy of *hanseki-hokan* (return of the land and the people to the tenno). In 1869 the daimyo of Satsuma, Choshu, Hizen and Tosa were persuaded to set the example by petitioning the tenno to accept their territories. The other daimyo followed suit; the han were replaced by prefectures in 1871. While the daimyo were initially granted the right to continue administering their former domains in collaboration with the government, they were soon replaced by governors appointed by Tokyo. A logical concurrent step, which the government undertook, was to centralise the country's finances; thus the land tax, hitherto payable to the han treasuries, was reformed and collected by Tokyo. Administratively and fiscally, therefore, within a very short time following 1868 the horizontal barriers were removed and Japan was centralised.

Another urgent step which the government needed to take was to remove the vertical barriers to modernity, namely to dismantle the *shi-no-ko-sho* social system. On the one hand men of talent (*jinzai*) should be recruited to serve the nation irrespective of their social background. On the other hand, just as the leadership wished that the subjects of the tenno should think of themselves as united in one nation, rather than disunited among so many han, so too should they think of themselves not as samurai, peasants, artisans or merchants, but as Japanese whose duty it was to serve the tenno and ensure the prosperity and greater glory of the nation. A great national effort was called for; geographic and social solidarity were a vital prerequisite for success. Reforms were also introduced to that end, the two major ones being the enactment of universal compulsory primary education and universal military conscription for men, promulgated in 1872 and 1873 respectively. It should be clear that these pronouncements were an expression of intent, not a reality capable of being implemented overnight. In the early 1870s the Japanese treasury did not have the resources necessary for educating every boy and girl even for only the three years initially involved, nor could it support a standing army of all able-bodied youths. There were also problems of human resources, an officer corps to train recruits and a teaching staff to instruct school pupils were not available in sufficient numbers, as well as material obstacles, barracks and school buildings, for example. While these laws represented an ideal, it remains the case that the ideal was pursued and ultimately crowned with success.

The new leaders, as we have seen, did not hesitate to betray their territorial origins. Nor did they show any significant reluctance to be disloyal to their social origins. The successive reforms resulted in the samurai's status being repeatedly undermined. With the *hanseki-hokan* they lost their fealty. The stipends they had been accustomed to receiving from their daimyo were now allocated by the Tokyo government. This was, however, an expensive proposition. In 1876 the samurai found that their stipends were being commuted: instead of being guaranteed a regular income they were given a lump sum; this they were encouraged to invest or deposit in the newly created banks, the intention being to help the samurai accomplish the difficult task of transforming themselves into capitalists. As their economic base was undermined, so were their social privileges under siege. From the leadership's perspective the samurai, in terms of their traditional patterns of behaviour, their exuberant indiscipline, and indeed their physical appearance, were not only an anachronism in the age of modernity, but indeed a source of embarrassment *vis-à-vis* the Western community which the government wished to impress by their civilisation, rather than amuse by their exoticism. For centuries the samurai had been taught to be proud; they were now being ridiculed, accused of being relics of a bygone age. The meanest blow was the conscription of peasants. This and other petty provocations – for example, their being discouraged to continue parading with their two swords, while encouraged to adopt a Western-style haircut – not unnaturally inflamed the passions of the noble warriors and moved them to anger.

In the short term, therefore, 1868 perhaps created more problems than were solved. There were two exacerbating factors. First, pre-1868 restorationist rhetoric had been very vague in terms of the social settlement which was envisaged. A loose federation of the han under the titular reign of the tenno was perhaps what was generally expected. Nor, needless to say, did the samurai ever conceive in the pre-1868 period that the settlement would involve their demise.

Shortly after the new government was installed, in March 1868, the *Go-kajo no Seimon* (Imperial Charter Oath of Five Articles) was issued. This document stipulated that henceforward (1) matters of state would be deliberated by a wide council, (2) high and low would be of one heart in carrying out national policy, (3) merchants and peasants would achieve their ambitions, (4) uncivilised customs of the past would be abandoned, and (5) knowledge would be sought throughout the world in order to enhance imperial policy. In subsequent years the document was to be often cited, especially by opponents of the government, as a blueprint for democratisation. Historians have also generally accorded it a liberal interpretation. It can, however, be read in different ways. Thus, article 1 could simply be read to indicate that in contrast to the practice of the bakufu whereby only the daimyo related or allied to the house of Tokugawa were involved in the council of the realm, henceforth all daimyo would be called upon to voice their opinion. In fact, the first draft had specifically referred to a *rekko kaigi*, a council of the feudal lords, and in 1869 the government established the *Kogisho*, a deliberative body, to which each daimyo or his appointee was entitled to a seat. Article 2 was not read as a Japanese variant on a mass egalitarian theme, but rather that within the samurai estate distinctions between upper and lower would cease when it came to securing offices. Similarly, article 3 can simply be read in terms of merchants and peasants being entitled to carry out their activities as merchants and peasants without having to suffer from restrictive practices; in other words peasants, for example, should be entitled to buy and sell land. The uncivilised customs referred to in article 4 were interpreted as relating to the policy of *sakoku*. Article 5 not only endorsed this view but also served to indicate that the West might well be seen as a possible model to emulate in order to strengthen the nation. *A priori*, therefore, there was nothing in the *Go-kajo no Seimon* of a nature to worry the samurai estate unduly.

The second factor was that the government wished at all possible cost to avoid foreign complications, namely interference in domestic affairs. It must be stressed that 1868 was perceived by its leaders as a national revolution, not a social revolution. That a social revolution occurred in its wake was a consequence of this major transformation carried out from above, not a cause espoused in ideological terms. The feudal order was being dismantled not for ideological purposes, but for highly practical ones. If the driving ambition of the leadership was to strengthen the nation, obviously all internal turmoil should be minimised for that could only serve to weaken the nation.

Confrontation, however, was inevitable. The trigger mechanism was provided by the *seikan-ron*, the debate over whether to conquer Korea. Korea, it will be recalled, was an integral part of the Chinese tributary state system. In theory, therefore, Korea's foreign affairs were administered by Peking. At the same time, however, commercial relations between Korea and Japan had been traditionally handled by the So han of the island of Tsushima. With the abolition of the han and the establishment of a central government in control of both domestic and foreign affairs, Tokyo wished to bring the traditional system to an end and enter into direct relations with Korea. Japanese overtures were rebuffed by Seoul. First, the Korean government insisted, all matters relating to external affairs should be referred to Peking; secondly, the proposed treaty was unacceptable in that the Japanese monarch was referred to as 'emperor', while it was in the East Asian order of things that there was only one 'emperor', namely the occupant of the Chinese throne; thirdly, Japan was held in contempt for her flirtation with the West and her unseemly espousal of occidental ways. The traditional arrangement, Seoul insisted, should be retained. Japan had been insulted. Or at least so it was alleged by the more ardent members of the government; Saigo Takamori became the passionate spokesman in favour of punishing Korea, a position which further enhanced his charismatic prestige. In 1873 the pro-war faction seemed to have won the day and the decision to go to war was adopted by the government.

In the meantime, however, the greatest turning point in early Meiji history was in the process of taking place. From late 1871 to 1873 Iwakura Tomomi presided over an imposing official delegation abroad. Iwakura and his entourage visited the United States and most European countries. Western capitalism was reaching its apogee. While Iwakura and his close assistants were mainly involved in negotiations with the different foreign ministries, the rest of the entourage, totalling approximately fifty, were absorbed in studying as many facets of the Western countries as possible: political institutions, legal structures and codes, matters relating to trade, finance and industry, schools, churches, hospitals. Japan, the mission realised, was very far behind indeed. The dream of *fukoku-kyohei*, 'rich country – strong army' had perhaps never appeared so illusory. Nevertheless, Iwakura and his retinue were convinced of one absolute priority facing the government. If the country was to develop modern industry, build up a strong army and achieve a status of equality with the Western powers by way of treaty revision, then all efforts should be concentrated on internal reform. Japan, in this perspective, could afford neither the energy, the funds, nor the time to engage in foreign ventures.

In terms of establishing priorities and developing the means to see them through, the year 1873 can perhaps be said to mark the first chapter of Japan's transformation to modernity, 1868 having served as a prologue. The problem, however, was that the priorities espoused by Iwakura and others of his group, notably Okubo Toshimichi (1832–78), Kido Koin (1833–77) and Ito Hirobumi (1841–1909), were fundamentally opposed to those harboured by Saigo and his sympathisers. Upon the return of the Iwakura mission, both sides held on to their positions with intransigence. While the decision to attack Korea was rescinded, compromise was clearly no longer possible. The crunch had come. Saigo, along with a number of other eminent 1868 veterans, including Itagaki Taisuke (1837–1919), Eto Shinpei (1835–74), Goto Shojiro (1837–97), and Soejima Taneomi (1828–1905), resigned from the government.

The political consequences of the split over the *seikan-ron* will be further investigated in Chapter 8. One may pause here simply to indicate that in the immediate aftermath of this incident the government was faced with a number of armed uprisings from dissident samurai; these culminated in the Satsuma revolt of 1877. The latter was suppressed and Saigo died. While, as will be seen, the government was by no means rid of political opposition, following 1877 no concerted armed confrontation against the state occurred. Violence continued, but this took the form of occasional sporadic terrorist attacks generally directed towards some particularly unpopular government leader. The point to emphasise here is that by 1877 the new Meiji state was secure.

With samurai revolts suppressed and the government's authority well established and recognised, in the ensuing decade the process of constructing a modern national edifice was pursued by the government with vigour. And during that period the government practically monopolised all affairs of state. Not only was administration firmly under its control, not only were the reforms which were implemented emanating from government policy, but the economy itself and most of the country's major industries were both financed and managed by the government. While the years up to 1877 were ones primarily concerned with the consolidation of power, the next decade was one of construction, whereby the foundations of the modern edifice were put into place: politically, socially, economically and militarily.

In 1881 the government announced, partly as a result of popular political pressure, that a constitution would be promulgated before the end of the decade; the Peace Preservation Ordinance of 1883, however, sought to make it abundantly clear that political developments were to take place on the government's own terms. In 1886 Mori Arinori (1847–89), as Minister of Education, completely reorganised and redirected the country's system of education; measures were adopted to secure tight central control of education and to make certain that especially at the primary level the syllabus should include a heavy dose of nationalistic indoctrination. Matsukata Masayoshi (1835–1924) carried out a number of major fiscal reforms, including in 1882 the creation of the Bank of Japan (partly modelled on the Bank of England) in order that the state should retain monetary control over the nation's economic affairs. Also in the early and mid eighties, Yamagata Aritomo (1838–1922), 'father' of the modern Japanese army, took measures to ensure that the military were fully committed to the government's policy and the tenno-ist ideology which it claimed to uphold; this was most visible in the Imperial Rescript to Soldiers and Sailors issued in 1882. Finally, although the government was under constant pressure to pursue a more forceful foreign policy, both in terms of revision of treaties and imperial expansion, and crises did occur, the oligarchy nevertheless resolutely continued to pursue foreign policy objectives by diplomatic rather than military means.

By the late eighties, Japan was entering yet another phase in her process of development. The government had been mainly concerned in the preceding decades in laying the industrial infrastructure. This was the period of what may be termed bureaucratic capitalism, in the sense that control of the means of production lay almost entirely in the hands of the state. In the meantime, however, private entrepreneurs had been accumulating capital mainly out of light industry and foreign trade. In the mid/late eighties most of the state's industries were transferred from the public to the private sector. Preferential treatment was granted to a number of firms. It is at this juncture that the *zaibatsu* originated. There was, therefore, a degree of economic devolution; whereas the government had laid the infrastructure, it was the *zaibatsu* who were to proceed with the development of Japan's major industrial enterprises and bring the initial policy of state-sponsored industrialisation to fruition.

In 1889 the constitution was promulgated. In 1890 the first elections were held, albeit on a limited franchise of approximately half a million people (out of a population of over forty million), for popular representation in the lower house of a bicameral legislature. While, as will be seen, the government perceived the lower house more as a form of window dressing for the West on the one hand, and for domestic consumption a sop to political *aficionados* on the other, nevertheless that first election did amount to the thin edge of the wedge. Whereas the first few years of the parliamentary experiment were marked by turbulence and violent confrontation, by the beginning of the twentieth century sufficient compromises had been achieved between the political parties and the governmental old guard (referred to as the *genro*, elder statesmen) to ensure that while political power might be devolved to some extent, the basic structures of the Meiji edifice remained intact. What form these structures took and how they should be defined will be looked at in a subsequent chapter. The point to note here is that the last two decades of the

Meiji era marked the culmination of the process of transformation to modernity. In economic, political and social terms, Japan emerged as a strong, viable nation-state. Under no circumstances should this be interpreted as inferring that Japan's was a liberal, just, progressive society. It was, in fact, nothing of the sort. That, however, was not the point, nor was it at any stage whatsoever a goal which the Meiji leadership had set before itself.

The culmination of the country's internal transformation to modernity was mirrored in its new international standing. In spite of pressures and occasional temptations, the Meiji government had resolutely stood by the principles and priorities established following the return of the Iwakura mission: that domestic reform should precede foreign expansion. The fact that by the end of the nineteenth and early twentieth centuries Japan emerged as a modern imperialistic power should not, certainly at this stage, be interpreted in terms of a blueprint for action formulated in the early Meiji period the conclusion of which was predetermined; the course of Japan's expansionism was far more complex, far more the result of changing policies than single-tracked ruthless determinism, and, in any case, a phenomenon which occurred as a result of both internal and external propelling forces. The point here, however, is that if the government felt that the time had come for it to make an entrée on to the world stage in reasonably dramatic manner, it was because the country was strong enough – sufficiently modern – to do so. It is in that sense that it is no accident that in the last two decades of the Meiji era Japan became a strong world power. In 1894 Japan went to war with China and won the following year; in 1899 the revision of the treaties in regard to extra-territoriality was ratified by all the treaty powers and in turn Japan became officially fully open to foreign residence and trade; in 1900–01 she allied with the major Western powers in suppressing the Boxer rebellion; in 1902 the Anglo-Japanese alliance was signed, confirmed and further extended in 1905; in 1904 Japan went to war with Russia and startled the world by her victories both on land and sea; having acquired Taiwan and a number of other islands from China in 1895, Japan further consolidated her empire in 1910 with the acquisition of Korea and extended her informal empire into Manchuria.

Illusory as the dream of *fukoku-kyohei* may have seemed to the Iwakura mission in 1872, by the time of the Meiji tenno's death little more concrete manifestation of the realisation of the dream could have been hoped for.

7 Society and Modernity

ECONOMIC GROWTH

The roots of the Japanese 'economic miracle' are deeply entrenched in the past. Thus, whereas the political historian may wish to distinguish between Edo 'feudalism', Meiji 'absolutism', Taisho 'democracy' and post-war 'liberalism', the economic historian is more interested in the continuous growth and acceleration of Japanese economic development. There were, of course, cycles, inflationary and deflationary periods, periods of rapid growth and others of comparative stagnation, periods of high investment, others of limited capital input into industry. These economic trends, however, rarely coincide with the prevailing political climate. The political obscurantism of the 1930s is a period of buoyant economic activity. The chaos and confusion of the end of the Second World War and the immediate aftermath are a temporary hiccup.

The characteristics and dynamics of Edo society have been stressed in order to demonstrate the comparative degree of preparedness of Japan in facing modern economic development. The 1868 revolution and the first two decades which followed consisted primarily of both transformation and consolidation: transforming outdated political and social structures, consolidating accumulated advantages of the preparatory period. Modern economic growth took off at both sustained and accelerated levels by the turn of the century. Seen from the perspective of the last eight decades, Japan's has been the fastest-growing economy of the world.

The social benefits of this rapid growth, however, have been bestowed on the Japanese people only very recently. During the period of transformation to modernity, poverty, physical abuse, monotony, spiritual suffocation, the devastating effects of war and pollution have been the lot of the majority of the Japanese population. The very rapidity of economic development must also be held accountable for severe psychological dislocations. The significant gap between economic and social developments helps to explain the chequered political history of Japan. It also helps to explain the more nefarious character of Japanese activities during the war. The transformation to modernity has been both brutal and replete with contradictions.

Japan's industrial revolution must be seen in terms of internal responses to

190

external stimuli. The challenge of the Western imperialistic order precipitated, in the first instance, a major political revolution, which resulted in an extensive programme of institutional reform. The first point to emphasise in terms of the causation of subsequent economic growth, therefore, is that the government itself adopted progressive economic policies. The state loomed large, partly because this was the traditional role of the state in the Edo era both at bakufu and han levels, but also because of the weakness and general confusion of the private sector.

The government was primarily involved in the laying of foundations necessary for economic development. It is not just the role which the state undertook on its own, but also the linkage which in due course it was able to accomplish with the private sector that accounts for the industrial take-off. This special relationship between the state and private enterprise, or what one might term the bureaucracy–business nexus, has remained a feature of the Japanese economy to the present day. This phenomenon already existed in the Edo era, albeit in disparate fashion given the nature of the baku-han system, but it was primarily in the early Meiji period that the relationship was consolidated within a national framework and further given that degree of internal coherence which has played such a vital role as a vehicle of economic development.

In the first fifteen years or so of the Meiji period, the government developed both the social and the industrial infrastructure. The government invested heavily in public works: railways, shipping, communications, ports, lighthouses, and so on. The government also invested a high percentage of national revenue in importing Western technology and expertise and in the establishment of model factories. Thus modern technology was not only imported but reasonably widely diffused.

Japan, it was stated in the previous chapter, developed in a manner which involved all the usual characteristics of the dual economy; in this process of transformation one can distinguish between the traditional, hybrid and modern sectors. The traditional sector refers almost exclusively to agriculture. In the course of the first two decades of the Meiji period the traditional sector remained dominant, not only in employing by far the largest percentage of the workforce, but also in providing the government with the bulk of its revenue, namely in the form of the land tax. Japan's early economic transformation, therefore, was achieved by agriculture subsidising industry, which is another way of saying that industrialisation was achieved by the exploitation of the peasantry. While this statement may evoke moral judgements in regard to the nature of Japan's industrialisation process, it should be pointed out that at first the government had no other significant potential sources of revenue to tap; to have introduced taxation of either light or heavy industry at this early stage would have been counter-productive, indeed suicidal, in view of the objectives of *fukoku-kyohei*, for this would have had a crippling effect on what was already at a heavy disadvantage in relation to the advanced industrial powers. Bucolic sentimentality was not a preoccupation of the Meiji leadership.

In spite of the onus placed on the agricultural sector in the early stages of industrialisation, it nevertheless experienced an impressive growth rate of just under 2 per cent per annum in the period 1870–1900. Following the land reform act of 1873, land tenure was rationalised and so was the collection of taxes. Significant efforts were also directed at improving agricultural technology, the introduction of new strains of rice, the application of fertilisers, and the establishment of educational centres for farming.

Another cause for agricultural growth, however, was the marked degree of diversification which occurred in the early Meiji years. It is in this context that the aforementioned Japanese quality of dynamic internal response to external stimuli is particularly noticeable. While the country is poor in natural resources, in the context of the mid-nineteenth century, Japan can be said to have had a stroke of good fortune. It will be recalled that silk manufactured goods played a crucial role in Western societies; indeed until the introduction of synthetic fibres, silk was *de rigueur* for the upper bourgeoisie – silk shirts, silk handkerchiefs, silk gowns, silk ties, silk scarves, etc. – while the lower orders had to content themselves with cotton. Precisely at the time that Japan was opened to foreign trade the silkworms of all the major sericultural districts of Europe and the Levant were ravaged by a devastatingly destructive disease known as the *pébrine*. Sources of raw silk were in desperate need. As noted in Chapter 2, Japan had been heavily dependent on the import of raw silk and silk goods from China until the early/mid seventeenth century when domestic production of silk was encouraged. Japan in the nineteenth century, therefore, was sericulturally comparatively rich. Although the French in particular – for whom the silk industry had played a vital economic role and indeed was the basis of the prosperity of Lyon – tried to import silkworms with a view to regenerating indigenous strands, with experiments carried out in the Pasteur Institute, these efforts failed. Up to the end of the nineteenth century raw silk represented just under 40 per cent of Japan's total export earnings, while in the years up to the First World War the figure dropped to just under 30 per cent. Tea was another commodity which Japan exported, though it represented far less in obtaining foreign revenue than silk. Foreign demand for raw silk and tea, therefore, stimulated agricultural diversification, which in turn contributed to agricultural growth, which in turn led to higher revenues which the government used for investing in industrial development.

In this respect, at least in the initial stages, Japan was no different from other client economies of the major metropolitan powers in that her export sector consisted primarily of raw materials. The question here, however, is what Japan chose to do with this product. Here again the role of the state cannot be minimised; the new leadership appreciated the value of that particular golden egg and as such was determined that under no circumstances should the proverbial goose be killed. While Western demand for Japanese raw silk assumed frenzied proportions, purveyors of the product perceived the short-term advantages that could be gained by fraud. The quality of raw silk varied considerably. In view of the vast quantities involved in transactions, it had become customary among a number of Japanese merchants to sell inferior quality under a superior label. As the substitution was generally not discovered until the produce had reached Europe, there was relatively little short-term risk involved. This was a practice which Chinese merchants, as China was also a major source of raw silk, carried on. The Meiji government, however, as early as 1871 set up inspection stations in all the major ports; were fraud to be discovered, the malefactor would be subjected to an onerous fine.

It is of course true that the production of raw silk offers certain potential forward linkage effects which are not necessarily evident in the raw materials produced in other countries during this period. (Though, on the other hand, silk has no backward linkage effects, which may partly explain the weakness of the Japanese chemical industry when compared to other sectors.) A potential, however, remains no more than a potential until it is exploited and translated into a reality. And the only factor which can determine whether a potential is to be properly exploited or not is that of the quality of the human resources. The linkage between sericulture and the growth of a vibrant textile industry must be seen in conjunction with another linkage, namely that between the public and private sectors. The Japanese government provided the foundations, the private sector in due course furnished the funds and the expertise for development. It is here that Japan stands in such stark contrast to, for example, Latin American countries; it is also here that one returns to a theme developed in the previous chapter, namely the quality and ambition of the élites. The Chilean nitrate boom resulted in the production of further nitrate and the inflow of a great deal of foreign revenue. In Brazil the production of coffee handsomely enriched the latifundists. There was the occasional Latin American government which sought to pursue a policy of national investment, diversification and industrialisation. Inevitably, however, these efforts failed to materialise into anything of substance. Chileans continued to import practically everything except nitrate, similarly the Brazilians in regard to coffee, while the Argentines failed to develop, for example, their own canning factories or even a competitive leather goods industry. While political instability and, conceivably, the tentacles of European and North American informal empire may be held partly responsible – though these factors also would have to be explained in causal terms – it remains the case that the Latin American élite was reluctant to invest in their countries' public utility services, namely the infrastructure, or even in native industries: surplus capital in these societies tended to be channelled into real estate or into foreign investments and, of course, into conspicuous consumption.

The revenue from raw silk and tea in Japan was used for the purchase of foreign machinery. While initially Japan's major role in the international economy was in providing raw silk to the Western countries, at the same time she developed on a substantial scale her own silk industry. By the time of the 1914–18 war Japan was a serious competitor to the hitherto major manufactured silk fabrics exporting countries, mainly France and Italy, while in the interwar period she took the lead. The spin-off effects from silk were particularly noticeable in the cotton industry. In the introduction and diffusion of Western technology priority was placed on the cotton-spinning industry. The initial motivation for this effort was to end the country's dependence on the import of Western manufactured textile goods. The aim of both public and private sectors was to achieve a situation whereby foreign revenue would be used as far as possible exclusively for the import of capital goods rather than consumer goods. At the end of the first decade of the Meiji period there were less than 10,000 cotton spindles in all of Japan; by the end of the second decade these had increased to just under 100,000, by the time of the Russo–Japanese war there were 1,500,000, and at the time of the outbreak of the 1914–18 war there were 2,500,000. At the beginning of the twentieth century Japanese industry possessed less than 5,000 power looms, by the time of the First World War the number had increased by a multiple of five. The Japanese were to find themselves fortunate once again, in that just as the ravages of the European silkworm disease were an undoubted godsend for the initial development of the economy, so were the ravages of the European 1914–18 war advantageous to the Japanese in that they were able to move into hitherto quasi-monopolised European markets. As the figures above indicate, however, the Japanese were well prepared to take advantage of these fortuitous circumstances. Similar types of figures could be provided in regard to the development of shipping and shipbuilding.

The textile industry was the leading sector so far as exports were concerned. Already by the late nineteenth century Japan had begun exporting cotton goods to China; by the beginning of the twentieth century exports of cotton manufactured goods exceeded imports. The textile industry was the major component of the hybrid sector of the economy. Increasingly, however, as steam and electric power were introduced on a greater scale, textiles came into the modern sector.

In more recent times perhaps the most marked characteristic influence of the Japanese economy on the West has been the competition – and ultimate victory – which the Japanese have waged precisely in the areas of apparent Western comparative advantage and strength: British motorcycles, Swiss watches, German cameras, Western European/US automobiles, musical instruments and so on have all been overtaken by Japanese products. As has been indicated here in regard to silk and cotton, the roots of this phenomenon go back a century. From textiles, Japanese industry moved into increasing emphasis on heavy industry, namely armaments, ship-building, iron and steel production. This industrial development was accompanied by the simultaneous growth in ancillary servicing industries. By the time of the 1914–18 war Japan possessed a sound and extensive industrial base, an advanced commercial sector with widespread foreign representation, a strong army, and so on. Whether any other country could or could not have achieved a comparable performance, the distinguishing characteristic of the Japanese is quite simply that they tried – in other words they responded positively to the external stimulation provided by the Western challenge. And the major ingredient in the recipe of success was the quality of the human resources and their skilful exploitation.

We have stressed in earlier sections of this book how nationalism must be seen primarily in terms of the motivation for industrialisation rather than in terms of causation. Nevertheless, this motivation in turn became translated into a causal effect. Another unique feature of Japan's modernisation is the degree to which it was self-generated within the narrow confines of the nation-state. Western capital, technology and expertise did, as we have seen, play a major role. Similarly, Japan's route to prosperity included not just a few forays beyond her shores. The point being made here, however, is that Japan is unique in the sense that no foreigners entered or were absorbed into the Japanese élite. Japanese enterprise was exclusively the creation of Japanese entrepreneurs. Nor was Japanese entrepreneurship exported. There was Japanese economic penetration of other countries, but this was always part of a carefully monitored process by Tokyo head-offices. When one thinks of the flight of Chinese or Indian entrepreneurial expertise, the export of capital from these countries, from Latin America, and more recently from the OPEC countries, the degree to which the Japanese proved capable of containing both financial and human capital to serve the nation's needs is remarkable and constitutes another important element in explaining the roots of the Japanese economic miracle. This factor can, in turn, be explained by the cultural cohesion of the country, the degree of ethnic, linguistic and ethical homogeneity. While these elements are of great significance, in themselves they would have provided little impetus to industrial growth had they not been accompanied by the solid foundations of institutional structures and a general climate conducive to economic development. In other words, to look at it negatively, it is not simply because the Brazilian coffee plantation owner did not share the same race or cultural values with the workers in his fields that Brazil's economy failed to develop.

Nor must the nationalism of Japan's élite be seen in too utopic a perspective. The élite did, it is true, share a certain common vision in regard to the future of the nation. The nation, in this sense, however was perceived in a rather abstract manner; the élite was not particularly concerned about the majority of their compatriots who inhabited the nation for whose greater glory the élite claimed to be working. And indeed here one comes to another ingredient in Japanese economic development and one which, *mutatis mutandis*, remained constant until about 1960: cheap labour. We shall be looking at industrial workers in more detail shortly. For the time being, however, one can offer as a general proposition that throughout the period of transformation to modernity the working classes – as indeed was the case with the peasantry – were brutally exploited. This applies mainly to the light industry sector, specifically textile, while in the capital-intensive heavy industry the conditions of the workers were noticeably better; Japan also, therefore, possessed her version of an aristocracy of labour.

If the Japanese élite exploited peasants and workers in their course of modernisation, so was modernisation achieved by Japan's exploitation of her neighbours. It is important not to forget the *kyohei* (strong army) part of the *fukoku-kyohei* equation. The militarisation of Japanese society created domestic demand for both heavy and light industry goods. Thus military requirements compelled a greater production of armaments and general hardware, thus increasing demand for iron, steel and coal. Uniforms, tents and so on provided a market for manufactured textile goods. The well armed, well equipped strong army was used to pursue expansionist ends from the late nineteenth century and then almost incessantly until 1945. Imperialism in turn produced significant material gain. The huge indemnity which the Japanese extorted from the Chinese in 1895 allowed, among other things, the country to adopt the gold standard two years later, while a large lump of the indemnity was also channelled into the steel industry. The colonies and spheres of influence which the Japanese acquired provided comparatively cheap sources of foodstuff and raw materials on the one hand and markets for Japanese manufactured goods on the other. Imperialism as a means of enriching the nation is by no means unique to Japan. All the major Western powers profited from the pursuit of imperialistic policies. Generally, however, the 'New Imperialism' of the Western powers occurred as a consequence or, at the very least, a sequence of their industrial revolutions. In Lenin's terms imperialism represented the highest stage of capitalism. Japanese imperialism, on the other hand, developed at a time when domestic capitalism was still very much in its infancy; imperialism, therefore, was by no means either an isolated factor or a product of industrialisation, but on the contrary it was inextricably interwoven in the whole pattern of Japanese modernisation.

To recapitulate, at the heart of Japan's industrial performance and economic growth lie a multiplicity of factors. The contribution of Edo society in preparing Japan has been noted. In the period of transformation, causal factors to industrialisation would include: (1) the political revolution and subsequent widespread institutional reform; (2) the powerful and progressive role of the state; (3) the investment in and development of the infrastructure; (4) import and diffusion of Western technology and expertise; (5) the rise of an able and dynamic entrepreneurial class with a close symbiotic relationship with the state – for example, both public and private sectors worked together in the development of the railways; (6) agricultural growth and diversification; (7) the role of silk in generating foreign revenue; (8) the advantage taken from forward linkage effects in the development of a viable and increasingly competitive textile industry catering in due course both to domestic demand and providing revenue from export; (9) the development and indeed emphasis given to heavy industry, the increased use of modern sources of energy, coal, steam, electricity; (10) cheap labour; (11) militarism and imperialism.

None of these factors should be seen in isolation. Rather they were strands which were woven into a common pattern and which accounted for both the causes and the nature of Japan's process of transformation. There were also, of course, many other factors involved. Little has been said here of certain cultural features which contributed to the transformation. One might note here, however, that the *ie* system was regenerated and redirected to the pursuit of economic ends. Another interesting, though highly speculative, element is the Japanese system of writing. Western pundits claimed – and, at least temporarily, a number of Japanese accepted – that for the Japanese to modernise they had no choice but to discard what was perceived as an archaic form of writing and reading. Paradoxically one can at the very least argue that this represented a positive rather than negative element. The fact that education was made obligatory and that learning even only the essentials of the script demanded great efforts of perseverance may have contributed to qualities which were advantageous to the task of industrialisation facing the Japanese. Nor, in drawing up the list, has any mention been made of ethical principles whether derived from Buddhism, Shinto, Confucianism, or an amalgam of all three. Similarly a host of other more intangible factors could be found, some of which will be elaborated in later sections.

While acknowledging the interplay of diverse factors and forces, the historian should nevertheless be prepared to take a stand in isolating what he perceives as the primordial cause, the *deus ex machina*, of Japan's successful transformation to modernity. So far as the crucial initial stages of the transformation process are concerned, and especially when Japan is placed in a comparative perspective, the fundamental feature was the vision, determination and flexibility of the new leadership. Both the vision and determination were in due course successfully communicated to a sufficient number of the population to ensure that Japan's transformation was achieved as the result of a great national effort. The Japanese in the late nineteenth and early twentieth centuries succeeded where the Brazilians, the Argentines, the Egyptians, the Chinese failed miserably. The profits of the Latin American *hacendado* were not ploughed into a national system of education, the result: desperately high rates of illiteracy and innumeracy, and widespread ignorance even in regard to such basics as hygiene. The vision, determination and the effective means of communication remain characteristics of Japanese society today and here the Japanese have continued to succeed, not only in comparison with other potential late-developers – potentials which were not translated into reality – but also where their major Western competitors have failed.

These qualities of the Meiji leadership, one should hasten to add, do not make them likeable. The vision and the determination encompassed a frightening degree of ruthlessness. To the new élite the end justified all the means: these included the exploitation of women and children factory operatives, the onerous taxation of peasants, the brutal drilling of military recruits, the development of an intellectually stifling, narrowly *étatiste* education system, the waging of war and the enslavement by colonisation of neighbours. None of this, however, makes Japan radically different from other industrialised societies; the process of industrialisation has inevitably involved a degree of brutality. One keeps coming back, however, to the same point. The Japanese may have been given in the late nineteenth century a rather narrow educational horizon, but they were, at the very least, *taught to read, write and count*. The ruling classes of the other countries mentioned in these pages never seem to have conceived the importance of achieving national integration by these means. Ultimately, therefore, Japan's success was derived not so much from financial capital, from technology, but from the accumulation and successful formation of human capital.

The following pages will be devoted to assessing the roles of the different component parts of this human capital in the period of Japan's process of transformation.

BUREAUCRATS

In view of the omnipresent and omnipotent role of the state in the initial years of the transformation and its continued dominance in ensuing decades, the bureaucracy was obviously of fundamental significance. *Kanryo-shugi* (bureaucratism), as we have seen, is nothing new to the Japanese tradition. The major distinctions between the Edo and modern bureaucracies are two: first, the bureaucracy became a national institution, as opposed to a bakufu/han particularistic one; secondly, entry to the bureaucracy came to be based on merit rather than birth, achievement rather than ascription.

In the first two decades of the Meiji era little distinction can be made between the government leadership and the bureaucracy. Okubo, Okuma, Ito, Inoue, Matsukata and others who became prominent government leaders began their careers in the new national bureaucracy. On the other hand, men such as Mitsukuri Rinsho (1846–97), Nishi Amane (1829–97) and Tsuda Masamichi (1829–1903), though prominent innovative bureaucrats, never obtained government posts. Thus, while the new bureaucracy was staffed by talented former officials from the han and the bakufu, all of whom shared a progressive outlook and generally some experience in the West or at least a Western-oriented education, it is also true to say that in these initial stages preference in the allocation of senior posts was undoubtedly given to those emanating from either Satsuma or Choshu. This, however, was a transitional phase during which Japan was managed by a narrow coterie, in fact a Sat-Cho freemasonry.

Not surprisingly, however, this Sat-Cho monopoly came to be intensely criticised by the 'outsiders'. In due course the bureaucracy became open to all men of talent irrespective of han origin. This was the result partly of widespread criticism, including in the rapidly proliferating press, and allegations of corruption within the government – something which certainly did exist, albeit never reaching too alarming proportions – but also from a number of other factors. Thus, in 1885 a major reorganisation of the government apparatus took place with the introduction of the Cabinet system. This was a move taken in preparation for the new constitutional structure which the country was to obtain at the end of the decade, but also involved a rationalisation of the procedure of government affairs. Ministries and ministerial responsibilities became more clearly defined. In turn, however, this organisational change was also a reflection of the growing complexity of state affairs – whether finance, agriculture, military, diplomatic and so on – and hence a corresponding demand for professional specialists rather than simply inspired amateurs. Given the reforms and innovations in the field of education, it was now possible to select from a pool of qualified candidates.

It is, therefore, in the mid-eighties that the modern Japanese bureaucracy was officially born.

The first Imperial University had been established in 1877. What is known today as Tokyo University – and remains to this day and will undoubtedly remain in the future the prestigious educational institution *par excellence* – was originally simply designated as the Imperial University. When an Imperial University was created in Kyoto in 1897, and subsequently in Sendai, Sapporo, Fukuoka, Osaka, Nagoya and in due course Keijo (Seoul) and Taipei, the first Imperial University became Tokyo Imperial University; since the Second World War the designation 'Imperial' has been dropped. In 1886 the Imperial University Ordinance was promulgated and Tokyo University combined the faculties of law, medicine, engineering, literature and natural sciences. The original *raison d'être* of this national university, as opposed to a number of private institutes of secondary and tertiary learning, was to serve the state directly. In consequence, in the following year civil service examinations were introduced. These applied mainly, however, to the lower echelons of the bureaucracy. Further reform was introduced in 1893 with the Civil Service Appointment Ordinance. Although a degree of nepotism was retained, nevertheless on the whole by the end of the century Japan had a fully-fledged modern professional civil service.

With modernity the phenomenon of *kanryo-shugi* was not only alive and well, but indeed probably far healthier than it had ever been. The Edo period motto of *kanson-minpi* ('revere officials – despise the masses') could also, accepting certain modifications, be said to have remained operative. Bureaucrats came to form a highly privileged, quasi-sacrosanct élite. Legislation was passed to ensure that they were well beyond the control of the Diet and the tumultuous political parties. Indeed, not only were bureaucrats beyond the control of the parties, but the parties can be said to have fallen under the control of the bureaucrats. As will be seen in the following chapter, shortly after the establishment of the Diet the parties changed considerably in character – once they began actually exercising a degree of power – from being hitherto popular parties, namely responsive to the populace and the issues which excited them, to becoming institutionalised, or entrenched, parties, namely absorbed into the establishment. Part of this scenario, indeed a fundamental dénouement in it, consisted of bureaucrats joining the parties and being invited to high offices in them. In the twentieth century, with only very few exceptions, practically every prime minister came from either a civil or military bureaucratic background. Similarly, throughout the modern era the power of the bureaucracy, independently of government office, has been extensive. This remains true today. Extensive, however, does not mean absolute.

The bureaucracy came to be divided between upper and lower echelons. Entry into one or the other was determined by examination. The dividing line between the two was clear: lower-ranking civil servants were second-class citizens within the bureaucratic order. A strict regime of apartheid was maintained: the lower did not join the ranks of the upper. Upper-ranking bureaucrats were almost exclusively from Tokyo Imperial University and also almost exclusively from the Law Faculty of that institution. The prestige of Law Faculty graduates from Tokyo especially, but also from the other former Imperial Universities – except of course, Keijo (Seoul) and Taipei – remains a marked feature of contemporary Japan. In fact, it would not be too much of an exaggeration to state that they constitute a caste, the brahmins of modern Japan. For this reason, a few points should be made clear. Although Law Faculties do produce lawyers and judges, this is by no means their primary function. The lawyer in Japan is not the omnipresent factor, both in the private and public sectors, in the manner of his American colleague; there are, in fact, few lawyers in Japan. The establishment of Tokyo Imperial University and recruitment into the top grades of the civil service took place at a time when Japanese affairs of state were still very much dominated by considerations regarding the revision of the treaties in particular, but also Western-imposed international relations in general. The syllabus of the Law Faculty took account of the contemporary realities and the bias necessary in the formation of the country's bureaucratic élite. Thus while jurisprudence was studied, including civil and penal law, constitutional law and, of course, international law, modern European history, international relations, political science and philosophy were equally important elements in the curriculum. Entrance to the Law Faculty included an examination in a European language. A Law Faculty degree was also generally complemented, especially for those who joined the diplomatic service, by a stint in a European or American university: to polish up linguistic abilities, to gather further knowledge at closer quarters of Euro/American institutions and to establish contacts with the Western élites.

Bureaucracies are, of course, a feature of all societies. In Japan it is held that while the government provides the head of the body politic, the bureaucracy is the backbone. This comment, however, could equally apply to many other societies, but the calibre and competence of Japan's bureaucracy ensured a particularly strong backbone – especially necessary in view of the comparative instability of governments throughout most of the period of transformation; indeed up to recent times very few governments lasted more than two years in office. Another interesting feature of modern Japan is that after the retirement into the background of the great architects of Meiji Japan, the country can boast hardly any statesmen of not just international, but even national standing. It is probable that one of the many causes for the failure of democracy in pre-war Japan is precisely this absence of powerful political figures emanating from the parties. The absence of a strong political movement made the bureaucracy's role in the administration of the affairs of state and the direction of government policy all the more significant. In comparison with other modern societies, therefore, one can underline the degree of power and initiative exercised by the bureaucracy. This reality and the ethic of public service, as opposed to private gain, inherited from *bushido*, also no doubt account for the fact that the civil service has remained throughout the modern period the most prestigious career.

It was claimed in the former chapter that in the course of the transformation to modernity the prestige attached to samurai status rapidly declined, while the key to political, social and financial success lay securely in the hands of university graduates, the *crème de la crème* emanating from Tokyo Imperial University. It was also claimed that the decades in the immediate aftermath of the 1868 revolution witnessed a comparatively high degree of social mobility, both upwards and downwards. Was the selection process into the universities and recruitment into the elevated civil service based on entirely meritocratic principles? The answer must be no. It is true that entrance into Tokyo University, and others, was conditional on passing a highly competitive examination. On the other hand, it was only at the turn of the century that primary education was made not only compulsory but also free of tuition charges; secondary and tertiary education remained fee-paying. Most secondary and all tertiary educational institutions were concentrated in the big cities, which, as we have seen, accounted for only a small percentage of the population. There were occasional examples of poor country boys – Tokyo Imperial University was closed to female candidates – rising in meteoric fashion up the meritocratic/bureaucratic ladder: perhaps the most striking illustration being Hirota Koki (1878–1948), variously foreign minister, prime minister, and one of the very few civilians to have been executed under orders from the Allied Military Tribunal for the Far East after the Second World War. In general terms, however, from geographical, economic and academic perspectives, the system was clearly biased in favour of the urban upper-middle classes. While it remains true that in comparison with Western European countries there was probably a higher degree of social mobility – and the élite Japanese universities never adopted or encouraged the social pretentiousness of Oxbridge or the American Ivy League colleges – in Japan, so far as the bulk of the native population was concerned, and, especially in contrast with the post-war situation, by the twentieth century this mobility was marginal. A similar trend can be discerned in the world of industry. While entrepreneurs were often parvenus, sons of their own works, the managers who succeeded them in the leadership of industry were almost invariably products of the new middle classes. By the early twentieth century the bureaucracy, as well as the other leading sectors of society, tended to issue from what increasingly became a self-perpetuating social élite.

WORKERS AND ENTREPRENEURS

It may appear more orthodox that the subtitle to this section should be inversed: entrepreneurs should come before workers. This would, among other things, recognise a reality, in that while entrepreneurs in industry cannot operate without workers, without entrepreneurs, whether the state or the private sector, workers cannot exist. Similarly, so far as this period of transformation to modernity is concerned, it is certainly the case that entrepreneurs provided a highly dynamic element in achieving economic growth which the workers, at this stage of Japanese history, could hardly claim. Throughout this period workers were a disparate, collectively passive force. Although the beginning of the twentieth century did witness an embryo of syndicalism, any even semi-cohesive form of labour movement did not really begin until after the First World War. This was partly due to both quantitative and qualitative characteristics of the Meiji period industrial workforce. In terms of quantity, it should be remembered that the percentage of the population employed in the secondary sector remained very low. In terms of quality, as will be described in more detail shortly, the major component, by far, of the industrial labour force consisted of peasant girls. It is also for these reasons that throughout most of this period the concept of a working class should be eschewed. Given the objective conditions of Japan's industrial workforce, there was no way in which any sense of solidarity among workers could develop. This, in turn, is no doubt the primary reason why employers were able to ride roughshod over their employees.

The inversion of orthodoxy, however, is quite deliberate. The acquisition and accumulation of capital and the development of industry have been subjected to a considerable amount of literature, while the social dimension has received little attention. From an economic perspective, entrepreneurs should rightly enjoy priority of place; this is not necessarily the case, however, when the perspective is a social one. The organisation of this section and the description to follow, however, should also serve to underline a major premise of this book: the role of culture in Japan's modernising society. Equally this section especially should make it clear why relatively little emphasis has been placed on concepts such as the Confucianist or samurai ethic. Japanese culture and social ethics have changed considerably in the process of modernisation; neither should be perceived as static elements. So far as the cultural values and social structures of the Japanese industrial firm is concerned, these did change remarkably in the course of the last century or so, but these changes occurred primarily *in response to economic and political forces*. That in due course both cultural values and social structures could claim to be derived from 'traditional' patterns of the Edo era does not constitute an argument in favour of the cultural continuity thesis, but rather illustrates the point made earlier in regard to Japanese modernity emerging as a dialectical process between culture and economy. All those positive features associated with Japanese industrial relations today – security through the life-long employment system, harmony through close manager–employee inter-personal relations, widespread consultation, reciprocal loyalty between worker and employer, etc. – most definitely did not exist during this period; certain indications, albeit on a rather limited scale, of what are today referred to as 'Japanese-style' industrial relations did become slightly perceptible in the interwar period.

The first two-thirds or thereabouts of the Meiji era, *c.* 1870–1900, correspond, as did the seventeenth and early eighteenth centuries, to a period of intense economic activity and change. As was also the case in the early Edo era, not only was this period marked by a high degree of innovation, of economic and social mobility, of impressive entrepreneurial flair, it was also one of conspicuous individualism. The motivating force of nationalism has been repeatedly raised in these pages. While orthodox historians have sought to stress the role of nationalism, more revisionist interpretations have rather insisted on the materialistic profit-seeking motive of Meiji Japan's new entrepreneurship. The two values, nationalism and materialistic individualism, however, need not be perceived as mutually exclusive. Most Northern European and American entrepreneurs were motivated both by the profit incentive and religious conviction, usually in the form of Calvinism. These Westerners, as their Japanese counterparts, were convinced, or simply convinced themselves, that while they were enriching themselves they were also providing ample benefits for society at large. This may be a contradiction, but then ideologies usually are. The point is that it was no more contradictory for successful Japanese entrepreneurs to be good patriots than it was for successful Western capitalists to perceive and portray themselves as good Christians. Just as the Protestant ethic of capitalism stressed the importance of the role – and hence the justness of material rewards – of the select, so did Meiji entrepreneurs readily accept the mantle of the national élite. The nation for them meant far more than its constituent parts, namely the population of peasants and workers, and hence the wellbeing of the latter need not be either a major preoccupation or a deterrence to achieving higher ends, for example, building more steamships to compete with the West, and, *inter alia*, earn more money in the process. It was only once it was made abundantly clear that more money could be gained by providing greater care for the workforce that more humane treatment was granted and 'traditions' of benevolent paternalism invoked.

There is, however, another dimension which needs to be added to an assessment of industrial relations in the early Meiji period. The seventies and eighties, it will be recalled, corresponded to a period of general emulation of Western ways. The obscure Edo past was being discarded in favour of the new Western-orientated enlightenment. Partly, but only partly, for this reason, labour tended to be perceived in a manner comparable to that of the West: labour was no more than a factor of production. The consensus, therefore, was that labour, just like any other commodity, should be judged according to the value attached to it by market forces. One thing Japan seemed to possess in abundance was labour, hence labour should be dirt-cheap. While this was true, the qualitative aspect of the labour market was not properly perceived by early Japanese entrepreneurs, nor were human beings, including lowly peasant girls, understood even in purely economic terms: while entrepreneurs were motivated by profits, they failed initially at least to understand that the logic of the labour market dictated that wage incentives constituted an important element to worker motivation as well. Productivity, the characteristic of the contemporary Japanese economy most envied today, was throughout the Meiji period abysmally low.

In terms of factory production one needs to make three distinctions: (1) in chronological terms; (2) in terms of state and private enterprise; (3) in terms of labour-intensive predominantly female-worked industries, especially textiles – weaving, silk reeling and cotton spinning – and capital-intensive predominantly male-labour industries – mainly iron, steel and general engineering works, such as ship-building, armaments, etc. In chronological terms, large-scale factory production does not begin until the late eighties. From then until the 1914–18 war there is a steady, accelerating progression of factory operatives; during the war a boom occurs. Also, although the *zaibatsu* already figure in the Meiji period, it is only during and after the war that they achieved the control of the Japanese economy with which they became associated. In the early Meiji decades the textile industry consisted either of modernising filatures set up by the state, such as the Tomioka Mill (whose main purpose, however, was to find employment, hence revenue, and training for girls of samurai stock), or very small-scale, technologically primitive private factories, or a continuation of cottage industry production. In the course of the Meiji period, however, as internal transport facilities became more extensive, as machinery was imported and figured more prominently in factory production, as capital was accumulated and concentrated, the pattern of labour in the textile industry changed significantly. The textile industry, it will be recalled, accounted for over 60 per cent of the entire industrial workforce throughout the Meiji period. Description of working conditions, therefore, should begin with the textile industry. In fact what will be said below applies mainly to the cotton-spinning industry, though its general outlines would hold true of textile industry in general.

The first point which deserves attention in regard to the textile industry is that approximately 80 per cent of the workforce consisted of female labour. Indeed female factory labour was a pronounced feature of industrialisation in Meiji Japan; even by the time of the outbreak of the 1914–18 war women represented 60 per cent of the factory operatives in Japan. The use of female – and child – labour is by no means peculiar to Japan's industrialisation *per se*, though the degree is certainly greater than it was in corresponding periods of Western industrialisation: in the decade 1840–50, for example, women constituted just under 30 per cent of the British industrial workforce. Why? Certainly no straightforward demographic explanation can be given; Meiji Japan does not appear to have had a large surplus female population. Rather, the reasons would seem to rest on a number of other factors. As already pointed out, the Japanese economy remained overwhelmingly agrarian with hardly any mechanisation being introduced, hence agriculture was labour-intensive. Primogeniture was the pattern in Meiji Japan, so elder sons stayed on the farm. As for younger sons, these would either seek employment in the urban-centred industries or swell the ranks of such non-industrial activities as rickshaw drivers, coolies, dockers and so forth. While these younger sons would be encouraged to go off and establish themselves on their own, farmers' daughters could be used to provide additional sources of revenue to the household until they were married off. So far as Meiji entrepreneurial perceptions of the market forces of labour were concerned, the advantage of hiring females was that they were cheaper – women were generally paid 50 per cent less than men, while children were paid 75 per cent less, thus as we shall see, the tendency to employ a fairly high percentage of young girls who would also be more malleable and hence less likely to cause or become involved in industrial disputes.

In terms of the age distribution of the workforce the available statistics would seem to indicate that at the end of the nineteenth century, about 30 per cent of the textile female labour force was aged less than fifteen years, with about 1·5 per cent less than eleven; the bulk of the female labour, over 60 per cent, was in the fifteen to thirty age group. The corresponding figures for males are: under fifteen about 12 per cent, fifteen to forty about 80 per cent. By the end of the Meiji period the percentage of very young girls, pre-teens, had diminished considerably; in absolute terms, however, the total number must have remained fairly constant in view of the considerable expansion which the economy experienced; indeed the number of factory workers increased by about 140 per cent in the first fifteen years of the twentieth century.

Although pay, working conditions and hours varied somewhat from industry to industry, generally speaking one can say that all three were abysmally low. Contracts existed, though these tended to consist primarily of oral promises extracted from employees with no reciprocity of guarantees being granted by employers. Written contracts would have been pretty useless in any case, since it is estimated that by the turn of the century less than 30 per cent of the total textile workforce had received their (compulsory!) primary education and those who had received it were predominantly the males. Generally the contracts were for a three- to five-year period; wages were fixed and hence took no account of inflation, high and endemic throughout most of the Meiji period. While a certain amount of pocket money may have been allocated, deductions of various forms were taken at source and placed into a savings account; this the operatives were to receive as a lump payment at the time of the expiry of the contract, something which relatively few workers waited for.

In terms of hours, allowing for considerable discrepancies from as much as eighteen to as little as six hours per day, the norm, especially after the introduction of the electric light into factories, consisted of two twelve-hour shifts, seven days a week. Although in theory provisions did exist for holidays, these were at the discretion of the employer. Working conditions in general were dire. While the electric light was introduced so that the mills could be kept operating twenty-four hours a day, neither ventilation nor heating were to be found in the Meiji textile factory, as these, from the employers' perspectives, did not generate profits, but on the contrary cost money; needless to say, in the summer months temperatures were stifling hot, in the region of 40°C, while in the winter it was freezing. Contemporary accounts of visits to textile factories describe the appalling physical condition of the young female workers. Disease was rampant. Inadequate diets caused severe digestive infirmities and painful and ugly skin ailments, while the general lack of sanitation and care led to the rapid transmission of infectious diseases, especially tuberculosis which accounted for over 40 per cent of the recorded factory deaths. Apart from the insalubrious atmosphere, the abysmal diet, and the oppressive hours demanded, the working conditions were made worse by a pronounced laxity in safety standards, hence accidents resulting in death or disfigurement were not infrequent. No compensation was paid to the families of workers who died from disease or had to leave work because of it. In cases of accidents at work, while compensation was in theory provided, this would be withheld if it was felt that the accident arose out of the worker's own negligence. Finally, it should be noted that most female workers were made to live in dormitories adjoining the factories; these were overcrowded, bedding was shared in shifts corresponding to working hours, fences were erected round the dormitories and bullies were employed to prevent the girls from running away – indeed physical beatings were easily resorted to even in the place of work.

In spite of all the repressive precautions taken by employers to keep their labour force, many workers nevertheless managed to escape. While bearing in mind the speculative nature of this statistical exercise, it would nevertheless appear that at the end of the century in the cotton industry about 40 per cent of the operatives managed to abscond within six months of their initial employment. The percentage of workers staying until the expiry of their contracts was as low as about 15 per cent. The paradox of Meiji Japan, therefore, was that in spite of an apparent abundance of labour, in reality employers were constantly faced with serious labour shortage problems. This resulted, among other things, in factories attempting to entice or kidnap workers from adjoining factories. The rapidity of the turnover in labour throughout Japanese industry in this period accounts for the extremely low level of productivity. In due course, as will be seen shortly, more enlightened employers woke up to the reality of the situation and opted for more progressive means of employment, but throughout most of the Meiji period the attempts to solve the labour shortage crisis consisted of depending heavily on intermediaries or, what in less flattering but reasonably accurate terms, might be described as industrial pimps. These middlemen would go out into the country to recruit female labour, sometimes by subterfuge, namely by providing false information regarding pay, working conditions, even destination, sometimes by bribing the parents, not infrequently by outright kidnapping. These intermediaries received a *per capita* fee; it was not uncommon, apparently, for the men to resort to different ruses to sell the same girl to more than one factory.

In this period of transformation, therefore, the conditions of labour in the textile industry were not only brutally inhuman, but also economically detrimental. In regard to heavy industry the situation varied considerably between government and private enterprises. In the public sector the policies pursued were reasonably enlightened, although certain social barriers existed for the smooth operation of industry. It must once again be recalled that one of the government's severest post-1868 problems was what to do with the samurai. An illustration can be drawn from one of the government's pilot schemes, the Yokosuka shipyards, in fact inherited from the Tokugawa bakufu. The Yokosuka shipyards had been established by the bakufu in 1866 with the assistance of French engineers, the latter retaining managerial supervision until the mid-eighties. Following 1868 the government operated training schemes on the site, with, however, more sophisticated engineering and managerial education being reserved for ex-samurai, while courses for skilled workmen were devised for commoners, mainly artisans. The problem, a source of frequent lamentation from the French managers, was that the ex-samurai were reluctant to communicate, let alone co-operate, with their social inferiors. This provides yet another illustration of the distance which the Japanese managerial system has travelled over the last century. Nevertheless, the government did seek to provide the means necessary for the development of an indigenous industrial expertise. Even though government enterprises generally operated at a considerable loss, nevertheless they were instrumental in the introduction and diffusion of modern technology and in the creation of a skilled workforce.

While the government began selling off a number of major enterprises to the private sector in the mid-eighties, it should be noted that throughout the Meiji era there was more employment in the government-owned heavy industries than in the private sector. In the initial stages private industry's approach to labour in the metalwork and engineering sectors was not significantly more enlightened than in textiles. Workers, who in these sectors were predominantly, indeed overwhelmingly, male, were certainly better paid, and general working conditions by no means corresponded to the inferno which young girls had to endure in the textile mills. What the private industries failed to obtain, however, was a steady and reliable workforce. Here again, therefore, there was an acute problem of labour shortage. One of the reasons for this state of affairs was that the enterprises failed to incorporate their workers into their organisations. This comes back to the point raised earlier on, namely that labour was perceived simply as a factor of production, a commodity to be bought and sold on the market. The idea of operating a team, a characteristic of contemporary Japan, was completely alien to Meiji employers. Thus, among other things, private enterprise provided virtually no training schemes for workers. A major reason here was the cost involved. Training skilled workers was an expensive business and an investment of highly dubious return value if the likelihood was that once the worker had been trained he would transfer to another firm. And indeed such was the likelihood, for the heavy industry workforce of Meiji Japan was highly mobile. Here again, therefore, one should note how radically different employment patterns were in the Meiji period from what they are today.

What has been retained from the Meiji period, however, are certain elements of industrial terminology. One of the first terms which the student of contemporary Japanese industrial relations becomes acquainted with is that of *oyabun-kobun* relationships, literally 'parent role – child role', more figuratively meant to denote the general paternalistic nature of Japanese employer–employee relationships. In the Meiji period, however, the *oyakata* (parent person) was a rather different kettle of fish from what he is today and fulfilled a different role. The common pattern for the private sector was to contract labour in bulk from the outside. Managers would approach labour gang leaders who, upon receipt of payment, delivered a team of workers. These leaders were referred to as the *oyakata*, their underlings as *kokata*. This system is perhaps somewhat reminiscent of and not necessarily all that dissimilar in nature from the role played by ethnic leaders in the United States for recently arrived immigrants. Through established networks the ethnic leaders found for their recently arrived compatriots jobs, housing and so forth, in turn receiving cash and of course the allegiance of their protégés for whatever cause their leaders espoused, whether in politics or in the underworld of crime.

The ties between the *oyakata* and their *kokata* were not simply economic or emotional, but often geographic. Thus, *oyakata* would generally recruit from their own villages or at least from the same region. These *oyakata-kokata* teams operated as a form of peripatetic *ie*. The individual worker belonged to the circle formed by his *oyakata*, it was with this group that he identified, to this group that he owed allegiance, to his *oyakata* he offered loyalty, in return for which he received benevolent care and protection. Thus the prevalent pattern in contemporary Japan, whereby an individual in introducing himself names his firm prior to himself, did not exist in Meiji Japan. On the contrary, the firm was perceived as something completely external, the main reason being no doubt that whereas the *oyakata* looked after his men, the firm did not.

So far as the private sector in the beginning of the twentieth century was concerned, therefore, both performance and outlook were bleak; productivity was extremely low, due in turn in great part to the very high labour turnover both in light and heavy industries. The high turnover was a product of the unenlightened policies of management. For the economic ends to be achieved, for Japan to be able to compete against the West, the means would have to change. They did. While major changes and the emergence of what may be termed a Japanese-style management occurred mainly during and after the 1914–18 war, and therefore beyond the scope of this book, the forces for a transformation of labour policies arose in the last fifteen years or so of the Meiji era. Indeed in the late nineteenth and increasingly in the early twentieth century management in the private sector found itself the target of a three-pronged attack: (1) the embryonic growth of class struggle; (2) government attempts at factory legislation; (3) poor industrial economic performance.

The process of industrialisation clearly resulted in the alienation of the workers. Female workers, as we have seen, responded mainly by escaping, or trying to escape, from their place of work. Apart from that no form of organised industrial militancy developed; the girls were too young, too weak, too scattered and too oppressed even to dream of seeking redress by establishing a concerted movement. From the late nineteenth and increasingly in the early twentieth century, however, militancy among urban-centred male industrial workers grew. This took the form mainly of frequent absenteeism, industrial delinquency, namely sabotage, and sporadic strikes. Workers became more vehement, but not necessarily more organised. There were a number of attempts at establishing trade unions. In 1897 Katayama Sen (1859–1933) established the *Rodo Kumiai Kiseikai* (Society for the Promotion of Trade Unions), and he tried, among other things, to organise metalworkers into the *Tekko Kumiai* (Metalworkers' Union). Katayama and other left-wingers, such as Abe Isoo (1865–1949), Kinoshita Naoe (1869–1937) and Kotoku Shusui (1871–1911) generally accepted the Marxist position of the inherent struggle between workers and managers and to that end established the *Nippon Shakai-to* (Japan Socialist Party). Other social reformers, notably Suzuki Bunji (1885–1946), found inspiration more in Christianity, and especially the Unitarian Church, than in Marxism, and thus preached a gospel of labour–management co-operation rather than conflict. Suzuki founded the moderate *Yuaikai* (Friendship Association), in 1911, which after the 1914–18 war was renamed the *Nihon Sodomei Yuaikai* (General Labour Organisation). These early attempts at a trade union movement, however, floundered. One reason was that the government, although keen as we shall see on improving the industrial climate, was virulently opposed to any form of worker organisation. In 1900 a special Public Peace Police Act was passed as a means of seriously curtailing union activities; government repressive legislation, therefore, was partly responsible for the abortive failure of Meiji syndicalism.

There were also, however, basic social reasons. Japanese labour, as we have seen, was organised not so much in terms of factories, let alone trades, as in disparate, hierarchically structured *oyakata-kokata* gangs. These vertical organisations militated against the development of horizontal trade union movements. Also, it should be recalled that even by 1910 or thereabouts one is still speaking in terms of a very limited number of male industrial workers, in fact numbering just over 300,000. It was after the 1914–18 war, when industrial expansion had experienced a boom and hence the number of factory workers increased in geometric proportions that a sufficiently extensive numerical base existed for the growth of a trade union movement – though once again it was to be aborted by political forces of repression. Nevertheless, the challenge, albeit confused and chaotic in character, posed by workers in the early twentieth century was one of the major forces which prompted a number of managers to re-evaluate their policies and seek more progressive forms of industrial relations.

The more immediate and forceful propulsion for improving industrial relations was the bureaucracy. In 1896 the government established the *Noshoko Koto Kaigi* (Superior Council on Agriculture, Commerce and Industry), with a view to carrying out an inquiry into the working conditions and state of health of the country's workforce. The government's motivation here should not necessarily be perceived in terms of altruism. For one thing, the transfer from the public to the private sector of major industries and mines had only recently begun taking place; the government, therefore, was concerned to see how private industry was coping. More fundamentally, however, the government, especially in view of its policy of expansionism, was concerned at the *kyohei* part of the Meiji equation. Japan was unlikely to be able to boast a strong army if the recruits were to consist essentially of weak soldiers. The nation's health needed to be properly monitored. Girls working in appalling conditions in factories, as a result of which debilitating and infectious diseases were rampant, were hardly likely to be in a position of producing and rearing able-bodied children.

The commission which had been appointed in 1896 completed its report in 1898 and submitted it to the government. As frequently happened in the parliamentary history of the Meiji era, however, there occurred a political crisis, resulting in a change of government which precluded the recommendations being debated by the Chamber. Nevertheless, in the ensuing decade the government persisted. These efforts from the bureaucracy met with very stiff opposition from the leaders of private industry. The latter objected to government intervention and factory legislation on two grounds. Firstly, they claimed that government intervention was anathema to the principles of *laissez-faire* and that in any case the disruption involved would seriously jeopardise Japan's growing competitive position. Secondly, however, business leaders stressed that while the government was insisting on the contractual aspect of industrial relations, the moral nature of Japanese traditional patterns of inter-personal relations was being discarded; in other words, legislation would disrupt the affectionate bonds which existed between worker and manager, based on the loyalty of the former and the benevolence of the latter. It is interesting to note how business leaders were using both Western and indigenous derived principles to counteract the government. This bureaucracy–business confrontation, however, should also be seen in the broader political context of the time.

The late nineteenth and early twentieth centuries witnessed an intense struggle for political power between the *genro* and the popular parties. The major paymasters of the latter were private industrial enterprises. It was not only in the field of industrial relations that the Diet (the 1890 established parliament) was always and *a priori* opposed to government-sponsored legislation, but in practically every domain. Towards the end of the Meiji era the conflict was in the process of being resolved and indeed in its place there developed a most cordial entente between business and bureaucracy. Thus, finally a Mining Act was passed in 1905 and a Factory Act in 1911; these theoretically provided protection to women and children, but neither was to be implemented until 1916 and even then the interpretation of the acts was left to the discretion of the employers.

This ruthlessly unviable exploitation of workers by Japanese entrepreneurs may appear to contradict the statement made earlier in this chapter, that the major factor behind Japan's stunning economic performance lay in the quality of the new élite. This, however, is not the case. By the beginning of the second decade of the twentieth century working conditions in both light and heavy industry sectors started to improve significantly. If one considers that large-scale factory production in the private sector began in the 1890s, then one can appreciate that it took only twenty years for Japanese managers to learn the irrefutable lesson that good working conditions result in much better industrial performances, higher productivity and, hence, bigger profits. It took industrialised Western countries far longer to reach this conclusion, while it still apparently completely eludes the leaders of such potentially rich countries as Brazil, the Argentine, Mexico, Venezuela and Indonesia. Thus, by the end of the Meiji era the emergence of Japanese-style management is apparent. While the features of this system are well known today, and will be briefly summarised shortly, one point should be noted. Given Japan's position as a latecomer and her disadvantageous situation *vis-à-vis* her Western competitors and the general absence of wealth in natural resources, successful economic performance and penetration of vitally necessary export markets still had to depend on the availability of cheap labour. While salaries were to improve and monetary incentives were introduced into the factory system, this could only be marginal. The major input of Japan's successful industries was not so much of a material nature as in the creation of a spirit of enterprise. Indeed a government report of the late nineteenth century had concluded that taking into account the necessary ingredients for successful enterprise, namely capital, technology and spirit, while capital and technology accounted for 25 per cent each, spirit was no less than 50 per cent – though, needless to say, this should be seen as moral exhortation rather than empirical analysis, spirit being by definition unquantifiable.

If the period from roughly 1870 to 1900 is the age of entrepreneurs, the ensuing decades correspond to the age of managers. Whereas the entrepreneurs may be said to have possessed a certain creative genius, which they undoubtedly did as pioneers, the managers had method. It was the latter who reorganised the structures of labour within the industrial context. While entrepreneurs and managers will be looked at shortly, an interesting, though not necessarily all that paradoxical, phenomenon should be noted. While a number of entrepreneurs may have been briefly exposed to Western-style education, nevertheless the atmosphere in which they were steeped during their formative years was that of Confucianism. On the other hand, the new generation of modern managers, born for the most part at the very end of the Tokugawa period or early Meiji period, were unlikely to have had any Confucianist education, but on the contrary were generally products of progressive, consciously anti-Confucianist, Westernised institutions such as the Keio Gijuku, founded by Fukuzawa Yukichi. Yet it was the entrepreneurs who pursued Western-inspired industrial labour market policies, while managers were to revive traditional social patterns of the Edo era. A somewhat comparable phenomenon was to occur among the country's intellectual élite: namely the earlier adulatory generation of things Western was succeeded by a more culturally conservative breed. The role of modern, progressive managers in reviving traditional social patterns should, once again, emphasise the dialectical, in fact symbiotic, nature of the cultural–economic process, as opposed to the tradition versus modernity model. One more point, however, in regard to the emergence of Japanese-style management should be noted: it applied mainly to the *zaibatsu*; while the *zaibatsu* became the leading economic force in the country by the time of the 1914–18 war, they were by no means the major employers in terms of the number of employees. Even leaving aside the rural sector, industry also in numerical terms continued (and continues) to be dominated by small workshops or medium-sized enterprises.

The large firms, under the skilful supervision of the new managers, proceeded to adopt the social patterns of the *ie*. They sought to instil in all their employees a sense of belonging, identification and loyalty to the firm as one *ie*. The first step in this process was to dispense with the extraneous role of the *oyakata*. Whereas the latter had been instrumental in helping their *kokata* acquire skills, large firms sought to displace the *oyakata* by inaugurating their own training schemes. In other cases, powerful and reputable *oyakata* were absorbed into the firm, given positions in management, and hence their *kokata* were thereby integrated into the organisation. The principal quality of the *ie* is the security that it offers. Edo-style apprenticeship systems were re-introduced. Thus a worker would be hired on a probationary basis, a trial period would ensue in order to determine the individual's attitude and the degree to which he could fit in, following which, if successful, he would be guaranteed life-long employment. Wages were paid not according to the amount or quality of work – thus piece-work, for example, was abolished – but according to seniority, namely the number of years spent working in the firm. Extensive welfare facilities were developed: enterprise schools for employees' children, medical facilities, recreation centres, training programmes and assistance in finding marriage partners. All these measures, while improving the conditions of workers, also had a clear economic rationale: a secure and stable workforce helped substantially to raise productivity, while actual wage levels could be kept down, but discipline, indeed harmony, within the firm-qua-*ie* was maintained.

It must once again be stressed that this transformation should by no means be perceived as a sudden ascension from inferno to an industrial paradise. The 1925 publication by Wakizo Hosoi (1896–1925), *Joko Aishi (The Tragic History of Female Factory Workers)*, movingly described the desperate plight of female factory operatives and thereby bore ample testimony to the fact that throughout the Taisho period conditions for many, especially females, still remained appalling. By the late Meiji period, however, a new pattern was set, albeit modelled on the past, which increasingly assumed the characteristic of Japanese industrial society. That it was the sectors which were more modern, more advanced in the use of sophisticated technology which clung most tenaciously to traditional patterns of inter-personal relationships also remains the case today; thus the Matsushita Electric Company, founded by Matsushita Konosuke (b. 1894) in 1919, today the world's pace-setter in electronics, is a highly modernised replica of the ideal Edo era *ie*. The son, therefore, resembles not so much the father, as the grandfather, or indeed the great-grandfather.

By the end of the Meiji period, therefore, certain significant changes had occurred in the mode of production and patterns were established which, *mutatis mutandis*, remained in force until the end of the Second World War. Since 1945 creative impulses have brought a new dynamic dimension to the established pattern. Among the more influential elements in the further development of a combined original and traditional system of industrial relations has been the role played by the trade unions. This movement has, among other things, ensured that workers would gain not only security but a proper share of a company's profits as well.

It is also in the late Meiji period that the ownership of the means of production came to be concentrated into a narrow oligopolistic circle. This was a feature of the Japanese economy which in the twenties, thirties and early forties became increasingly more prominent. The major *zaibatsu*, notably Mitsui, Mitsubishi, Sumitomo and Yasuda, controlled Japanese economic affairs to an extent which no other group of financial or industrial combines have ever been able to establish in any other capitalist country. Following Japan's defeat in 1945 and as part of the American Occupation's policy of democratisation anti-trust laws were introduced and the *zaibatsu* were dissolved. Mitsui, Mitsubishi, Sumitomo – Yasuda today consists of the Fuji banking and insurance companies – remain names to conjure with, though their structures, especially the pre-war system of interlocking directorships and holding company control, differ from what they used to be. Post-war economic reconstruction has also witnessed the growth of new mammoth industrial organisations, especially in the automobile manufacturing sector, Toyota and Nissan, and in electronics, Matsushita, Toshiba, Hitachi. While numbers have swelled and the character of the Japanese economy, as a result of both structural and legal reforms, has markedly changed, nevertheless the role of industrial giants remains more pronounced in Japan than in other major capitalist industrialised countries. Why did Japanese industry develop in this fashion?

The combination of state guidance and encouragement through subsidies, of political stability, of a free market economy and the new openings and stimulation provided by foreign trade all contributed to creating a climate highly conducive to vibrant entrepreneurial activity. This was an age of initiative. The numerous activities which men of vision could engage in is perhaps not so much illustrated as caricatured – in view of the somewhat exceptional nature of his character – by the extraordinary career of Shibusawa Elichi (1840–1931). The son of a rich farmer, he gained samurai status, and entered the service of the bakufu. Initially xenophobic in outlook, he was persuaded to accompany the last shogun's younger brother to the Paris International Exposition of 1867, visited Lyon's sericultural districts and industries on his way from Marseille to Paris, was dazzled by the material splendour of the Second Empire, and then never looked back. After a stint in the Meiji administration, he moved into private enterprise and at one stage or another was involved in practically every aspect of industrial activity, stretching from banking to cotton.

There were many other entrepreneurs whose careers were perhaps less illustrious than Shibusawa's, but impressive nonetheless. While initiative and vision are undoubtedly most valuable assets for the development of an enterprise, capital remains an essential ingredient. In the course of the late nineteenth and early twentieth centuries capital was becoming increasingly important as industry was becoming more mechanised; machinery had to be paid for and it was expensive. Those companies which were able to import machinery were able to operate economies of scale which their less mechanised competitors could not. The late Meiji period witnessed a steady and indeed accelerating diminution in the total number of firms, in order words the concentration of ownership of the means of production. This was one major factor in the rise of a small number of *zaibatsu*; a *zaibatsu* literally means a financial clique, thereby indicating that the origin of these companies lay in the capital which they had at their disposal. Another factor towards the growth of the *zaibatsu* which should be mentioned here is that they received preferential treatment from the Meiji government. This in turn is no doubt partly attributable to the fact that they were more lavish in their bribes than competitors, but also reflects a tradition which the Meiji government carried over from bakufu and han practices: the conferring of a special status to certain designated merchant houses. Thus, for example, when the government proceeded to sell their heavy industries, mines, and modern mills to the private sector, these were not auctioned off on the open market but negotiated *in camera* through a series of private deals. The beneficiaries were primarily the houses of Mitsui, Sumitomo and Mitsubishi.

Mitsui and Sumitomo were merchant houses dating from the Edo era. In both cases, however, the families themselves were not so much involved in the modernisation of their firms, but depended on the entrepreneurial vision and dynamism of outsiders, Minomura Rizaemon (1921–77) for Mitsui and Hirose Saihei (1828–1914) for Sumitomo. Mitsubishi and Yasuda were post-1868 creations, the former established by Iwasaki Yataro (1834–85), the latter by Yasuda Zenjiro (1838–1921). Mitsui obtained from the early Meiji period, mainly via the kind offices of the well-remunerated Inoue Kaoru, a number of sizeable government contracts out of which they earned large profits. Iwasaki had been responsible for the administration of the finances of Tosa han in the bakumatsu period. Following the 1868 revolution he obtained the use of the former han's ships in order to start up a transportation business; in 1874 he put his fleet at the disposal of the government to ferry troops to Taiwan, thus earning official goodwill and protection, in due course enabling Mitsubishi to found the Nippon Yusen Kaisha, which eventually became one of the world's largest shipping firms. Sumitomo accumulated capital from mining, and mainly by taking the initiative of introducing Western technology into the Besshi copper mines, which had been Sumitomo property since the seventeenth century.

The major feature which the four *zaibatsu* shared, and hence their designation as financial cliques, is that they established their own banks. They were highly successful in accumulating and generating their own capital. It was with the capital that they cornered that they were able to enlarge their industrial activities, acquire government plants, and thus lay the foundations for their empires. Shibusawa, although engaged as early as 1872 in the establishment of a bank, the Dai Ichi Ginko, administered it as president, but did not seek to own it; hence no Shibusawa *zaibatsu* emerged.

The *zaibatsu* became engaged in all stages of production and in all sectors of industry, primary, secondary and tertiary. Their tentacles, therefore, spread to mining, real estate, textiles, metalwork, shipbuilding, construction, shipping, insurance, banking, trade, etc. Their special relationship with the government continued throughout the decades and they both contributed to and benefited from the country's military and imperialistic expansion. They were especially well placed to reap the ample harvest of the economic boom which Japan was able to experience in the 1914–18 war. As already noted, it was especially after the war that the *zaibatsu* came to dominate almost completely both product and capital markets.

By the beginning of the twentieth century the age of the entrepreneurs had by and large come to an end. In the twenties and thirties there were a number of prominent entrepreneurs who emerged and proceeded to build vast industrial enterprises, though these tended to be in new ventures, thus Matsushita Konosuke in electronics and Toyoda Sakichi in automobile manufacturing providing two of the more dazzling examples. Indeed, Matsushita's background and career are reminiscent of the heady days of Meiji entrepreneurship: born the seventh son of a destitute peasant family, he left school at eleven, at sixteen was working in Osaka in a bicycle repair shop (specialising in British bicycles!), and at the age of twenty-five he founded Matsushita Electric. While a number of other cases could be identified, including Honda Soichiro, the rags-to-riches syndrome is not a prominent part of the late Meiji or interwar scenes.

Similarly, in regard not only to the *zaibatsu* but big firms in general, family control of the enterprises was loosened. While family members might be granted prestigious posts, such as president, in fact their roles tended to be of a mainly ceremonial nature. In the case of Mitsui where, we have seen, the family had not played a decisive role in any case, the character of its directorship radically changed: Minomura Rizaemon had been illiterate and based his decisions mainly on his remarkable powers of intuition, while Nakamigawa Hikojiro (1854–1901), who assumed the post of director in 1891, was highly educated both at home and abroad, having graduated from Keio and subsequently studied for three years in Britain. The new managers tended to be university graduates, emanating from Keio, the Tokyo Higher Commercial School (later Hitotsubashi) founded in 1887, and indeed major enterprises began vying with the bureaucracy to recruit graduates from Tokyo Imperial University. While these three remained the more prestigious institutions, throughout the country commercial colleges were being established to provide for the new needs of industry. The managers were educated, they were professionals. What the entrepreneurs had created, the managers proceeded to consolidate. As we have seen, they were responsible for the reform of industrial relations by re-introducing concepts from the Edo era. The pattern also developed whereby university or college graduates would enter a firm upon graduation and stay with that firm until retirement; the managers, therefore, became the *banto* of these modern *ie*. It was also under their initiative that certain decision-making processes with traditional roots, such as the *ringi* system, whereby proposals for policies originate from subordinates and move up the enterprise hierarchy in circular fashion to be finally submitted for approval to the chief, were re-introduced.

Again, it should be emphasised that what has been described above should be perceived mainly as a trend, not a sudden widespread reality. In so far as education was concerned, for example, the percentage of the age-group able to attend university remained infinitesimal throughout the late Meiji and interwar periods. While college graduates were very much in demand, their supply was limited. The trend nevertheless persisted and was enlarged: while at the time of the First World War only approximately 15 per cent of business leaders had university qualifications, by the Second World War this figure stood at approximately 80 per cent. Within a short time, therefore, the percentage of qualified managers in Japanese industry was higher than in Western countries.

Who were these managers? Again, as with the bureaucrats, the costs of education must be borne in mind. The modern Japanese manager, as opposed to the earlier entrepreneurs, was unlikely to be a son of his own works. In most cases they were no doubt the offspring of urban-based, mainly Tokyo, bankers, businessmen or bureaucrats; in the twenties, as the phenomenon of absentee landlordism grew, this group was also likely to produce recruits into business. The career prospects and status of any (male) individual were determined not by social origin but by educational achievements. In comparison with Western Europe and the United States, it is probable that there continued to exist in Japan a greater degree of social mobility, and indeed a number of comparative studies indicate that this was in effect the case. Nevertheless, in view of the costs and rather limited availability of higher education, it is also reasonable to assume that by the late Meiji period the new business leadership became a self-perpetuating élite. It remained, however, a highly qualified and highly motivated élite; Japan's continued economic growth is a testimony of their qualities and determination.

What was the motivating force of these managers? This is a highly speculative exercise, by no means easily verified by empirical research. One can nevertheless seek to establish a model by means of reasonable conjecture; models, contrary to orthodox definition, are imperfect and must assume numerous exceptions. Managers, young executives and the workers in Japan's labour aristocracy, namely those who secured life-long employment in one of the big firms, became associated with the *ie*, indeed not only associated, but vitally integrated parts of it. The nature of the inter-personal relationships which came to characterise these modern *ie*, as they had their Edo predecessors, and other burgeoning features, the company song, the motto, the early morning pep talks, the group activities, the general paternalistic attention given to employees, undoubtedly led to the creation of strong bonds of solidarity between the total *ie* and its constituent parts. All this in turn generated a strong sense of loyalty to the *ie*. At the same time, although occasionally collusion existed, generally in the face of some foreign menace, nevertheless the general pattern was one of extreme competitiveness – in terms of productivity, market penetration, innovations, etc. – between the big firms. Members of the *ie* were exhorted to work harder for the good of the *ie*. Thus, while recognising that nationalism remained a force in modern Japan, nevertheless nationalism, except perhaps at times of war, remains a rather abstract concept. In real terms it is difficult to see why the young executive of Fuji Spinning Company, for example, should be motivated by die-hard nationalism. Or, rather, while it may be reasonable to assume that he would be thus motivated in 1941, *a priori* there is no reason why he should have felt the same in 1921 or indeed in 1911. Yet, at the end of the day it is simply unconvincing to explain Japan's economic performance simply by taking into consideration economic factors. That intangible quality of spirit was undoubtedly there, as indeed it is definitely felt in Japan today. That spirit, it would seem, is tightly encapsulated in the *ie*. The driving spiritual force of Japan's economic performance from the late Meiji period onwards has been, and remains, that strong sense of *ie* solidarity and loyalty.

To that general proposition, one postscript should be added. The new managers introduced many innovations in the organisation of the firms they worked for. One major innovation, however, notably carried out, for example, by one of Mitsui's new managerial recruits in the early twentieth century, Ikeda Shigeaki (1867–1950), later to become a Mitsui director, was to bring about a radical redistribution of profits within the firm. In the course of the ensuing decades, not only managers' salaries, but the wages of all permanent personnel rose substantially. Thus, in once again paraphrasing Cecil Rhodes, one can conclude that while *ie*-ism is fine, *ie*-ism plus 5 per cent is even better.

PEASANTS AND LANDLORDS

Japan, as has already been noted, remained throughout the period of transformation to modernity an essentially agrarian society. In view of the fact that the primary sector remained by far the largest employer and also that the overwhelming majority of the Japanese population resided in small rural villages, it is necessary to stress that Japan was above all a nation of peasants. Whereas today farmers represent some of the richer sectors of Japanese society – the astronomic costs of land ensure them a very sizeable fixed capital, and the government subsidises agriculture generously, thus farmers represent the most reliable supporters of the ruling Liberal Democratic Party (and indeed thanks to an element of gerrymandering their political influence is disproportionate to their numbers, for today they correspond to under 10 per cent of the population) – the situation during the Meiji era was rather different. The relative deprivations of the pre-war peasant community and the contradictions of the Japanese agrarian economy contributed in a significant manner to the political extremism of the thirties. At the same time it was the rural sector which bore the main initial burden of industrialisation. The export of raw materials and the surplus generated from agriculture subsidised the process of industrialisation. For these and other reasons, it is clear that the rural sector is of fundamental importance.

Agricultural production, as noted earlier, rose throughout the period of transformation and generally managed to keep in step with the increase in population. This rise in agricultural production was partly due to the area under cultivation being increased, in the course of the Meiji period by approximately 13 per cent. With the dispossession of the daimyo in 1872, following the return of the registers to the imperial government, agriculture was fully opened to the forces of a market economy. Landlords played a vigorous entrepreneurial role by means of modernisation, diversification, investment and developing rural manufacturing. Significant advances in irrigation, application of fertilisers, the introduction of better crop strains on the one hand and pest control on the other, and other improvements all led to a substantial increase in agricultural productivity. Furthermore, while it is correct in one sense to view the state as milking the rural sector in order to subsidise military and industrial developments, it should also be borne in mind that the state contributed to rural progress. By the mid-seventies a number of agricultural colleges had been established by the government. For obvious reasons governmental efforts were particularly directed towards sericulture; here the state played a vital role in the introduction and diffusion of technological innovations, notably in disease control, quality improvement and mulberry culture. In 1896 a sericultural college was established in Tokyo, and two years later a sister institution was set up in Kyoto. The National Sericultural Experiment Station, established at the end of the Meiji era, was the most sophisticated institute of its kind in the world. The production of raw silk increased by a multiple of more than twelve in the course of the Meiji era, while the revenue obtained from the export of raw silk in the same period increased by a multiple of twenty-four.

While the agricultural sector, therefore, was by far the major source of foreign exchange earnings, it was also responsible for the generation of national capital. Until 1890 the land tax represented 70–80 per cent of the total government revenue. Following 1890 it dropped to just under 40 per cent and in the last decade or so of the Meiji period it corresponded to about a quarter. This apparent staggering decrease in revenue from land should be viewed in proper perspective: this was a decrease in relative, not absolute, terms. Nevertheless, the onus of taxation was eased, though this may have been more for political than economic reasons. The year 1890 marks the opening of the Diet and the first elections; the franchise was based on a poll tax and among the half-million or so who were entitled to vote there was a substantial number of landlords. Although landlord interests remained well represented in the Diet throughout the Meiji era, occasionally the government nevertheless had to resort to increasing temporarily the contribution of land taxes: for example, in 1899 the then prime minister Yamagata sought a rather steep increase, which was initially strongly opposed by the Diet, but when he also proposed to raise dietmen's salaries by more than double, resistance vanished.

The contribution of the rural sector to modernising Japan was not solely financial in nature. The bulk of the army's conscripts came from the peasantry. The girls who were recruited to work in the textile factories or indeed to cater to increasing demand for prostitutes in the urban *yukaku* were also exclusively taken from the villages. To the peasant community it appeared that whereas they were contributing a great deal they were receiving very little in return, apart that is from added hardships. While peasant grievances will be looked at shortly, it should be noted that rural discontent and not infrequent revolts remained a feature of Japanese society throughout the Meiji period, though especially in the initial stages of the transformation.

While sericulture and tea plantation and a few other cash crops were engaged in as a means of diversification, Japanese agriculture nonetheless remained essentially involved in rizicultural production. While technical improvements might yield a greater degree of productivity from the soil and a certain amount of land reclamation took place, the basic topographical problems remained the same. And the major problem was, and remains, the scarcity of arable land, the latter corresponding to only about 15 per cent of the country. The colonisation of Hokkaido helped to relieve some of the pressure, but only marginally. Throughout the Meiji period Japan was in fact overpopulated, especially in the rural regions, which constituted a significant force for seeking emigration outlets for the surplus population. The pressure on cultivatable land can be seen by the fact that by the end of the Meiji period and excluding Hokkaido more than 30 per cent of the farms were smaller than 1¼ acres and more than 65 per cent were smaller than 2½ acres. Thus the rural pattern of Meiji Japan consisted of very small plots with labour-intensive cultivation.

In 1872, as noted, the ban on the sale of land was lifted, agriculture became completely subject to a money economy and indeed a strictly capitalistic approach was adopted. As was indicated in Chapter 3, the pattern which emerged in the Meiji period was to a large extent a natural outgrowth of developments which had occurred in the Edo era: the 1872 reforms legalised a situation which had been in existence *de facto* for some time. The ensuing decades of the transformation period witnessed the proprietorship of more land into fewer hands. Thus, at the time of the lifting of the ban on the sale of land approximately 20 per cent of the peasantry consisted of tenants rather than proprietors; by the end of the Meiji period that figure had more than doubled, in fact it was not far from 50 per cent. This pattern of land tenure remained constant until the US Occupation imposed land reform in 1947. Given the labour-intensive nature of Japanese riziculture during this period, however, the new landlords did not eject their tenants from the land but kept them as agricultural workers. Rents were generally paid in kind, ranging from 25 to 80 per cent of the yield, but averaging out at about 50 per cent. As with entrepreneurs, the early Meiji years witnessed a degree of social mobility within the peasantry, with, for example, those able to capitalise most on the new foreign markets for raw silk or tea able to accumulate capital and thereby increase their holdings. By the end of the Meiji period, however, social stratification within the peasant community was consolidated; landlords of the twenties and thirties were unlikely to be the sons of their own works, unlikely to have made it by visionary perceptions of new market or produce opportunities, but in all likelihood they were sons of landlords.

With the bureaucrats and the business managers representing the urban élite, the landlords were their rural counterparts. A certain amount of revisionist work notwithstanding, Japanese landlords have tended to be the victims of a rather bad press, especially in Japanese historiography. The parasitic image which has been projected, however, is not necessarily consistent with historical reality. While it is true that there was a fairly wide unequal distribution of wealth within the rural communities, in the Meiji period the capital accumulated by landlords tended to be reinvested in projects for improved agricultural production and diversification. The landlords were able to benefit from a greater degree of education – for it was they rather than the tenants, needless to say, who attended the agricultural colleges – and hence able to experiment with and implement innovative techniques. The fact that they were able to travel also meant that they were agents for the diffusion of better strains of rice and other produce. Their mobility also led to the villages being integrated into a wider national network, for example landlords were in a position of being able to interpret government policies. The social structure of the village hardly changed from the Edo to the Meiji periods. While in the Edo era the village headman and his assistants administered affairs, in the Meiji years these functions were taken over by the landlord class. The authoritarian paternalism exercised by landlords also ensured a degree of continuity and social assistance; thus landlords were instrumental in the development of education and various welfare facilities, such as medical services, in the villages.

The picture sketched above obviously involves a high degree of generalisation and is also perhaps somewhat on the favourable side. Nevertheless, when the balance sheet is drawn up, it would be correct to view the landlords of the Meiji era as an essentially progressive force in economic terms, even though it may well be argued that in social terms they constituted a rather regressive force; to put it in different terms, rural Japan was composed of a capitalist base and feudal superstructure.

From the late Meiji period, however, absentee-landlordism became more prevalent as landlords moved themselves and their capital, either to invest in industry or to live it up by conspicuous consumption of imported luxury goods, leaving the collection of rents from tenants to ruthless, impersonal agents. The situation in the rural districts tended towards deterioration in the interwar period. In any case, however, there was a basic weakness in the Japanese rural economy which was not the case in the urban sector.

Sericulture, as we have seen, played a vital role in Japan's industrialisation. While the export of silk goods remained an important element in the national economy, nevertheless by the late Meiji period the urban sector was reasonably diversified, including not only cotton textiles and other light industry products for both domestic consumption and exports, but heavy industry and especially military procurements added an important dimension. For the rural sector, however, sericulture was *the* major source of added revenue; riziculture was not a significant earner especially once cheap rice from Japan's colonies began being imported in the twentieth century. Thus, for all intents and purposes, the rural community depended on a single product for its livelihood. This dependence was further exacerbated by the fact that the product was sold mainly in one market; by the early twentieth century approximately 70 per cent of Japan's silk exports went to the United States. Practically only a single cash crop and practically only a single market meant that the Japanese rural economy possessed two of the more acute characteristics of an underdeveloped economy. When the US depression occurred and then in the later thirties economic warfare against Japan was waged by Washington, the consequences on the rural economy were disastrous. It is clear, therefore, that while in the short term the increase in agricultural production contributed significantly to the process of industrialisation, in a longer-term perspective the foundations of the rural economy were most unstable, in fact weak. Furthermore, while the nature of the capitalist agrarian economy of the Meiji period may have been progressive, its growth was stunted. As poor tenants came to represent such a high percentage of the rural community, the highly unequal distribution of wealth, the oppressive conditions, the absence of fair remuneration for work, resulted in the failure to develop a rural domestic consumption market and also a lack of incentives for further improvement.

In political terms, not surprisingly given the conditions, a certain radicalism existed in the rural areas even though it may not have been either effectively or coherently articulated. In the early Meiji period, as will be seen in the following chapter, tenants and landlords joined in significant numbers to swell the ranks of what was called the *jiyu-minken-undo*, the movement for freedom and popular rights, a movement consisting of disparate and often contradictory elements whose only real common bond was its opposition to the government. Towards the end of the century landlords became politically more quiescent at least as far as extra-parliamentary action was concerned in view of their influence and representation in the Lower House of the Diet.

For tenants and small proprietors, however, discontent remained a powerful sentiment. Given the rather feudal nature of rural social relationships, however, anti-landlordism was not a significant feature of rural radicalism. There was, however, a strong anti-urban, anti-capitalist bias to rural radical political ideology. From the peasant perspective, and indeed to a considerable degree in reality, the separation between the rural and the urban communities assumed the proportions of a chasm. City-dwellers enjoyed much higher revenues, far better educational facilities, an incomparably richer cultural life, many more welfare services and the utilities of modern life such as electric lights, public transportation, brick buildings, and so on. Between landlords and tenants, managers and workers class divisions certainly existed. The more glaring and potentially explosive discrepancies, however, were those between the urban and rural communities; in social, economic and political terms it was primarily here that one could speak of the existence of two Japanese nations. The real crisis of the transformation to modernity was the failure to remedy this situation. One can surmise that had there been an extensive programme of land reform some time in the twenties rather than in the late forties, new forces would have been generated for further economic development, a more equal distribution of wealth would have contributed to the growth of a domestic consumption market, and all this in turn would possibly have resulted in a more stable and progressive political development. As it is, however, this exercise can only be pure speculation for nothing of the sort was attempted. By the end of the Meiji era and in the ensuing decades the landlords were not only parasitic, but politically powerful; it would have taken a revolution to dislodge them – which is precisely what happened in the late forties; though the agent of revolution on this occasion happened to be the US army.

WOMEN

The participation of females in industrial labour has already been examined. In terms of work, however, in view of the predominance of agriculture throughout the Meiji period, it goes without saying that the major function of women continued to be in those areas of agrarian activity listed in Chapter 3. Towards the end of the era there were a few clerical jobs available to women, otherwise they might find employment as telephone operators, ticket vendors in railway stations or salesgirls in the urban department stores.

In 1873 the Meiji government abolished the *yukaku*. In view of the chaos which ensued, however, with the inmates taking to the streets, the order was rescinded within a year – the licensed quarters were finally eliminated only after the Second World War. Throughout the Meiji, Taisho and early Showa years, therefore, prostitution continued to flourish. There were a few elements of modernisation. For example, some establishments abandoned the practice of exposing the girls in cages and instead provided photograph albums for the perusal of potential customers. In the mid-seventies Lock hospitals were established in all the major *yukaku*. Venereal disease, however, remained very much of a problem throughout the Meiji era; in the early twentieth century syphilis was claiming approximately 10,000 lives per annum. Otherwise life in the *yukaku* continued much as before, indeed some hailed them as the last refuge of traditional Japan, for example, the novelist, Nagai Kafu (1879–1958), who, like his Edo literary predecessors, chose the *yukaku* as the setting for some of his works. In the early Meiji period a number of intellectuals and polemicists urged the abolition of prostitution, though their motivations here would appear to have been mainly because of the embarrassment they feared prostitution would cause Japan *vis-à-vis* the Western powers; once it was discovered that prostitution also existed in Western countries, presumably it became less urgent to close Japanese brothels. In the late nineteenth and early twentieth centuries anti-prostitution movements did emerge, though these were mainly under the umbrella of Christian organisations, for example the Japanese branch of the Salvation Army and also the *Fujin Kyofukai*, the Christian Women's Social Reform Organisation. Their efforts, however, were in vain.

Apart from farming, fishing, textiles, employment as domestic servants and waitresses, the few clerical positions noted above, and prostitution, there were not many openings for women. They did, as will be seen shortly, eventually swell the ranks of the teaching profession. As far as the other professions were concerned, their impact was minimal; this was partly because the education they received was not geared towards professional life, partly because of discriminatory social attitudes, partly because of government legislation, with women being barred from entering the civil service and from practising law. An important exception, albeit not of great numerical significance, lay in the field of medicine; the first Japanese female doctor began practising in 1885. There were also a number of women engaged in the arts, notably, for example, the novelist Higuchi Ichiyo (1872–96). In these respects, however, Japan can hardly be said to have been very different from Western industrialised societies.

Japan was ahead of most countries, however, in introducing compulsory education for girls – as indeed was the case for compulsory primary education in general; with the exception of England (1870), most Western countries did not make primary education compulsory until much later in the century. As has been seen, however, the 1872 Education Act was the expression of an intention, not an immediate realisation. Thus, while in the mid-seventies approximately 50 per cent of boys were enrolled for the three years of compulsory primary schooling, the figure for girls was in the region of 20 per cent. The percentage for both sexes increased in the next two decades at roughly even pace. In 1900, however, ten million yen were taken out of the Boxer indemnity in order to make the first part of primary education free. Numbers then rose dramatically and by the end of the Meiji era almost 100 per cent of the female age group were attending primary school.

Secondary education, for either sex, was only made compulsory after the Second World War. Already in the Meiji era, however, secondary education was provided for girls, though the number who took advantage of this was limited. In 1885 there were nine girls' high schools with six hundred pupils enrolled, which by 1912 had increased to 297 girls' high schools with 74,816 pupils enrolled. The curricula of these schools, however, were based on the principles of what was called *ryosai-kenbo-shugi*, 'good wife – wise mother-ism'. Thus, apart from the three Rs, girls were given a heavy dosage of moral instruction, lessons in domestic matters, such as sewing, and in such cultural activities as flower arrangement.

The first teacher-training college was founded in 1872, though it was exclusively for males – teaching was one of the professions which it was not considered demeaning for a samurai to join. Two years later, however, the Tokyo Joshi Shihan Gakko was founded, which was the first women's teacher-training college. Thereafter other prefectures either established such colleges for women or had a part of the college reserved for girls – schooling, even at this level, involved a clear separation of the sexes. By the mid-Meiji period women were making significant inroads into the primary teaching profession, partly because they were cheaper than men and also because the growing army was absorbing more ex-samurai.

In regard to the tertiary sector, women were barred not only from the Tokyo and Kyoto Imperial Universities, but also from the private universities such as Keio and Waseda. They could gain admission to a number of vocational schools, for example the Tokyo Academy of Music, and in 1900 the Tokyo Women's Medical College was established. Otherwise, progress in that direction was achieved as a result of the efforts of primarily two individuals, one male, one female, both of whom were influenced by their experiences in the United States. Naruse Jinzo (1858–1919) became concerned at what he perceived as a popular reaction against higher education for women – when in the late nineteenth century a conservative cultural mood was sweeping the nation – and so in 1890 travelled to the United States and spent some three years there visiting women's colleges. In 1895 he published a book on women's education and began soliciting funds for the establishment of a university for girls. His efforts proved fruitful and in April 1901 the Nihon Joshi Daigaku, Japan Women's University, was officially inaugurated. Tsuda Umeko (1865–1929) had been one of the five girls selected to go to study in the United States at the time of the Iwakura mission. She returned to Japan in 1882, then went back to the US in 1889 where she obtained a degree from Bryn Mawr. In 1900 she established what subsequently came to be called Tsuda College and which specialised mainly in English language and literature. In 1913 female students were admitted to the imperial universities of Tohoku, Hokkaido and Kyushu, though the numbers were minute.

Prevailing social attitudes towards women reflected, not surprisingly, the changes in the general climate. In the first fifteen years or so of the Meiji era there was a marked degree of anti-Confucianist iconoclasm especially among intellectuals. This was also the period of *bunmei-kaika*, the years when practically all Western concepts and customs enjoyed a high prestige in Japan; to be Westernised was to be civilised. In the Rokumeikan (the Pavilion of the Baying Stag) erected by the government as a social centre to facilitate intercourse between the foreign community and the Japanese upper classes, wives and daughters of bureaucrats and businessmen appeared in Western-style evening dresses and danced to waltzes, polkas and other Western music. This was emblematic of a general climate of encouragement to Japanese women to emulate their Western sisters.

The liberation of women from the traditional Confucianist bondage was a theme rather stridently taken up by a number of the country's leading intellectuals. Fukuzawa stands out particularly both in terms of the force of his exposition and the prolific literature he wrote on the subject. He virulently attacked the traditional Japanese conjugal relation, namely the samurai pattern, and many of its ills, including the system of concubinage. In announcing the new age of female emancipation, among his many tracts on the subject he wrote a direct refutation of Kaibara Ekken's *Onna Daigaku* (see Chapter 3) and which he entitled *Shin Onna Daigaku*, namely the 'New Greater Learning for Women' – a work which was banned in girls' high schools while Kaibara's continued to be required reading. The pages of the *Meiroku Zasshi* – the 'Meiji Six Magazine' (six because it was founded in the sixth year of Meiji), which included articles by the period's most *avant-garde* intellectuals – were replete with attacks on the inferior status of the wife in the traditional Japanese family system, on concubinage, on prostitution, and other social ills afflicting Japanese women. Much of this polemic was influenced by Western writers on the subject, notably John Stuart Mill (1806–73) in his *The Subjection of Women*. A few, but not many, of these intellectuals put theory into practice. Mori Arinori, for example, a member of the Meiroku group, married his first wife in a Western-style ceremony and based the marriage on a contract which recognised mutual rights. (He later divorced her, however, and married his second wife according to traditional samurai custom.) It is difficult to see the pro-feminist literature of these early Meiji intellectuals as more than a passing, albeit exuberant, fancy. Fukuzawa, for example, gave his own two daughters a traditional upbringing and married them off without consultation; and in spite of his exhortations for girls' education, he did not open the doors of Keio to female students. However, the hypocrisy of Fukuzawa and other pro-feminist Japanese intellectuals by no means makes them unique of their genre. In any case, by the second half of the Meiji era the Rokumeikan and pretty much all that it stood for had been destroyed – the Rokumeikan by arson shortly after a fancy-dress ball when to the astonishment and anger of ardent patriots senior Japanese bureaucrats appeared as gondoliers, Nubian slaves, and in other outlandish disguises. When the ball was over orthodoxy returned: an orthodoxy epitomised in the dictum of an intellectual of more conservative hue, Kato Hiroyuki (1836–1916), namely that government is to the people what parents are to their children and husbands to their wives.

The feminist cause was by no means espoused solely by fashionable male intellectuals. A number of women became involved in the early stages of the *jiyu-minken-undo*. One of the early pioneers was Kishida Toshiko (1864–1901) who advocated both women's rights and love marriages. Kageyama Hideko (1867–1927) also joined the *jiyu-minken-undo*, but became disillusioned when she saw her male companions, theoretically supporting the feminist cause during the day, spending so much time in the *yukaku* at night; she later became a militant leader of the Taisho period *fujin undo* (women's movement). While a number of women activists publicly engaged in the political movements of the early Meiji period, this was abruptly brought to an end in 1887 with the promulgation of the Peace Preservation Ordinance, which remained in force until 1922; women were hereafter forbidden to join political movements, attend political meetings, or even listen to political speeches.

Nevertheless, women could be found engaged in political activism in the late Meiji period, though generally in underground left-wing movements. Otherwise the early flame of feminism had by no means been completely extinguished. While women were forbidden to become publicly involved in politics, they could read and write. The late Meiji era witnessed the emergence of a female literary circle which in 1911 established itself as the *Seitosha*, the Blue Stocking Society, partly inspired by the British eighteenth-century movement of the same name, and which began the publication of a monthly entitled *Seito*. Among the founders of the society was Hiratsuka Raicho (b. 1886) who throughout her career remained Japan's most ardent and constant advocate of women's rights.

In the more liberal atmosphere of the decade or so which followed the 1914–18 war feminists and feminist movements were able to operate with a somewhat greater degree of freedom. While in 1925 universal suffrage was granted to males, it was not extended to females. Women activists protested and obtained some encouragement from certain political quarters. The ultra-nationalistic, obscurantist atmosphere of the thirties and early forties, however, once again aborted all chance of women being granted equal civil rights. While the 1947 Constitution, drawn up mainly along American lines, granted women equality with men, this was not just a fortuitous gift, but could also be seen as the culmination of courageous women seeking to swim against the phallocratic tide.

Indeed, for the vast majority of women the Meiji period witnessed little progress in their status, in fact one could speak of a regression. This was accomplished both by the diffusion of samurai social customs and by legislation. The distinction between peasant and samurai marriages was drawn in Chapter 3, when it was also indicated that in the course of the Meiji period women were subjected to a process of samurai-isation. It is, of course, difficult to establish how quickly and how extensively this process took place; it was, however, most definitely the trend of the times.

The basic pattern of the samurai-type or *yome-iri* marriage has already been noted. A few other elements, however, are worthy of consideration. Thus one should note, for example, that the actual marriage ceremony was a purely social affair, not a contractual one – it was in this sense that Mori Arinori in his youth had sought to set a radical example. A marriage was legally binding only once the wife had been registered in her husband's family register (*koseki*), this usually occurred once her in-laws were satisfied that she was acceptable; frequently just before, or indeed after, the birth of the first, preferably male, child. A young wife, therefore, can be said to have had to undergo a probationary period. In spite of this, divorce rates throughout the Meiji period were high, second only to the United States among industrialised nations; women, it will be recalled, did not enjoy the right to divorce – except under certain very exceptional circumstances – thus showing that wives not only lost their independence but gained little security in exchange.

Perhaps the most prominent feature of the female condition to be stressed in regard to the Meiji period is the fact that women were producing many babies. In the course of that era there was a demographic increase of almost 60 per cent. The average Japanese family counted more than five children, which, among other things, indicates that the average woman was probably spending about a decade of her life in more or less constant pregnancy. During the Edo period population was limited by infanticide (*mabiki*) and while the practice seems to have continued to some extent in the early Meiji period, by the nineties it would appear to have generally disappeared. Although vulcanised rubber sheaths were introduced to Japan by the late nineteenth century and these were issued to soldiers in the Russo–Japanese war, the intention here was to prevent the spreading of venereal diseases rather than for purposes of birth control. Indeed, attempts to propagate birth control in the early twentieth century were heavily censored, in fact outlawed, by the Meiji government.

While attempting to illustrate the condition of the female sex in this period of transformation, one must be careful not to engage in caricature. Two points should be borne in mind. Thus, while it is true that the state, for example, sought to restrict severely women's legal rights in the new Civil Code promulgated in 1898 – whereby, although women were granted the right to inherit, own property and even to become household heads, this could occur only within certain strict qualifications, nor were they permitted to manage their own property, nor enter into any sort of contract or profession without the prior consent of their husbands – the same limitations on women's rights applied in the Code Napoléon and even more in the German Bürgeliches Gesetzbuch. If Japanese husbands assassinated their adulterous wives when discovered *in flagrante delicto* they were exonerated on the grounds of extenuating circumstances, while wives enjoyed no such privilege. But the same applied, *mutatis mutandis*, in many Western countries. In terms of political rights, while Japanese women were granted the right to vote in 1946, French women had to wait another two years and Swiss women in some of the cantons are still waiting. It was not only in Japan that birth control was banned. The list could be prolonged. Hence, though there were certain peculiarities in regard to the condition of Japanese women in the Meiji era, these did not necessarily deviate too markedly from more universal patterns. The second point is that although there undoubtedly existed certain social customs and legal restrictions which were obviously detrimental to women's interests and well-being, it does not follow that the image to conjure up of the entire Meiji Japan female sex should be that of despairing unhappiness. There is nothing to indicate that there was not as much gaiety, love and tenderness in Japan, when circumstances permitted, as elsewhere.

Certainly, however, the rather draconian and misogynous nature of government legislation and legal codification strongly illustrates not only its conservative character, but also the determination with which it sought to instil in the population unwavering qualities of loyalty and obedience. The government was quite clear that what the country needed were good soldiers and good workers. The late-nineteenth-century reaction against the insouciance and exuberant Westernism of the *bunmei-kaika* years was visible not only in relation to women, but also in educational policies and in the political domain. For the Meiji leadership the quality which came to be the most prized was that of discipline. For a disciplined society to be created, there was obviously no better place to start than in the home.

THE *ETA* AND OTHER MINORITIES

While the social and political reorganisation of Japan was taking place, the government also consolidated the nation's borders in both northerly and southerly directions. Following the daimyo's return of their estates to the tenno, in 1873 the king of the Ryukyus was invited to Tokyo in order to follow the example set by the daimyo. The status of sovereignty over the Ryukyus, as we have seen, was somewhat complex, traditionally the Chinese claiming the islands as one of their tributary states. When a Japanese military expedition was mounted to invade the island of Taiwan in 1874 – partly as a palliative measure for fiery samurai disappointed at not being able to invade Korea instead – the government used as its *casus belli* the fact that Ryukyuan fishermen had been eaten by Taiwanese cannibals, thereby making it clear that the Japanese government assumed protection over the Ryukyuans, which in turn granted them sovereignty over the islands. The formal annexation of the fifty-five islands of the archipelago, with a population of about half a million, took place in April of 1879 when the Ryukyus were reorganised administratively as the prefecture of Okinawa. China formally protested, but Ulysses S. Grant (1822–85), former Civil War General and US President at the time of the Iwakura mission, whose arbitration was sought, declared in favour of Japan. The Ryukyuan people, as noted in Chapter 3, do not differ significantly from the Japanese in either ethnic or linguistic terms. The Ryukyus became fully absorbed into Japan, in due course both education and conscription being extended to the islands, until Japan's defeat in the Second World War. Following the Occupation the Ryukyus were maintained as a kind of military colony by the United States until they were returned to Japan in 1972 – at which point one of the first steps the government undertook was to change all the road signs so that henceforth Ryukyuans would drive on the left (the Japanese practice) and not on the right as had been the case during the American occupation.

In 1869 the northern island of Ezo was renamed Hokkaido, which means 'road to the northern sea'. In the same year the *Hokkaido kaitaku-shi*, Hokkaido colonisation office, was established. The government invested a substantial sum of money in the development, mainly agriculture and fisheries, of the area and also set up the *tondenhei-seido*, colonial troops system, whereby ex-samurai were encouraged to migrate and take up the pioneering challenge which this new frontier offered. The colonisation office was abolished in 1882 following Meiji Japan's most infamous public political scandal.

Early Meiji Japan's investigative press which specialised in exposure of scandals associated with the oligarchy – and was labelled the *akashinbun*, literally 'red press' arising from the fact that newspapers were published on pink paper, but figuratively would correspond to the English 'yellow press' – discovered the collusion between Kuroda Kiyotaka (1840–1900), chief administrator of the colonial office, and Godai Tomoatsu (1834–85), a successful businessman of Satsuma origin, who were planning secret sales of Hokkaido property to relatives and friends of the administration at very low discount prices. The public outcry which ensued resulted in (1) the cancellation of the proposed sale, (2) the announcement that a Constitution would be promulgated by the end of the decade, (3) measures passed to ensure that henceforth the press should be more effectively muzzled, and (4) reorganisation of Hokkaido into three prefectures, those of Sapporo, Hakodate and Nemuro.

The colonisation of Hokkaido continued, however, and by the end of the century the population numbered approximately 850,000, less than 20,000 of whom were Ainu. It is clear, therefore, that the indigenous people were completely submerged in the new and sizeable waves of migration. In any case, the government pursued a policy of assimilation. Contrary to the discriminatory legislation of the Matsumae han regarding Ainu, noted in Chapter 3, education was made compulsory for Ainu in the same manner as ordinary Japanese and indeed through the law of conscription Ainu young men were granted the privilege of serving in the Imperial Army. Although vestiges of the Ainu race and some of their culture remain to this day, the policy of assimilation can be deemed successful in that, for example, the indigenous language has practically disappeared. There exists an Ainu liberation movement in contemporary Japan, but they are so localised and their numbers so exiguous that one cannot really speak of a significant Ainu problem.

While the assimilation of the Ryukyuan and Ainu peoples may be said to have succeeded, the same would not apply to two other minority groups, namely the Koreans and the *eta*. As far as Koreans are concerned it will be recalled that Hideyoshi's aborted conquest of that country had resulted in a number of the generals returning to Japan with groups of Korean artisans whom they set to work in order to produce the porcelain ware for which they were famous. By the Meiji period 'Korean villages' could still be readily identified given the comparatively static nature of geographical mobility in the Edo era. It was during the Meiji era, however, that relations between Japan and Korea and the attitudes between the two peoples were to change radically. The *seikan-ron*, debate over the conquest of Korea, did not die down; on the contrary it persisted throughout the Meiji era and culminated in the Japanese annexation of that country in 1910. While some migration took place in the teens and the twenties, it was mainly in the thirties and early forties that Koreans were brought into Japan in sizeable numbers to work in factories as part of the war effort; and when Korean women were liberally used as *ianfu*, literally 'consolation women', to accompany Japanese soldiers at the front during the war. Racism, which appears to be an invariable consequence of colonialism in the modern era, also occurred in Japan; today Korean residents in Japan are perceived by the indigenous population in terms perhaps approximating those of the British in regard to Indians and Pakistanis – with, indeed, Korean restaurants being as popular in Japan as curry restaurants in Britain – the roots of this phenomenon lying in the Meiji era.

By far, however, the most poignant problem of discrimination remains that meted out to the *eta* people. In the 1871 census, as pointed out in Chapter 3, the *eta* population was estimated at some four hundred thousand; in the mid-thirties estimates varied from one to one and a half million, while today figures range from two to three million. The rate of demographic growth of the *eta* was substantially higher than that of the rest of the Japanese population; this would by no means be a peculiar phenomenon, as in all societies, given a minimal subsistence level of existence, the poor and the downtrodden breed in greater numbers. In 1869 the Kogisho deliberated on the future status of the *eta* and voted overwhelmingly in favour of their emancipation, namely that they should be absorbed into the *heimin* (commoner) class. Since then there has been no official national discrimination against the *eta*, though municipal legislation varied and in some areas, especially, not surprisingly, those with high *eta* populations, discriminatory policies were actively pursued. So far as the government is concerned, once emancipation was established the policy of succeeding decades, until recently, can perhaps best be described as *laissez-faire*.

With the relaxed policy of the government and especially the freedom of movement which came to be the law of the land, certain *eta* individuals benefited. With the frequent changing of residence, the original *buraku* (village) in which one was born would disappear from one's record, hence a degree of anonymity was achieved – though successful *eta* lived in perpetual anguish that they would be 'discovered'. Nevertheless, cases of rapid social promotion did occur: by the Taisho era there were *eta* in the faculty of Kyoto University, in industry, in the officer corps of the army, in fact including at least two generals. No official ban existed against *eta* joining any of the professions, including the bureaucracy, with the exception of the *Kunaicho*, the Imperial Household Agency, which *eta* were formally forbidden to enter. Indeed, on one occasion when the Taisho tenno was to be present at a meeting of the Diet, one of the members of parliament, known to be an *eta*, was advised by the *Kunaicho* that he should refrain from attending this special ceremonial session.

In the course of the Meiji era the plight of the *eta* continued mainly as a result of popular prejudice. A number sought solace by converting to the Catholic Church, though this was a mixed blessing so far as the missionaries were concerned in that although they sought to enlarge their flocks, and therefore welcomed all converts, they were nonetheless dismayed to see that the entrance of *eta* into the Church tended to lead to the desertion of others. Towards the end of the Meiji era the sufferings of the *eta* as a result of social injustice aroused the conscience of a number of intellectuals, some of whom were moved to action partly as a result of the example set by Emile Zola's 1898 denunciation (*J'Accuse*) of Dreyfus's incarceration. Nakae Chomin (1847–1901), a great liberal and remarkably courageous intellectual whose many accomplishments included the translation into Japanese of Rousseau's *Social Contract* (1882), became an outspoken champion of the *eta* cause. No doubt the most moving account of the infernal circumstances of anxiety to which *eta* were doomed was the 1906 publication of the novel by Shimazaki Toson (1872–1943), *Hakai* (*The Broken Commandment*), which traced the story of a schoolteacher of *eta* origin.

The first *eta* protest movement was founded in 1902, namely the *Buraku Kaiho* (Emancipation of the Buraku People). Shortly afterwards, however, the government suppressed the movement; this should not necessarily be interpreted as being a specifically anti-*eta* move on the part of the government, which was by then accustomed to suppressing practically anything which smacked of social and/or political radicalism. As with the feminist movement, the *eta* regrouped their forces in the Taisho era. They were spurred on by two events. First, *eta* did not fail to notice the irony of the Japanese delegation at Versailles sponsoring a racial equality clause to be inserted in the Covenant of the League of Nations – a request which was turned down by the British delegation as a result of pressures from their colonies of settlement, Australia, South Africa and Canada; the *eta* pointed out that there was here a blatant case of hypocrisy in view of the discrimination of which they were the victims. Secondly, the somewhat more liberal atmosphere of the mid-Taisho era – Taisho, it should be recalled, means 'Great Justice' – resulted in the abolition of the Peace Preservation Ordinance in 1922. In the same year the second *eta* movement was formed, namely the *Suihei Undo*, literally the 'Water Level Movement', figuratively indicating the aim of achieving equality between *eta* and other Japanese. In 1928, however, the *eta* movement was once again suppressed, this time on the grounds of its alleged affiliation with the outlawed Communist Party.

In the period of transformation to modernity, therefore, one can note that whereas certain individual *eta* were able to take advantage of the new social circumstances, including the provision of education for all citizens, and by means of subterfuge rise to prominent positions, as far as the bulk of the *eta* were concerned their condition certainly did not improve, in fact it probably worsened. The same general pattern persists to this day. While a number of intellectuals, a few politicians, and to some extent both the national and certain metropolitan governments have sought to improve the situation, popular prejudices remain strongly ingrained.

One tragic footnote to the history of the *eta* should be added. When on 6 August 1945 the atomic bomb was dropped on Hiroshima, quite a number of those who perished in the holocaust were *eta*, as Hiroshima is one of the cities with the highest proportion of *eta*. Among those who survived but were exposed to the nuclear blast not only have there been numerous cases of leukaemia, cancer and other fatal diseases, but the progeniture of these unfortunates have also been affected: the incidence of still-births, deformed children and so on has been proportionately much higher among those who are called the *hibakusha* (survivors of the holocaust) than in the rest of the population. Consequently the *hibakusha* have been subjected to a form of discrimination in that it is generally difficult for them to find marriage partners. There are those, therefore, in contemporary Japan who suffer from double discrimination, namely by virtue of being both *eta* and *hibakusha*.

THE SOCIAL SETTING IN MODERN JAPAN

By the beginning of the twentieth century most vestiges of daimyo and upper samurai power and privilege had disappeared. The new ruling class, at least in socio-economic terms, consisted of an urban-based upper bourgeoisie. It was composed primarily of industrial managers and bureaucrats. In the mid-eighties a new peerage system was introduced – partly so that the government could fill the upper house of the eventual bicarmeral parliament with its own appointments – and higher bureaucrats especially, though also industrial magnates, were liberally invested with titles of count, baron, and so forth. No importance should be attached to this charade, however, as it should be interpreted as no more than the icing on an otherwise bourgeois–capitalist cake. To the bureaucrats and managers should be added the members of the liberal professions, doctors, professors, architects and so on. All of these, by the late Meiji period, tended to be almost exclusively drawn from the universities or colleges. Thus Japan's élite can be said to have been meritocratic in character. Also by the latter part of the Meiji era the urban ruling class found as its natural allies what was earlier termed the rural wing of the bourgeoisie, namely the landowners. It has been pointed out how this group, mainly perhaps because of their methods of village social control, have tended historiographically to be perceived as an atavistic residue of the feudal order. This, it was suggested, is not a correct perception and that, while in the interwar period there may have been a change in the character and outlook of the landlords along with a rise in absenteeism from their land, initially at least they were rural capitalist entrepreneurs. The fourth major component of the ruling order was the military hierarchy, of which more will be said in the following chapter.

While an evolutionary process of social differentiation had occurred in the course of the Edo era, it is nonetheless clear that the 1868 revolution was not only profound in consequence, but rapidly so. At least so far as the composition of the ruling order was concerned, by the beginning of the twentieth century there was little which distinguished it from other industrialised societies, namely the major Western powers, where coalitions of industrial managers and financiers, higher civil servants, landowners and high-ranking military officers ruled their respective countries. There were, of course, differences among the Western powers – where, for example, in Britain and the United States the military were far less influential than in France or Germany – but in nature, if not necessarily in degree, all modern industrialised powers, including Japan, shared a common ruling class composition. Two somewhat marginal differences which set Japan rather apart can be noted. Most Western countries counted among their élites the magnates of their various churches. No such comparable phenomenon existed in Japan. More significant is the fact that Japan's bureaucrats and managers tended to be completely divorced from the land, whereas in European countries the possession of estates continued to confer social prestige and political influence and remained a source of revenue for practically all members of the élite.

It is when one descends the social ladder, however, that the differences between Japan and other industrialised states become far greater. For one thing, as has been stressed, Japan remained an overwhelmingly peasant society and economy. What is particularly striking about Japan is the existence of the dual economy and the dual society, the separation between the two being, as stated earlier, in the form of a chasm. The actual industrial urban proletariat of Japan was very small, even in the more industrialised interwar period. Another striking feature is the degree to which female labour was utilised in the process of industrialisation; it was only in the 1930s, when the great military build-up was under way, that the number of male factory operatives surpassed that of females, though even then women still constituted over 40 per cent of the industrial labour force.

It has also been stressed how the demographic picture of Japan showed a heavy concentration of the population in small villages. There was what can be termed an urban petite-bourgeoisie, namely schoolteachers, proprietors of small businesses, retailers, manufacturers of such products as *sake* and soya sauce, minor clerks, and so on. Another feature of the social setting of Japan in the period of transformation, however, is the relatively small number of an urban middle-middle class. Japanese society should be perceived from two angles. Firstly, one should again note the distance between the urban and rural areas. Secondly, one should stress the gap that existed between the upper and lower orders with only a very slender line in between. The upper orders were well educated, the lower orders were just basically indoctrinated. The upper orders were rich, the lower orders were poor. The upper orders were cultivated in both Japanese and Western art forms, the lower orders were primitive. The upper orders tended to be cosmopolitan in outlook, the lower orders were parochial. While a certain demographic and financial redistribution occurred in the interwar period, this was of not much more than marginal proportions. The rapidity with which the revolution occurred also caused a severe psychological trauma to the nation. So far as the bulk of the population was concerned, therefore, while modernity brought little comfort, it did bring a great deal of confusion.

The Japanese élite successfully pursued economic objectives, but failed to remedy the social ills, some of which were inherited from the Edo era, but many of which were the creation of the transformation period to modernity. While a number of far-sighted managers in the urban-based heavy industry sector improved the conditions of their workforce, as has been pointed out, this corresponded to a very small proportion of the overall population.

Although there were a number of political reforms in the interwar period, notably in 1925 the introduction of universal male suffrage, there was no concerted attempt at social or economic reforms. The contradictions in modern Japanese society not only continued, they were exacerbated. For the era of 'Great Justice' – the Taisho years of 1912 to 1925 – to have lived up to its name, efforts should have been directed primarily at land reform, but also the redistribution of industrial income; the recognition of trade unions and political movements representing the interests of the lower classes, educational reform, and more sympathetic understanding, at the very least, to women's rights and *eta*'s social conditions would have constituted appropriate measures for achieving social objectives commensurate with the earlier 'economic miracle'. Nothing of the sort happened or was even seriously attempted. The failure to recognise the imperative need for social progress made all political reforms no more than cosmetic in effect. The economic gains of the first phase of the period of modernisation were not translated into social amelioration in the course of the second phase.

8 The Making of the Meiji State

CULTURE AND POLITICS

The oligarchy's weak-kneed policy *vis-à-vis* Korea in 1873, its apparent intention to embark on an extensive programme of Westernisation, its continued denigration of the samurai soul and status resulted in a series of furious explosions. Eto Shinpei (1835–74), hitherto the government's chief administrator of the Justice Department, left Tokyo, returned to his Saga fief and called upon his fellow samurai to rise in revolt; the rebellion was quickly and ruthlessly suppressed, Eto was beheaded by order of his successor in the Justice Department, Oki Takato (1832–99), also from Saga, and the head was paraded about at the end of a long spear in order to *décourager les autres*, without, however, achieving success. In 1876 Maebara Issei (1834–76) led a samurai rebellion in Hagi; he too was beheaded and his head was also publicly exposed. In the same year a group of fiery young samurai formed the *Shinpuren*, Divine Wind League, in Kumamoto; they stormed the local imperial garrison, managing to kill the commander, then moved to the prefectural office, slew the governor, and finally those who were still alive ran up a hill and committed *seppuku*.

All this culminated in the grand finale, namely Saigo's 1877 Satsuma rebellion which was the government's greatest military and political – especially in view of Saigo's extensive national popularity – challenge. While at first Saigo's troops moved swiftly, they were soon stopped and the retreat began. In his last stand Saigo stood on Shiroyama, the hill overlooking his beloved city of Kagoshima; he then knelt down, proceeded to disembowel himself, while his *kaishakunin* – the assistant at a *seppuku* whose duty it is to put him who is about to die out of too prolonged a misery by a swift, preferably accurate blow of the sword to the neck – having completed his operation, hid Saigo's head in a hole he dug in the ground so that it would not be defiled. The samurai never rose again.

The causes of samurai revolt, as seen in Chapter 6, were at least partly economic in nature. The ideology they espoused, however, was romantically

240

nativist. They strongly resented the Westernisation of the country and the emerging capitalist character of society. The military defeats which they repeatedly suffered, however, and especially the rout of Saigo's army undoubtedly brought the age of the samurai to an end – something which in 1877 simply had to be accepted, no matter how reluctantly. For although the 1877 campaigns were rather a military fiasco, nonetheless the samurai had been defeated by a modern, mainly peasant conscript army. This spelled the doom of armed uprisings. The spirit of romantic nativism as a rejection of materialistic modernism, however, was by no means dead.

In 1881 Toyama Mitsuru (1855–1944) founded the *Genyosha* (Dark Ocean Society) in Fukuoka. This was the first of a number of comparable semi-secret societies which sprouted in the course of the later Meiji and Taisho years, such as the *Kokuryukai* (Black Dragon Society), the *Kokusuikai* (National Essence Society) and so on. These societies were avowedly virulently nationalistic and, as the name of especially the third of these indicates, they perceived the nation as a mystical entity. It was one response to the crisis of identity in the face of modernity. The heroic sincerity of the young *Shinpuren* members, the deified defiance of Saigo, served as inspiration to those who sought to save the soul of Japan from the clutches of Westernised materialism or indeed the decay of its own body. Thus the spirit of Saigo and of the *Shinpuren* burned ardently in the breasts of those who perceived themselves as the true inheritors of the *shishi*, those who had fought so valiantly and selflessly in the name of the tenno and all that the spirit of Japan stood for. From Saigo and the *Shinpuren* an ideological current can be perceived which passes through the Meiji period, guides the nationalistic luminaries of the twenties, emboldens the young officers of the thirties and in the post-war era can be seen motivating the melodramatic extravaganzas of Mishima Yukio (1926–70).

While after 1877 armed uprisings were no longer part of the scene, intense xenophobic political pressure nonetheless remained a significant force. These self-appointed guardians of the national essence did not, for example, hesitate in resorting to murder. Okubo Toshimichi was assassinated in 1878 shortly after the defeat of Saigo and as a direct consequence of it. In 1889 a member of the *Genyosha* threw a bomb at the passing carriage of then Foreign Minister Okuma as a means of protesting over the latter's handling of the treaty revision negotiations. In the same year Mori was assassinated on the grounds that he had not shown proper respect during a visit to the Ise Shrine – the 'Mecca of the Shinto faith'. An interesting feature of these militant organisations and the individuals who either joined them or espoused their cause was that it was very rare for them to choose Westerners as their targets. One spectacular exception to this rule was the attack carried out by the ex-samurai policeman Tsuda Sanzo on the person of the then czarevitch

Alexandrovitch (later Nicholas II, 1868–1918) at the beginning of his official visit to Japan in 1891; the czarevitch, needless to say, was not killed, but he was very severely wounded, the visit had to be cancelled and the heir to the Russian throne returned home to recover.

From the late nineteenth century until the end of the Second World War these societies operated on both the domestic and foreign fronts. In terms of internal activities, apart from the occasional assassination of a political or business leader, they were engaged mainly in fighting what they perceived as left-wing threats to the *kokutai* (national body or essence), this taking the form of strike-breaking, conflicts against socialist movements, and indeed, for example, the *Kokusuikai* terrorised the *eta Suihei Undo*. On the foreign front they espoused a Japan-led Pan-Asiatic expansionist ideology, providing here the embryo for the later state-adopted doctrine of the Greater East Asia Co-Prosperity Sphere.

As far as modern Japanese political history is concerned, an important point to note is this. At no stage, whether in the later Meiji, Taisho or very early Showa periods, did any government ever seriously try to restrain the activities of the militant nationalist organisations. Paradoxically it was only on the very eve of the Second Sino-Japanese War (1937–45) that a few of the more strident apostles of ultra-nationalism were to be silenced, as was for example the case of Kita Ikki (1883–1937). Otherwise neither the societies nor their infamous leaders – for there was never anything really very secret about the societies – were harassed by successive governments; on the contrary they were cajoled. One can illustrate this phenomenon by pointing to the creation and character of the Bureau of Thought Control established in 1926. This was an office situated in the Home Ministry whose role was to combat 'dangerous thoughts', namely the modernised generally Marxist-inspired versions of the *jashumon*, referred to in Chapter 2. In terms of chronological sequence, it will be noted that this was achieved four years after the abolition of the Peace Preservation Ordinance. Now the governments of this period of 'Taisho democracy' were, in theory at least, committed to the principles of parliamentary democracy. The militant nationalist societies were openly, indeed brazenly, hostile to parliament and to democracy, these being perceived as nefarious foreign importations. They were not, however, targets of official censorship. Saigo's body had long since been eaten by worms, but his spirit survived. Why?

Part of the reason is that these societies gained a significant degree of influence and indeed infiltrated government circles, the military and the police force. Another major reason, however, is that the societies were ideologically outflanking the governments. The sole basis of legitimacy for the post-1868 governments was that they were appointed by the tenno; the tenno was in theory the state. While alternative political ideologies were sought by a number of intellectuals and concepts of democracy were espoused in certain quarters, these did not include the government, nor were they reflected in the country's constitution. By claiming to be more tenno-ist than even the tenno's own ministers the societies, albeit a nuisance, were nonetheless untouchable. There is another reason. No government can successfully resist two opposing flanks. Its efforts must be concentrated in the direction where it perceives itself to be most vulnerable. Throughout the period of transformation to modernity, successive governments feared not so much the romantic nativists, but those they deemed to be radicals, inspired not by native but by certain Western doctrines.

It is in this sense that one must place Japanese political society within its proper cultural context. The early adulatory fascination for Western things and concepts had lasted some fifteen to twenty years. This was the period variously referred to as that of *bunmei kaika*, or that of *keimo*, enlightenment, when scholars of the new age, namely those imbued with Western social and political doctrines, sought to educate the masses – though mainly the articulate and literate ones – to an understanding of the meaning of this universe which they were in the process of entering. Fukuzawa had proclaimed that Japan should hereafter 'shed Asia', *Datsu-A*, the title of one of his publications. It was in the very early seventies that Mori, at the time diplomatic representative in Washington, urged Japanese students in the USA to try to find white American wives so that by miscegenation they might improve the Japanese racial stock. The *romaji-kai* (Society for the Romanisation of the Japanese Script) advocated what its name indicated, while some went even further and preached that nothing short of the total abandonment of the Japanese language in favour of English would usher Japan into the modern age. While the ban on Christianity was still operative, a member of the Iwakura mission in Berlin met the German scholar of jurisprudence, von Gneist (1816–95) to seek his opinion as to whether the Japanese nation *in toto* should embrace the Christian faith. And in France in 1882 Itagaki Taisuke met Victor Hugo (1802–85) and asked him how he could arouse the political conscience of the Japanese people, to which Hugo advised that they should be encouraged to read political novels; Itagaki asked him which ones and Hugo replied, 'Mine' – Itagaki returned to Japan laden with the complete works of Hugo.

In 1895 one of the most famous painters of the *yoga* (Western painting) school, Kuroda Seiki (1826–1924), caused rather a scandal in Tokyo by exhibiting his vividly naturalist paintings of nudes – in traditional Japanese painting, even pornographic works never portrayed subjects totally naked. By that time, however, while Kuroda and his fellow *yoga* painters continued to enjoy a degree of celebrity, more traditional Japanese painting had forcefully come back to its own. The renaissance of Japanese painting was achieved primarily by the efforts of two men, Okakura Tenshin (1863–1913) and Ernest Fenollosa (1853–1908); the latter, an American professor of art invited to Japan to teach Western-style art, underwent a complete conversion and advocated the aesthetic superiority of Japanese over Western art. In the world of literature and especially fiction, whereas the early period consisted mainly of naïve imitations of Western styles and plots, by the late nineteenth century the literary productions of writers such as Mori Ogai (1862–1922), Natsume Soseki (1867–1916), Shimasaki Toson, Nagai Kafu and others represented clear evidence that modern Japanese literature was by no means an ersatz Westernised product, but contained a highly dynamic genre of its own. The imperial restoration was responsible for the revival of *gagaku*, ancient court music, which like the occupants of the throne had been kept in hibernation for centuries. Western music, however, continued to have an impact, though ironically enough it was mainly in schools and in the army, the two major vehicles of nationalism, that Western martial music *à la* Elgar was most widely diffused. In the field of drama, while *shingeki* (new theatre) continued to develop, the traditional forms of Kabuki and Noh were by no means abandoned. While various Christian sects counted a few converts – and in certain cases men of some influence – the rather unseemly sectarian bickerings in which the missionaries engaged resulted, among other things, in a number of Japanese Christians led by Uchimura Kanzo (1861–1930), one of the most interesting and courageous intellectual figures of the period, founding the *Mukyokaiha-Kirisutokyo*, that is, the Christian Church without any sectarian affiliation. At the same time, however, the period of transformation to modernity also witnessed the revival of certain Buddhist and Shinto sects and the proliferation of new ones.

It has been tempting for historians to contrast the nativist reaction of the later Meiji period with the excessive Westernism of the earlier period. While there is undoubtedly a marked difference between the cultural climate of the two periods, it should not be perceived in too stark a contrast, but rather as an evolutionary formation towards a sense of national identity. The romantic nativism of the *Genyosha* and similar societies is by no means representative of the atmosphere at any stage of the Meiji period. In fact romantic nativism consistently remained somewhat beyond the cultural mainstream – even at the outbreak of the Second World War the Japanese authorities had great difficulty in dissuading urban citizens from engaging in ballroom dancing. From its Japanese birth in the nineties and in ensuing decades baseball became the most popular sport and retained this position even in the late thirties – though in order to accommodate nativist sentiments its appellation was changed from the Western *besuboru* to the Japanese term *yakyu*.

The point to emphasise, therefore, is that while it would by no means be correct to claim that in her transformation to modernity Japan underwent a thorough process of Westernisation, it is nevertheless the case that Western cultural and political influences in Japan – as everywhere else in the world at that time – were eminently powerful. Cultural and political discourse took place within a predominantly Western-orientated context. The West might be feared, certain aspects of it might be despised, but nonetheless its power inspired awe and motivation for emulation – which is not the same thing as imitation. The distinction was drawn earlier in this book between nationalism and xenophobia. While Japanese nationalism undoubtedly developed in both extensive and intensive form in the late nineteenth century, xenophobia remained no more than a distant echo.

A major change which occurred in the development of Japanese politics, and one which illustrated a growing degree of political maturity, was the realisation by the early eighties or thereabouts that the West was by no means a political monolith; in other words that from the various Western political traditions, doctrines and systems it was possible to make a choice, or a selection, to identify those extraneous elements which would accommodate themselves most fruitfully to the indigenous milieu and, perhaps more important, serve the political interests of the ruling oligarchy. The equation that Western influences were liberal while Japanese reactions were conservative is based on false premises. Western liberal doctrines found a response among liberal-inclined Japanese, while Western conservative doctrines met with the approval of conservative-minded Japanese. The fact that many young liberals became old conservatives should not be interpreted as a rejection of the West; Japan could by no means claim a monopoly of young liberals becoming more conservative with age!

Politics in Japan were primarily conditioned by nationalist considerations. The question was which form of government would best serve the interests of the nation. The answer, given the post-1868 pluralistic nature of Japanese politics, varied in different times and between different political factions. In all the debates, however, the Western dimensions figured prominently. Thus, for example, as historians have explained, one of the major reasons for the growing political liberalisation – albeit, as pointed out in the previous chapter, mainly of a cosmetic nature – of the post-First World War was the fact that the victorious nations were Britain, France, Italy and the United States, namely nations with either republican regimes or constitutional monarchies, while the autocratic regimes of Germany, Austria–Hungary and Turkey were the losers – and, of course, the autocrat *par excellence*, the Romanov czarist dynasty, had been overthrown in a bloody revolution. While ideology *per se* certainly figured in the Japanese political debate in the course of the transformation to modernity, the major consideration remained the desire to discover the source of Western strength.

In accordance with the fifth article of the *Go-kajo no Seimon*, that knowledge should be sought throughout the world, the immediate aftermath of the 1868 revolution witnessed a veritable deluge of foreign works entering the country. Many were translated, mainly in serial form, in the burgeoning press. Otherwise, the *keimo* scholars sought to interpret by means of paraphrase the basic tenets of various Western political philosophies, even though these may only have been partially digested. Political slogans derived from Western concepts were emblazoned in the tracts and speeches of the new political parties and movements. It was the new intelligentsia which provided the locomotive force for the great political debate which occurred in these years. Their thirst for Western knowledge appeared unquenchable. Among the Western authors most widely read, respected and influential were Buckle, Carlyle, Disraeli, Guizot, Mill, Comte, Macaulay, de Tocqueville and Rousseau.

In terms of the diffusion of ideas, however, in the *bunmei-kaika* years Mill and Rousseau appealed the most, albeit not necessarily to the same audiences. Rousseau's *Social Contract* became something of a bible for the early *jiyu-minken-undo* and was rather liberally quoted by the leaders, especially Itagaki, of the party formed in 1881 called the *Jiyuto*, Liberal Party. While Itagaki and his followers tended to espouse, in the context of the period, fairly radical views, Mill's utilitarianism had more of an impact on the more moderate, urbane political movement led by Okuma Shigenobu, which existed briefly in the form of a party called the *Kaishinto* (Progressive Party). The oligarchy, however, came to view both as dangerous, and indeed in 1881 it banned from schools the Japanese translation of *On Liberty* – translated by Nakumura Keiu (1832–91), who was also the translator of the supreme Western best-seller in Japan, Samuel Smiles's *Self Help*, which by the end of the Meiji period had sold more than a million copies, thereby finding a much greater market in Japan than in its country of production.

In regard to the heady political discussions of the early Meiji years, several points should be made clear. Although there was some repressive legislation and censorship by the government, certainly in the seventies, such measures were comparatively mild; and it is only in the eighties that the authorities became more oppressive. This is partly because at this stage a number of the younger oligarchs either shared the views of those with liberal tendencies or sympathised with them. It should also be emphasised, however, that in spite of the ideological background to the restoration of the tenno, as seen in Chapter 5, the underpinnings of the tenno-ist ideology were still weak, certainly ill-defined, and most definitely not widely diffused. It is only in the eighties that a more concerted effort at erecting the Meiji tenno-ist edifice took place. Finally, however, it should also be made clear that the political deliberations were articulated within a rather limited circle.

The major organ for the diffusion of political ideas and ideals was the press. Although the seventies witnessed a proliferation of newspapers and reviews, this proliferation consisted more of titles than of readership. It has been estimated that in the mid-seventies approximately 50,000 people received daily newspapers. We are most definitely not, therefore, speaking here in terms of mass democracy, or anything approaching it. In the seventies modern ideological politics, namely in contrast for example to peasant rebellions, should be seen mainly in terms of an intellectual pastime for the élite. (Things, however, began to change at an accelerating pace: by the beginning of the twentieth century there was an estimated daily newspaper circulation of 1 ½ millions.) In the early Meiji period most newspapers were organs of the opposition political parties. The latter were obtaining increasingly large and increasingly rowdy followers. It was at this stage that the government translated concern into constraint. By the early eighties it was clear that modern politics were more than a parlour game. Ignoring certain fringe groups, the political scene in Japan had become polarised between two major forces, the oligarchy and its opponents.

The central and indeed probably only real issue which separated the government from the opposition was the width of the political power base. The government desired to keep it narrow, the opposition desired that it should be widened. The roots of the debate over political participation are to be found in the final stages of the overthrow of the bakufu. While the anti-bakufu forces were agreed, it will be recalled, on the need to overthrow the shogunal government, by no means was there a well defined consensus on what should take its place. Activists of the Tosa han, notably Sakamoto Ryoma (1836–67) and Goto Shojiro (1838–97), led what was known as the *Kogi Seitai Ron*, namely deliberations over government by open discussion. It was also Goto's memorial to the shogun which persuaded the latter to resign. What was being advocated at this stage was an aristocratic form of government, a council of state which would be composed of the leading daimyo/samurai figures. The transitional years 1868–73 involved a degree of experimentation, including the establishment of the *Kogisho*; it was, however, the year 1873 which, as we have seen, marked the major turning point and the consolidation of power into the hands of what became the Sat-Cho oligarchy. This incident precipitated the departure of a number of the government's leaders, notably Saigo and Itagaki.

Saigo was the charismatic and legendary hero of the samurai resistance, who, at a comparatively young age (forty-nine), perished by his sword in true samurai fashion. Itagaki, on the other hand, may perhaps deserve to be called the father of political parties in modern Japan. Itagaki had consistently supported Saigo in the *Seikan-ron*; indeed there was a significant degree of mutual admiration between Saigo and Itagaki. From the moment that both resigned from the government, ostensibly over the same issue, their paths diverged completely. Itagaki's can be said at the very least to have been healthier in that unlike his comrade he lived until the ripe old age of eighty-two. From 1874 until 1900, when he retired from active political life, Itagaki was the dominant figure in the political opposition movement. A few brief words, therefore, should be said about his character.

It is difficult to imagine two more different personalities than those of Saigo and Itagaki. Saigo was undoubtedly rather a fanatic and he was not only someone of strong moral convictions and singularity of purpose, but also – something not uncommon among fanatics – he was incorruptible. Itagaki had all the qualities of the chameleon. He was an opportunist *par excellence* and his greatest weakness would appear to have been his vanity, something his enemies were quick to perceive and when necessary to exploit. While he formed the Jiyuto in 1881 in order to fight the government and influence the drafting of the constitution which had been announced that year, the following year he and Goto left on an extended tour of Europe. This was a ploy on the part of the oligarchy which persuaded Mitsui to disburse the funds necessary for the tour. This left the Jiyuto in a state of disarray, while the government was rid, at least temporarily but at a crucial moment, of what it perceived as a pest. This same pattern repeated itself throughout Itagaki's career. In 1887 the government inserted Itagaki's name in that year's peerage list. On the day the announcement was made, 9 May, Itagaki gave a long interview to the press explaining why he would never accept a peerage – which included the interesting argument that the luxurious living of the nobility was the cause of poverty in Ireland – as this was contrary to his democratic views; on 15 July 1887 he gratefully accepted from the tenno, out of devotion to him, the title of count. Itagaki, the government realised, could be bought off, he could be flattered, and when absolutely necessary he could be asked to join a government, especially since the oligarchy could ensure that it would be of very brief duration. Itagaki was undoubtedly a nuisance for the government; nevertheless, his constant waltzing through politics enabled the oligarchy to ensure that most of the time it was calling the tune.

Upon his resignation from the government in 1873, the first party which Itagaki and a few of his comrades formed in Tosa was the *Aikoku-koto*, the Public Patriotic Party. A feature of this and all subsequent opposition parties which should be stressed is that while attacking the government's domestic policies they also fiercely criticised the oligarchy's foreign policy on the grounds that it was seriously lacking in forcefulness. The issue of treaty revision remained an opposition *cause célèbre* until these were revised in 1894. With even greater vehemence, however, the opposition parties denounced the government for not pursuing a more vigorous and patriotic policy in regard to Korea and China. While in due course the parties claimed that they were championing people's rights, it should be clear that they were equally vociferous in their advocacy of militant nationalist expansionism.

The *Aikoku-koto* had a very brief existence and in 1874 the same group founded another organisation called the *Risshi-sha*, the Self-Help Society. The main issue between the government and the opposition can be summarised quite briefly. The opposition claimed that the strength of the Western countries lay in the fact that their governments had an extensive degree of political participation; participation, it was argued, resulted in commitment. In other words, Western countries were strong because the majority of the people were united behind their governments and the reason for this unity lay quite simply in the fact that it was the people's opinions which formed government policy. The conclusion of this particular syllogism was clear: for Japan to be strong there should be a broad political base whereby decisions would be arrived at by consensus, which would in turn ensure the effectiveness of government policy in view of the fact that it would be backed by a strongly united and committed people. The oligarchy's counter-argument was that while what was being posited no doubt applied to Western countries, the conditions in Japan were very different – in the West the democratic participation of the people in the formation of government and formulation of policy followed centuries of political evolutionary change which had permitted the people to achieve the necessary degree of maturity and that therefore their political power was exercised in a responsible manner; in Japan no such preparatory period had occurred, as a result of which the Japanese people were politically immature. A wise government should exercise the correct degree of caution, reforms should only very gradually be introduced, and while broad political participation was the aim, the right amount of time should be allowed to lapse before it could be achieved. The opposition replied that the government's logic necessitated that the introduction of, for example, railways should be delayed by at least several decades until the Japanese people had been able to comprehend the physical laws of steam power. And so the arguments raged.

By no means, however, should it be believed that Itagaki and his colleagues were calling for mass democracy. Theirs was a very élitist organisation; the popular participation they had in mind was meant to be essentially restricted to samurai. Also, a major motivation on the part of those who joined ranks with Itagaki was that they resented the monopoly of power being exercised by the sons of the Satsuma and Choshu fiefs; in that respect the 'modern' politics of Meiji Japan were initially heavily influenced by vestiges of 'feudal', namely particularistic, attitudes. In the meantime, however, there were groundswells of discontent emerging and frequently exploding throughout the country. In 1875 a mass rally of some 90,000 people was held at Osaka with representatives of sundry political organisations attending from many parts of the country. While Tosa continued to be the hotbed of political opposition to the government, the movement gathered strength and increasingly became a nationwide affair. It is here that the *jiyu-minken-undo*, the movement for freedom and popular rights, came into existence.

The initially narrow samurai élitist organisation of government opposition centred mainly in Tosa han began to spread horizontally throughout the country and vertically to different strata of society. The various social elements represented in the *jiyu-minken-undo* included westernised progressive intellectuals, disaffected samurai, tenants and landlords, small-scale manufacturers and rural entrepreneurs, who joined ranks to protest against the oppressive conditions for which they held the government responsible. Thus, the *jiyu-minken-undo* represented sundry dissatisfied groups which Itagaki sought to rally round his person and his party. He projected himself as the champion of the oppressed and the spokesman for their cause. There were, however, many causes: the element of unity which bound them together was essentially a negative one – their total opposition to the government. With the possible exception of the idealistic intellectuals, this opposition was based on primarily economic grievances.

The government can be said to have been subjected to a two-pronged attack. On the one hand, the energies of the Home Ministry, its police force, and the army had to be deployed to suppress a whole series of violent uprisings which occurred mainly in the rural areas, though the cities also witnessed political rowdyism. Thus, in figurative terms, the government was made the target of physical abuse. On the other hand, the verbal abuse did not cease nor did it become less sophisticated; the opposition was constantly replenishing its ideological armoury. To Mill and Rousseau a third major influential Western figure was added, Herbert Spencer (1820–1903). In fact, Spencer was eventually also adopted by the Government, though for different ideological reasons, but initially it was the *jiyu-minken-undo* which made use of his works and interpreted them in a manner to further their own position. *Social Statistics, Study of Sociology* and *Representative Government* were translated and Spencer's theories of individualism and egalitarianism widely and enthusiastically disseminated.

The government responded to both attacks. In the prevailing culture of early Meiji Japan, as was stressed earlier in this chapter, nativist arguments would simply not have had any effect. The government knew this perfectly well and therefore under the circumstances it was useless to seek to invoke the names of Motoori, Hirata, or any of the other ideological founders of *sonno*. By the very nature of things, in any case at this particular juncture, the debate *had* to take place within a Western context. By the late seventies/early eighties, however, there was a much more sophisticated appreciation of the realities of Western political doctrines and systems than previously rather nebulously held views of a monolithically liberal West. Although, as will be seen, the oligarchy derived its political philosophy and structures mainly from Germany and Austria, it did not hesitate to use British ideological weapons to counter the ideological attacks emanating from the same national sources. Thus in 1881 the government commissioned Kaneko Kentaro (1853–1942) – who, as was pointed out in Chapter 5, became a regular correspondent and close friend of Spencer – to translate works by Edmund Burke (1729–97): *Reflection on the French Revolution* and *Appeal from the New to the Old Whigs*. The following year under the auspices of the Ministry of Education there appeared a partial translation of *Leviathan* by Thomas Hobbes (1588–1679).

If 1873 marked the first important turning point in post-1868 Japanese political history, the second major landmark was undoubtedly the year 1881. It was that year, as was seen in the previous chapter, that the major scandal and intense embarrassment caused by the Hokkaido land sale deal, among other things, led the government to announce that a Constitution would be promulgated by the end of the decade. In preparation for the event the same year witnessed the formation of Japan's first two political parties: the *Jiyuto*, of relatively radical persuasion with a mainly rural support and led by Itagaki, and the *Kaishinto*, more moderate, with a predominantly urban backing of wealthy merchants and led by Okuma. In the following year the government formed its own party, the *Teiseito*, Imperial Government Party, ostensibly led by Fukuchi Gen'ichiro (1841–1906), but in fact masterminded by Ito. Also in 1882 the government announced that as a preliminary step to the drafting of Japan's Constitution, Ito would carry out an extended tour of European countries in order to learn from their different constitutional systems; that Ito spent almost all of his time in Bismarckian Germany was no accident. The fact that Ito was sent to Europe, however, further illustrates the point made earlier. In other words, though the government knew what it wanted in terms of a constitution and although it was to use this document and other pronouncements as a means of extolling the political legitimacy of the tenno and the power of his government, it was essential that there be both for domestic and external (the process of treaty revision) consumption the necessary coating of a Western veneer.

In the face of the opposition in the course of the decade which preceded the establishment of the constitution, the oligarchy resorted to four tactics. First, it sought to use the means of diversion: it set up prefectural assemblies ostensibly as a means of educating the public in political responsibility, but actually in the hope of diffusing energies away from the centre and containing them in isolated provincial units. Secondly, it resorted to concession, announcing that it would promulgate a constitution in 1889 and establish an elected legislative assembly the following year. Thirdly, it made liberal use of repression, both by police action and by a whole series of minatory laws and regulations in order to curtail the activities of the press, hamper public assemblies, and generally restrict the political rights of the citizens, all of which culminated in the draconian Peace Preservation Ordinance of 1887 which in effect granted the government unlimited powers of political suppression. Fourthly, it engaged in sophisticated means of subversion, for example by getting Mitsui to fund Itagaki's and Goto's European tour and by using a variety of devices to play the *Jiyuto* off against the *Kaishinto*.

The combination of these tactics proved eminently successful. Within a couple of years the parties were either dissolved or moribund. A large number of editors of the political press were safely locked up in prison, or subjected to onerous fines, or both. The Peace Preservation Ordinance entitled the Home Ministry to deport from the cities anyone who was held to be politically subversive, so the government was able to give a wide berth to a number of its political opponents who found themselves languishing in the countryside. Thus, in the mid- and late eighties the government was able to proceed with the erection of its modern ideological/political edifice in reasonable peace and quiet. Although the forces of opposition would later regroup, at this crucial stage they were in a state of complete disarray.

The fact that a constitution was granted and a parliament established has been perceived by some historians as a victory for the opposition, an opposition which in turn has been presented as representative of democratic forces. Certainly, seen from an international historical perspective, the promulgation by Japan of a modern constitution is remarkable. Apart from a brief constitutional experiment from 1860 to 1864 in Tunisia under the reign of Muhammad al-Sadiq Bey and with the exception of the various Latin American republics, where writing and tearing up constitutions is something of a national pastime, in the late nineteenth century Japan's was the only modern constitution outside the West European/US hemisphere. In comparative terms, therefore, the Japanese constitution of 1889 represented a significant degree of progress and also clearly established Japan's credentials as a modern state.

It is very difficult, however, to see the opposition as representing democratic forces; it was far too much of a hodge-podge to claim any such distinction. Rather it was the developing modernity of the Japanese nation which led the government to seek modern means to strengthen its own foundations. The economic developments were unleashing new social forces; these social forces should not be permitted to operate in a state of anarchy; new structures were necessary to ensure that the process of modernisation should take place in orderly fashion, that discipline should be maintained, that the state should be able to continue leading the nation, rather than being led by it. This was necessary, so the oligarchy believed, not simply in order to ensure that the gains accumulated in the process of achieving *fukoku-kyohei* were not dissipated by the folly of political irresponsibility, but also that the maintenance of political order was an essential prerequisite to the ultimate revision of the injurious treaties. In order for the country to be strong, the government had to be strong. Police repression or ceaseless battles of ideological wits between government and opposition were not sufficient to obtain that degree of political consolidation which the government desired. A constitution tailored to meet the oligarchy's requirements would provide the basic pillar to the modern political edifice it wished to construct. Even that, however, would be useless unless the constitution were buttressed by other elements of the modern nation-state. The last two decades of the nineteenth century, therefore, witnessed not only the promulgation of the oligarchy's self-designed constitution, but also major reinforcements of the legal, educational and military institutions.

MODERNITY AND LAW

The post-1868 Japanese state was in desperate need of a modern legal apparatus. This was necessitated both by the fact that Japan was becoming a centralised state and that a national *corpus* of jurisprudence was an essential ingredient in the organisation of society. There was, however, another major motivating factor: the most sensitive element in the injurious treaties consisted of the extra-territoriality clauses. In order to be able to convince the Western treaty powers that their nationals, when the occasions arose, would be treated in a civilised manner by Japanese magistrates, Japan had to be able to show that she possessed a modern and sufficiently Westernised legal system.

The existing Japanese legal tradition was totally unsuited to the requirements either of modernity or of the new international order. The *ritsu-ryo* system of the Heian period, even though it was partly the legal basis for the imperial restoration, was clearly outdated; Western governments were unlikely to have much confidence in any Japanese modern legal institutions, let alone ones which were elaborated more than a millennium earlier. The Edo period's *buke* and *kuge sho-hatto* were of no particular value, partly because they were in any case designed exclusively for the upper feudal orders, partly because the *bakuhan* system had recognised the sovereignty of the daimyo's jurisprudence over his han, so that Edo law was not entirely nationalised, but indeed consisted of each individual han's codes (*hanpo*). The new, highly centralised Meiji state required a unified national legal system and one which would be operative among all classes of society. And, as indicated above, among its various qualities it was indispensable that the country's legal system should be packaged in such a manner as to placate Western anxieties. The Meiji government required all that – and quickly!

Of all the Western imports to Japan, the introduction of Western jurisprudence was probably by far the most problematical. A legal system consists of more than codes, magistrates, procedures. It is the product of an entire philosophical and historical tradition. While Western jurisprudence originates from Roman Law, that in turn was the progeny of Greek philosophy. Apart from religion, probably nothing is so intimate to any given society as its legal philosophy and the system from which it is derived; indeed religion and law are inextricably bound together. Western concepts of justice and of rights had deep roots. In Japan and indeed in Confucianist society in general neither the concepts of justice nor rights could claim any indigenous pedigree. The whole fabric of traditional Japanese society was woven according to Confucianist moral patterns of reciprocal relationships of benevolence (from above) and loyalty (from below). Personal bonds were sacrosanct, contractual relationships were non-existent. The concept of rights was not only alien to the Japanese tradition, the very term did not exist and had to be invented. Society was not perceived in terms of individuals enjoying rights, but of individuals bestowed with a strong sense of obligation. The word for 'rights', *kenri*, is a modern fabrication, extraneously derived, neither understood, nor digested, nor indeed entirely trusted; while the Japanese vocabulary abounds in terms for obligations, such as *giri, gimu, on*, all of which have various connotations, the differences being more than simple nuances. The monumental barriers which existed in the introduction of Western law to Japan, however, could not, by the very force of things, distract the Meiji government from its determination that the operation should be expeditiously carried out. This operation was nothing less than the transplantation of a Western legal heart into the Japanese body.

As with practically everything else, and especially in this totally new and unchartered field, the Japanese required a foreign model. The English system of common law was far too complicated and diffuse to be understood and incorporated within the short period of time desired by the government. Other alternatives, for example the American, the Swiss and, at that stage, the German and the Italian were unsatisfactory in that the legal systems of these countries were not unified, but provided for provincial (state, canton, etc.)

diversification. On the other hand, the Napoleonic codes, with their highly centralised character, appeared ideal for the Meiji government's purposes. In fact the first minister of Justice, Eto Shinpei, was so enthusiastic about the codes that he instructed Mitsukuri Rinsho (1846–97), a Justice Ministry official who had studied in France during the *bakumatsu* period, to proceed immediately with a complete translation of the codes, without over-worrying about possible mistranslations, in order that these might be incorporated into Japan as the law of the land. Eto, however, as pointed out earlier in this chapter, lost his head.

The government, albeit recognising that a somewhat more gradual introduction of Western jurisprudence would be necessary and that a degree of adaptation to the local environment was preferable, nevertheless proceeded with the intention of using the Napoleonic codes as their basic model and to that end in 1873 retained the services of one of France's most distinguished scholars of jurisprudence, Gustave Emile Boissonade de Fontarbie (1825–1910). Boissonade remained for more than twenty years in Japan and ceaselessly worked not only at the modern codification of Japan's civil and penal laws, but also at seeking to instruct the Japanese with the spirit of Western jurisprudence as well as its letter.

His task was an onerous one. An illustration of the difficulties he encountered can be seen from problems arising in regard to torture. Torture had been practised for centuries in Japan, while, by the mid/late nineteenth century, it had been abolished in most West European countries – *de jure*, in any case, even if not always *de facto*. The practice of torture had already been the subject of considerable criticism from some of the *keimo* intelligentsia; the problem, however, was that traditionally in Japan a criminal could not be punished, no matter how flagrantly obvious the evidence might be, unless he confessed his guilt. As punishments were harsh and the death penalty imposed for a wide variety of crimes, not surprisingly there was not much enthusiasm or spontaneity on the part of culprits to confess their guilt, hence torture was perceived as a means of persuasion. These subtleties, however, were not appreciated by Boissonade who launched a major offensive against the practice of torture in April 1875; the government's eagerness to learn Western ways can be seen from the fact that by June of the following year an ordinance was issued which forbade the use of torture as a means of obtaining evidence, a confession, or indeed as a punishment.

Other reforms were introduced, notably, for example, the promulgation in 1875 of a decree that henceforth all criminal and civil cases would be heard in public trials. The sequence of reform followed by retrenchment, a characteristic pattern of behaviour on the part of the Meiji government, should be also noted here, however. Thus, the principle of public trials remained unaltered from its inauguration in 1875. According to article 59 of the 1889 Constitution, however, stipulations were inserted that when it was felt that such publicity might prove prejudicial to national peace and order or to morality, the public trial might be suspended by government order. Although similar safeguards exist in all societies, from the late Meiji period – and especially in the case of the trial of Kotoku Shusui (1871–1911), when he and a number of his collaborators and fellow anarchists were executed on rather dubious charges of plotting to assassinate the tenno – the use of this device of hearing cases *in camera* increasingly became an abuse.

The first major step in legal codification in Japan occurred with the adoption of a Penal Code and Code of Criminal Procedure, largely inspired by the Napoleonic model and a fruit of Boissonade's efforts, in 1882. While this Code was met with significant approval both in Japan and indeed abroad for its progressive character, it should not be forgotten that the government simultaneously retained an impressive array of extra-judicial powers which enabled it to promulgate a whole series of ordinances for specific purposes, covering such matters as public meetings, the press, censorship, libel and so on. While the Napoleonic codes of penal law could hardly be presented as excessively liberal, they nonetheless reflected the spirit of the French Revolution and by most contemporary standards they were indeed progressive. The Code of Criminal Procedure (*Keiji Soshoho*) was revised by the government in 1890 and the Penal Code (*Keiho*) submitted to comparable treatment in 1908. It is an indication of the oligarchy's policy of significant retrenchment that when the revisions were carried out the comparatively liberal Napoleonic model was discarded in favour of the absolutist character of the German Wilhelminian jurisprudence, with the result that the *Keiji Soshoho* re-emerged as a 'japanised' replica of the *Strafprozessordnung* and the *Keiho* that of the *Strafgesetzbuch*. The foreign model was still imperative, but in Wilhelminian autocracy the oligarchy found one that suited its taste far more than the more liberal French alternative.

While a modern criminal code was in operation within a relatively short time, the question of a civil code (*minpo*) was far more complex. Civil affairs, by definition, relate to the very basis of society. A draft civil code had been presented to the government in 1879. It was rejected, however, on a number of grounds; one of the more forcefully expressed criticisms was that the provisions in the draft threatened the integrity of the traditional family. In fact, what the law-makers desired was that the customs of the traditional samurai family should be legally codified. At that stage, however, this position was not necessarily articulated. Boissonade and his team set to re-draft the code, the new version being completed in 1889, the same year that the Constitution was to be promulgated. At the time that the code was submitted a national storm of vituperation and indignation ensued, with the result that for almost a decade it became a subject of intense debate. Eventually a civil code was adopted in 1898; by that time, however, it differed markedly from the Boissonade draft.

The fierce debate which raged over what became known as the 'postponement controversy' was a highly complex affair in which numerous positions, emotions, interests and political ideologies came into play. There was, for example, an element of *gakubatsu*, academic cliques, namely a confrontation between the legal schools which claimed either mainly French, mainly British or mainly German derivation; the exchanges between these schools were expressed in print in their respective journals, but also in the popular press. And, it should be noted, the popular press at the end of the nineteenth century (a period coinciding with the Sino-Japanese war in particular but the more expansive nature of Japanese foreign policy in general) had adopted a far more jingoistic tune and was also heavily influenced by this time by the Social-Darwinian theories of Herbert Spencer than by his tenets of egalitarianism and individualism. This jingoism was also coloured by strong anti-Western feelings which were particularly felt at the time of the Triple Intervention. The very foundations of the national essence were at stake, it was argued, hence the controversy was certainly not limited to considerations of jurisprudence, but contained passionate elements of emotional and political dimensions.

The argument centred round the question of the structure and the values of the family. Hence it was argued that the draft code presented far too much of a slavish imitation of Western social mores, whereas what was necessary at all costs was to preserve the structures and values of the traditional, that is, samurai, family, for therein resided the country's soul and its strength. In concrete terms the draft was attacked on the grounds that it gave far too much emphasis to individual rights, whereas traditionally it was not the individual but the family which was the basic social unit of Japan and that values within the family were based on patterns of reciprocal obligations and especially the cardinal virtue of filial piety. It was also strongly objected that the Western model had been far too liberally appropriated in that the draft emphasised the conjugal relationship, whereas in traditional (samurai) society the lineage relationship was the key factor. Among other things, it was objected, the draft gave far too many legal prerogatives to the wife in terms of management of property, inheritance, decision-making within the family, and so on. Perhaps the most inflammatory attack on the draft was penned by Hozumi Yatsuka (1860–1912) in a pamphlet entitled *Minpo Idete Chuko Horobu* ('The Civil Code In, Loyalty and Filial Piety Out'). Hozumi protested that if the Civil Code were adopted, not only would the traditional family system be undermined, but loyalty to the tenno would be lost. A major theme in the attacks on the draft was that what Japan above all needed was to return to traditional indigenous morality, with its emphasis on virtue, rather than adopt Western legalism which was the sure road to Armageddon as far as the spirit of Japan was concerned.

The 1898 Civil Code which did eventually emerge paid far greater attention to samurai customs: laws were incorporated safeguarding such vital aspects of the family as filial piety, primogeniture, and even the greater subservience of the wife to the husband. When the civil code was further revised in 1912, the parts relating to the family and inheritance laws were even further 'samurai-ised' in such a way as to keep in harmony with the prevailing spirit of *junpu-bizoku*, 'gentle ways and beautiful customs'.

Certainly, therefore, the nativists won the day in so far as the vital provisions regarding family matters were concerned. This is very important. The family, in legal terms, was an autocratic, hierarchically structured unit. The power of the head of the *ie*, the household, was virtually absolute, over both his children and his wife. In this respect the family represented the microcosm of what the oligarchy desired should be the total nature of the Japanese state. The power of the *ie*-head was a reflection of the power that the tenno should exercise over his children, namely the subjects of the Japanese Empire.

To perceive this purely in terms of a nativist reaction against Westernism, however, is not totally correct. For one thing, and as cruelly paradoxical as it may seem when one remembers his influence on early Meiji Japan's radicals, the general highly conservative tenor of late Meiji codification and legislation obtained the blessing of Herbert Spencer. In a letter to Kaneko in 1903, which was to be shown to Ito, Spencer strongly argued against allowing American or European influences to infiltrate Japanese society and indeed insisted that in regard to the future of Japan, 'my advice is strongly conservative in all directions' (Spencer's letter was posthumously published in *The Times* of 18 January 1904). Also, however, the 1898 Civil Code was strongly influenced by the German *Bürgeliches Gesetzbuch* which was completed and published in 1896. The marriage of traditional samurai values with Wilhelminian-inspired public and private absolutist legal theories, codes and institutions set the foundations of the Meiji jurisprudential edifice. This did not necessarily reflect the will of the inhabitants, but it was the blueprint on which the architects carefully modelled practically every pillar.

From then until the end of the Second World War Japanese society was administered according to the principles of *hochishugi*, 'rule by law', these being principally derived from the German legal concept and framework of the *Rechsstaat*. The 1889 Constitution did guarantee certain basic rights to the citizens of Japan; these, however, were subjected to the German principle of *Gesetzesvorbehalt*, legal reserve, namely that they were granted only within the framework of law. Rights in this sense, therefore, are not inalienable, but rather should be perceived as temporary privileges which the lawmakers, namely the tenno's government, could rescind by simple legislative action. It is clear, therefore, that in matters of jurisprudence the state appropriated to itself the role of an absolute central authority. It is also clear that by insisting on the autocratic and hierarchic nature of the family according to the provisions of the civil code, the government intended that this basic social unit should serve as the cornerstone for the *kokutai*. Finally, one should not fail to mention that none of the 'liberal' governments of the 'Taisho democracy' ever sought to liberalise the existing legal codes.

EDUCATION AND THE STATE

In regard to education during the Meiji period, several points should be borne in mind. First, as was stressed in Chapter 4, the Edo period had witnessed a significant development in both qualitative (for example *Rangaku*) and quantitative aspects of education. The literacy rate of the total population on the eve of industrialisation stood somewhere in the region of 40 per cent. By the end of the Meiji period the literacy rate had doubled to about 80 per cent. Although there can be no doubt that education significantly contributed to Japan's process of industrialisation, it is difficult to determine how important the quantitative element of modernising Japan's 'mass education' actually was. For example, in terms of evaluating literacy, one has to distinguish between basic literacy and functional literacy; the percentage figures indicated above refer to the former rather than the latter. In other words, a conscript who is able to sign his name is considered to be basically literate, even though this by no means indicates whether the same conscript is capable of deciphering a manual on the use of a particular piece of military hardware. This does not mean that Japanese literacy figures should be revised in a downward direction as literacy rates tended to be computed in analogous fashion throughout the modern world – for example, in France during the nineteenth century literacy rates were compiled on the basis of whether or not the bride and groom at a marriage registry office were capable of signing their names.

As far as Japan's education system and its contribution to economic growth is concerned, while admitting the highly complex nature of the exercise, perhaps two rather uncontroversial points can be posited. The first is that it is probably far more on the qualitative index that Japan's impressive economic performance resides; namely, the high quality of instruction offered in the élite establishments of the universities, the colleges and the military schools.

The university faculties of engineering produced excellent engineers, the agricultural colleges first-class agronomists, the military schools some of the world's finest officer material. In view of the fact that throughout the Meiji and subsequent periods those who entered these establishments represented less than 2 per cent of their age group certainly raises doubts in regard to the significance of the quantitative input. At the same time, however, it must be recognised that an élite on its own is of comparatively little use – a problem of severe dimensions facing most under-developed countries today. Below the level of engineers and high-grade officers, however, there was an important layer of able foremen and petty-officers. These groups tended to be graduates of secondary and/or vocational schools. Even in the interwar period, however, the proportion of the age bracket attending these institutions was well below 10 per cent. Although the early Meiji education organisation was somewhat haphazard, following reforms in the eighties a linear progression from basic primary school on was established. Efforts were directed at seeking to discover and encourage (male) talent wherever it might be. The fact that by the beginning of the twentieth century virtually 100 per cent of Japanese children attended the compulsory period of primary education – first three years, then four and in 1907 raised to six, which remained the only compulsory unit of education until the end of the Second World War – meant, if nothing else, that the net to catch talent was cast widely. This, therefore, marks the second point, namely that at the very least the potential pool of talent was extensive.

As has already been pointed out, the Education Act of 1872 should be seen as no more than the declaration of an intention. It was part and parcel of the *fukoku-kyohei* ambition. Thus, the Act proclaimed that education should no longer be the monopoly of any class or indeed of only the male sex, that henceforward there should be no illiterate family in any village nor illiterate members in any family. Progress, however, was marred by financial and personnel difficulties. It was only, as has been seen, by the early twentieth century that primary school enrolment surpassed the 90 per cent mark; even then a distinction must be drawn between enrolment and attendance, indeed there is reasonably strong evidence to indicate that until the last few years of the Meiji period absenteeism remained a substantial problem. In regard to overall government educational policies, it should also be noted that its lofty ambitions were not matched by fiscal generosity. Throughout the Meiji period the government expenditure on education remained, to say the very least, parsimonious, especially in comparison with the rather lavish outlays in the military budget.

In the early Meiji period, however, the government was not simply hampered in its educational aims by material obstacles, but also by psychological ones. To put it simply, there was stiff opposition in the rural areas to education: the peasantry considered that it had more immediate priorities, for example feeding itself, than achieving enlightenment. Peasant resistance was, of course, partly based on economic grievances, for primary education was made compulsory, but it was not for that matter free; along with taxes and everything else the peasantry perceived education as just one more financial burden which they were being forced to bear. There was also, however, an instinctive premonition that this new-fangled education was some form of witchcraft, hence schools were viewed by the peasant masses with suspicion, indeed hostility. Riots broke out and these frequently took the form of destroying school buildings.

Undaunted, the government persisted in its efforts. The Iwakura mission, composed of both a diplomatic and a fact-finding expedition, included as its chief educational officer Tanaka Fujimaro (1845–1909). Upon his return to Japan in 1873 Tanaka was named Vice-Minister of Education and in the same year retained the services of an eminent American pedagogue, David Murray (1830–1905) of Rutgers University, who remained as chief adviser to the Ministry of Education until his departure from Japan in 1878. Whereas the original Meiji model had been the highly structured and highly centralised French Napoleonic format, during the seventies a more American informal, decentralised system prevailed. This was partly due to Murray's influence, but also to Mori, who at this stage – he will change – was going through a very pro-American, liberal phase. The liberal atmosphere which pervaded the embryonic educational system was, of course, a reflection of the general *bunmei-kaika* ethos. Once again, it was Fukuzawa who set the tone, especially in his *Gakumon no Susume* ('An Encouragement to Learning'), published in 1872–6; education was an end in itself, the primary beneficiary was the individual who by instruction enriched himself. Again bearing in mind the understandable anti-Confucianist iconoclasm of that period, not surprisingly the emphasis in school syllabi was on discovering all about the West, while not only was there no attention paid to traditional morality, but on the contrary past principles were discarded in enthusiastic favour of individualism, egalitarianism and other assorted European concepts worthy of importation.

It should also be pointed out that the state was by no means the only dispenser of education at this stage. For one thing, missionaries went very much into the education business. Otherwise, however, private academies of one form or another proliferated throughout the seventies and pretty much throughout the country; this was a period when every qualified or semi-qualified person went about setting up a school. Early Meiji Japan was a veritable educational maze. While traditional Confucianist institutions still existed, state schools were being erected, private academies of mainly Western orientation were proliferating and, of course, the missionaries were in a highly competitive position as well – especially in view of the premium placed on the acquisition of a European language, mainly English. While dependence on Western missionaries was somewhat humiliating, far more worrying from the government's viewpoint, was the fact that the private academies were almost exclusively run by militants or sympathisers of the *jiyu-minken-undo*; and indeed the movement was proving highly successful in infiltrating the state school system as well. And to make matters worse, the *jiyu-minken-undo* spirit was even contaminating the conscripts of the imperial army (there occurred a rather serious mutiny in 1878) – a phenomenon which could no doubt be explained by the subversive thoughts they had been subjected to during their primary school days.

Reaction, therefore, was bound to set in. As in the case of the civil code, however, it should be noted that the reaction was composed of both a moral and a political nature; in the former there was a strong nativist element, namely a rejection of Western values in favour of a return to indigenous traditional patterns, while in the latter there was more a concern with the proper organisation of the state. The result was an amalgam of the two: indoctrination of nativist values with, once again, a German-inspired educational organisation.

In the moral sphere, the first major onslaught on the excessive westernism and liberalism of the primary education curriculum came from the tenno's tutor, the Confucian scholar Motoda Eifu (1818–91). In the late seventies the tenno had toured a number of schools and, or at least so Motoda claimed, he had been most distressed to discover how little the pupils knew of their own history and traditions. In 1879 Motoda published *Kyogaku Taishi* ('Essentials of Education') which, among other things, could be perceived as the complete antidote to the poisonous substance of Fukuzawa's *Gakumon no Susume*. In fact, Motoda's prescription was a strong combination of tenno-ist and Confucianist principles: the primary goal of education should be the moral education of the young, in the form of instruction in the virtues of benevolence, duty, loyalty and filial piety; furthermore, these principles would result in achieving the most important function of education, namely instilling in the hearts of Japan's youth burning sentiments of reverence for the tenno and love for the country. Motoda proceeded with his programme of an educational purge by writing two years later *Yogaku Koyo* ('Essentials of Learning for the Young'), which was published by the Imperial Household Ministry, copies of which Motoda distributed to schools throughout the country.

Motoda's views, it should be made clear, were not received with much enthusiasm by all government officials. Not only Mori, but indeed also Ito, viewed with some apprehension this Confucianist revivalism. While they were concerned that the nation should produce good patriots, an excessive emphasis on Confucianist ethics could prove detrimental to the more modern aspirations which they held for the future of Japan. Motoda, however, found a more sympathetic ear in the person of the new Minister of Education, Fukuoka Takachika (1835–1919). In 1881 the ethics textbooks which hitherto had consisted essentially of translations from Western primers were banned. Indeed, as has been indicated, 1881 witnessed a considerable censorship in educational institutions when not only foreign works such as Mill's *On Liberty* and Spencer's *Education* were placed on the index, but also a number of Fukuzawa's works and others emanating from the liberal *keimo* scholars. At first the Ministry issued ethics textbooks written by conservative nativist scholars. During Mori's tenure of office as Minister of Education, from 1885 until his assassination in 1889, ethics textbooks were not circulated to schools. Following the 1890 Imperial Rescript on Education (*Kyoiku Chokugo*), however, the Ministry published its own textbooks and from then until 1945 the moral content of primary education enjoyed pride of place. From the beginning of the twentieth century all school textbooks were issued by the state; those in subjects such as language and history also contained a strong moral flavouring. The ethical standardisation which the government sought to impose was extensive and can be illustrated by the fact that Uchimura Kanzo was dismissed from his teaching post at Tokyo's First Higher School in 1891 owing to his refusal to accept the Imperial Rescript on Education as holy educational writ.

While the moral instruction in Japanese primary schools undoubtedly represents a degree of nativist reaction, it was certainly not the government's intention that the national education should be allowed to return simply and purely to some idyllic Confucianist past. The moral instruction should not be seen in isolation. In terms of building up the modern nation-state, far more important than the ethical input into the curriculum was the politicisation of education. This was primarily the work of Mori Arinori, hardly a romantic nativist, but very much a realist, indeed an adept at *Realpolitik*. It was in 1885, the year of Mori's appointment as Minister of Education, that the new Cabinet system was introduced with Ito as the first Prime Minister. Mori, therefore, was Ito's choice, a choice which the Imperial Household Ministry, dominated as it was by the likes of Motoda, tried to veto, in view of Mori's alleged excessive westernism, but Ito's decision prevailed. Antipathy towards Mori among the tenno's household staff was grounded on his American bias. While this had certainly been the case in the past, it should be remembered that the formation of Ito's 1885 Cabinet took place after the latter's return from his extended study-tour of Germany and Austria. It was also while Mori was Minister of Education that Kato Hiroyuki was appointed President of the newly organised and newly named Tokyo Imperial University. Kato had been one of the government's most reliable supporters especially in his foreceful antagonism to the *jiyu-minken-undo*. Kato had been strongly influenced by the *Allgemeines Staatsrecht* of Johann Caspar Bluntschli (1808–81), which in fact he had translated into Japanese; while Bluntschli had occasionally found himself in opposition to Bismarck, his legalistic, élitist and *étatist* conception of the nation-state was very much in keeping with the structures and nature of the Second Reich.

Mori's extensive educational reforms included the following developments. In his belief that education should serve the interests of the state – Mori no longer subscribed to the *Gakumon no Susume*-type pedagogical philosophy – he sought to achieve a high degree of national integration of the educational system. This was to be achieved by complete centralisation of the curricula and other matters pertaining to schooling, including textbooks, under the authority of the Ministry of Education. While these positive directions were taken in favour of the state system, a number of negative steps were taken in regard to the private sector. Some private academies were quite simply closed under government orders. While it was difficult simply to enforce the closure of missionary schools – this would have caused difficulties with the Western powers and the treaties were not yet revised – a number of disincentives were put into operation, for example requiring that only pupils from the state educational system could gain entry to the colleges and vocational schools, or sit for the university entrance examinations. A complementary step was to have all the prefectural teacher-training colleges brought under Tokyo control. The Ministry of Education set the curricula in these institutions and also the very rigid, indeed spartan, discipline which pervaded the atmosphere and schedule of the colleges was determined by Tokyo under Mori's guidance. Tokyo appointed all school principals, while candidates to the teacher-training colleges were selected by the prefectural offices. Once they were qualified, teachers were subject to the authority of the Ministry of Education which decided where they were to be posted. The Ministry also appointed government inspectors who made annual visits to all schools throughout the country. Political education was fostered by, among other things, the inclusion in textbooks of hagiographic stories of the reigning tenno and his illustrious ancestors. Mori's measures can be said to have accomplished two things: the consolidation of the national educational base and the imposition of strict governmental control, indeed regimentation, over the teaching profession. Henceforward teachers were the servants of the state.

While consolidating the base, however, Mori also planned the erection of an educational structure which would cater to the needs of the advanced sectors of society. It was at his initiative that the middle schools and vocational schools both grew in number and were more effectively organised. And his Imperial

University Ordinance of 1886 resulted in a close connection, noted in the previous chapter, between the Imperial University and the bureaucracy. Mori's meritocratic élitism precluded him from approaching university education in too dogmatic a fashion. In fact, throughout the later Meiji period and in the twenties universities enjoyed a high degree of academic freedom.

Mori's educational philosophy and institutionalisation remained essentially the pattern to which successive governments in the Meiji, Taisho and early Showa periods held. Thus, throughout these decades it remained government policy that while an educated élite was essential, for the preservation of peace and order within the land it was also essential that this élite be kept to the strict minimal national requirement. The philosophy of an enlightened élite and an indoctrinated mass was a key pillar to the Meiji edifice. Thus, for example, Hozumi Yatsuka's nativist interpretation of the constitution, which emphasised the divine status of the tenno and advocated the principles of theocratico-patriarchal constitutionalism, was rapidly superseded in universities by the more modern conservative interpretation of Minobe Tatsukichi (1873–1948). Minobe presented the tenno as one of the organs of state, albeit the highest, and thus de-emphasised, if not totally rejected, the nativist *sonno* ideological tradition. In the thirties Minobe was forced to resign from his Chair at Tokyo Imperial University because of his scholarship. This fact has tended to make him somewhat of a hero among liberals. Minobe's academic background, however, was very much in the Wilhelminian constitutional tradition, especially the influence of Georg Jellinek (1842–1909); Minobe presented the Japanese monarchy not as absolutist, but as constitutional, albeit an autocratic constitutional monarchy. The point here, however, is that while Minobe's was the basic university textbook, it was Hozumi's ideas which were filtered down and prevailed as orthodoxy in the primary and secondary sector. This was something else which the 'liberal' regime of the 'Taisho democracy' overlooked.

By the late nineteenth century the government had devised an educational system which suited its needs and ambitions. A highly qualified leadership with a well disciplined and indoctrinated mass were, in their perception, the ideal recipe for the creation of their viable nation-state. No system is foolproof and the Meiji educational edifice was no exception to this rule. Certainly, however, the oligarchy cannot be accused of not having tried.

THE MILITARISATION OF MEIJI JAPAN

The role of the military in the modern age presents something of a paradox. On the one hand, the military in underdeveloped countries can be said to figure among the more forceful and effective agents of modernisation. It is generally in the army and its ancillary industries that one finds the most advanced technology. There also tends to be in the military – though this is by no means a universal rule – a greater degree of social mobility than in other sectors of society. The education received in military academies, especially in applied sciences, will invariably be of a high calibre. While the military will, also invariably, be presented as the paragons of nationalism, at the same time there is inevitably a high degree of internationalism: young officers from underdeveloped countries will study in the military academies, for example Sandhurst, of advanced countries, which will in turn dispatch military missions to cooperate in the modernisation of the host country's military institutions. This was certainly the case in Meiji Japan where the army came first under French and later German tutelage, while the Imperial Navy, not surprisingly, benefited from the instruction of the Royal Navy – indeed at the Naval College of Etajima a lock of Nelson's hair could be found and admired in the museum (until it was removed in 1941), while the red bricks of the *seitokan*, the main cadet building, had been imported all the way from England. In spite of all this, and bearing in mind the occasional exception, military intervention in governmental affairs has almost always led to socio-political repression and regression. In many countries of Latin America, Africa and Asia the military junta rules. The same phenomenon has been present in the less developed countries of Western Europe, in Spain and in Greece, and at the time of writing is manifest in Turkey. It can be put forward as a general proposition that the advanced society is one in which the military is made to serve the state and not the state serve the military. In other words, an advanced society possesses strong and viable civilian institutions and values which the indigenous army will be preoccupied in protecting rather than demolishing.

The military coup tends to have fairly universal characteristics. The civilian government appears incapable of solving serious social and economic problems, law and order break down, rioting in the streets becomes a daily occurrence, the military move in, civilian leaders are deposed, executed or imprisoned, the fortunate ones flee the country and set up a government in exile, followed and supported by artists and intellectuals. Nothing of the sort ever happened in Japan. While there were a number of abortive putsches by young officers in the thirties, no successful military coup ever occurred. From its promulgation in 1889 to its abolition in 1946 the Constitution was never violated by the military hierarchy. At no time in modern Japanese history was there an exclusively military government. Indeed at the height of 'militarism', in the late thirties, among the prime ministers of the period were the civilians Hirota Koki (1878–1948), in office from March 1936 to January 1937; Konoe Fumimaro (1891–1945), in office from June 1937 to January 1939 and from July 1940 to October 1941; and Hiranuma Kiichiro (1967–1952), in office from January to May 1939. Tojo Hideki (1884–1948), presented as the militarist figure *par excellence* and prime minister of the wartime cabinet from October 1941 to July 1944, included in his Cabinets civilians with important portfolios.

While the alleged militaristic period of the late thirties continued to include a significant civilian element, a list of Japanese prime ministers is illustrative of the phenomenon of 'militarisation' of Japanese politics. From the setting up of the Cabinet system in 1885 until the end of the century, the prime ministership oscillated between the *genro*, namely Ito, Kuroda, Yamagata, Matsukata and Okuma – the last, following a brief and moderate renegade period in the early eighties, had rejoined the establishment by the end of the decade, and formed a government twice, once from June to November 1898 (with Itagaki as Home Minister) and from April 1914 to October 1916. Ito's last government lasted from October 1900 to June 1901; this was also, with the exception of Okuma, the last *genro* prime ministership. The *genro* retired to the background and influenced policy partly by ensuring that their protégés assumed the headship of government. While Saionji Kinmochi (1849–1940), civilian and president of the newly formed *Seiyukai* (Society of Political Friends) and protégé of Ito, was prime minister from January 1906 to July 1908 and August 1911 to December 1912, the last dozen years of the Meiji era can be said to have been virtually dominated by the general Katsura Taro (1848–1913), protégé of Yamagata, prime minister from 1901 to 1906, 1908 to 1911 and December 1912 to February 1913. From the fall of Katsura's last government until 1937, the year that Japan embarked on full-scale war with China, and including, therefore, the years of 'Taisho democracy', the heads of government included the following: admiral Yamamoto Gonnohyoe (1852–1933), in office from February 1913 to April 1914 and September 1923 to January 1924; general Terauchi Masatake (1852–1919), in office from November 1916 to October 1918; admiral Kato Tomosaburo (1861–1923), in office from June 1922 to September 1923; general Tanaka Giichi (1863–1929), in office from April 1927 to April 1929; admiral Saito Makoto (1858–1936), in office from May 1932 to July 1934; admiral Okada Keisuke (1868–1952), in office from July 1934 to March 1936; and general Hayashi Senjuro (1876–1943), in office from February to June 1937.

Thus in the course of the period from 1901 to 1937, governments headed by either admirals or generals account for twenty-one years. Among modern industrialised states – in which Japan figured by the early twentieth century – the phenomenon of prestigious military figures becoming heads of government is unique to Japan; cases such as Dwight Eisenhower (1890–1969) or Charles de Gaulle (1890–1970) are the exception rather than the rule. Nor can Germany be compared to Japan; while the prestige of the military and their political power were certainly much more in evidence than in other Western European countries, a situation which was maintained even after 1918, with Paul von Hindenburg (1847–1934) becoming President only seven years after defeat, Adolf Hitler (1889–1945) was not a prestigious military officer, but an ex-corporal. While there are undoubtedly patterns of socio-political continuity in modern German history, the first half of the twentieth century nevertheless was punctuated by significant and violent changes in government and policy: the Second Reich, the brief Spartakist Revolution, the Weimar Republic, the advent of the Third Reich. In terms of Japanese political history, what appears striking above all is the very strong element of continuity. Although military influence in governmental affairs and policies may have been stronger at certain times than at others, the difference was one of degree and not one of nature. Thus even during the years of 'Taisho democracy', identified as the period from 1918 to 1932, the year of the assassination of the civilian prime minister Inukai Tsuyoshi (1855–1932), roughly a third of that period witnessed governments formed by military officers, in spite of the alleged strong popular antipathy to the armed services.

The role of the military in Japan's transformation to modernity was pervasive. In regard to the statements made above, certain qualifications are in order. First, it is not the intention to suggest that the governments of generals or admirals from Katsura to Hayashi should be perceived as militaristic. In most cases these men were not officers on the active list, but generally retired and not infrequently presidents of political parties. Secondly, there certainly did exist tension between civilian and military elements. Thirdly, at least until the late thirties, numerous instances could be cited where military demands in regard to national policy or budgetary allocations were rebuffed. Nevertheless, the prominence of military figures as heads of government had more than simply emblematic significance. Japan was not a military state. On the other hand there was a significant degree of militarisation which occurred in the economic, political and social spheres of modernising Japan.

The process of industrialisation in the heavy-industry sector especially was largely determined by military requirements. Whether industry was owned and controlled by the state or subsequently by the *zaibatsu*, throughout the period beginning with the construction of modern arsenals, dockyards and so on, in the *bakumatsu* years until Japan's defeat in 1945, the military remained by far industry's most important client: it is sound business policy not to alienate one's major client. In comparison with other modern industrialised powers, the existence of a 'military–industrial complex' was by no means unique to Japan, but the degree to which it pervaded the national economy was far more substantial. For reasons pointed out in the former chapter, namely low wages for workers and high rents and/or taxes for peasants, there was virtually no domestic consumers' market in Japan.

The historical phenomenon of the militarisation of the Japanese nation must be perceived from different perspectives. The fact that so many admirals and generals came to form governments in the country is obviously an indication of the prestige which the military enjoyed in society at large. The prestige of major military figures and the elevation of martial values can be partly accounted for by the long tradition of samurai power, by the fact that since the ascension to the shogunate of Minamoto no Yoritomo in the late twelfth century, indeed even before, Japan had been politically dominated by the bushi, namely by the warrior estate. Political power, as was shown in Chapter 2, was accompanied by the development of a martial ideology, *bushido*, and by an assortment of cultural currents ranging from the introduction of the Buddhist Zen sect to the literary output of military epics such as the *Heike Monogatari*. These martial traditions and the veneration of the martial spirit were vestiges of a past which *all* modern governments until 1945 sought to keep alive, and indeed burning, in the breasts of all Japanese. It was, for example, during the period of 'Taisho democracy' that military officers were seconded to schools throughout the country and that a programme of military training for school pupils was introduced. In any case, therefore, a major factor involved in the militarisation of Japanese society in the period of its transformation to modernity was the existence of deep and solid martial roots.

In the modern context, however, there are two other powerful factors responsible for the high social prestige of the military, and both are obvious. The first is that the Japanese people, it must not be forgotten, believed that they risked the danger of foreign military invasion. That military prestige among some of the urban sectors may have dwindled somewhat in the twenties is no doubt mainly to be attributed to the fact that this was the only time in modern Japanese history that foreign military invasions did not appear to constitute a threat on the horizon. The second is that from 1894 to 1945 not only did Japan never lose a war, but she obtained successive stunning victories both on land and on sea. It was thanks to the military that Japan came to enjoy international prestige and hence it was natural that they be granted the national prestige which they deserved.

The militarisation of Japanese society, however, went far deeper than simply the national psychological proclivity for admiring the military and martial values. From the immediate aftermath of the 1868 revolution, policies were pursued which would ensure that the *kyohei* side of the Meiji modernisation equation resulted in a strong army both in terms of external defence and internal influence.

In 1871, at the same time that they submitted their fiefs, the daimyo of Satsuma, Choshu and Tosa also proposed that their infantry and artillery battalions should be placed at the disposal of the tenno; thus with the establishment of the *Go-shinpei*, Imperial Guard, was the nucleus of the modern Japanese army formed. In 1872 the tenno proclaimed that henceforth Japan would return to the military organisation of the Heian period: military service for all subjects irrespective of social rank with the tenno himself as commander-in-chief. In 1873 the Conscription Law was promulgated.

The introduction of conscription, it should be noted, involved a major revolution in Japan. While this was partly a result of adhering to foreign models, this radical innovation had already appeared in the *bakumatsu* period. At the time that Choshu was contemplating warfare against the Western powers and subsequently against the bakufu, under the recommendation and organisation of Takasugi Shinsaku (1839–67) and Omura Masajiro (1824–69) the *kiheitai*, an armed corps composed of able soldiers irrespective of social rank, was formed and drilled. While both Takasugi and Omura were killed, the establishment of a national conscript army was strongly advocated by Tani Kanjo (1837–1911), Yamada Akiyoshi (1844–92) and Yamagata Aritomo. In fact in 1870 Yamagata and Saigo Tsugumichi (1843–1902), Takamori's younger brother, had been on a military fact-finding mission to Europe and therefore had been lucky enough to witness the Franco-Prussian war at first-hand.

The bakufu, it will be recalled, had invited a French military mission to help train its own modern army in 1866. Not much time was allowed to the French officers, however, and with the advent of the new government they were asked to return home. In 1872, in spite of France's defeat a year earlier, the French were nonetheless invited once again to send a military mission. This appears somewhat baffling in view of Meiji Japan's reputation for selecting what was best from the various European countries. The major factor here, however, was one of time. The new army was in rather desperate need of foreign assistance because of all the peasant and samurai uprisings which were occurring in the early and mid-seventies. There was already a corps of officers, inherited from the bakufu, who knew French, hence could understand the lessons given by French military tutors and read French military textbooks, whereas hardly any Japanese spoke German. It should be noted, however, that while a French military mission was in Japan, from the very early 1870s onward an increasing number of Japanese officers went to study in Germany. Nevertheless, throughout the seventies the organisation of the new Japanese army proceeded along mainly French lines. In spite of the government having won against Satsuma in 1877, it was widely recognised that the new army, with, after all an overwhelming majority in numbers, had really put up a pretty bad show. It came to be strongly felt that for the sake of *kyohei* a process of de-gallicisation might not be a bad thing. Also, however, with the quelling of the Satsuma uprising, as noted earlier, the military threat to the government was by and large removed. It was from the late seventies and in the course of the eighties that the much more internally secure Japanese army was able to engage in the relative luxury of a very substantial reorganisation. Once their contracts expired the French military officers, much to their chagrin, were for the most part once again asked to go home. The late Meiji army, both in terms of its system of conscription and in its hierarchical organisation, followed a German pattern and it was in 1885 that the most influential foreign military figure, Wilhelm Jacob Meckel (1842–1906), arrived in Japan, where he remained for three years before returning to Germany.

From what has been said above, the first fundamental point about the formation of the modern Japanese army should be clear. The Meiji government's primary concern was to achieve internal pacification. The origins of the conscript army were not, as in France in 1793, a popular patriotic *levée en masse* to defend the nation from foreign invasion, but the instrument of the state to quell domestic disturbances. From its inception in 1873 until 1945 internal policing remained an important function of the army. As a result of political disturbances in the seventies and eighties emanating from the activities and propaganda of the *jiyu-minken-undo*, Yamagata – who by the mid-Meiji period had become the dominant figure in the formation of the Meiji military machine – sought to bring the military to heel by issuing in 1878 the *Gunjin kunkai* ('Admonition to Soldiers'), by forming in 1881 the *kenpeitai*, a kind of army intelligence unit whose initial function was to gather information on dissidents within army ranks but was later used to investigate civilians as well, and in 1882 the *Gunjin Chokugo* ('Imperial Rescript to Soldier and Sailors') was issued as emanating from the tenno himself. There also followed a number of military ordinances, including army and navy penal laws.

The Rescript to Soldiers and Sailors was for the army and navy what the Imperial Rescript on Education was for schools. The military rescript was read on certain ceremonial occasions, and as the rescript on education admonished children to be good pupils, so the military rescript admonished conscripts to be good soldiers. Being good soldiers, according to the rescript and the military laws, involved total abstention from politics in a formal sense. Throughout the period 1890 to 1945 soldiers, both men and officers, were not granted the franchise, nor were they to stand for elections, nor engage in any form of political propaganda or even attend political meetings – except, of course, when they were sent there under orders to break them up. On the surface all this by itself is neither particularly significant, nor indeed necessarily ominous. In France as well, for example, professional soldiers were deprived of the political rights of voting or standing for office. These measures, however, must be seen in conjunction with others.

The consolidation of the national military base by the introduction of conscription was devised both as a means of modernisation and as a means of inculcating among peasant youth the martial values of *bushido*, reverence for the tenno (especially as it was repeatedly stressed how soldiers and sailors enjoyed a special relationship with him) and the spirit of nationalism. There can be no doubt that by any standard the exercise must be deemed a great success. For example, although the strategic genius of admiral Togo and general Oyama Iwao (1842–1916) played a crucial role in the Russo-Japanese war, victory could never have been achieved without the remarkable courage, indeed total fearlessness, and spirited determination with which the ordinary Japanese soldiers and sailors fought. The major difference, indeed, between the Russian and Japanese armies was that of morale.

At the same time, however, the impressive performance of the Japanese army and navy in all their wars – including, of course, the Second World War – rested on the quality of their officer corps. As in the bureaucracy and industry, the selection of the military élite came to be determined by academic achievement; in other words, the military also became a meritocracy. The *bakumatsu* years had witnessed the establishment of modern military academies both in the bakufu and in the han. In 1875 officer education was formalised in the establishment of the *shikan gakko* (military academy) which in 1883 was upgraded in the opening of the *Rikugun Daigakko* (War College). Although there developed throughout the Meiji period a whole number of educational institutions for officer training, the *Rikugun Daigakko* was to the Army what the Law Faculty of Tokyo Imperial University was to the bureaucracy: *the* élite course.

In 1876 the *Kaigun Heigakko* (naval academy) was formed; in 1888 it too was upgraded to the *Kaigun Daigakko* (Naval College), while at the same time it moved from Tsukiji, near Tokyo, to the south-western island of Etajima – Etajima was frequently referred to as the 'Dartmouth of Japan', in view of the British influence and indeed continued presence, as from its foundation in 1888 until 1938 there were always two British instructors among the staff. Both the academic and physical training which the students at both institutions received were extremely demanding and undoubtedly went a long way to separating the goats from the sheep; every year, for example, naval cadets had to swim the ten miles from the island of Miyajima to Etajima, though not all made it – *morituri te salutant!* By the late Meiji period, therefore, the military élite, like its bureaucratic counterpart, was of a very high calibre indeed.

The consolidation of military influence over the Japanese nation, in other words the process of militarisation, must be seen for the extensive and indeed intensive exercise that it was. While in the early period of the modern military formation many conscripts were called but few were chosen to serve the tenno – mainly for financial reasons (the finances of the state, that is, not the individuals concerned) – by the late nineteenth century most able-bodied youths experienced some form of military service. Army social organisation increasingly took on the form of the octopus rather than that of the squid, namely with its tentacles not simply drooping downwards but extending in all, or at least many, directions. From the late nineteenth century and throughout the ensuing decades a whole series of ancillary military groups was established: youth organisations, reservist associations, veterans' clubs and in due course even women were privileged to enjoy some form of para-military respectability. Membership to all of these groups was on a voluntary basis. In the rural areas, however – and in fact they never had much success in the cities – local landlord families played prominent parts in the running and recruiting of these organisations so that the social pressure to join was not insignificant. This was especially the case in view of the numerous practical activities in which the groups engaged, fire-fighting being only one example.

While the army was sowing seeds in the social foundations, Yamagata also took a series of steps to ensure that the military should enjoy a powerful leverage at the apex of the political pyramid. The policies which he pursued ultimately resulted in securing the quasi-total independence of the military from civilian control, while at the same time imposing extensive military control over the government. The first substantial move in that direction occurred when in 1878, again using the German model, the General Staff Headquarters, the jurisdiction of which included staffing, military plans and strategy, was removed from the authority of the War Ministry. The Chief of the General Staff, therefore, superseded in rank and responsibility the Minister of War and was deemed solely accountable to the tenno as supreme commander-in-chief. Not only was the Chief of the General Staff not subject to Cabinet control, therefore, but indeed he enjoyed direct access to the tenno. This relationship was further rendered legitimate in Article 11 of the 1889 Constitution. These measures meant, in effect, that the army was above and beyond the government. The government, however, was not to be beyond the stretch of the army or navy. It was stipulated that the Cabinet's choice of ministers of the army and the navy should be submitted to their respective general staffs. In 1900 a special ordinance was inserted that only officers on active duty could serve in these capacities. While that particular ordinance was dropped in 1913, to be resurrected in 1936, the practice of selecting only officers on the active list for either portfolio continued. Indeed in 1914

Kiyoura Keigo (1850–1942) was unable to form a government owing to the Navy General Staff's veto, namely by refusing to nominate a minister, arising out of disagreements over the proposed naval budget.

In the erection of the Meiji political edifice one is entitled to conclude that the most influential architect was Yamagata. Ito had desired a greater degree of civilian control and indeed had incurred Yamagata's wrath by seemingly siding with the opposition, namely by descending to the murky world of party politics by forming and presiding over a political party himself. It was under Ito's authority and pen that the 1889 Constitution was drafted. As a result of a series of concessions and separate ordinances, Yamagata ensured that the military should enjoy what in real terms amounted to an extra-constitutional, or certainly extra-parliamentary, privileged status.

A brief survey of this nature will inevitably reveal as much, perhaps even less, than it conceals. The student of Japanese history and especially of Japanese military history will know that there are certain very important qualifications which need to be underlined in the socio-political diagram which has been drawn. Certainly the major caveat to be inserted, even in a macro-historical exercise of this nature, is that it would be unfortunate if the impression were to arise that the military in Meiji Japan or even more so in the interwar period were some kind of gigantic and completely homogeneous monolith. For one thing, the army too was plagued by atavistic fief particularism. Choshu domination was bitterly resented by officers of non-Choshu birth; while the navy tended to be perceived by the sons of Satsuma as their special preserve. Apart from han rivalry, by the early twentieth century there also developed within the army a strong resentment and sense of envy among the officers who were not products of the élite staff colleges against those who were. There also developed strong ideological differences between various military factions and indeed these assumed explosive proportions in the thirties. Thus, although it is the case that a fair number of civilian prime ministers were assassinated (by civilians), it was the admiral prime minister Okada whom young officers sought to murder in the abortive military uprising of 26 February 1936 – though by mistake they killed his brother-in-law instead. Disputes between the army and the navy and disputes between inter-service factions were at least as serious, and certainly far more violent, than disputes between the military and civilian hierarchies. These qualifications having been made, the fact remains that the degree of political, social, ideological and economic control exercised by the military during the process of transformation to modernity was both extensive and intensive.

Why did Yamagata and his followers take, and seek to maintain, such measures of control? The answer lies at least in part in pure greed. The military, albeit occasionally divisive, were united in wanting the largest possible slice of the budgetary cake, and the best means to achieve that was to obtain the greatest possible degree of political influence and control. If society is viewed as a set of conflicting forces, then the military must be included and perceived as an economic pressure group. There were also strong expansionist tendencies in the military (though by no means were they alone in this respect) and in order to fulfil their dreams reality demanded that they should obtain the means; in the Meiji and Taisho eras practically all disputes between the army and the would-be civilian governments centred round questions of fiscal allocations for military expansion. There were also ideological considerations. Yamagata certainly perceived the possible advent of party political dominance with nothing short of horror. If that had to be so, and Ito seemed to be weakly oscillating in that direction, then it was the duty of the military to ensure that it should never be allowed to go too far. Yamagata desired that the military should preserve the essence of the nation-state, the *kokutai*. He was successful. The army appeared not just as the guardian angel of the *kokutai*, but with all the awe and power of the archangel Michael.

THE *TENNO-SEI*

The *tenno-sei*, tenno system, is a term coined by Marxist historians as a means of describing the political system and culture which was imposed from above on the Japanese people and characterised the Meiji socio-political edifice which remained, *mutatis mutandis*, intact until it was dismantled by the American occupation authorities. The use of the term is not meant to imply that the tenno was an absolutist monarch. While in theory sovereign power resided in his person, in reality the three successive tenno of the modern period exercised not only far less power than the czar, the sultan, or the kaiser, but indeed, as has been suggested, perhaps enjoyed even less political influence than the European constitutional monarchs. Although the tenno was occasionally paraded about – usually in resplendent kaiserish uniform – he was, in reality, a prisoner in his palace. He never addressed his subjects directly, the only occasion this precedent was broken being the wireless address of the Showa-tenno (b. 1901) to the nation announcing the country's surrender. Thus, although he was portrayed as the father of the nation, he was a very aloof one. Although the tenno did occasionally intervene, this was invariably indirectly, and while accepting that they had their personalities and their views, it is nevertheless correct to view them primarily as deified figure-heads.

What is meant by the term *tenno-sei* is that the imperial throne provided the legitimacy and the backing for a political system referred to as *zettai-shugi*, absolutism, an absolutism exercised not by a single individual but by successive governments. In other words, by virtue of being able to speak in the tenno's name the government conferred upon itself total and unimpeachable political power.

The real cornerstone of the government's edifice was its constitution. The oligarchy desired, indeed needed, a constitution and while the announcement that one would be promulgated took the guise of a concession to popular pressure, in fact such a step was very much part of government policy. Two things must be borne in mind. First, the ideal of the almighty tenno was not, in the first couple of decades or so of the Meiji era, widely diffused or understood throughout society. *Sonno* may have been the ideological justification for the restoration, but then relatively few people, even samurai, had actually participated in the events leading up to 1868 and in any case, as stressed in the first section of this chapter, the cultural atmosphere was decidedly Western-orientated and a West which was held up as the child of the Enlightenment if not of the French Revolution. Thus, the new Japan, it was felt, should model itself on the advanced nations of the West. While republican sentiments did not figure prominently in the political debate, nevertheless the advocacy of a British-style constitutional monarchy was well represented. This devolution of power, which in the oligarchy's perspective represented dangerous radicalism which would culminate in anarchy, was anathema to what the architects of the Meiji state desired, namely strong central control. The second factor which must be borne in mind and one which represented a problem for the government was that although the legitimacy of the tenno's spiritual and temporal rule could be found in texts dating back to the Nara and Heian periods and the exegetical studies, noted in Chapter 5, of the Edo era contributed significantly to strengthening the tenno-ist ideology, all these works were old and/or highly disparate in nature, and in any case comprehensible only to more erudite scholars. Some more basic, compact and modern document was called for. Such an exercise would also have the double advantage of placating, at least temporarily, internal opposition – especially if the leaders of the opposition could be sent on a European spree – and at the same time impress the West.

It is with this background that Ito left for Europe in 1882 where he remained for eighteen months. As noted earlier, though his trip was presented as a study-tour of the major European constitutional countries, in fact he spent most of his time in Berlin and in Vienna, where he was tutored in constitutional theory and history by Friedrich von Gneist (1816–95) and Lorenz von Stein (1820–1902) respectively. Upon his return to Japan he undertook the supervision of a constitution drafting committee whose main membership consisted of Inoue Kaoru, Kaneko Kentaro and Ito Miyoji (1857–1934). The committee was assisted by a German adviser, Hermann Roesler (1834–94), who had come to Japan in 1878 and served for seven years as special counsellor to the Foreign Ministry and then for another eight years, until 1893, to the Cabinet. Roesler, among other things, was responsible for the drafting of Meiji Japan's Commercial Code. While Roesler's position has generally been interpreted as further evidence of the German influence on the composition and contents of the Meiji constitution, a slight refinement of this view is necessary. Roesler was a Bismarckian reject in that owing to his conversion to Roman Catholicism he had lost his university Chair according to the provisions of the *Kulturkampf*. Furthermore, while displaying sound knowledge of constitutional theory, Roesler's academic background was not in that discipline but in economics. Also, as recent scholarship has shown, Roesler's recommendations and interpretations were by no means necessarily accepted by the oligarchy. In fact one can suggest that Ito's European tour and Roesler's presence as special adviser to the constitutional commission represented a degree at least of simple window-dressing, a measure meant to impress both domestic and external audiences. All this is not to deny the heavy Germanic influence in the 1889 Constitution; in terms of organisation and presentation, also in terms of theoretical arguments, the German dimension is prevalent. In terms of substance, however, there is a distinction. An early European visitor to Japan described the modern soldier as having a Japanese soul wrapped in a Western uniform. The same might be applied to the 1889 Constitution.

The soul of the Constitution was the tenno. In the Preamble and in Chapter I the absolute sovereignty of the tenno is specifically spelt out. The legitimacy derived from ages eternal and for ages eternal, his position as coeval with heaven and earth, and the fact that the Constitution is a gift to his subjects from the tenno are all made perfectly clear. It has been argued that the 1889 Constitution should not, in fact, be perceived as a rigid document and that, on the contrary, it allowed for a reasonable degree of flexibility. While this may be true in terms of provisions of actual governance, nevertheless the tenno's supremacy is presented as dogma. While the application of the dogma may have been more moderate at certain times than at others, it nonetheless remained a potential Damocles sword to be lowered over the head of whoever was accused of sacrilege. By sacrilege was meant 'dangerous thoughts', which in turn meant those thoughts prejudicial to the preservation of the *kokutai*, which in turn meant practically anything – on the left, but not, as noted in the first section, on the right – which in turn meant that any government might wish to invoke laws regarding the sacrilegious violation of dogma.

Some of the other provisions of the 1889 Constitution, notably the fact that basic rights were limited by legal statute, have already been noted. In terms of executive and legislative power, the Constitution was devised so as to allow as little muscle as possible to the Diet. The government was to be appointed by the tenno and it was only to him that the government could be held accountable. While the Diet had certain powers over the budget, in terms of all other legislative matters its role was a purely advisory one. The Diet, so the oligarchy desired, should be no more than a debating chamber.

The first election was held in 1890 and this was a stunning defeat for the government; the parties and the many candidates who presented themselves as independents won massive victories while the candidates fielded by the oligarchy were by and large unsuccessful. In the election of 1892 the then Prime Minister Matsukata's Home Minister, Shinagawa Yajiro (1843–1900), decided to resort to outright violent intimidation: the police and hired rowdies were sent out to break up opposition political meetings, beat up opposition candidates, and terrorise individual electors at the polls. This was Japan's bloodiest election, resulting in at least twenty-five people killed and hundreds seriously wounded. The result at the polls, however, was another massive defeat for the government. In the case of a vote of no-confidence, the government could either dissolve the Diet and call for fresh elections or resign. In the first decade of the parliament's existence there were no fewer than seven changes of government. Ito's prime ministership from 1892 to 1896, lasting four years and one month, was by far the longest; it also occurred, however, during the build-up and subsequent outbreak of the Sino-Japanese war of 1894–5, a period during which there was an internal political armistice. The second longest, Yamagata's government of November 1898 to October 1900, lasted one year and eleven months. The shortest, Okuma's with Itagaki as Home Minister, had a life span of four months. The oligarchy had clearly miscalculated; rather than having created a docile debating chamber, it appeared as though they had opened a Pandora's box.

Why did the Diet and their electors rebel against the government? For one thing, it must be remembered that by the early parliamentary phase the oligarchy had been in power for a quarter of a century. There was, therefore, a feeling, by no means unique to Japan, that that particular show had lasted just a bit too long; it was time for new faces and new methods. Secondly, the composition of the electorate must be borne in mind. The franchise, as already indicated, was determined by a form of poll-tax. The electors were, therefore, comparatively speaking, men of wealth or property. Among the younger ones especially they were also likely to be educated: products of institutions such as Keio and Waseda – the latter in particular a renowned centre of 'radicals' – or the various commercial colleges, vocational schools, and so on. These men, products of the modern meritocracy, resented the rigid paternalistic authoritarianism of the oligarchy. Thirdly, the struggle which occurred represented a determination on the part of the electorate to have the political power base brought into alignment with the emerging economic edifice; in other words those who had the money also wanted the power. The tumult, therefore, had nothing to do with mass democracy; rather it was a struggle between contending élites, the upper bureaucracy versus the private sector.

Yamagata remained steadfastly opposed to compromise with the opposition parties. The official line was that they should have no say in the formation of governments, for by definition parties would pursue purely partisan interests, hence to the detriment of the nation, while the bureaucracy was motivated exclusively by the interests of the nation as a whole. Ito, however, began to undergo a degree of political metamorphosis. From the mid-nineties there occurred a rapprochement between Ito and the political opposition. In 1900 Ito indeed formed his own party, the *Seiyukai*. This consisted of an amalgam of personalities and factions derived from the earlier *Jiyuto*, *Kaishinto*, and a variety of rather ephemeral political groupings which had surfaced in the course of the nineties. The principle of a party forming a government was by no means recognised as yet and indeed was only to occur in 1918. The process, however, was well under way. While Ito may have conceived this transition, it was the professional party politician, neither from Satsuma nor Choshu, nor indeed a samurai, Hara Satoshi (1856–1921), who was the midwife to the birth of governments formed by the party with a majority in the Diet.

After a career in various departments of the bureaucracy, culminating as Japanese minister in Korea, Hara left the civil service in 1897 in order to take up a post as editor of a newspaper, the *Osaka Mainichi Shinbun*. He became involved in politics and joined Ito in the establishment of the Seiyukai. He was given a Cabinet post in Ito's 1900–01 government; in 1906 he ascended to the highly powerful and prestigious job of Home Minister in Saionji's government, a post which he held on a number of occasions. In 1918, as prime minister, he formed the first party government. In 1921 he was assassinated in Tokyo Station, a rather unhealthy spot for politicians in view of a number of other statesmen meeting a violent end there. Hara, therefore, professionalised politics and more than any other individual ushered in what was to become known as 'Taisho democracy': a period when the principle of party government was accepted even if not always respected.

Ito, who was assassinated by a Korean nationalist in Harbin in 1909, had been the first president of the Seiyukai; upon his death the mantle was passed to his protégé Saionji who in turn became the protector of Hara. Katsura, it will be recalled, was the Yamagata-man. While Yamagata was staunchly opposed to political parties, it was nevertheless clear that it was becoming increasingly difficult to oppose the winds of change which were quite clearly blowing in the direction of greater party participation in government. There was also another problem. One of the reasons the *Seiyukai* was able to do so well at the polls was that it had enlisted the financial backing of the Mitsui *zaibatsu*. For both political and financial reasons, therefore, Katsura had to compromise. He founded the *Rikken Doshi-kai* (Association of Friends of the Constitution), and obtained financial backing from Mitsui's main rival, the Mitsubishi *zaibatsu*. Thus a two-party system was coming into formation. After Katsura's death, the opposition to the *Seiyukai* was taken over by Kato Takaaki (1860–1926); in 1923, as a result of a coalition among a number of groups, he assumed the prime ministership and renamed the party the *Kenseikai* (Constitutional Association), which Kato's successor, Hamaguchi Osachi (1870–1931) – also fatally wounded in Tokyo Station – changed to the *Minseito* (Democratic Party) in 1927. In 1940 both the *Seiyukai* and the *Minseito* were dissolved by government order and integrated into the *Taisei Yokusan-kai* (Imperial Rule Assistance Association), supposedly to indicate a united effort, or mass party, to assist in the war effort, but which in fact never amounted to much. After the war the *Minseito* re-emerged as the *Minseito*, while the *Seiyukai* reverted to its old name of *Jiyuto*, the idea of a 'liberal' party being somewhat more in tune with the post-1945 times than an association of political friends. In 1955 the two parties merged, becoming the *Jiyu-minsei-to*, more often referred to as the *Jiminto*. The *Jiminto* (Liberal–Democratic Party) has been in power ever since.

The transition from a bureaucratic government to a coalition bureaucratic-party government, to the recognition of the principle of party government was in the very early stages rather violent, but short-lived. For one thing, the nature of the political parties had notably changed. Radical Rousseauist ideas and other Western-imported ideologies were discarded. The parties were primarily concerned in representing the interests of their pay-masters, namely the landlords and the new urban upper-middle classes. The union of the propertied and managerial classes with the bureaucratic hierarchy, natural in any case, was hastened by the emergence of forces hostile to all of them. By the late nineteenth century labour and tenant unrest was growing, revolutionary political ideas from the West were infiltrating the country. Albeit disparate, these groups and the ideals they espoused were perceived as a serious threat by the whole establishment. In spite of all the measures carefully taken by the oligarchy to ensure strict socio-political control, in education, in law, in military training, they had obviously not been entirely successful. Rebellious tenants, workers, students and, in due course, even rebellious soldiers were threatening the destruction of the Meiji edifice. There was, it must be stressed, no great revolutionary movement in Japan at any time in the pre-war period. But this was precisely something the establishment desired should be prevented at all costs. This was felt even more so after the Russian Bolshevik Revolution.

Thus were the various factions of the establishment welded together. 'Dangerous thoughts' came to include not only attacks on the *kokutai*, but also attacks on the principle of private property. In dealing with the anti-establishment forces, successive governments followed the pattern set in the late seventies/early eighties, namely concessions followed by repression: in 1925 universal male suffrage was granted, in 1926 the Home Ministry created the Bureau of Thought Control. Otherwise, the *Seiyukai* and the *Minseito* (alias *Kenseikai*, etc.) were in real political terms no more than Tweedledum and Tweedledee. The first was backed by the Mitsui *zaibatsu*, the second by Mitsubishi. What this meant was that when there was a *Seiyukai*-dominated Cabinet there was a better chance of major government contracts, for example, going to Mitsui rather than their rivals, while the *Minseito* would see to it that Mitsubishi got preferential treatment. Both parties cultivated their rural constituencies mainly by means of pork-barrel politics. One would be stronger in one area than another. Apart from that there was little to distinguish the two parties. Certainly, they were both equally corrupt. While the parties succeeded in establishing political machines, they failed to develop strong ideological roots. When the wind came, they were quickly swept away. Perhaps their greatest shortcoming was their failure to seek to revise the Constitution. Thus, while universal male suffrage was granted, no attempt was made to ensure the constitutional principle of a popularly elected government. Similarly, while they sought, and indeed briefly succeeded, to loosen the military grip on the reins of government, they never tried to achieve civilian control of the army or navy.

The Meiji architects achieved an impressive programme of modernisation. In that sense the Meiji era must be viewed as highly and successfully progressive. Progressiveness, however, by no means went as far as democratisation. In fact, the policies pursued by the Meiji oligarchy and subsequent successive governments deliberately sought to prevent any such thing from occurring. The major motivation here was a combination of political rationale and economic greed. The efforts necessary to build the *fukoku-kyohei* edifice required strong, central discipline. At the same time society in Japan was far too immature to understand the principles of democracy, let alone exercise political power with a sense of responsibility. That, at least, was the justification. As to the parties, representing the interests of the propertied and managerial classes, political reform would only have made sense had it been accompanied by social and economic reforms. In political terms this would have been quite clearly suicidal. A major landlord was unlikely to back a *Seiyukai* or *Minseito* candidate who favoured land reform. The *zaibatsu* were unlikely to provide funds to a party that advocated a minimum hourly wage or the legal recognition of trade unions. There were a few small parties in the twenties which incorporated in their platforms such reform measures. They did not perform well at the polls: partly because the bureaucracy was right – Japanese society was politically immature – partly because they lacked funds, partly because they lacked experience, and mainly because they were not given a chance to acquire that experience as a result of their being disbanded by the government.

Is it correct to describe the Meiji political system as absolutist? One needs to distinguish here between the exercise of political power and ideology. As far as the former is concerned, by the standards of the time and indeed in comparison with most countries today the exercise of political power by successive governments from 1868 until the late 1930s was a reasonably mild affair.

In spite of the manifold injustices of pre-war Japanese society, in spite of the very uneven distribution of wealth, in spite of the sacrifices imposed on the people, why was the establishment able to get away with what amounted to a comparatively moderate policy of repression? The main answer here is that, especially after the various samurai revolts had been suppressed and the political parties incorporated into the establishment, there was not really all that much internal resistance. This, in turn, can be explained by a number of factors. First, Japan's demographic picture must be borne in mind: the majority of people lived in small isolated rural villages. Secondly, the government was well organised in terms of policing the country; dissidents could be quite quickly weeded out. Thirdly, although the various measures of socio-political control were not foolproof, they were nonetheless reasonably successful. Fourthly, Japan's geographic isolation must figure prominently in terms of explaining this phenomenon. Although some of Japan's rich and the powerful, *zaibatsu* managers or officials of the Foreign Ministry, might hobnob with the rich and the powerful of Western countries at one level, while at another a few radicals might join the international coterie of revolutionaries, the majority of the Japanese people remained remote from the major political movements and ideas occurring in Europe and elsewhere. Fifthly, and perhaps most importantly, we return to the high degree of homogeneity among the Japanese people as outlined in Chapter 1. This sense of '*asabiyya*, of national solidarity, was bound to be especially strong were the tribe to perceive itself threatened, or indeed insulted from the outside. The Western powers in the mid-nineteenth century were responsible for Japan achieving in a very rapid time the unification of the country and the development of nationalism. In the ensuing decades the Western powers, though not necessarily always in concert, were responsible for sustaining this strong sense of national solidarity, and the ideology of nationalism. The constant prevarications over treaty-revision, the Triple Intervention, the discrimination practised against the

Japanese in the west coast of the United States and Canada, the British veto against the incorporation of the Japanese-sponsored racial equality clause in the Covenant of the League of Nations – all these were far more likely to unite than divide the people of Japan.

While for these and other possible reasons, the absolutist character of the political system was qualified to some extent by moderation, in ideological terms the *tenno-sei* was undoubtedly and indeed narrowly absolutist. It was particularistic, obscurantist, irrational, hence by definition in contradiction with the modern mind. It was a doctrinal strait-jacket imposed on the Japanese people. With the militarisation of society and the army, along with the lunatic Genyosha-type fringe, as the self-appointed guardians of the tenno-ist faith, it assumed terrifying intellectual proportions. To what extent the majority of the Japanese people actually believed in the doctrines of the *kokutai* is difficult to determine. That roots of modernisation, even in the ideological and political fields, and in spite of the tenno-sei, had been laid in the course of the period of transformation is manifestly the case in view especially of the enthusiasm with which many Japanese responded to the intellectual liberation offered to them in 1945. Whether a major war, with all the suffering that it entailed, followed by total defeat was really necessary to achieve this liberation is a question impossible to answer.

PART 4

JAPAN AND THE MODERN WORLD

Introduction

The modern world was fashioned by the West. From Buenos Aires to Lagos to Nairobi to Cairo to Delhi to Manila, the Western nations were omnipresent. Not only had the major powers, Britain, France, Germany and the United States, divided the world among themselves, but the old guard, the Netherlands, Spain and Portugal, retained slices of varying sizes, while newcomers, Belgium and Italy, were determined to get their share. The means of control extended from outright colonisation, to spheres of influence, to more informal methods. The causation for this international extension of Western control was to be found in patterns of economic relationships – set in the nineteenth century and a remaining characteristic of the twentieth – whereby the non-industrialised regions of the world provided raw materials, for production, consumption or simply as luxury items, to the industrial nations: nitrate from Chile, rubber from the Congo and Malaya, jute from Bengal, tea from Ceylon, coffee from Brazil, cocoa from Ghana, gold and diamonds from South Africa, fruit from the 'Banana Republics' – and, by the early twentieth century, oil from the Middle East. Japan, as an industrialising nation with few natural resources, was also going to have to secure her own access to sources of vital raw materials.

While varying degrees of political control and economic exploitation were the norm, Western penetration went much deeper than that. Christian missionary proselytism, though enjoying only a limited success in Asia (with the exception of the Philippines and to some extent in Vietnam), attracted converts by the thousands in Africa. Throughout the non-European world social mores and thought patterns were changed, or at the very least challenged. The West, and all the philosophies and values that it stood for, could be admired, could be feared, could be despised, but the West could not be ignored. Even, or perhaps especially, the great non-European nationalist leaders of the early twentieth century were all, to some extent, products of Western culture: Mohandas Gandhi (1869–1948) began his career as an 'English' barrister, Sun Yat-sen (1866–1925) held a degree in Western medicine, while others were products of military academies, Christian schools, and so on.

Along with Western economic, political and military imperialism, there also occurred a significant degree of cultural imperialism. The Western veneer is undoubtedly far more noticeable among the upper classes – the scions of even such traditional indigenous élites as the Saudi royal family attend Western universities; nevertheless, from sports to politics, westernising influences have filtered down to all but the very poorest layers of society in all countries of the world.

Japan, as we have seen, was very much part of this Western cultural orbit. Yet Japan was at the same time the only non-Western nation to have successfully industrialised and to have become a major imperialist power. Among the many differences separating Japan from the other imperial powers, however, is the fact that the Japanese cultural impact on the rest of the world is far less noticeable, even if perhaps not totally absent, than that of the Western countries. Baseball became one of Japan's major national sports, while *sumo* – with the exception of the odd Hawaiian – is not practised in the United States. As Britain, France, Germany and the United States expanded economically, politically and militarily throughout the world, they also exported their languages, their philosophies and politics, their literature, painting and music, their sports, their religions, their dress and social manners, all of which came, to varying degrees, to be integrated or emulated in non-Western societies.

While in more recent years some Japanese products have begun to penetrate other societies, the martial arts perhaps in particular, also various forms of Buddhism, ranging from Zen to the Soka Gakkai, and certain industrial practices, nevertheless, comparatively speaking Japan's cultural influence on the rest of the world has remained minimal. This phenomenon can be partly ascribed to tradition. Japan, as was indicated in Chapter 1, has traditionally been a beneficiary rather than a benefactor of the world's major cultural innovations and intellectual movements. Hideyoshi's Korean campaigns, among other things, resulted in Japan importing artisans and techniques for porcelain manufacture, while the Japanese cultural legacy in Korea was non-existent. Throughout her history Japan has modelled herself on other societies: China and Korea in the past, Britain, France, mainly Germany in the modern age, more recently the United States. The model, as has been insisted all along, has undergone a significant process of indigenisation, but the external model nonetheless existed. Even in the period of *sakoku*, it was Chinese-derived Confucianism which was meant to serve as the basic social ideology, while it was Western science, by way of *Rangaku*, which began paving the way for subsequent modernisation. Secondly, even though individual Western nations were more influential in certain quarters of the globe than others, while there existed differences and, of course, rivalries, there was nevertheless a certain monolithic quality about the West.

The total Western impact on the rest of the world is composed of its constituent parts. In that respect, Japan had no obvious cultural ally; she was then – and now – on her own. Thirdly, Japan's own indigenous stamp on the world was obviously limited by the very nature of her modernising society: she too was a product of Western cultural imperialism.

While Japan's impact on the rest of the world may not be easily discernible in cultural or political terms, it was nonetheless real, indeed dramatic. The modern world may have been fashioned by the West, yet all the major and rapid changes in the international scene which have occurred in the last four decades are unquestionably the products of Japan's modernisation. The Japanese challenge to Western imperialism culminated in the destruction of the Western-imposed world order. It was Japan which was mainly responsible for the extinction of the Western empires firstly in Asia but ultimately in Africa as well. While these momentous events occurred in the early forties, the roots of the Japanese challenge lie deeply in the nineteenth century.

9 The Expansion of Modern Japan

JAPAN AND THE WEST

In the beginning Japan was a kind of semi-Western colony. As noted in Chapter 5, the treaties which Japan was made to sign were based on conditions which were detrimental to Japàn's economic interests and to her sovereignty, with, of course, the converse being that they were favourable to the Western powers. The semi-colonial status was highlighted by the presence of Western troops, namely British and French garrisons in Yokohama, which, in spite of persistent official requests by the government, did not depart until 1875. It has also been noted that the treaty ports in which the Westerners resided became small enclaves or quasi-independent republics. The foreign settlements were administered and policed by the Westerners themselves; the Japanese had no jurisdiction over them. Yokohama, Nagasaki, Kobe and so on became Western colonial territories in all but name. This foreign presence, indeed implantation, was by no means unique to Japan. The same applied, on an even more extensive scale, in China and in most other non-Western countries not in a colonial status – in which case, of course, everything was a great deal simpler.

The exclusively economic disadvantage which Japan suffered as a result of the terms of the relationship, namely the treaty provisions preventing the country from imposing its own tariff levels, did not play a prominent part in arousing Japanese nationalism. The issue of extra-territoriality, on the other hand, rapidly became a popular *cause célèbre*; until the abolition of extra-territoriality in 1894, that single issue, far more than anything else, inflamed the passions and rallied the nation round to the cause of revision.

In view of the overriding importance in modern Japanese history of extra-territoriality, the characteristics of the system and the steps taken towards its eventual repeal deserve attention. By the terms of the clauses of extra-territoriality, no citizen of one of the treaty-powers, no matter under what circumstances, could be tried or punished according to Japanese jurisprudence or by Japanese magistrates. Thus, even a Westerner accused of a criminal offence against a Japanese, including the most heinous crimes such as murder or rape, would be brought before his own consular court rather than have to face Japanese justice. The juries of the consular courts were composed of the interested individual's own compatriots, irrespective of whether he was plaintiff or defendant. It is simply in the nature of things that injustice should have prevailed. The members of the jury, apart from being compatriots, were also likely, given the small number of foreign residents in the treaty ports, to be the individual's friends or associates. In cases involving Japanese there were also other considerations: by granting a decree favouring the Japanese party certain vested interests could be prejudiced, dangerous precedents set, or worst of all, the natives might get ideas above their station – for example, that Japanese and Europeans were equals. Even when in the consular courts justice was seen to be done, it could subsequently be undone. Thus, a certain Englishman by the name of Michael Moss was found guilty by the Yokohama consular court of murdering a Japanese. At the court of appeal, however, at that time in Hong Kong, he was exonerated of all charges. A Frenchman by the name of Brunet had acted as a military adviser to the rebellious army of Enomoto in Hokkaido. When he was caught he was handed over to the French consular authorities, punished (mildly), the sentence was quashed in Saigon. For, to make matters worse and as this case makes clear, the jurisdiction of the consular courts covered not only the treaty ports, but extended to the whole country, even in those areas where, according to the treaties, the foreigners had no right to enter.

It was not only the abuse which caused annoyance, but that the labyrinthine complexities of the extra-territorial system posed serious problems. Each individual consular court applied its own laws. Thus, for example, French Catholic missionaries were caught violating the stipulations of the treaties by entering and proselytising in areas closed to foreigners. Even had the consular court been so inclined, what legal measures could possibly be taken against the missionaries in view of the fact that there is not a single French law which forbids Frenchmen from preaching the gospel in parts of Japan and, therefore, according to the sacrosanct principle of *nullum crimen sine lege*, they could not be tried for any offence. What was equally depressingly baffling for the Japanese was that they had to contend with about twenty or so different legal systems and procedures. The system, it should be noted, also produced headaches for the Westerners themselves: should, for example, a drunken Dutch sailor, working on a British ship, accused of molesting a French girl, be tried before the Dutch, British or French consular court? That sort of problem, needless to say, was the least of the preoccupations for the Japanese. The point to stress here, however, is that the system of extra-territoriality grieved the Japanese not only out of an abstract sense of nationalism, but also out of very concrete causes. They perceived themselves as real or potential victims of injustice by foreigners in their own country.

While Japanese demands for the repeal of the clauses of extra-territoriality became increasingly passionate and vociferous, it should be noted that pressures from the Westerners in the opposite direction were expressed in equally strong terms. As soon as the issue of treaty revision was raised, even as only a remote possibility, the treaty-port newspapers produced leading articles full of righteous indignation and gratuitous advice to the Japanese. In regard to the latter, it is a matter of some irony that Western editors used against the Japanese desire for treaty revision exactly the same arguments as the oligarchy used against the *jiyu-minken-undo* over the issue of wider popular participation in the affairs of state, namely that a greater degree of maturity was necessary before any such step could be seriously contemplated.

The first step towards the revision of the treaties took place on the occasion of the Iwakura mission to the United States and Europe in 1872. This could hardly, however, be described as a well-planned concerted effort. The Japanese were still fairly ignorant of the usages of Western diplomacy. In fact, as a result of a number of diplomatic misadventures in Washington, by the time the mission had reached Europe it was decided that it should concentrate on the study-tour aspect rather than on negotiations. It was also realised that in order to achieve any progress in the revision of the treaties, a significant degree of internal reform would be a necessary prerequisite. Other lessons no doubt were not lost on the members of the mission, notably perhaps that offered by Bismarck (1815–98): on 15 March, 1873, Bismarck held a banquet in honour of the Iwakura mission, in the course of which he invited Iwakura and an interpreter to join him in an antechamber. He warned Iwakura of the predatory instincts of Britain and France and that, while these nations would be full of platitudinous advice on the sovereign rights of nations according to international law, in fact only might could preserve them.

Following the return of the Iwakura mission, though a degree of diplomatic activity on the treaty front continued, including an abortive attempt at concluding a revised commercial convention in 1878, the emphasis was on preparing the Japanese case. As was noted in the previous chapter, the *sine qua non* of treaty revision resided in legal reform. In January 1882 the new Criminal Code had been promulgated and in the same year Inoue convened a multilateral conference in Tokyo with a view to revising the extra-territorial clauses of the treaties. As the rationale for extra-territoriality was the absence of a system of jurisprudence which would guarantee that justice would be done, with the new Criminal Code, so the Japanese argument went, the rationale disappeared and so should extra-territoriality. The conference, however, ended in a deadlock, mainly because of the uncompromising attitude of the British minister, Sir Harry Parkes. Four years later Inoue, with the assistance of one of Japan's most experienced diplomats, Aoki Shuzo (1844–1914), convened another multilateral conference in Tokyo. The Japanese introduced a new element in the negotiations, namely the offer of opening all of Japan to foreign residence and trade in exchange for the abolition of extra-territoriality. The Japanese negotiators were also prepared to compromise on the question of the administration of justice to Westerners in that provisions would be made for mixed courts, namely that the court would be composed of both Japanese and Western judges. The 1886 round, however, also had to be adjourned, partly because of opposition to the concept of mixed courts from other members of the government and from some of their foreign advisers, including Boissonade, but also because an incident had occurred which had enraged Japanese public opinion: a British passenger ship had sunk and while all the Japanese passengers had drowned, all the British crew had been saved.

As the new Meiji era approached its twentieth anniversary, the vexed issue of extra-territoriality seemed nowhere near being solved. While nationalist anti-Western feelings were thereby being not only aroused, but fuelled, the government too was finding itself under constant attack for its failure to safeguard Japan's dignity and sovereignty. In 1888 Kuroda appointed Okuma as foreign minister in his government. Okuma attempted a different strategy from Inoue's: instead of convening a multilateral conference, he would seek to achieve revision by a series of bilateral negotiations. He also hoped that by proceeding in this manner, the negotiations would be less susceptible to public scrutiny. His first step in this direction was to sign a treaty with Mexico which excluded extra-territoriality clauses and which Okuma hoped would serve as the model for the revised treaties. As the negotiations progressed an article appeared in *The Times* in 1889 indicating that revision of the Japanese treaties was approaching a conclusion and that a compromise had been reached in regard to the administration of justice whereby provisions had been inserted for foreign judges to sit in on cases in which their nationals were concerned. The *Times* article was taken up in the Japanese press, a storm of protest blew up, a bomb was thrown in Okuma's coach as a result of which he lost a leg – as far as Japanese popular opinion was concerned, it was too late for compromise, it had to be all or nothing.

By the time the first Diet was elected the humiliating status of extra-territoriality had not been eradicated; Japan was still a second-class nation. The government's failure in this extremely sensitive area no doubt contributed significantly to its very bad showing at the polls in the early elections. Aoki was named foreign minister in both Yamagata's and Matsukata's governments and he concentrated his diplomatic efforts mainly in the direction of London. In May 1891, however, Aoki was forced to resign from the foreign ministry as a result of the attempted assassination of the czarevitch. The post was given in Ito's new government to another highly experienced and skilful diplomat, Mutsu Munemitsu (1844–97), with, however, Aoki as Japan's representative at the Court of St James. The Mutsu–Aoki team continued to press Japan's case in London on the grounds that if Britain conceded, the other nations would follow suit. Finally, on 16 July 1894 a new revised treaty was signed between Britain and Japan which abolished extra-territoriality and in exchange the whole of the country was to be opened to foreign residence and trade. This was not the end of the affair. Under the terms of the most-favoured-nation clause, the new treaty would only become operational once all the other treaty powers concurred in this new arrangement. Negotiations lasted another three years and, though difficulties were encountered, in its essentials it was a mopping-up operation. The Western powers here, true to form, sacrificed certain political advantages in order to gain economically, namely the opportunities offered by increased trade, purchase of real estate, and so on as a result of no longer being circumscribed by the treaty ports. Other economic advantages were safeguarded, namely the clauses relating to tariffs, which remained operative until they too were revised as a result of the efforts of foreign minister Komura Jutaro (1855–1911).

It is often alleged that Japan was able to gain an equal status with the Western powers, at least so far as extra-territoriality is concerned, because of the military prestige she had gained from the Sino-Japanese war. While Japan's victory undoubtedly had an impact on international affairs and in terms of her own international standing, the relevance to treaty revision is not by any means an obvious one and it is not chronologically compatible, at least as far as the United Kingdom is concerned. While the revised treaty between Britain and Japan was signed on 16 July 1894, the war between China and Japan broke out on 25 July. Even though more astute European observers may have predicted that a war was bound to erupt before the actual date, it was widely believed that either China would win or that it would result in a stalemate. Paradoxical as it may seem, throughout the late nineteenth century and first four decades of the twentieth, Japan's military strength tended to be underestimated. Victory in 1895 was ascribed not so much to Japan's strength, as to China's weakness. The same conceptual pattern tended to prevail throughout the ensuing decades until in late 1941 it was revealed to what extent Japan's military strength had indeed been underestimated. It is tempting to draw a parallel here with the situation in the last two decades or so where Japan's economic strength was underestimated until in 1980 the flagrancy of the error was made clear. It is probable that a combination of europocentricism and racial prejudice can be held accountable in both cases.

As far as the treaty revision was concerned, however, if it was not military strength, what was it? The answer to this question rests to some extent on whether or not the revision of the treaties in 1894 should be perceived as a success. From the perspective of Japanese popular opinion in the eighties and early nineties it was not deemed all that successful: it should have occurred much earlier. The government won no praise for its efforts. On the other hand, Japan was the only non-Western country to have been granted the abolition of extra-territoriality in that period. Indeed, one of the arguments levelled against the Japanese demands was that extra-territoriality was operative in many countries, namely China, Siam, the Ottoman Empire and so on. At the same time, however, Japan's internal reforms were impressive. It had to be admitted that, by comparative standards, significant progress towards 'civilisation' had indeed been achieved. China, by contrast, was still in a state of anarchic 'barbarism', as the Boxer uprising was to make only too clear. In purely jurisprudential terms, therefore, the Japanese were able to present a case which none of the other nations under the extra-territorial system could.

In view of the European imposed system of international relations of the time, in view of the prevalence of racial theories and prejudices, and in view, not of Japan's strength, but indeed of her weakness – as the 1895 Triple Intervention amply demonstrated – then the revision of the treaties must be deemed a significant success. And probably the most influential ingredient in this success is to be found in the skill of the Japanese diplomats. These men, particularly in the later stages, were no amateurs, they were professionals who knew their trade extremely well. Both Aoki and Mutsu had extensive experiences in Western countries, both spoke a number of European languages well, both were at ease in European company – in fact Aoki had an upper-class German wife. Thus the creation of a thoroughly professional and impressive diplomatic corps must be counted as one of the more significant of Japan's modernising achievements.

The revision of the treaties, however, did little to placate strong anti-Western feelings among the Japanese. This was not xenophobia in the *joi* sense; it was a form of nationalism which, from the Japanese perspective, arose from perfectly understandable circumstances. Although in the course of the first forty-five years of the twentieth century Japan formed an alliance with a number of Western nations, with the UK from 1902 to 1922 and with Germany and Italy in the so-called Anti-Comintern Pact of 1936, renewed and strengthened in the Tripartite Pact in September 1940, in fact relations with the major Western countries were at best ambiguous, at worst hostile. As was suggested earlier, the racial dimension of social-Darwinism also came to play a role as a constant and forceful leitmotiv in the Japanese perception of international relations. Thus, although there occasionally existed cordial relations between Japan and one or more of the Western nations there was also a constant lingering doubt, an apprehension, in fact mistrust.

In assessing the chronology of relations between Japan and the Western countries, the causes for Japanese animosity become apparent. In so far as the period from 1894 onwards is concerned, two factors must be borne in mind. The first is that Western prevarications, indeed outright opposition, to revising the treaties over such an extended period of time and in spite of the inordinate lengths the Japanese went to in order to meet Western objections, resulted, not surprisingly, in feelings of acute frustration and anger. Secondly, at least so far as the urban sectors were concerned, it would appear that no modern nation's foreign policy was followed by such a degree of popular attention, indeed fanaticism, as was the case in Japan. There is also an important political dimension which needs to be added here. Whereas in the West – admitting significant exceptions – conservative parties pursued forceful foreign policies and favoured expansion, liberal parties were, at least in theory if not necessarily in practice, more moderate. In Japan throughout the Meiji period the situation was the reverse. The *jiyu-minken-undo* was strongly expansionist in temperament; so was the *Jiyuto*. Thus even one of the most radical members of the *jiyu-minken-undo*, Oi Kentaro (1843–1922), who advocated such measures as tenant relief, labour legislation and universal male suffrage, was also a strident exponent of expansionism. Among the popular parties, as indeed was the case with the popular press, there was a constant element of high-pitched jingoism.

It has occasionally been alleged that Japan's expansionism should be seen in terms of a national motivation to emulate the West. While there were different elements involved in the causation of Japanese expansionism, a major motivation was not so much to keep company *with* the West, but to fight *against* the West, in other words to combat discrimination in international affairs and ensure that Japan too would be able to obtain her place in the sun. Japan was small, Japan was comparatively weak, Japan was being discriminated against, thus there developed what one might term a sense of frustrated machismo. Japanese expansionism, therefore, was, among other factors, strongly motivated by a reaction against Western policies and attitudes.

Thus, if the revision of the treaties in 1894 may have appeared as at least a partial victory following a long and arduous campaign, within less than a year it was clear how ethereal a victory it was. The peace treaty concluding hostilities between China and Japan was concluded in Shimonoseki on 17

April 1895. On the 23rd of the same month the Japanese government received a note jointly signed by Russia, Germany and France instructing the Japanese government that one of the provisions of the treaty, the cession to Japan of the Liaotung Peninsula was unacceptable. While the exchange of notes took place, Britain played possum. In this affair in fact only Russia had direct vested interests. Vladivostock is not an ice-free port all the year round while Port Arthur, at the tip of the Liaotung Peninsula, is, hence it was coveted by Russia especially in view of her own easterly expansionism. The whole of Manchuria was also of vital interest to Russia, among other reasons because of the ideal terrain it offered for the extension of the Trans-Siberian railway. Germany, in order to defuse the potential powder keg in the Balkans, encouraged Russian expansion in an easterly direction, hence her support for Russia's position *vis-à-vis* the Liaotung. It was also, it should be noted, in 1895 that the kaiser William II (1859–1941) had commissioned the famous drawing entitled the 'Yellow Peril' which he sent with a dedication to his cousin Nicholas II – Nicholas, who had just recently ascended to the throne, may well have been inclined to agree with the message of the drawing in view of his near-death at the hands of a Japanese only four years earlier.

The cordiality of relations between Russia and Germany was a matter of considerable consternation to France in view of the fact that French foreign policy from the beginning of the Third Republic had consisted of seeking to bring about a strong rapprochement with Russia as a means of curtailing Germany. France could not abide the possibility of Germany and Russia achieving a common eastern policy which excluded France. Hence, France too supported Russia, hence the Triple Intervention. A point to emphasise here is how in the policy making of Paris and Berlin, the least of their worries was Tokyo. The Ito government had no choice but to bow in humiliation before the combined strength of these three major powers. The government, realising the impact that this terrible blow would have on the public, only so recently elated by their magnificent victory, asked that the public announcement of the decision to accept the return of the Liaotung Peninsula to China be made by the Imperial Household in the form of a message from the tenno. Although, by way of compensation, it was agreed that China's war indemnity should be raised by half, from 30 million yen to 45 million, the marginal economic benefit could not erase the deep wound suffered in the national pride – the money was used mainly to increase the country's military potential.

While it is also true that Japan still gained a number of concessions from the war, for example the formal cession to the island of Taiwan and sovereignty over the Pescadores, in the former it was a *de jure* recognition of a *de facto* situation which had been in existence for two decades, and the latter were not

quite the booty which the Liaotung would have represented. It was not a
desire to emulate the West which motivated the Japanese, but already and
once again the bitter feeling that they were being made the victims of a double
standard. Grabbing territory was precisely the name of the game that the
Western powers were gleefully engaged in. The Berlin conference resulting in
the partition of Africa was just a decade old, while in Asia Britain had recently
acquired Upper Burma and France Tonking and Laos. The feeling among the
Japanese that the West had devised two sets of rules, one which applied only to
them the other to the Japanese, persisted throughout the modern period and
was succinctly expressed in the remark made in the thirties by admiral
Yamamoto Isoroku (1884–1943): the Western powers taught us how to play
poker, once they had all the chips they decided to take up contract bridge.

And, in the context of the late nineties, what made the situation all the
worse was that albeit victorious in 1895, very shortly afterwards Japan was to
find herself in an even more precarious position *vis-à-vis* the Western powers
than she had ever been hitherto and, on top of that, being generally excluded
from the scramble that was going on. In a series of moves, the details of which
need not detain us, between 1897 and 1899 the Western powers proceeded to
'slice the Chinese melon' in a patchwork of spheres of influence – including
Russia's seizure of the Liaotung Peninsula and the port of Port Arthur;
although the Japanese managed to obtain the 'non-alienation' of the province
of Fukien, namely that it would not be granted as a sphere of influence to
another power, this was very much small beer in comparison with what the
other powers, especially Russia and Germany, had gained. This was certainly
one instance in which the Japanese had won the war but lost the peace. Also,
while the European powers were copiously helping themselves in China, the
United States annexed Hawaii in 1898 and, following the Spanish-American
war, replaced the Spaniards in the Philippines the following year. These two
moves were of particular significance in view of the important interests which
Japan had in both areas, partly for economic reasons, but mainly as areas for
settlement of Japan's surplus population. Indeed, once the Americans took
over Hawaii and the Philippines they proceeded to enact restrictive tariff and
immigration legislation.

The dawn of the twentieth century was not particularly auspicious for the
Japanese. The treaties had been revised, a significant military victory had
been won, but in geopolitical terms Japan was in a more vulnerable position
than she had been a few years earlier. Japan's expansionist ambitions in both
southerly and northerly directions were being effectively blocked. While
resentments against France and Germany were still harboured and Britain
was viewed with suspicion, nevertheless it appeared clear by the end of the
nineteenth century that the two major antagonists were Russia and the United
States.

Japan concentrated first on Russia for a number of reasons. In the first place, Russia was much nearer, in geographic terms of course, but also as a potential enemy. While the USA had carried out her annexations, thus presenting Japan with a *fait accompli*, and she was also in the process of building up her Pacific fleet, she posed no immediate threat to Japan herself. Similarly, it was important to try to maintain the goodwill of the USA, no matter how serious the provocations, because of the sizeable Japanese colony in the American West Coast and in the new American territory of Hawaii, which together accounted for approximately 75 per cent of Japanese emigrants, while Russia was not perceived as an area for settling surplus Japanese population, hence the chances of Russian reprisals against Japanese nationals were non-existent. The reason why Russia was perceived as an immediate threat, however, was because of the ambitions she was known to harbour in regard to Korea. It was over the 'Korean question' that Japan had fought China. Korea was perceived as the 'dagger pointing at the heart of Japan'. The most vital and urgent issue facing the Japanese government was to prevent, by diplomacy or by war, Russia from gaining even a foothold in Korea. Finally, however, there was another major consideration. At the end of the nineteenth century relations between the United States and Great Britain had witnessed a net improvement. British attitudes to Russia, on the other hand, were of a somewhat different order. Britain was apprehensive of Russian expansionism in the Far East and indeed of possible Russian designs in the north-western regions of the Indian Raj. Russia had to be checked. It was this communality of views in regard to Russia that led Britain and Japan to form their alliance in 1902. The Triple Intervention, whereby Japan had been isolated and overpowered, should not be allowed to be repeated. It is the Anglo-Japanese Alliance which in fact marks the beginning of Japan rolling back the West from Asia, ultimately including Britain also.

JAPANESE IMPERIALISM

'Capitalism has grown into a world system of colonial oppression and of the financial strangulation of the overwhelming majority of the population of the world by a handful of "advanced" countries. And this "booty" is shared between two or three powerful world plunderers armed to the teeth – America, Great Britain, Japan – who are drawing the whole world into *their* war over the division of *their* booty' (Lenin, *Selected Works*, vol. I, pp. 680–1).

Lenin in this passage did not hesitate in placing Japan alongside Great Britain and America as a major capitalist country, indeed an 'advanced' one, armed to the teeth, and engaged in imperialistic rivalry with the other great powers in such a manner which could only culminate in the outbreak of a war which would willy-nilly encompass the rest of the globe. While Lenin died over fifteen years before Japan's ultimate challenge to the Western imperial world order, namely the attack on Pearl Harbor in December 1941, in a sense, therefore, he can be credited with a good deal of foresight. The two questions which arise, however, are (1) whether Japan deserves to be labelled along with the United States and Great Britain as a major advanced capitalistic power, and (2) whether in fact there was an element of inevitability in the global confrontation of the early 1940s, in other words whether the roots of Pearl Harbor are to be found in the period covered in this book.

A brief chronological survey of Japanese expansionism should precede more analytical considerations. In Chapter 2 it was noted how Japan had become a major trading nation in the course of the fifteenth and sixteenth centuries, that economic expansionism also involved piracy and emigration to numerous parts of South-East Asia, that this process culminated in Hideyoshi's abortive attempts to conquer Korea and China, a policy reversed by Ieyasu ultimately leading in 1639 to the adoption of *sakoku*. It was, however, in the Edo era that the initial steps towards the colonisation of Ezo, subsequently renamed Hokkaido, were taken. It is also the case that in spite of *sakoku* throughout the Edo era there were writers who advocated a policy of expansionism for Japan. Yoshida Shoin, among others, visualised the extension of the Japanese empire mainly in a northerly direction. The 1868 restoration was, certainly in rhetoric but also in reality, a national revolution; from there a policy of nationalism was espoused not only by the government, but equally by practically all articulate sectors of Japanese society. Only a few years after the new regime's birth, in fact practically from its inception, a heated argument, the *seikan-ron*, took place over the question of conquering Korea. The Iwakura-dominated government resolutely refused to embark on such a course and, in spite of offering the less dangerous course of invading Taiwan instead as a palliative to fiery samurai sentiments, the decision not to proceed with war against Korea ultimately resulted in a number of uprisings and indeed a brief civil war.

With the exception of the expedition to Taiwan (1874), the annexation of the Ryukyu islands and the colonisation of Hokkaido, and the pressure on Korea resulting in the occasional skirmish and certainly a good deal of Japanese intrigue in Seoul and the stationing of Japanese troops in that country after 1885, it was not until 1894 that Japan actually went to war. From 1894 a course of imperialism was embarked upon – 1894–5: war with China; 1900–1; suppression, along with the major Western powers, of the Boxer uprising; 1904–5: war with Russia; 1910: annexation of Korea; 1915: declaration of war on Germany and presentation of the Twenty-One demands on the government of Yuan Shih-kai (1859–1916) which, if accepted, virtually transformed China into a Japanese colony; 1919: as a result of the Paris Peace conference transference of Germany's spheres of influence in China to Japan; 1922: the Siberian expedition against Russia's new Soviet regime; 1931: annexation of Manchuria and creation of the puppet state of Manchukuo; 1937: war against China; 1941: attack on Pearl Harbor and, under the title of the Greater East Asia Co-Prosperity Sphere, colonisation of the Philippines, Indonesia, Malaysia, Burma; 1945: Japan accepts 'total surrender'.

There is, therefore, even in regard to the extended *sakoku* era, a certain continuity in Japanese expansionism. In this context there are certain purely geographical considerations which need to be brought into perspective. Japan is poor in natural resources and, in view of the mountainous and volcanic nature of her terrain, exiguous in terms of accommodating her population. Demographic pressures emerge as a constant leitmotiv. The stagnating population of the second half of the Edo era was an inevitable result of the confines imposed on the Japanese people. The fact that an estimated doubling of the population could take place in the first half of the Edo era is simply an indication of the significant advances which, in comparison with earlier times, were achieved in increasing productivity and land reclamation. Once these innovations had been pushed to their limits, however, a population ceiling was imposed and hence the various Malthusian checks indicated in an earlier chapter were resorted to. *Sakoku*, notwithstanding the fact that it lasted 215 years, from 1639 to 1854, was an aberration which in fact the Japanese could ill afford; the cost of this policy had to be the practice of infanticide, abortions, famines, and so on. For Japan to develop and prosper she *must* expand, though this expansion can take a variety of different forms, from peaceful migration, to trade, to the acquisition of colonies, to exporting, as is the case today, on a sufficient scale to ensure the import of necessary raw materials, including of course energy. While the equation between development, prosperity and expansion may apply to other countries, in no case is it as vital a link as in modern Japan; it is also for that reason that throughout modern history, none of the major powers has been as vulnerable as Japan.

The imperative of expansionism, however, and the development of imperialism are not two inextricably tied phenomena. This, as suggested above, can be indicated by the fact that Japan today is an expanding nation, though not an imperialistic one. The use of these terms obviously raises certain semantic questions. In the Japanese context of the period covered in this book, the term 'expansion' is meant to indicate the peaceful pursuit of a policy which involved the emigration of surplus population, the development of trade and such ancillary activities as the construction and expansion of a merchant navy, the acquisition of raw materials from external sources and the penetration of foreign markets. Imperialism arose when these policies were pursued no longer in simply a peaceful manner but when the use of force or the threat of the use of force were resorted to. Imperialism includes colonisation, but does not exclude other more indirect means of achieving national ends through policies of intimidation.

Following Perry's overtures and especially after the political revolution of 1868 was resolved, Japan became absorbed in the world economy. For roughly the first quarter of a century of this new phase in her historical development Japan responded by expansion. From 1894, however, Japan's response was unequivocally that of imperialism, a policy which was pursued and maintained for the next half-century. Why?

From the moment that Japan was 'opened' and especially once the exclusivist, xenophobic policy of *joi* was abandoned in favour of a concerted programme of modernisation, as encapsulated in the slogan *fukoku-kyohei*, new urgent needs arose. The most pressing of these needs was undoubtedly foreign exchange. As indicated in Chapters 6 and 7, the import of Western technology, Western expertise and Western machinery, along with the ambitious programmes in the development of a modern army and navy, the laying of the infrastructure for economic growth and a variety of other aims sought by the new leadership, were all very expensive propositions. In order to pay for all this there were certain internal resources which could be tapped: taxation of the land on the one hand and the export of silk and tea on the other provided the government with some revenue. The potential in regard to both, however, was limited. In any case, as has been seen, the excessive taxation of the peasantry was having dangerous political destabilising consequences. At the same time Japan was experiencing a population explosion. The areas designated for migration ranged from the Philippines, to Indonesia, to Hawaii, to the West Coast of the United States, Mexico, South America and Australia. This combination of new economic needs and a surplus population, it was argued, could be turned to Japan's advantage. The policy envisaged was that by encouraging the migration of Japanese to what would have amounted to colonies or enclaves of settlement they would secure for the home-land both access to sources of raw materials and markets for Japanese manufactured goods. In this sense, therefore, migration was presented as a patriotic means of helping Japan develop and prosper.

A number of journalists and polemicists eagerly embraced this policy of overseas expansion by migration. Societies were established with a view to encouraging migration, notably the *Tokyo Chigaku Kyokai* (Tokyo Geographical Society) in 1879 and especially the *Shokumin Kyokai* (Colonisation Society) founded in 1893 under the direction of Enomoto Takeaki. The arguments put forward involved not simply Japan's current demographic needs, but also visions of a future order. The protagonists of migration and colonisation insisted that were the Japanese not to take this course of action, as in ensuing decades the population would grow and the needs for external expansion would become obviously even greater, Japan would find that in fact all possible areas of resettlement had already been appropriated by one or other of the Western powers. In fact, however, these policies of peaceful expansion were not proving successful. On the one hand and in spite of the demographic pressures there were great difficulties in recruiting migrants. On the other hand there was a considerable amount of resistance to Japanese immigration. In the Philippines, for example, a prime target for Japanese colonies of settlement, the Spanish Catholic Church objected on the grounds that, first there was no evidence, in view of the meagre results of Christian proselytism in Japan, that the settlers would embrace Catholicism, and secondly that the Japanese might incite the natives to revolt against the established colonial orders. Once the United States annexed the Philippines, dreams of Japanese colonisation had to be abandoned, at least temporarily. With the annexations of Hawaii and the Philippines, the hostile attitudes of the Americans towards Japanese migration to their West Coast and even to Mexico – when in the early twentieth century the popular Californian imagination conjured up phantasmagoric images of armed uprisings consisting of an alliance between Japanese, Negroes and Mexicans – the hostile attitudes of the Dutch regime in Indonesia, and even stronger sentiments on the part of the Australians and the Canadians, the avenues for Japanese expansion by migration were effectively blocked.

The sense of national vulnerability, suggested earlier, and perceptions of the encirclement of Japan by antagonistic forces remained two overriding concerns in the formulation of Japanese foreign expansionist policy. It is also in this context that the first of the two questions arising from Lenin's quotation can be answered: whether Japan should be compared with the United States, Great Britain, and possibly other Western imperialist nations. In fact, it is not so much the similarities as the contrasts which are striking. First, one may approach the problem from a purely economic perspective. Even by the time of the 1914–18 war, in other words two decades after Japan had begun forcefully embarking on an offensive imperialistic policy, as opposed to a peaceful expansionism, Japan was not an advanced capitalist power comparable to the United States or Great Britain, nor indeed to France or Germany. While numerous indices could be used to indicate that fact, suffice it to point out that Japan, unlike the four countries mentioned above, was not so much exporting capital but rather, as indicated in Chapter 6, very much involved in the capital-importing business. In the perspective of the international economy, it is not Japan's strength which needs to be stressed as her weakness. Having said that, it is also true that by the late nineteenth century Japan was already engaged in investments on the Asian mainland, namely in Korea and Manchuria. Indeed the construction of Japanese railways in these areas proceeded at an accelerating pace and, especially in North China, led to confrontation with the United States.

While the simultaneous import and export of capital is by no means a feature unique to the Japanese economy and indeed applied to the advanced capitalist nations as well, three points should be made. First, Japan was far more dependent on the import of capital, in that especially in the period 1895 to 1914 had there not been the necessary inflow of foreign capital the Japanese economy would quite simply have collapsed. Secondly, the economic motivation for the penetration of North China was primarily of a prophylactic nature. In other words, the same argument applied here as the one raised in regard to migration: were Japan not to seek penetration into these areas, the Western powers would acquire all the territories for potential future Japanese economic development. Thirdly, the development of railways in Korea initially, and subsequently in Manchuria, was determined by considerations comparable to the earlier development of Japan's own national railway network, namely a perceived strategic imperative.

It has already been pointed out that Japan's expansionist policies were strongly determined by economic factors. In regard to her actual imperialist thrust economic forces were also at play, but in a manner which should be distinguished from that of the major Western imperialist powers. The 'new imperialism' of Great Britain, the United States, France and Germany occurred primarily as a consequence of their respective periods of industrialisation. In the case of Japan, imperialism was not so much a consequence as a cause. The huge indemnity obtained from China in 1895 provided the capital necessary for a very significant increase in Japanese industrial output in iron and steel production, in the construction of steamships and, of course, in the rapid increase in armaments and overall development of the army and navy. The Russo-Japanese war, in spite of Japan's victory, provided no indemnity, as a result of which Japan had to go heavily into debt. In this sense, therefore, Japan's imperialism was perhaps not so much capitalist as mercantilist.

There is another major distinction which must be drawn when comparing the imperialistic policies of the major Western powers and Japan. In the European annexations in Africa or in South-east Asia, the metropolitan powers were engaged in conflicts with primitive societies all of which were at a great distance from the homeland. For Britain to have lost the Boer War, for example, would have obviously entailed a number of adverse consequences, but the sovereignty of the British nation as such would not have been placed in jeopardy. Japan's imperialistic offensive involved far higher stakes than was the case among the Western powers. China in 1894 and Russia in 1904 were both on paper superior in terms of military might to Japan. Not only were the risks of defeat considerable, the consequences, especially in regard to the Russians, could have been nothing short of disastrous. Why were the Japanese prepared to take such risks?

The answer to this question should, in turn, enable one to consider the second question raised by Lenin's quotation: whether the road to Pearl Harbor can be said to begin quite perceptibly in this early phase of Japan's transformation to modernity. The answer needs to be studied from two angles: external pressures and internal forces.

The aspirations of a peaceful expansionist policy through migration, shipping and trade were effectively stifled. The issue of migration indeed remained throughout the late nineteenth century and until the outbreak of the Second World War a source of antagonism between Japan and the United States. In so far as the external pressures were concerned, however, it was only at the very end of the nineteenth century that these could be perceived in such a manner as to act as a decisive factor in the development of Japan's policy and direction of imperialism. The themes of vulnerability and encirclement appear in a particularly strong light in the events which began with the Triple Intervention of 1895, rapidly followed by the partition of China into exclusive spheres of influence and by the United States' annexation of the Philippines and Hawaii. With Russia in Manchuria, Germany in the northern province of Shantung, Britain controlling central and south-eastern China, France in southern China and Indo-China, the United States in the Philippines, not only did Taiwan and such outposts as the Pescadores appear insignificant, but there was really no more room for manoeuvre. In less than five years, Japan was effectively encircled and more vulnerable than she had ever been.

Korea, the Hermit Kingdom, had been the target of atavistic Japanese imperialism in the early 1870s. Between the *seikan-ron* forcefully espoused by Saigo and others and the actual annexation of Korea in 1910 there is, certainly, a thread, but this thread is primarily ideological in nature and not necessarily to be found in the development of government policy. In other words, there were individuals and various organisations, including Itagaki's Jiyuto and the nativist societies like Genyosha, which systematically and incessantly advocated a policy of Japanese imperialism on the continent of Asia, but the degree of success which they enjoyed can be gauged from the fact that for over two decades the government did not take any decisive action. Korean politics, however, throughout this period were highly unstable, indeed explosive. Without denying the existence of internal forces propelling the Japanese towards an imperialistic advance in Korea, there was nevertheless a justified anxiety on the part of the Japanese decision-makers that Korea's instability and China's apparent inability or unwillingness to exercise effective control on her tributary state did constitute a grave risk to Japanese sovereignty.

Japan's economic interests in Korea at this stage were limited. This was still the period when perceptions of economic expansionism were mainly being directed in a southerly direction. Interest in Korea, as indicated above, was partly ideological, more importantly strategic, in other words the vital element here was the relationship between Korea and Japan's security; the decision to go to war with China in 1894 arose primarily from strategic considerations. Sino-Japanese rivalry had been in existence in Korea for two decades and this rivalry was reflected in the internal political divisions of that country. In terms of the immediate causes of the war, however, this should be seen primarily as a straightforward Sino-Japanese affair, not necessarily as the beginning of a systematic policy of imperialism. Japan's victory caused more serious problems than had been solved. The events including and following the Triple Intervention changed everything; what, from the Japanese perspective, made things worse was that with the Chinese removed from the Korean scene, it now appeared that the Russians were casting covetous eyes in that direction. Russia's interest and intrigues in Korea were occurring at the same time that Japanese expansionism to the south was blocked. While securing the Anglo-Japanese alliance in 1902 was one step in the direction of seeking to lessen Japan's vulnerability, the provisions of the alliance did not guarantee British military support in the case of a conflict between Russia and Japan over Korea. The Korean question became a far more burning issue after the Sino-Japanese war than it had been before. The Japanese had, as in all comparable situations, two options: diplomatic negotiations or armed confrontation. The government opted for the former. Essentially what the Japanese were prepared to offer the Russians was a reciprocal recognition of the two countries' vital territorial interests: Russia could hold on to Manchuria if Japan could be guaranteed exclusivity in Korea. What was labelled the *Man-Kan kokan* (Manchuria in exchange for Korea) proposals were rebuffed by Russia. Why did Japan then opt to go to war with Russia? The answer can be stated quite simply: because she had to. Especially in view of all the events which had taken place with such dazzling speed following 1895, Japan's vital strategic and economic interests, indeed her very national autonomy, were too seriously jeopardised. With Russia in Korea the encirclement would be complete and Japan would be a prisoner unable to do anything but await the day of execution. The external pressures, therefore, were those of imperialistic rivalries between the major powers, but rivalries which were being exercised in close proximity to Japan.

While Russia was defeated in 1905 and following the termination of the

1914–18 war Germany was expelled from East Asia, from the Japanese perspective the encirclement did not cease. The major rival in the interwar period was the United States, the same country which had blocked Japan's southerly expansion. One must, nevertheless, reject the view that the confrontation which culminated in the Pacific war was inevitable. In the course of the first four decades of the twentieth century numerous opportunities were afforded for compromise. The outcome could conceivably have been different; from the Triple Intervention to Pearl Harbor the road was by no means straight, nor was it predetermined. Among the various signposts which indicated not a continuity in direction, but indeed a significant shift, one would have to include, for example, the Great Depression. Yet, at the end of the day, when the background to the holocaust of the Pacific War needs to be assessed, when one seeks to establish the point of departure, even accepting that a number of bifurcations were indeed available, the year 1895 stands out as marking the first major landmark. In Chapter 7 it was suggested that Japan's industrial revolution should be perceived in terms of internal responses to external stimuli. The course of Japan's imperialistic policies can be perceived in similar terms. That, however, is only part of the story. While it is the case that Japanese imperialism was fuelled by a series of Western provocations, there is another element to the equation: the internal forces propelling Japan to adopting policies of ruthless exploitation in regard to her neighbours.

Japanese expansionism by the late nineteenth century was translated into imperialism. Japan's interests beyond her borders were pursued by military means. These interests were motivated by both economic and strategic factors. The road to the south having been blocked, Japanese attention focused first on Korea; with Russia's defeat, the vital area for Japanese expansion for both strategic and economic reasons – finance, trade and sources of raw materials – was Manchuria. Japanese imperialism was further motivated, as we have seen, by perceptions of vulnerability and encirclement by hostile forces. There was, however, also a strong ideological commitment to imperialism.

Throughout the quarter of a century when official Japanese policy advocated expansion but stopped short of imperialism there were strident voices calling for a far more forceful manifestation of 'Japan's destiny'. These voices came from both the so-called liberal quarters, namely the *jiyu-minken-undo*, and from the nativist movements. From the perspective of the *jiyu-minken-undo* the vocation of the new westernised Japan was to bring enlightenment and civilisation to the country's neighbours and erstwhile cultural fellows; in the words of Fukuzawa, just as Japan had 'shed Asia' (*Datsu-A*) so should she proceed to help China and Korea to divest themselves of their old habit in order to re-emerge in modern, enlightened Western garb. The ideological commitment from these quarters was highly idealistic. It was also, in that sense, positive. It was not, at this stage, by any means directed against the West. In fact, at the time of serious political turmoil in Seoul in the mid-eighties, Itagaki called on the French head of legation in Tokyo in order to suggest that France and Japan might consider collaborating in the pacification and colonisation of Korea. One finds here also an element of continuity. Liberal imperialists throughout modern Japanese history have generally preferred a policy of collaboration with the major Western powers in the peaceful exploitation of China rather than confrontation; this was, for example, the cornerstone of the policy advocated in the 1920s by the Foreign Minister Shidehara Kijuro (1872–1951).

The ideology of the nativists was, needless to say, rather different. The Genyosha had already begun penetrating China as early as 1882. It and other nativist societies carried out policies of intrigue and intimidation as a means of promoting Japanese imperialism both at home and on the continent. They developed an extensive intelligence network and indeed a high degree of collaboration with a variety of Asian revolutionary or nationalist leaders. They also enjoyed support, protection and funds from the army and even from the *zaibatsu*. The ideology they espoused consisted of a blend of intensive nativist romanticism and a form of Pan-Asianism. Thus, from their perspective Japan's mission was to carry out the strengthening of the Japanese/East Asian spirit. It is here that the concept of Asia for the Asians had its roots; though here, as in the Greater East Asia Co-Prosperity Sphere of the late thirties/early forties, it was Asia for the Asians under the tutelage of Japan.

The year 1895 was a turning point in many respects. To start with, one should stress that Japan's war effort against China in 1894 obtained nationwide popular support. The nativists were in exultant mood, as after all this is what they had been working for all along, while the 'liberal' idealists perceived Japan's mission as coming to fruition at last. The idealism of the 'liberals' notwithstanding, jingoism was in the air. Cartoons in such popular newspapers as the *Maru Maru Chinbun* portrayed tall, muscular Japanese soldiers grabbing two handfuls of Chinese by their pigtails and twirling them about prior to launching into another stratosphere. The anti-Chinese racism displayed in these illustrations was no different from similar illustrations to be found in the 'yellow press' in California or Australia, including the stereotypes of pigtails, slant eyes, filth, opium dens, and so on. The point here, however, is that for whatever reason all sectors of Japanese society enthusiastically, indeed fanatically, supported the war against China.

In terms of the ideology of imperialism 1895 is a watershed in two respects.

The idealists believed that Japan had an altruistic mission to accomplish and that this was qualitatively not in the same category as the predatory imperialism of the Western powers. In other words, the enlightenment was taken seriously. This idea of Japan being on the one hand westernised, but on the other different, had been nourished in some of the literature of the early Meiji period. For example, in one of the most popular novels, Shiba Shiro's *Kajin no kigu* ('Strange Encounters with Beautiful Women') the Japanese hero encounters two beautiful women, while gazing on the Liberty Bell in Philadelphia and cogitating upon its implications; one of the women is the daughter of an Irish patriot fighting against English oppression while the other is the daughter of a Spanish liberal fighting against dictatorship. During a dinner in a restaurant it is revealed that the head-waiter is a Chinese revolutionary fighting against the Manchu dynasty. The point, indeed culmination, of this story, once the woes of the world have been scrutinised and deplored is that Japan will right the wrongs; Japan is new, Japan is young, Japan is brave, Japan is benevolent. Hence the shock to the idealists when at the Treaty of Shimonoseki it was discovered that Japan in fact intended doing all those terrible things associated with predatory Western imperialism – grabbing territory and demanding onerous reparations. In that sense 1895 marks the end of any credible ideology of altruistic westernisation. Disillusioned by the materialism of Japanese imperialism, a number of intellectuals turned instead to theories of socialism.

The shock of Shimonoseki, in any case felt only by a handful of idealistic intellectuals, was nothing in comparison with the reverberations of the Triple Intervention. The main ideological current of imperialism from 1895 until 1945 will therefore be reflected far more in the nativist/pan-Asiatic version. The idea of Japan acting as an agent of westernisation in association with the West was abandoned; such a vision, for example, never figured in the rhetoric of imperialism even during the twenty years of the Anglo-Japanese alliance. Japan became projected as the leader of Asia, as the one East Asian nation worthy of the mantle of Eastern civilisation, the mission of which consisted of re-invigorating the Asian world through a return of the traditional spirit and the expulsion of the Western imperial powers. Thus, as opposed to the *Datsu-A* (shedding Asia) formulation of Fukuzawa, which in any case he himself came to abandon, one finds associations such as the *Toa Dobunkai* (East Asian Common Culture Association), founded in 1898 by the highly respected figure of Konoe Atsumaro (1863–1904), father of the pre-Second World War prime minister Konoe Fuminaro; the *Toa Dobunkai* and comparable organisations fulfilled two complementary roles: one was to gather intelligence on the activities of various political groups in East Asia, the other was to carry out propaganda in regard to Japan's imperial mission. The *Toa Dobunkai* benefited from secret subsidies provided by the Foreign Ministry. Thus were the ideological foundations for Japan's modern imperialism laid.

The causation of Japanese aggressive imperialism must also be seen in its domestic context. In 1901 Kotoku Shusui published *Nijusseiki no kaibutsu teikokushugi* ('Imperialism, the Monster of the Twentieth Century'). This work appeared the same year as Hobson's *Imperialism* and fifteen years prior to Lenin's *Imperialism: the Highest Stage of Capitalism*. One of Kotoku's economic arguments against imperialism finds echoes, albeit in different forms, in both Hobson's and Lenin's treatises, namely that imperialism diverts capital to unproductive ends. This is particularly the case for a comparatively poor country like Japan where there was a great need for capital to be invested in both industrial and social development. Hobson's reflections were motivated primarily by what he perceived as the wasteful Boer War, Lenin was writing as the 1914–18 war was raging, Kotoku's study was the product of his views on the Sino-Japanese War. Kotoku himself had figured among those idealistic intellectuals mentioned above: he had initially supported the war effort against China in the belief that Japan was accomplishing a mission of civilisation, as a result of which, however, he was bitterly disillusioned by the terms of the Shimonoseki treaty.

Imperialism, Kotoku stated, not only diverted capital from domestic need to unproductive activities, but it also diverted the attention of the people away from the imperatives of social reform to the hollow glories of foreign ventures. Imperialism in this sense could be perceived in terms of a conspiracy theory elaborated by the ruling classes as a palliative for the economic burdens and social deprivations which the masses were being forced to endure. Militarism and imperialism, Kotoku contended, were not compatible with civilisation; militaristic war did not ennoble a nation, it diminished it to the level of barbarism.

The major outlines of Kotoku's diagnosis appear applicable to the internal forces of Japanese imperialism. Of course, many of the points he raised would have universal application, some of which are elaborated in the works of authors such as Schumpeter and Manoni in respect to Western imperialism. While there are undoubtedly certain parallels between Japan and the major Western powers in respect to both the causes and motives of imperialism, one must once again rather underline the differences. For one thing, as stressed earlier, Japan was not an advanced capitalist nation in the sense of the United States or Great Britain. By comparison the standard in Japan in many respects was much lower, certainly in terms of *per capita* income and in the distribution of the workforce between the various sectors. Japan, in this period and indeed until the last three decades or so, was in economic and social terms far more of an 'underdeveloped' country. In political terms Japan differed also in three major respects. First, Japan was a far more authoritarian society, even when compared to Wilhelminian Germany. Secondly, in spite of this authoritarianism, in fact the Japanese political scene was highly unstable: the parliamentary experiment was not working well and terrorist acts continued to plague the nation and its leaders. Thirdly, Japanese politics were based on an exclusive, dogmatic, *étatiste* ideology.

There is another very important point. In assessing the various component parts of the ruling classes attention was drawn to the role of the military and the degree of militarisation of Japanese society. The ideological tenets of the *kokutai* were essentially composed of a combination of tenno-ism and nationalism. The military sought to project the army as the custodians of the national ideology and martial values as the embodiment of the spirit of the Japanese people. An army which sits around doing nothing is hardly likely to inflame the popular imagination. An army returning from the field of battle covered in glory, on the other hand, is a different matter. If Japanese society were to undergo a process of samurai-isation, then for the warrior spirit to be kindled the occasional war would not be out of place. The fighting spirit, the sentiments of blind and absolute loyalty, courage in the face of death, were prominent and highly prized. The economically oppressed, socially deprived, ideologically indoctrinated Japanese people could gain vicarious pleasure, honour, and a sense of national dignity from the country's exploits on the battlefield. One returns here, therefore, to Renan's definition of a nation as set out in Chapter 1: victorious battles provided a sense of common glory in the past and a determination to achieve more glories in the future. The Japanese nation, as described in Chapters 6, 7 and 8, was in fact deeply divisive in political, economic and social terms. Imperialism was perceived as that element of national cohesion which would divert attention from internal divisions to a concentration on the need for solidarity. Imperialism, in other words, was the aggressive expression of Japan's contradictions.

These contradictions can also be situated in socio-psychological terms. The spirit of Saigo was not dead; it burned in the breast of ardent Japanese nationalists; it was cherished by officers and men alike fighting the wars for the salvation and greater glory of the Japanese nation. The psychological dislocations caused by the excessive speed of modernisation were traumatic. The major motivating force for Japanese imperialism was, in the Schumpeterian sense, to be found in an atavistic feudal ideology and supported by the residual social classes of the pre-modern era, namely those samurai (whether real or ersatz) who constituted the bulk of the Japanese imperial army and navy officer corps. In that sense, therefore, modern Japanese imperialism was a product of modernity – for, without the development of a modern industry to support the country's military offensives there could have been no successfully sustained policy of imperialism – but it must also be seen as a reflection of the failure and crisis of modernity.

It was suggested earlier that Japanese imperialism should be seen in terms of internal responses to external stimuli. Had the treaties been revised more rapidly and amicably, had the Triple Intervention not occurred, had the United States proved less insulting over the immigration issue, had the policy of peaceful expansion been allowed to develop . . . conceivably, of course, things could have turned out very differently. On the other hand, however, for Japan to have developed in a peaceful manner domestic conditions would have had to differ significantly, or certainly improved. Given the divisiveness of pre-war Japanese society there is no doubt that imperialism did serve as a catalytic agent. Albeit supported by an ideology and a society derived from the past, imperialism nonetheless projected Japan as a major power in the contemporary and future age.

The Japanese nation of the late Meiji period should not be perceived as populated exclusively by atavistic, chauvinistic, racist warmongers. There were many facets to Japanese society. In fact the nativist/romantics, the assertive and oppressive military officers were in a minority. The fact remains, however, that they could legitimately claim to be more in tune with the officially espoused ideology than any other sector of society, in fact they were the apostles and the evangelists of the *kokutai*. The fact that they enjoyed ideological legitimacy and power made them an indomitable force in Japanese society. Thus, while the roots of Pearl Harbor are to be found in the late nineteenth century, so are the roots of the rape of Nanking also discernible at this stage.

CONCLUSION

When Menelek II (1844–1913), Emperor of Ethiopia, heard of Japan's victory over Russia he expressed great satisfaction and stated that Ethiopia, in her own way, was trying to emulate Japan's example. Menelek had, of course, presided over the first major defeat of a European army by non-European forces in the modern era, namely the rout of the Italians at Adowa in 1896: although this was a cause of considerable humiliation for the Italians, its impact on the rest of the world was not of great significance. Japan's defeat of Russia, however, was an event of momentous proportions and consequences, as indeed was recognised at the time. One of the longest and most detailed studies of the Russo-Japanese war was compiled by two young Turkish officers, while the Egyptian nationalist intellectual, Mustafa Kamil Pasha, was moved to write a eulogistic study of modern Japan, entitled *al-Shams al-Mushriqa* ('The Rising Sun').

So far as Europe was concerned Japan's victory precipitated the outbreak of the 1914–18 war and the Russian revolution; Russia's military defeat appeared to illustrate vividly the czarist regime's incompetence and bankruptcy. Equally significant, this single event set the bell tolling for European dominance over Asia and ultimately Africa: the seed of decolonisation was firmly planted in 1905. If Europe witnessed the scene with apprehension, for Asians as well it was clear that a new dawn had risen. There was, throughout that continent, a mood of exultation. Chinese students, already increasingly turning towards Japan after their country's defeat a decade earlier, flocked in much greater numbers after 1905. The nationalist movement of Sun Yat-sen (1866–1925) the Tongmenghui, was founded in Tokyo the same year. In India the National Congress adopted a more radical programme. Tokyo became a veritable mecca for nationalist leaders from China, Vietnam, the Philippines, India, Burma.

The Japanese government, it should be noted, was never totally pleased about this overt association between Asian nationalist figures and Japan; for example, in 1910 at the behest of the French Government a Tokyo-based Vietnamese nationalist movement was dismantled. At least until the thirties there was always a degree of ambivalence in government circles over this question of Asianism. The Foreign Ministry in particular was generally concerned that Western feathers should not be ruffled. Nevertheless, especially after her stunning victory of 1905, Japan was projected as a model. In the sense of having both weakened Europe – and thereby having destroyed the myth of Western power as an impregnable fortress – and in strengthening the resolve of nationalist leaders, Japan's contribution to world history in the modern era is immeasurable.

While Chinese anti-Manchu nationalist leaders may have perceived Japan as a model in the course of the events leading up to and immediately following the 1911 Revolution, by 1915, as a result of the Twenty-One Demands the Tokyo government sought to impose on Peking, it was now clear that she should rather be seen as a menace. Japan's role in galvanizing the Chinese nation into a sense of unity, albeit unintentional, must also stand out as a major force in modern history. When students at the newly created Peita (Peking University) learned that the Paris Peace Conference had resulted in Japan being granted Germany's former spheres of influence in China, they took to the streets; the date was 4 May 1919, one which historians of China generally concur marks the birthdate of modern Chinese nationalism.

Ultimately, therefore, Japan was responsible for the liberation of millions of people from the yoke of Western imperialism – even if, in the process, a number were subjected to the more oppressive yoke of Japanese imperialism. Within Japan herself the transformation which allowed her to assume the role of a world power had been exceedingly brutal; poor peasants, young female factory operatives, political dissidents, and many others were ruthlessly exploited, while even those who escaped physical abuse were nonetheless subjected to spiritual enslavement in the shape of the tenno-ist ideology. Undoubtedly Japan's defeat in 1945 can be also said to have achieved the liberation of the Japanese people.

   Both in 1854 and 1945 the United States precipitated the transformations which ensued. Both in the period of transformation to modernity and in the contemporary age, the societies which emerged reflected a combination of indigenously developed values and institutions along with the selective application of certain Western models. Both in the Meiji era and in the contemporary age these combinations have proved a source of strength. Although the Meiji period displayed a certain eclecticism, at least in the early stages, by the end of the nineteenth century the major model was quite clearly Wilhelminian Germany. The post-Second World War model was obviously the United States. These foreign inputs have undoubtedly contributed to the dynamic qualities of Japanese society. At the same time, however, the output invariably contains a high degree of originality.

   Japanese society in the contemporary age differs markedly from what it was even only three or four decades ago. Thus, it was stressed how Japan in the transformation to modernity was a basically peasant society, that economic activity occurred principally in the primary sector, that freedoms and rights were narrowly circumscribed, that insularity remained the fate of the vast majority of the population, that workers, with the exception of the most advanced sectors, were underpaid, overworked, generally exploited, partly as a result of which Japan enjoyed no domestic consumption market. Today the opposite of all these attributes would apply. In a very fundamental sense Japan has undergone a major transformation. The militarisation of Japanese society and the imposition of the tenno-ist ideology were possible in the Meiji era precisely because the bulk of the population was poor, rural, more indoctrinated than educated, insular, and so on. Objective conditions have changed to such an extent that neither militarism nor tenno-ism could conceivably resurface.

   Among the various qualities of contemporary society which account for Japan's success in both economic and social terms one would include the following: a sense of national solidarity; a high degree of coordination between business and bureaucracy for the achievement of national economic ends; the strength of social cohesion within the individual enterprise or organisation, namely the *ie*; the role of education and the emphasis placed on academic achievement rather than social background – the meritocratic nature of society; the international vision and intellectual curiosity about the West, the original flame of which was lit with *nanban-gaku*; the empirical spirit of scientific enquiry, dating at least from the publication of *Zoshi* ('Reflections on Entrails') in the eighteenth century; the readiness for the absorption and diffusion of technology. All of these have their roots in the Edo and early Meiji periods. While democracy is obviously of foreign origin, the Meiji period found vigorous adherents and exponents of its principles in men such as Nakae Chomin, Ueki Emori, Yoshino Sakuzo, and others; in that sense democracy was not lacking indigenous roots. The condition and status of women in society have also undergone significant change; while Japan is unlikely to be presented as a feminist paradise, certainly in historical terms the transformation has been profound, though it could hardly have been achieved without the pioneering strides undertaken in the course of the Meiji era in spite of official harassment. While all these transformations can be perceived as beneficial to the country, the record so far as the *eta* are concerned is somewhat less admirable.

The policy of *sakoku* may have given the cocooned Japanese a sense of security, though in the course of the first half of the nineteenth century it was bound to be a false sense of security. Once Japan became absorbed in the arena of world politics, the feeling of national vulnerability became acute. Japan is still vulnerable. The country's total dependence on the import of sources of energy is the most manifest index of this condition of vulnerability. Thus, while pundits proclaim that Japan, presently the third-ranking state in terms of GNP, may well achieve first place and that the world is in the process of entering the Pacific Era, from the Japanese perspective the sense of security in the future is somewhat attenuated. Dependence on oil from the Middle East and the proximity of the Russian military superpower make an uncomfortable combination. In the contemporary age any resurgence of Japanese imperialism, for a whole series of reasons, must be discounted. For economic and demographic reasons, however, expansion is an absolute national necessity. Whether this expansion can prove constructive and be achieved in a collaborative spirit will of course very much depend on the Japanese. It will also, however, and indeed to a very significant degree depend on the reactions, attitudes and policies adopted by the Western countries. It would be extremely unfortunate if the spirit lying behind the Triple Intervention were to be revived.

Glossary of Japanese Terms

Aikoku-kōtō: Public Patriotic Party, the first party founded by Itagaki after he resigned from the government in 1873.

Ainu: name of the original aboriginal inhabitants of the Japanese isles, the few who remain to be found only in parts of the northern island of Hokkaidō; in the Ainu language, *Ainu* simply means 'man'.

Akashinbun: literally meaning 'red newspaper', though corresponding to Meiji Japan's 'yellow press'; it was called red because the newspapers were printed on pink paper.

Ama: a female pearl diver.

Ashigaru: foot soldier, among the lowest-ranking *samurai*, in fact somewhat on the periphery of the *samurai* estate, in the Edo era.

Bakufu: literally camp or tent government; when a *shōgun* was mainly engaged in battle and hence peripatetic in nature he administered from his camp; with the establishment of the Kamakura shogunate shogunal governments maintained more permanent residences but the term *bakufu* was retained.

Baku-han-sei: the system of *bakufu* and *han*; in the Edo era the form of national government consisted of a compromise between local (*han*) government and central (*bakufu*) government, hence labelled 'centralised feudalism'.

Bakumatsu: the closing years of the Edo era, those between Perry's treaty, 1854, and the Restoration, 1868.

Bansho Torishirabesho: Office for the Study of Barbarian Writings, established by the Tokugawa *bakufu* in 1856 and the progenitor of the modern Japanese Foreign Ministry.

Bantō: The manager of an enterprise in the Edo period.

Bekke: a branch *ie* (firm, establishment, family), derived from the *honke*, the head or main *ie*.

Besubōru: baseball, imported into Japan in the early Meiji period and today the country's favourite spectator sport.

Budō: the martial arts.

316

Buke: military families, as opposed to the *kuge* who were the civilian nobility.

Buke sho-hatto: the corpus of regulations issued by the Tokugawa *bakufu* in 1615 to govern the conduct of *buke* affairs.

Bunmei-kaika: 'civilisation and enlightenment', the slogan adopted with enthusiasm by the Japanese intelligentsia in the 1870s and 1880s, corresponding to a period of fairly strong adulation of all things Western.

Buraku kaihō: Movement for the Emancipation of the Buraku People (*eta*), founded in 1902 but very shortly afterwards suppressed by the government.

Burakumin: village people, a euphemism for *eta*, but the term currently in use in Japan and preferred by the *burakumin* themselves.

Bushi: a man of arms, an equivalent term for *samurai*.

Bushidō: the way of the *bushi*, in other words the Japanese code of chivalry.

Cha-no-yu: 'the way of tea', that is, the tea ceremony, originally an exercise performed in temples, subsequently secularised.

Chigyō: the fief that only a handful of *samurai* retained in the Edo era which provided their revenue, different from the majority of *samurai* who received stipends (*hōroku*).

Chōnin: townsman, a generic term used for urban dwellers of the merchant and artisan estates in the Edo era.

Chōnindō: the way of the *chōnin*, in other words the merchant/artisan variant on the *bushidō*.

Chū: loyalty, one of the cardinal Confucian virtues.

Daikan: a middle-ranking administrator of the Edo era, acting mainly as deputy to a *bugyō*.

Daimyō: literally 'great name', feudal lords of the Edo era whose origins and fiefs generally dated from the *sengoku* era.

Dairi: the part of the imperial palace where the *tennō* resided and one of the euphemisms formerly in use to designate him.

Danson-johi: 'revere men – despise women', phallocratic slogan of the Edo era; vestiges of this spirit can perhaps still be occasionally discerned.

Danzaemon: name given to the chief of the *eta* in Edo.

Datsu-A: 'Shedding Asia', one of Fukuzawa's publications, but equally emblematic of the westernising spirit of the *bunmei-kaika* years.

Deshi: a pupil, a disciple, apprentice.

Ebisu: literally 'barbarian'; until the term *Ainu* became widespread in Japan, it was the term *ebisu* which was used when referring to these aboriginal people.

Edo-machi bugyō: chief administrator and magistrate of the city of Edo during the Tokugawa period; one of the higher-ranking echelons in the Edo *bakufu* administration.

Eta: original term for the *burakumin*, Japan's outcast group.

Fudai daimyō: hereditary vassals, those *daimyō* families which had allied themselves to the Tokugawa cause prior to the battle of Sekigahara; generally not as rich as the *tozama*, nor as close to the *shōgun* as the *shinpan*, *fudai daimyō* were nevertheless in a position to exert a significant degree of political influence throughout most of the Edo era and it was from their numbers that the *rōjū* (see below) were selected.

Fujin Kyofukai: Christian Women's Social Reform Organisation, a group existing in the late Meiji era, one of whose aims was to abolish prostitution.

Fujin undō: the women's movement of the Taishō period.

Fukoku-Kyōhei: 'Rich Country – Strong Army', the slogan meant to encapsulate the major motivations and ambitions of the Japanese leadership in the Meiji era.

Fumi-e: the practice in the Edo era of trampling on sacred Christian images to prove one was not a Christian.

Furoya: bath-house keepers, the first trade group in Edo Japan to receive the right to form a guild (in 1651).

Fūsetsugaki: the annual report which the chief Dutch factor in Dejima submitted to the *bakufu.*

Gaikoku-bugyō: administrator of foreign affairs, an office created by the *bakufu* after the initial treaties had been signed.

Gakubatsu: academic clique, namely referring to rival schools.

Gaku-reki shakai: 'School-record society', a term used in contemporary Japan to indicate that one's whole life and career are determined by performance in school and which university one gains admission to.

Geisha: 'artistic person', originally a term used in reference to male entertainers at the imperial court, subsequently for mainly female professional entertainers.

Gekokujō: 'rule of the higher by the lower'; a constant theme in Japanese history whereby actual power in determining events is controlled by subordinates; a complex phenomenon to describe, presented in this book as one of the historiographical elements in the dénouement of Japanese history.

Genrō: 'elder statesmen'; this term referred to those leaders of the Restoration who retained power in the course of the Meiji era and collectively directed the affairs of state even when not necessarily holding government office; it was they, for example, who advised the *tennō* on who should form a government.

Genyōsha: Dark Ocean Society, one of the more militant radical nativist societies founded by Tōyama Mitsuru in Fukuoka in 1881.

Go-kajō no seimon: Charter Oath of Five Articles, the first major official document to emanate from the new government in April 1868 which set out, albeit in somewhat ambiguous language, the course Japan should follow.

Go-kenin: 'personal attendants'; one of the two categories of the Tokugawa *shōgun*'s direct retainers and who held posts in the *bakufu* administration.

Gōnō: 'rich peasant'; the upper stream of the peasant estate in the Tokugawa era.

Go-rin: the five basic relationships of Confucianism: ruler–ruled, father–son, elder brother–younger brother, husband–wife, friend–friend.

Go-sanke: the three families related to the Tokugawa, from the *han* of Owari, Kii and Mito, and from whom a shogunal successor might be chosen.

Go-sekke: the five families descendant from the Fujiwara who monopolised the offices of *sesshō* (regent) and *kanpaku* (chief councillor).

Gōshi: 'rustic *samurai*', lower level of the *samurai* hierarchy in the Edo era, found mainly in the Satsuma *han*, who, unlike most *samurai*, lived not in the castle-towns but in the country and engaged in agriculture.

Go-shinpei: the Imperial Guard, formed in 1871 and consisting of battalions from Satsuma, Chōshū and Tosa; the original nucleus of the modern Japanese army.

Gosho: 'hallowed place', name of the Imperial palace and one of the euphemisms formerly in use for designating the *tennō*.

Goyō-kin: a forced loan extracted from merchants by the *bakufu* on an *ad hoc* basis in the latter part of the Edo era.

Gozō-roppu: 'the five viscera and six entrails', term used to refer to classical Chinese anatomy according to which every bodily function and organ corresponds to an act of nature.

Gundai: essentially the same as *daikan* (see above).

Gunjin Chokugo: Imperial Rescript to Soldiers and Sailors, emanating from the *tennō* himself, a document which became holy writ for the military and was publicly read on ceremonial occasions.

Gunjin Kunkai: Admonition to Soldiers, issued by the government in 1878 following a mutiny and admonishing soldiers to be good soldiers and not meddle in politics.

Gyoen: imperial park, the area in Kyoto where the *kuge* resided.

Han: the domain or fief; a *han* is a geographical area, *not* a family or a clan, hence a *han* never bore the name of the ruling *daimyō* family: the Shimazu were the *daimyō* of Satsuma, the Mori of Chōshū, the Maeda of Kanazawa, and so on.

Hanpō: han law, namely the jurisprudence of the individual *han*.

Hanseki-hōkan: 'return of the land and the people to the *tennō*'; in 1869 the *daimyō* of Satsuma, Chōshū, Tosa and Hizen petitioned the *tennō* to accept the return of their fiefs and subjects, thus marking the first official step in the centralisation of the Japanese state.

Hara-kiri: disembowelment; the traditional form of committing suicide by *samurai*, consisting of inserting the shorter of the two swords into the right side of the abdomen, moving it to the left and then up towards the heart; *hara-kiri* was a privilege reserved for the *samurai* estate in the Edo era.

Hatamoto: bannermen, direct retainers of the Tokugawa *shōgun* who were expected to assume important posts in the *bakufu* administration.

Heimin: collective term for commoners, namely all those not of the *samurai* estate.

Hibakusha: residents of Hiroshima and Nagasaki who survived the atomic holocaust.

Higyō-sha: residence of the *tennō*'s wife.

Hinin: 'non-human'; a social group of the Edo era, distinct from the *eta*, but also outcast.

Hirazamurai: middle-ranking *samurai* of the Edo era.

Hitogaeshi: 'sending people back'; Mizuno Tadakuni's programme for forcing people out of the cities and sending them back to the countryside as a means of curing Edo Japan's economic and moral ills; the programme was never implemented.

Hōchishugi: 'rule by law'; a principle operating from the late nineteenth century to the end of the Pacific War, derived from the German concept of *Rechsstaat*.

Hōkan: male professional entertainer operating in the *yūkaku* (see below).

Hokkaidō kaitaku-shi: Hokkaido Colonisation Office; a bureau set up in 1869 to undertake and supervise the development of the northern island.

Honke: the head or main *ie*, as opposed to the *bekke* (branch *ie*).

Hōroku: the stipend a *samurai* was due to receive from his lord during the Edo era; these were commuted in 1876 and thereby provided one of the causes for the Satsuma uprising of the following year.

Hōtoku: religious movement founded by Ninomiya Sontoku in the early nineteenth century and which spread especially among the peasantry.

Ianfu: 'consolation woman'; women, many of whom were Korean, sent out to accompany soldiers in the campaigns of the Pacific War.

Ie: term meaning alternatively family, household, firm, establishment, organisation, etc; one of the key concepts in an understanding of Japanese social history.

Insei: 'cloister government'; indicating the practice of a reigning *tennō* abdicating in favour of his successor.

Ishin: the Meiji Ishin is generally translated into English as the Meiji

Restoration; the term, however, implies not simply 'restoration', but also 'renovation'.

Itowappu: the semi-governmental monopoly established to control the silk trade shortly after the advent of the Tokugawa *bakufu.*

Jashūmon: 'evil or pernicious sect'; term used to describe and define Christianity from the late sixteenth century until 1873 when the ban against Christianity was lifted.

Jin: benevolence, one of the key cardinal Confucianist virtues, especially expected in the conduct of a superior towards an inferior and above all the reigning monarch.

Jinzai: 'man of talent'; a concept gaining strength in the latter part of the Edo era, thus leading the way for administration by a meritocracy as opposed to an hereditary aristocracy.

Jisankin: the sum of money which a bride might take with her upon marriage, rarely, however, amounting to any great significance, hence not really constituting what might be termed a dowry.

Jisha-bugyō: chief administrator of Shintō Shrines and Buddhist Temples during the Tokugawa *bakufu* regime.

Jitsugaku: 'the study of real things'; a school of thought which developed in the Edo era, consisting of what might be termed a Confucianist form of empiricism.

Jiyū-minken-undō: movement for freedom and popular rights; an umbrella term for the opposition movements to the Meiji oligarchy in the 1870s and 1880s.

Jiyū-minsei-tō: the Liberal Democratic Party, more often referred to as the *Jimintō,* formed in 1955 through a merger of the *Jiyūtō* and the *Minseitō,* and having remained in power ever since.

Jiyūtō: the first political party in modern Japanese history, literally translated as the Freedom Party, but more often as the Liberal Party, founded by Itagaki in 1881, the year the government announced that a constitution would be promulgated prior to the end of the decade.

Jōi: 'expel the barbarians'; xenophobic, millenarian slogan and policy of the imperial court and militant *samurai* in the *bakumatsu* era.

Jōka-machi: castle-town, towns formed surrounding fortifications erected during the *sengoku* (civil war) era and in which most *samurai* were made to live after they had been taken off the land.

Jōrō: generic term for prostitute.

Jōshi: upper-ranking *samurai.*

Junpū-bizoku: 'gentle ways and beautiful customs'; a spirit of nativist reaction against excessive westernisation in the early twentieth century.

Junshi: the self-immolation of an attendant on the death of his lord, a practice according to which a lord's chief retainers would commit suicide upon his death; the fourth Tokugawa *shōgun*, Ietsuna, had the practice of *junshi* officially proscribed; in the modern era the most famous case of *junshi* is that of General Nogi committing suicide upon learning of the Meiji *tennō*'s death.

Jusha: the Confucian scholar, normally an hereditary position as teacher in the *bakufu* and *han* schools during the Edo era.

Kabu nakama: the guilds of the Edo era which did not receive official sanction until under the reign of *shōgun* Yoshimune.

Kaigun Daigakkō: Naval College established in 1888 in Etajima.

Kaigun Heigakkō: Naval Academy, founded in 1876, upgraded into the Kaigun Daigakkō in 1888.

Kaiken: a small dirk used by ladies of the samurai estate as a means of protection or else to thrust into their jugular vein when committing suicide.

Kaishakunin: the assistant at *hara-kiri*, namely the one, generally the most trusted retainer or friend, who cuts off the head with a swift blow of the sword to spare too great agony.

Kaishintō: the Progressive Party, founded by Ōkuma Shigenobu, following the establishment of the *Jiyūtō*.

Kakeya: financial agents for the *daimyō* in Osaka during the Edo era.

Kakure kirishitan: crypto-Christians, namely those who held to the Christian faith in hiding throughout the years of the Edo era when Christianity was banned.

Kami: a term very difficult to translate, possibly a deity or saint; *kami* is derived from the same character of *shin* in Shintō, which can also be pronounced *Kami-michi*, meaning the way of the deities; Shintō is the indigenous Japanese religion.

Kamikaze: 'divine wind', referring to the typhoon which destroyed the bulk of the Kublai Khan's fleet which sought to invade Japan in the late thirteenth century, hence the origin of the term used for the suicidal pilots who carried out missions at the end of the Pacific War, but in vain.

Kanjō-bugyō: administrator of finance under the Tokugawa regime.

Kanpaku: chief councillor to the *tennō*, an office established and subsequently monopolised by the Fujiwara family in the Heian period.

Kanryō: bureaucracy or officialdom; *kanryō-shugi* means bureaucratism, this being another key historiographical concept in an understanding of modern Japanese history.

Kanson-minpi: 'revere officials – despise the people'; a slogan indicating the absolute nature of official bureaucratic power in Edo Japan, features of which certainly survived in the Meiji period and at least until 1945.

Karō: the chief councillors of the *daimyō*.

Kashi: lower-ranking *samurai* of the Edo era.

Katana-gari: Hideyoshi's sword-hunt of 1588, aimed at bringing about a clear differentiation between the peasant and *samurai* estates, namely by disarming the peasants and taking *samurai* off the land.

Keihō: Criminal Code; see below.

Keiji Soshōhō: the Code of Criminal Procedure, one of the new westernised codes of the Meiji era, designed partly to serve for the purpose of revising the treaties.

Kenpeitai: an army intelligence unit formed in 1881 with the aim of rooting out dissidents in both military and civilian life; in the late thirties and early forties the *kenpeitai* can be said to have been to the Japanese what the SS was to the Germans.

Kenseikai: Constitutional Association, name given to the party in opposition to the *Seiyūkai* in 1923 by Katō Takaaki, subsequently re-named the *Minseitō* (Democratic Party) in 1927.

Kiheitai: an armed corps composed of able soldiers irrespective of their social origins, namely including peasants, formed in the Chōshū han in the years prior to the restoration and thereby the origin of the later conscript army.

Kikoku-senkin: 'revere grain – despise money'; slogan of the Edo era underlying the regime's physiocratic economic philosophy and social attitudes in regard to the merchant estate.

Kirisute-gomen: 'slay and take leave'; a practice occasionally engaged in by the *samurai* of the Edo era, possibly to try out a new sword, alternatively to keep the non-*samurai* orders, merchants and peasants, in their place.

Kō: filial piety, one of the cardinal Confucian virtues.

Kōbu-gattai: 'amalgamation of civil and military power'; an unsuccessful policy pursued in the *bakumatsu* era with a view to achieving a closer union between the Edo *bakufu* and the Kyoto imperial court to co-ordinate policy.

Kogaku: ancient school; a school of Confucianism which insisted on the necessity of reading the original texts rather than subsequent exegetical writings.

Kogisho: the first deliberative body established by the Meiji government in 1869.

Kōgō: chief consort to the *tennō*.

Koku: the unit used to calculate the rice yield of a domain, equivalent to 4·96 bushels.

Kokugaku: the school of national learning; originally a school involved in the academic pursuit of the Japanese (as opposed to Chinese) cultural legacy, which in the later Edo period assumed political proportions and served as the ideological justification for the restoration of both temporal and spiritual power to the *tennō*.

Kokuryūkai: Black Dragon Society; another militant romantic nativist society.

Kokusuikai: National Essence Society; as above.

Kokutai: the national structure, a term meant to indicate the fundamental characteristics of the Japanese state.

Koseki: the family register; a woman was not legally a wife until she was inscribed in the *koseki*, which need not necessarily take place at the time of the wedding.

Kōtei: the Japanese word for emperor, but only foreign emperors; the *tennō* is never referred to as *kōtei*.

Kuge: the Kyoto civil nobility, as opposed to the *buke*, the military families.

Kuge sho-hatto: the *kuge* equivalent of the *buke sho-hatto* (see above).

Kunaichō: the Imperial Household Agency.

Kuramoto: the merchant administrators of Osaka who managed the *daimyō*'s financial/commercial affairs in that city.

Kyōiku Chokugo: the Imperial Rescript on Education, issued in 1890, recited in all schools on ceremonial occasions; a moral tract admonishing schoolchildren to various virtues, including reverence for the *tennō*.

Mabiki: 'thinning out'; euphemism for infanticide as practised in the Edo and early Meiji eras as a means of population control.

Makura-zōshi: 'pillow books'; books with illustrations given to prospective brides for educational purposes.

Man-kan kōkan: policy unsuccessfully pursued prior to the outbreak of the Russo-Japanese war, according to which Japan would recognise Russian interests in Manchuria if Russia reciprocated in regard to Korea; Russia refused and ended up losing both Korea and Manchuria.

Metsuke: censors; officials of the Edo *bakufu* mainly responsible for keeping an acute eye on things.

Mi no hodo wo shire: 'know your place'; an injunction of the Edo era against social mobility; rising above or falling below one's station was not supposed to be contemplated according to the Tokugawa scheme of things whereby each family belonged to a particular estate and, in the case of *samurai*, to a particular rank within that estate.

Mikado: 'sacred gate' leading to the imperial palace in Kyoto, one of the euphemisms formerly used to designate the *tennō*, especially current among foreigners in the *bakumatsu* and early Meiji periods; also the title of a Gilbert and Sullivan operetta.

Minpō: Civil Code of Law; see remarks under *Keiji Soshōhō*.

Minseitō: Democratic Party, new name given to the Kenseikai by Hamaguchi Osachi in 1927.

Mitō-gaku: the school of the Mitō *han*, prominently involved in Japanese (as opposed to Chinese) studies, and responsible, among other things, for the compilation of the voluminous *Dai Nihon-shi*.

Muko-iri: 'bringing in the groom'; the practice to be found in some rural regions, whereby the groom would be brought to the bride's house for marriage, rather than vice versa.

Mukyōkaiha-Kirisutokyō: the Christian Church without any Sectarian Affiliation, founded by Uchimura Kanzō in the Meiji era in order to transcend the petty doctrinal and other squabbles frequently engaged in by Western missionaries of the different sects.

Mura: the village, the basic economic unit of the Edo era.

Muradaka: the calculated agricultural yield of the village, the basis used for taxation purposes.

Mura-yakunin: the village administrators, generally elected from among the villagers, responsible for the collection of taxes.

Myōga-kin: literally protection money; regular contributions paid by the guilds (*kabu-nakama*) to the *bakufu* treasury.

Myōji: a family name or surname; a privilege theoretically only members of the *samurai* estate were entitled to in the Edo era.

Nakōdo: a go-between; a person and function used in traditional *samurai* marriages.

Nanban-gaku: the Iberians and other Europeans who visited Japan in the sixteenth century were, following Chinese practice, referred to by the Japanese as the *nanban-jin*, southern barbarians; *nanban-gaku* was the term used to refer to the first elements of Western scholarship brought into Japan.

Nanushi: the village headman in the Edo era.

Nihon Sōdōmei Yūaikai: General Labour Organisation, established after the 1914–18 war, previously known as the *Yūaikai* (see below).

Nippon Shakai-tō: Japan Socialist Party, the first left-wing party founded in the Meiji era by Katayam Sen and others.

Nōhonshugi: agrarianism; reflecting the gulf between rural and urban areas and the priority given by the Meiji government to industry as opposed to agriculture, agrarianist ideologies and movements – there was never a single, carefully articulated ideology, nor a significant mass movement – it sought to restore the balance by giving primacy to the rural sector, the agrarian economy and the livelihood of the peasantry.

Nōshōkō Kōtō Kaigi: Superior Council on Agriculture, Commerce and Industry; a committee set up by the Meiji government in 1896 whose remit was to carry out an inquiry into the working conditions and state of health of the country's workforce.

Ōmetsuke: a cut above the *metsuke* (see above), these 'grand censors' reported to the *bakufu* on the activities of the *daimyō*.

Onkyū: the granting of fiefs to vassals as a reward for military services, resorted to by the imperial court in the later Heian period and ultimately a major cause for the rise of the *buke* and the demise of the *kuge*.

Ōoku: 'grand interior', namely where the *shōgun*'s wife, concubines and female relatives resided.

Ōsei-fukko: 'return to the ancient system of monarchic rule'; this was the term initially used in the *bakumatsu* years for the restoration of both spiritual and temporal power to the *tennō*; subsequently the term *ishin* (see above) was substituted.

Oyabun-kobun: 'parent part – child part'; a term used to describe the paternalistic relationship existing between an employer and his employees.

Rangaku: Dutch Studies; the term used to describe scholarship emanating from the West during the Edo era, particularly after the advent of Yoshimune to the shogunal throne.

Ranpeki: 'Dutch mania', something which gripped a number of *Rangaku-sha* (scholars of Dutch studies) in the mid-eighteenth century, which included such affectations as using Dutch pseudonyms.

Rikken Dōshi-kai: Association of Friends of the Constitution, the political party founded originally by Katsura Tarō, which in subsequent years fairly frequently changed names until finally in 1927 it was called the *Minseitō* (see above).

Rikugun Daigakkō: War College, founded in 1883, the élite course for aspiring Japanese army officers.

Ringi-sei: a decision-making process whereby proposals for policies originate from subordinates and move up the enterprise hierarchy in circular fashion, with all those in favour placing their stamp on the document, and finally submitted to the director.

Risshi-sha: Self-Help Society, a political movement founded in 1874, part of the general *jiyū-minken-undō* phenomenon; the *Risshi-sha* was specifically designed for *samurai* who had fallen on hard times because of Meiji government policy.

Ritsu-ryō: legal society operating under the codes devised at the time of the Taihō reforms of 701, namely the legal system adopted by the government of Heian-kyō.

Rōdō Kumiai Kiseikai: Society for the Promotion of Trade Unions, founded by Katayama Sen in 1897.

Rōjū: the council of elders; the major advisory body to the *shōgun*, generally consisting of about six in number and chosen from among the *fudai daimyō*.

Rokumeikan: the Pavilion of the Baying Stag, a building erected under the auspices of the government in the early Meiji period in order to facilitate social intercourse between the foreign community and the new Japanese leadership in government, commerce and so on; a characteristic feature of the *bunmei-kaika* years (see above).

Rōmaji-kai: Society for the Romanisation of the Japanese Script; a society set up by a number of the westernised intelligentsia in the *bunmei-kaika* period; an organisation which many students of Japanese no doubt wish would have had more success.

Rōnin: a masterless *samurai.*

Ryōgaeya: professional and licensed money-exchangers in the Edo era.

Ryōsai-kenbo-shugi: 'good wife – wise mother-ism'; the major pedagogical ideology regarding girls' education as it developed in the Meiji era.

Sai-sei-itchi: 'the unity of rights and administration'; the term found in the early Japanese chronicles by *kokugaku* (see above) scholars, which ultimately provided the ideological justification for the claim that both temporal and spiritual power should reside in the person of the *tennō.*

Sakoku: 'closed country'; the policy of isolationism adopted by the Tokugawa *bakufu* in 1639 and which remained operative until 1854.

Samurai: etymologically derived from the verb 'to serve', *samurai* is another term for *bushi* (see above).

Sankin-kōtai: the system of alternative residence in Edo enforced on the *daimyō* by the Tokugawa *bakufu.*

Sei-i-tai-shōgun: 'barbarian-repressing generalissimo'; the original term for *shōgun*, referring to his main obligation as being the suppression of the *ebisu* (see above).

Seikan-ron: the debate over whether to conquer Korea; this occurred in 1872–3, following the decision not to invade Korea a number of restoration leaders, including Saigō and Itagaki, left the government; the negative outcome of the *seikan-ron* acted as the trigger mechanism for the *samurai* uprisings which ensued.

Seiryoku-tōzen: the eastern advance of the Western powers, namely indicating how in the Japanese perspective Western imperialism was inexorably moving in an easterly direction, ultimately to Japan.

Seitosha: the Blue Stocking Society, a female literary circle established in 1911.

Seiyūkai: Society of Political Friends, the first major party to be formed following the establishment of the Diet in 1890.

Sekisho: internal custom barriers dating back to the Nara era; in the Edo era *sekisho* were used purely as a policing exercise and not for purposes of trade.

Sengoku jidai: the era of civil wars, from the period following the Onin wars to the unification of the country in the late sixteenth century.

Senmin: literally, 'despised people', a generic term in the pre-Edo era for all outcast groups.

Seppuku: a more refined term for *hara-kiri.*

Sesshō: regent; another office (see *kanpaku* above) created and monopolised by the Fujiwara family.

Shikan gakkō: the military academy, founded in 1875, forerunner to the *Rikugun Daigakkō* (see above).

Shikken: regent to the *shōgun*; an office created by the Hōjō family during the Minamoto (Kamakura) *bakufu.*

Shingaku: 'heart or mind learning'; a sect founded by Ishida Baigan in the mid-Edo era whose adherents came from the merchant estate.

Shinkoku: 'divine country'; Shintō concept regarding the sacredness of the Japanese territory.

Shi-nō-kō-shō: Samurai–Peasant–Artisan–Merchant; the social order of the four major estates in hierarchical order during the Edo era.

Shinpan daimyō: daimyō coming from the collateral branches of the main Tokugawa family (see *go-sanke* above).

Shinpū: a more refined term for *kamikaze* (see above); note, more refined in the sense that *shinpū* like *seppuku* correspond to the Chinese readings of the characters for *kamikaze* and *hara-kiri* respectively.

Shinpūren: Divine Wind League; a militant *samurai* group in Kumamoto prefecture, who in 1876 undertook a suicidal uprising; they have served as an inspiration for romantic Japanese radicals throughout the modern era.

Shishi: 'men of sincere will'; term used to refer to the heroic patriots who fought for the cause of the Restoration.

Shōen: private estates which emerged in the latter part of the Heian era.

Shōgun: the chief military figure originating in the Heian era; when power passed from the *kuge* to the *buke*, the *shōgun* came to exercise a greater degree of temporal power, until finally the authority of the imperial court was eclipsed; the first shogunal dynasty was created by Minamoto no Yoritomo at the end of the twelfth century, while the last *shōgun*, Tokugawa Yoshinobu, abdicated in 1867.

Shokumin Kyōkai: Colonisation Society, founded in 1893 by Enomoto Takeaki as an organisation to encourage emigration for the creation of colonies of settlement.

Shōya: village headman, a term equivalent to *nanushi* (see above).

Shuinjō: 'red seal permits'; only those Japanese ships which carried Ieyasu's official red seal permits (*shuinjō*) were entitled to engage in foreign trade; in other words this was a means devised by the first Tokugawa *shōgun* to monopolise foreign trade.

Shuinsen: 'red seal ships', namely those ships which did in fact carry the *shuinjō*.

Shukueki: relay stations along the routes of the *sankin-kōtai* which provided numerous services, generally including that of prostitution.

Sōmō no shishi: 'unattached patriots'; a term used by Yoshida Shōin in appealing to those *samurai* who were prepared to abandon their purely fief loyalties and struggle for the survival of the whole nation.

Sonnō: 'revere the emperor'; the slogan aiming at the restoration of the *tennō*.

Suihei undō: 'Water Level Movement'; the second *eta* emancipation movement, founded in 1922 and suppressed by the government in 1928.

Taikō: term to designate a retired *kanpaku* (chief councillor); Hideyoshi fraudulently claimed Fujiwara descent, assumed the office of *kanpaku*, but then resigned in favour of his son in the hope of thereby guaranteeing the succession; hence the custom of referring to Hideyoshi as *taikō-sama*.

Taikō-kenchi: the major land survey carried out under orders of Hideyoshi in the years 1582 to 1598.

Taikomochi: male professional entertainer in the *yūkaku* (see below).

Taikun: literally 'great lord' an alternative term for *shōgun*; with its anglicisation 'Tycoon' it was generally used rather than *shōgun* by the foreigners in the *bakumatsu* era; one of the few Japanese contributions to the English language, as in 'business tycoon'.

Tairō: 'chief elder'; this was an office in the Edo era which the *bakufu* occasionally filled on an *ad hoc* basis by appointing to a prime leadership position one of the *rōjū* (see above).

Taisei Yokusan-kai: Imperial Rule Assistance Association; in 1940 by government order the political parties, namely the Minseitō and Seiyūkai, were dissolved and integrated into the IRAA as a means of uniting all political groups to support the war effort.

Tansu: a chest of drawers in which a bride would collect a few personal belongings to take with her when entering her husband's *ie*.

Tashidaka: incremental stipends given to really able *samurai* as a recompense for meritorious service.

Tedai: journeyman; the position which an apprentice having successfully completed his apprenticeship would rise to in an establishment in the Edo era; the *tedai* were under the direction of the *bantō* (manager, see above).

Teiseitō: Imperial Government Party; a party founded under the Meiji government's auspices in 1882 in order to combat the Jiyūtō and Kaishintō.

Tekkō Kumiai: Metalworkers' Union, an attempt by Katayama Sen to form a labour union as part of the programme of the *Rōdō Kumiai Kiseikai* (see above).

Tennō: 'lord of heaven'; the most current modern term for designating the Japanese emperor.

Tennō-sei: a term coined by Japanese Marxist historians to describe the absolutist (see *zettai-shugi* below) character of the political society which emerged after the Restoration and remained in force until Japan's defeat in 1945.

Tenryō: the shogunal domains.

Tenshi: 'child of heaven'; another euphemism formerly in use to designate the *tennō*.

Terakoya: 'temple schools'; the village schools of the Edo era, but which, in spite of their name, were secular institutions and not administered by the temples.

Tezuke: low-ranking Edo *bakufu* officials who served as assistants to the *daikan* and *gundai* (see above).

Tōa Dōbunkai: East Asian Common Culture Association; a would-be Pan-Asiatic movement, but under clear Japanese direction, established by Konoe Atsumaro in 1898.

Tōbaku: the movement to overthrow the *bakufu*, generated in the final years of the *bakumatsu* period.

Tokyo Chigaku Kyōkai: Tokyo Geographical Society, established in 1879, and like the *Shokumin Kyōkai* (see above) active in encouraging emigration.

Tondenhei-seido: colonial troops system; a means of encouraging former *samurai* in the Meiji era to migrate to Hokkaidō and assist in the development of that island; see *Hokkaidō Kaitaku-shi* above.

Tonya: Osaka wholesalers in the Edo era.

Tozama Daimyō: 'outside lords'; those *daimyō* who submitted themselves to the Tokugawa either in the course of or immediately following the battle of Sekigahara.

Uji: ancient term for Japanese clans.

Unjō-kin: the charter fees paid by guilds at the time of their formation in the Edo era.

Wafū no narai: Japanese-style learning; in the Edo era this referred to the education for women who were encouraged to read and write the Japanese syllabaries (the *kana*) and read Japanese literature as opposed to what was perceived as the more challenging and masculine Chinese classics.

Waka-doshiyori: 'junior elders'; Edo *bakufu* officials directly below the *rōju* (see above).

Wako: Japanese pirates of the pre-Edo era.

Yakyū: the Japanised word for *besubōru* (see above).

Yashiki: mansions kept by the *daimyō* in Edo as part of the sankin-kōtai arrangement.

Yobai: 'night crawling'; practice whereby a suitor would go at night to sleep with an eligible girl in her house as a possible means for betrothal; a common custom in the rural areas of the Edo era.

Yōga: Western-style painting.

Yōgaku: Western studies in the *bakumatsu* and early Meiji eras, following the earlier *nanban-gaku* and *rangaku* (see above).

Yomei-gaku: the Japanese version of the Wang Yang-ming school of Neo-Confucianism, introduced in the seventeenth century by Nakae Tōju.

Yome-iri: 'bringing in the bride'; system, as opposed to that of *muko-iri* (see above), whereby the bride was brought to her groom's *ie* for the marriage.

Yūaikai: Friendship Association, a very moderate labour organisation founded by Suzuki Bunji in 1911.

Yūkaku: 'pleasure enclosures'; the red-light districts set up during the Edo era and abolished shortly after the Pacific War.

Zaibatsu: financial clique; term used to designate the mammoth enterprises, primarily Mitsui, Mitsubishi, Sumitomo and Yasuda, which developed in the Meiji era and blossomed after the 1914–18 war.

Zettai-shugi: absolutism; term used by historians to characterise the nature of political society as it emerged in the course of the early Meiji era and remained until 1945.

Bibliographical Note

There is today a considerable variety of publications in English on Japanese history. It goes without saying that an inability to read Japanese will constitute a severe handicap in terms of understanding the process and forces of historical development of that country. The first reason is the obvious one that a nation's language is perhaps the most important element of its culture. This is more emphatically the case in Japan where the national language is spoken exclusively by Japanese and also forms an integral element in the people's sense of identity and nationhood. The second reason is equally clear, namely that an inability to read the language deprives the reader of access to the works of Japanese historians; this is compounded by the fact that few Japanese historians have published in English. This barrier, however, must not be allowed to assume insurmountable proportions. Given the importance of Japan and the uniqueness of her historical development it is imperative that a broader appreciation of Japanese history should be achieved. People in the West should not be discouraged by this handicap, but rather strongly encouraged to take advantage of what there is at their disposal to seek enlightenment on the nature and course of Japanese history.

The early Western pioneers of Japanese history were essentially inspired and highly talented amateurs. One can, for example, find many fascinating articles whose authors display a high degree of erudition in the volumes of the *Transactions of the Asiatic Society of Japan* (Asiatic Society of Japan, Tokyo, from 1874). The maestro of this art was undoubtedly Sir George Bernard Sansom, whose three-volume history of Japan and especially his *Japan: A Short Cultural History* (London, 1946) and *The Western World and Japan* (Alfred A. Knopf, New York, 1950) remain masterpieces. These works tended to be histories written along classical lines, that is essentially narrative rather than interpretative. The major milestone in Western historiographical interpretation of modern Japanese history was undoubtedly E. H. Norman's *Japan's Emergence as a Modern State* (Institute of Pacific Relations, New York, 1940). Norman's thesis was moderately Marxian in nature, the essential objective of his work (bearing in mind the period in which it was researched and written – the late 1930s) being to discover the roots of contemporary Japanese fascism. Some of the details of Norman's thesis are no longer tenable today. There is little evidence, for example, to support the view that the Meiji Restoration was carried out mainly as a result of an alliance forged between lower samurai and wealthy merchants. The picture, as indicated in the pages of this book and indeed in many works, is in any case somewhat more complex. The scope and ambition of Norman's work, however, remain impressive and challenging.

In the last twenty-five years or so the situation in the West, and especially in the United States of America, in the study of Japanese history has changed significantly. The new school, pioneered by historians such as Marius B. Jansen and John Whitney Hall, originating essentially from the East Coast Ivy League universities, has set more modern, professional standards. In other words, the majority of writers on Japanese history today are professionals rather than amateurs: men and women who in many cases will have specialised in both their undergraduate and postgraduate degrees in Japanese language and Japanese history. Similarly, in these last twenty-five years the number of Japanese archives which have been scrutinised by Western scholars has increased in geometric proportions. There can be no doubt that we now know a great deal more and it is probably also the case that as a result we are somewhat the wiser. As just implied, however, there is room for some qualification. Professionalisation inevitably runs the risk of excessive specialisation. History must be more than archivism and it becomes tiresome if it develops into footnote fetishism. There is a visible tendency today in the profession that whereas an individual may know a great deal about his own limited subject, unless he is capable of perceiving it in the context of a broader historical canvas a good deal of the more significant meanings of his research may not be properly appreciated. Having entered this caveat, it must nonetheless be stressed that a great deal of the material available is of excellent value.

In bibliographical terms there are, of course, numerous articles on various aspects of Japanese history to be found in the history and economic history professional periodicals. *The Journal of Asian Studies* (formerly known as *The Far Eastern Quarterly*), *The Journal of Japanese Studies*, *Modern Asian Studies* and *Monumenta Nipponica* are either, as in the case of the second and the fourth, exclusively or, in the case of the first and the third, substantially concerned with Japanese studies. In view of the fact that articles in professional periodicals are generally focused on somewhat narrower themes, the select bibliography below has concentrated on books; needless to say, further bibliographical material can be obtained from these.

In terms of an introduction to modern Japanese history one can do no better than read G. R. Storry, *A History of Modern Japan* (Penguin, Harmondsworth, Middlesex, revised edition 1978). J. W. Hall in *Japan from Prehistory to Modern Times* (Weidenfeld & Nicolson, London, 1970) encapsulates in a remarkably brief but penetrating account the broad sweep of Japanese history over the centuries.

The novice to Japanese economic history should begin with G. C. Allen's *A Short Economic History of Modern Japan* (George Allen & Unwin, London, 3rd edition 1972) for a most lucid and penetrating analysis. A stimulating recent publication on the subject is K. Yoshihara's *Japanese Economic Development: A Short Introduction* (Oxford University Press, Oxford in Asia Paperbacks, Tokyo, 1979). G. C. Allen and A. G. Donnithorne, in *Western Enterprise in Far Eastern Economic Development: China and Japan* (George Allen & Unwin, London, 1962), analyse the different responses of China and Japan to the two countries' absorption into the world economy by the Western powers. J. Hirschmeier and T. Yui, in *The Development of Japanese Business, 1600–1973* (George Allen & Unwin, London, 1975) provide a highly informative, interpretative and fascinating account of the Japanese model in business history. J. F. Roberts, *Mitsui: Three Centuries of Japanese Business* (Weatherhill, New York, 1973) is a compelling account of Japan's most famous industrial giant. L. Klein and K. Ohkawa (eds), *Economic Growth: the Japanese Experience since the Meiji Era* (Yale University Press, New Haven, Connecticut, 1968) and H. Rosovsky, *Capital Formation in Japan 1868–1940* (The Free Press, Glencoe, New York, 1961) are two classics on the subject. The six volumes edited by K. Nakagawa emanating from the International Conference on Business History and published since 1976 by the Tokyo University Press are of great value and of particular relevance to this book is the second volume, *Social Order and Entrepreneurship* (Tokyo University Press, Tokyo, 1977). Highly recommended as an introduction to modern Japanese economic history are the chapters contained in W. W. Lockwood (ed.), *State and Economic Enterprise in Japan* (Princeton University Press, Princeton, New Jersey, 1965) and H. Patrick (ed.), *Japanese Industrialisation and Its Social Consequences* (University of California Press, Berkeley, 1976).

The volumes on modernisation in Japan published by the Princeton University Press, and of which the work mentioned above by W. W. Lockwood is a part, are fully extensive in their treatment of the many different facets both in causal and consequential terms of modern Japanese history; they include: R. P. Dore (ed.), *Aspects of Social Change in Modern Japan* (1967), M. B. Jansen (ed.), *Changing Japanese Attitudes Toward Modernization* (1965), D. H. Shively (ed.), *Tradition and Modernization in Japanese Culture* (1971) and R. E. Ward (ed.), *Political Development in Modern Japan* (1968), while J. W. Morley (ed.), *Dilemmas of Growth in Prewar Japan* (1971), as its title implies, is more specifically concerned with events in the interwar period. E. Skrzypczak (ed.), *Japan's Modern Century* (Sophia University Press, Tokyo, 1968) includes articles on diverse aspects of modern Japan. A. M. Craig and D. H. Shively (eds.), *Personality in Japanese History* (University of California Press, Berkeley, 1970) provide highly informative insights on a number of the major figures in Japanese history. R. P. Dore, *Land Reform in Japan* (Oxford University Press, London, 1959) and T. R. H. Havens, *Farm and Nation in Modern Japan: Agrarian Nationalism 1870–1940* (Princeton University Press, Princeton, New Jersey, 1974) present from two different angles the evolution of the agrarian sector in the modern age. J-P. Lehmann, *The Image of Japan, 1850–1905: From Feudal Isolation to World Power* (George Allen & Unwin, London, 1978) assesses how the West reacted to the momentous changes taking place in the course of Japan's modernisation. M. B. Jansen, *Japan and Its World: Two Centuries of Change* (Princeton University Press, Princeton, New Jersey, 1980) analyses the evolutionary and indeed at times revolutionary changes which have occurred in Japan's perception on the outer world. The fullest account in English on the history of the *eta* and a major source for the relevant sections in this book is S. Ninomiya, 'An Inquiry Concerning the Origin, Development and present Situation of the *Eta* in Relation to the History of Social Classes in Japan' (*Transactions of the Asiatic Society of Japan*, London, 2nd series, vol. X, 1933). Reference should also be made to G. de Vos and H. Wagatsuma (eds.), *Japan's Invisible Race: Caste in Culture and Personality* (University of California Press, Berkeley, 1972) who present a remarkably penetrating account focusing primarily on the contemporary condition of the *eta*.

In terms of the studies concentrating on narrower periods of Japanese history the list below focuses on works from the Edo era. On the earlier periods and specifically in terms of political developments one should read J. W. Hall, *Government and Local Power in Japan 500 to 1700* (Princeton University Press, Princeton, New Jersey, 1966). G. R. Storry, *The Way of the Samurai* (Orbis, London, 1978) provides a fascinating insight into the evolution of the manners, customs, values and roles of Japan's warrior élite. The early contact and ultimate confrontation between the Europeans and Japanese in the sixteenth and seventeenth centuries is the subject of C. R. Boxer's classic, *The Christian Century in Japan, 1549–1650* (University of California Press, Berkeley, 1951); while M. Cooper's *They Came to Japan: Anthology of European Reports on Japan 1543–1640* (Thames & Hudson, London, 1965) contains a great deal of insight both on the Japanese and on the Europeans in Japan during this period. A unique and highly stimulating book is that edited by A. Boscaro, *101 Letters of Hideyoshi* (Sophia University Press, Tokyo, 1975), which sets out an intimate portrait of this monumental figure of Japanese history.

The first and essential text on the Edo era is that edited by M. B. Jansen and J. W. Hall, *Studies in the Institutional History of Early Modern Japan* (Princeton University Press, Princeton, New Jersey, 1968); the subjects vary from developments in commerce to education and generally provide both an extensive and intensive perspective of the period. T. C. Smith's *The Agrarian Origins of Modern Japan* (Stanford University Press, Stanford, California, 1959) is another 'must' in terms of an understanding of the historical forces of the period and their legacy in the course of modernisation. Two significant economic studies with a primarily demographic orientation are S. B. Hanley and K. Yamamura, *Economic and Demographic Change in Preindustrial Japan, 1600–1868* (Harvard University Press, Cambridge, Massachusetts, 1977) and T. C. Smith, *Nakahara: Family Farming and Population in a Japanese Village, 1717–1830* (Stanford University Press, Stanford, California, 1977). C. P. Sheldon's *The Rise of the Merchant Class in Tokugawa Japan, 1600–1868* (Russell & Russell, New York, 1958) provides a penetrating analysis and has certainly figured prominently in the material obtained in writing the third chapter of this book. From a political perspective a most authoritative and informative analysis is the study of H. Webb, *The Japanese Imperial Institution in the Tokugawa Period* (Columbia University Press, New York, 1968). T. G. Tsukahira in *Feudal Control in Tokugawa Japan: the Sankin-Kōtai System* (Harvard University Press, Cambridge, Massachusetts, 1970) assesses the full impact of the *sankin-kōtai* system on the evolution of Tokugawa society. R. Bellah, *Tokugawa Religion: The Values of Industrial Japan* (The Free Press, Glencoe, New York, 1957) seeks to find a Japanese counterpart to the Protestant ethic in terms of assessing a value system conducive to economic development and industrialisation. M. Maruyama, *Studies in the Intellectual History of Tokugawa Japan* (University of Tokyo Press, Tokyo, 1974) is a work of very high erudition which focuses on the condition of and challenges to the Neo-Confucianist doctrines of Tokugawa Japan. The work which embodies all the major features and forces of the Edo era and perhaps more than any other sets the stage for an understanding of the process and nature of the modernisation which follows the eclipse of the Tokugawa order is R. P. Dore's *Education in Tokugawa Japan* (Routledge & Kegan Paul, London, 1965). D. Keene's *The Japanese Discovery of Europe, 1720–1830* (Stanford University Press, Stanford, California, 1969) not only offers an insight into the intellectual and geographic expansion of the period at least in some quarters, but is also of high literary quality. In regard to the Dutch presence and its impact, apart from Keene's study, one should certainly read C. R. Boxer's *Jan Compagnie in Japan, 1600–1817* (Oxford University Press, London, 1968) and also G. K. Goodman, *The Dutch Impact on Japan* (Brill, Leiden, 1967). Finally, a remarkable and unparalleled study of the *yūkaku* can be found in J. E. de Becker, *The Nightless City or the History of the Yoshiwara Yūkwaku* (first published Tokyo, 1899, reprinted by Charles E. Tuttle & Co., Rutland, Vermont and Tokyo, 1971).

In regard to the events leading up to 1868 and the analyses of the Meiji

Restoration the pioneering work, as indicated above, was E. H. Norman's which, along with other of his publications, can be found in J. W. Dower (ed.), *Origins of the Modern Japanese State: Selected Writings of E. H. Norman* (Pantheon Books, New York, 1975). The most exhaustive and authoritative analysis of the Meiji Restoration is W. G. Beasley's *The Meiji Restoration* (Oxford University Press, London, 1973). M. B. Jansen, *Sakamoto Ryōma and the Meiji Restoration* (Stanford University Press, Stanford, California, 1961) and A. M. Craig, *Chōshū in the Meiji Restoration* (Harvard University Press, Cambridge, Massachusetts, 1967) provided important historiographical interpretations of the causes of the Meiji Restoration, while tracing with detail their chronological evolution; both studies undoubtedly present major milestones in terms of a much deeper understanding of the forces at work during this period and their complexity. H. Harootunian, *Toward Restoration* (University of California Press, Berkeley, California, 1970) concentrates primarily on the development of the ideology behind the Restoration. C. Totman, *The Collapse of the Tokugawa Bakufu 1862–1868* (University Press of Hawaii, Honolulu, 1980) approaches the problem from a somewhat different angle, namely not so much why the Meiji Restoration occurred, but rather why the Tokugawa Bakufu fell. W. G. Beasley, *Select Documents on Japanese Foreign Policy, 1853–1868* (Oxford University Press, London, 1955) brings to light the realities the Japanese had to face in view of Western demands, the painful process this involved, the confusions, and the overall impact of this perceived external menace on the development of Japanese internal politics in the crucial years from Perry to the Restoration. R. T. Chang's *From Prejudice to Tolerance: A Study of the Japanese Image of the West 1826–1864* (Sophia University Press, Tokyo, 1970) to some extent can be said to carry on from where D. Keene stopped, namely in analysing the intellectual changes occurring as Japan was about to abandon the policy of *sakoku*. And M. Miyoshi's *As We Saw Them: the First Japanese Embassy to the United States, 1860* (University of California Press, Berkeley, California, 1979) presents the confusion of these first Japanese emissaries abroad in coping with the Western atmosphere and at the same time the degree to which they perceived their sense of identity as Japanese rather than as simply officials representing the Tokugawa house.

In terms of the period *circa* 1870–1914, or roughly corresponding to the years of the reign of the Meiji Tennō, many themes are covered in the books cited earlier in this bibliographical note. The setting up of the new infrastructure and the nature of the early stages of modern economic development are the subject of T. C. Smith's *Political Change and Industrial Development in Japan: Government Enterprise 1868–1880* (Stanford University Press, Stanford, California, 1965). The articles by K. Ohkawa, on capital formation, K. Taira, on factory labour, and K. Yamamura, on entrepreneurship and ownership, in P. Mathias and M. M. Postan (eds), *The Cambridge Economic History of Europe*, vol. VII, *The Industrial Economies: Capital, Labour and Enterprise, Part 2, The United States, Japan and Russia* (Cambridge University Press, Cambridge, 1978), provide a wealth of material and analysis on these crucial aspects of Japanese economic development. J. Hirschmeier, *The Origins of Entrepreneurship in Meiji Japan* (Harvard University Press, Cambridge, Massachusetts, 1964) is a work of great significance in terms of understanding both the causation and the motivation involved in Japan's transformation from a pre-industrial to a capitalist society. While Hirschmeier stresses the role of the samurai and their values in this transformation, a rather revisionist interpretation on this subject is presented by K. Yamamura in *A Study of Samurai Income and Entrepreneurship* (Harvard University Press, Cambridge, Massachusetts, 1974).

A number of studies of these periods have focused on biographies of the more prominent figures. In this category one should include: R. F. Hackett, *Yamagata Aritomo in the Rise of Modern Japan 1838–1922* (Harvard University Press, Cambridge, Massachusetts, 1971), which, owing to its subject, provides considerable insight into both the political and military developments in the course of modernisation; I. P. Hall, *Mori Arinori* (Harvard University Press, Cambridge, Massachusetts, 1973) deals with one of the more complex and controversial leaders of modern Japan, whose roles as a prominent member of the intelligentsia, and also as a diplomat, a politician and especially his strong imprint on the evolution of education in modernising Japan, combine to form a rich picture of the period; F. G. Notehelfer, *Kotoku Shusui: Portrait of a Japanese Radical* (Cambridge University Press, Cambridge, 1971) assesses Japanese political history from the perspective of one of the country's early revolutionaries whose execution in 1911 provided a major turning point; J. D. Pierson in *Tokutomi Soho 1863–1957: A Journalist for Modern Japan* (Princeton University Press, Princeton, New Jersey, 1980) concentrates on a very different individual whose political thought evolved from pro-Western liberalism to nationalistic social-Darwinism ultimately to ultra-nationalistic obscurantism, although the reader is perhaps struck above all by the superficiality both of the man and of his thought. Of all these biographies in fact perhaps the most revealing in regard to the nature of Japanese political life in the Meiji period and the amount of graft and corruption which it encompassed is K. Strong's study, *Ox Against the Storm: A Biography of Tanaka Shozo, Japan's Conservationist Pioneer* (Paul Norbury Publications, Tenterden, Kent, 1977).

The social mores of the Japanese people in the course of the major transformation to modernity is a subject vividly and eloquently described in the pages of K. Yanagida's *Japan's Manners and Customs in the Meiji Era* (translated by C. Terry, Obunsha, Tokyo, 1957). C. Blacker in *The Japanese Enlightenment: A Study of the Writings of Fukuzawa Yukichi* (Cambridge University Press, Cambridge, 1964) completely captures the spirit and intellect of Japan's leading intellectual figure, a major influence on his contemporaries and subsequent generations. Fukuzawa's autobiography, though somewhat superficial and inclined to the occasional narcissistic touch, nevertheless provides both insight and colour: *The Autobiography of Fukuzawa Yukichi* (translated by E. Kiyooka, Columbia University Press, New York, 1966). T. R. H. Havens, *Nishi Amane and Modern Japanese Thought* (Princeton University Press, Princeton, New Jersey, 1970) also provides an illuminating account of the intellectual transition of Japan and the early absorption of Western thought. One of the most useful sources for the study of intellectual and social change in the Meiji era is W. R. Braisted (ed.), *Meiroku Zasshi: Journal of the Japanese Enlightenment* (Harvard University Press, Cambridge, Massachusetts, 1976); this consists of a translation of the Meiroku periodical which featured articles by the more *avant-garde* intellectuals of the early Meiji period. K. B. Pyle, *The New Generation in Meiji Japan: Problems of Cultural Identity 1885–1895* (Stanford University Press, Stanford, California, 1969) focuses his attention on the second generation of students and intellectuals: a period when the initial innovation and excitement of the West had begun to wane and the problem of defining the new Japanese identity became more acute. D. T. Roden, *Schooldays in Imperial Japan: A Study in the Culture of a Student Elite* (California University Press, Berkeley, 1980) brings a stimulating addition to the general collection on the cultural aspects of modernisation.

On the political scene three of the more comprehensive texts are: G. Akita, *Foundations of Constitutional Government in Modern Japan, 1868–1900* (Harvard University Press, Cambridge, Massachusetts, 1967), N. Ike, *The Beginnings of Political Democracy in Japan* (Johns Hopkins University Press, Baltimore, 1950) and J. Pittau, *Political Thought in Early Meiji Japan* (Harvard University Press, Cambridge, Massachusetts, 1967).R.H.P.Mason's *Japan's First General Election 1890* (Cambridge University Press, Cambridge, 1969), as its title indicates, concentrates on a more narrow issue but nonetheless a major event in Japanese political history. M. B. Dardess, (ed.), *A Discourse on Government: Nakae Chomin and his Sansuijin keirin mondo* (Western Washington State College, Occasional Paper no. 10, Bellingham, Washington, 1977) is a most valuable document, providing as it does a translation of perhaps one of the most famous, certainly incisive, political treatises by one of the most influential figures among the opposition and subsequently radical groups. G. O. Totten, *The Social-Democratic Movement in Prewar Japan* (Yale University Press, New Haven, Connecticut, 1966), although focusing more attention on the interwar period, provides an interesting thematic study on the Japanese setting and political culture. M. Maruyama, *Thought and Behaviour in Modern Japanese Politics* (Oxford University Press, London, 1963) is primarily, though not exclusively, concerned in this work with the evolution and nature of Japanese 'fascism'; it is one of the great classics of Japanese history and should be read by all interested in the development of modernisation in Japan. Also to be highly recommended, though here again not primarily focused on the Meiji period, is D. A. Titus, *Palace and Politics in Prewar Japan* (Columbia University Press, New York, 1974). In regard to the militarisation of Japanese society an interesting account is R. J. Smethurst's *A Social Basis for Prewar Japanese Militarism* (University of California Press, Berkeley, 1974), while M. R. Peattie, *Ishiwara Kanji and Japan's Confrontation with the West* (Princeton University Press, Princeton, New Jersey, 1975) focuses his attention on the career and attitudes of one of the country's major military figures. E. L. Presseisen, *Before Aggression: Europeans Prepare the Japanese Army* (University of Arizona Press, Tucson, Arizona, 1965) assesses the transformation of the Japanese army resulting from European influences and tuition.

On the subject of Japanese expansionism, the first book to be recommended which provides a penetrating analysis of the Japanese diplomatic setting and includes translations of key foreign policy documents is I. Nish, *Japanese Foreign Policy, 1869–1942: Kasumigaseki to Miyakezaka* (Routledge and Kegan Paul, London, 1977). K-H. Kim, *The Last Phase of the East Asian World Order: Korea, Japan, and the Chinese Empire, 1860–1882* (University of California Press, Berkeley, California, 1890) presents an illuminating study of the changes occurring in the realm of international affairs as they affected East Asia and the role played by Japan in this process. F. C. Jones, *Extraterritoriality in Japan and the Diplomatic Relations Resulting in Its Abolition, 1853–1899* (Yale University Press, New Haven, Connecticut, 1931) is an important and detailed study. J. J. Stephan, *The Kuril Islands: Russo-Japanese Frontiers in the Pacific* (Clarendon Press, Oxford, 1974) looks at a narrow issue through an extended time perspective, the result of which is a penetrating and fascinating study. G. Fox, *Great Britain and Japan, 1858–1883* (Oxford University Press, London, 1969) seeks to assess not just the diplomatic relations between the two countries but the total impact and influence of Britain on Japan during this period. H. J. Jones, *Live Machines: Hired Foreigners and Meiji Japan* (Paul Norbury Publications, Tenterden, Kent, 1980) studies the roles of individual foreigners in assisting Japan's transformation.

M. Mayo (ed.), *The Emergence of Imperial Japan* (D. C. Heath, Lexington, Massachusetts, 1970) and G. K. Goodman (ed.), *Imperial Japan and Asia: A Reassessment* (East Asian Institute, Columbia University Press, New York, 1967) provide a number of essays assessing different facets of Japanese imperialism. On Japanese policies towards Korea the major text is H. Conroy, *The Japanese Seizure of Korea, 1868–1910* (University of Pennsylvania Press, Philadelphia, 1960); also to be recommended on the subject are C. I. and H. K. Kim, *Korea and the Politics of Imperialism, 1876–1910* (University of California Press, Berkeley, California, 1967) and A. C. Nahm (ed.), *Korea under Japanese Colonial Rule* (Western Michigan Press, Grand Rapids, 1973). A. Iriye (ed.), *The Chinese and the Japanese: Essays in Political and Cultural Interactions* (Princeton University Press, Princeton, New Jersey, 1980) contains a series of highly significant articles on the relationship in a very broad sense between these two East Asian nations; also highly recommended on this subject is M. B. Jansen, *The Japanese and Sun Yat-Sen* (Stanford University Press, Stanford, California, 1970). I. H. Nish, *The Anglo-Japanese Alliance: The Diplomacy of Two Island Empires 1894–1907* (The Athlone Press, London, 1966) and *Alliance in Decline: A Study in Anglo-Japanese Relations 1908–1923* (The Athlone Press, London, 1972) provide the fullest account and analysis of Japan's foreign policy. S. Okamoto, *The Japanese Oligarchy and the Russo-Japanese War* (Columbia University Press, New York, 1970) and J. A. White, *The Diplomacy of the Russo-Japanese War* (Princeton University Press, Princeton, New Jersey, 1964) are the two major texts in English on the subject. A. Iriye, *Pacific Estrangement: Japanese and American Expansion 1897–1911* (Harvard University Press, Cambridge, Massachusetts, 1972) raises and analyses numerous significant issues relating to the nature and direction of Japanese expansionism.

The translation from *Onna Daigaku* on p. 99 is taken from B. H. Chamberlain, *Things Japanese* (first published Tokyo, 1904, reprinted by Charles E. Tuttle & Co., Rutland, Vermont and Tokyo, 1971).

The Tokyo First High School versus Yokohama Athletic Club baseball encounter cited on p. 141 is taken from Donald Roden's fascinating article, 'Baseball and the Quest for National Dignity in Meiji Japan' (*American Historical Review*, vol. 85, no. 3, June 1980, pp. 511–34).

OTHER WORKS CITED IN THE TEXT

Batchelor, J. *An Ainu–English–Japanese Dictionary* (Kyobunkan, Tokyo, 1926).

Hourani, Albert. *Arabic Thought in the Liberal Age* (Royal Institute of International Affairs, London, 1962).

Kaempfer, E. *The History of Japan* (Glasgow, 1906).

Lenin (Vladimir Ilich Ulianov). *Selected Works* (Moscow, 1968).

Lévi-Strauss, Claude. Article in *Le Matin Magazine*, 25–26 October 1980.

Morris, Ivan. *The Nobility of Failure* (Secker & Warburg, London, 1975).

Oliphant, Laurence. *Narrative of the Earl of Elgin's Mission to China and Japan* (first published 1859, reprinted by Oxford in Asia Historical Reprints, Oxford University Press, London, 1970).

Renan, Ernest. *Qu'est-ce qu'une nation?* (Paris, 1882).

Rostow, Walter. Article in *The Economist*, 15 August 1959.

Smith, Thomas C. 'Japan's Aristocratic Revolution' (*The Yale Review*, New Haven, Connecticut, spring 1961, vol. 50, pt 3, p. 371).

Vogel, Ezra. *Japan as Number One* (Harvard University Press, Cambridge, Massachusetts, 1979).

Index

(Note: The major themes of this book, such as economic forces, intellectual and political developments, the condition of women, *eta* and *Ainu*, etc., are detailed in the Table of Contents. The Index here is primarily concerned with people, places, events and institutions.)

343